Untangling Tolkien

Other Books from Inkling

Across Asia on a Bicycle

Thomas Gaskell Allen Jr. and William Lewis Sachtleben

When they graduated from college in 1891, the authors set out east from New York City for an epic journey around the world on the then-new 'safety' bicycle. In 1893 they arrived back in New York, having covered just over 15,000 miles by bicycle, at that time the "longest continuous land journey every made around the world." This book describes the most difficult and dangerous part of that journey, their 7,000 miles of travel from Constantinople to Peking, as they biked alone across lands few outsiders ever visited. Along the way, they became the first Americans to reach the top of Mount Ararat, and in China, they were the first to introduce the modern bicycle to a nation that now has 300 million bicycles. This book is back in print for the first time since 1894.

Paperback: 1-58742-020-1 Hardback: 1-58742-021-X

Celebrating Middle-earth

Edited by John G. West Jr.

In speeches first given at Seattle Pacific University in November 2001, six Tolkien scholars describe the literary, political and spiritual background to *The Lord of the Rings*. Contributors are John West, Peter Kreeft, Janet Leslie Blumberg, Joseph Pearce, Kerry Dearborn, and Phillip Goggans.

Paperback: 1-58742-012-0 Hardback: 1-58742-013-9

Beginning in the Fall of 2003, Inkling will release a series of books to commemorate the literary influence that William Morris had on J. R. R. Tolkien. That series includes the following books.

More to William Morris

William Morris

In a letter written at the end of 1960, Tolkien said the Dead Marshes landscape may have been influenced by World War I battlefields, but it owes "more to William Morris and his Huns and Romans, as in *The House of the Wolfings* or *The Roots of the Mountains*." Here, in one inexpensive volume, are those two books. Those who wish Tolkien had written more about Rohan, about Aragorn and his Rangers, or about Éowyn should enjoy reading them.

Paperback: 1-58742-023-6

On the Lines of William Morris

William Morris

In a 1914 letter to his future wife, Tolkien noted that he was working on a story "on the lines of Morris' romances." Here, in one inexpensive volume, are two of the best known of those tales of great quests like much that of Bilbo and Frodo: *The Well at the World's End* and *The Wood Beyond the World*.

Paperback: 1-58742-024-4

Single Volume Editions of William Morris Books

Inkling also plans to release single-volume editions of many William Morris books, newly typeset in both paperback and hardback editions.

Bookstores can order from Ingram or Baker & Taylor (U.S.) and Bertrams (Europe). Also available online.

Untangling Tolkien

A Chronology and Commentary
for
The Lord of the Rings

by

Michael W. Perry

Inkling Books   Seattle   2003

Description

Untangling Tolkien is the first book-length chronology ever published for J. R. R. Tolkien's popular epic, *The Lord of the Rings*. It contains commentary to help readers understand the story and describes how the book came to be written.

Copyright Notice

Disclaimer

Publisher's Note

Periodicals, newsletters, and Internet websites wishing to publish portions of the end of chapter commentaries should contact Inkling Books for permission.

Dedication

This book is dedicated to the marvelous fair use provisions of copyright law, and to the many friends who encouraged and supported me while it was being written.

Library Cataloging Data

Perry, Michael W [Wiley] (1948–)
Untangling Tolkien: A Chronology and Commentary for The Lord of the Rings
251 pages, 7.5 x 9.25 in. 235 x 191 mm.
Includes 20 chapters and 15 graphics
Library of Congress Control Number: 2001097041
ISBN 1-58742-019-8 (alkaline paper)
PR6039.O32 Z49 2003 and 823.091

Publisher Information

Inkling Books, Seattle, WA, U.S.A.
Internet: http://www.InklingBooks.com/
Published in the United States of America on acid-free paper
First Edition, Second Printing, October 2003

Contents

Preface

J. R. R. Tolkien's great tale, *The Lord of the Rings,* is wonderfully complex. Within its pages, readers meet a marvelous array of creatures from little Hobbits to giant Ents. Its narrative sweeps across a territory roughly the size of western Europe and draws on events spanning thousands of years. But for most readers, however enthralled, making sense of it all is not easy. Fortunately, there are encyclopedias to help us understand the people and places, as well as an atlas to sort out the geography. This book will do the same for the chronology and should become a 'must have' for all serious Tolkien fans.

J. E. A. Tyler's *The Tolkien Companion* is a good source of information about people and places, as is Robert Foster's *The Complete Guide to Middle-earth.* Karen Wynn Fonstad's *The Atlas of Middle-Earth* is excellent for making sense of the geography and history. This book would have been far more difficult to write without the help each provided.

No one, however, should see this book as a substitute for *The Lord of the Rings.* It most emphatically is not. If you are reading this and haven't yet read Tolkien's great epic, stop and read no further. Read *his* book at least once from cover to cover before you even *look* at this book. Enjoy one of the best-written and most widely popular books of modern times and leave details such as the chronology for later. The first rule in reading is always "Enjoy!"

Only *after* you find yourself wanting to know more about the intricacies of this complicated tale, should you use this book in tandem with other reference books. Remember that the description of events given here is deliberately terse. It is in no way a substitute for Tolkien's much more engrossing narrative. It intended to give you a concise description of what happened on a particular date, along with chapter references to the places where those events described in books such as *The Hobbit, The Lord of the Rings, The Silmarillion* and *Unfinished Tales.* Without at least the first two books (and preferably all four), this book is of little value.

C. S. Lewis introduced *The Fellowship of the Ring* to the world with these words: "This book is like lightning from a clear sky; as sharply different, as unpredictable in our age as *Songs of Innocence* were in theirs. To say that in it heroic romance, gorgeous, eloquent, and unashamed, has suddenly returned at a period almost pathological in its anti-romanticism is inadequate. To us, who live in that odd period, the return—and the sheer relief of it—is doubtless the important thing." See "Tolkien's *The Lord of the Rings,*" in *C. S. Lewis,* Lesley Walmsley, ed. (London: HarperCollins, 2000), 519. The original book review is in the August 14, 1954 issue of *Time and Tide.*

Readers would also do well to heed the advice of Gandalf when he rebuked Saruman, warning that "he that breaks a thing to find out what it is has left the path of wisdom." Do not focus overmuch on the minutia and forget the wonder of the story as a whole. Use this book as a tool to better understand all that Tolkien is saying.

Like most reference works, you can use this book several ways. The most obvious is as a chronology, letting you go from a date to what happened on that day. This is particularly important if, for instance, you want to know what Merry and Pippin were doing when Frodo and Sam entered Mordor. As careful as Professor Tolkien was about the time line of events that lay behind his story, he rarely gives us an actual date. Events are typically described as the third day after some event or the fifth day of a journey whose start date may not even be given. Here you will find the actual day in the Shire calendar when almost everything happens. Try doing that yourself, and you'll discover the work that went into this book.

You can also use this book to go from an event to both a date and a reference to where that event is described by Tolkien. In many cases you will find that the sidebar reference is not to one passage but to several. Tolkien liked to spread his story around. Details about an particular event are often given hundreds of pages apart and even in different volumes. With this chronology, you'll be able to put everything together, perhaps for the first time.

In addition, many time-related details have been added to increase the book's value. When Sauron darkens the sky, the days of darkness are numbered. When Rohan races to Minas Tirith, the days of their ride are counted. When someone enters the story, his age is given. When one event is closely linked to another weeks or even months later, a reference to that other date is given. A computer-generated calendar of the times when the sun and moon set and rise was consulted and included when useful. The same is true of phases of the moon, which play a critical role in parts of this story, particularly the night journeys.

Finally, because Tolkien placed so much stress on the realism and historicity of his tale, the plausibly of his narrative is repeatedly tested. "If Middle-earth really existed," the book asks, "could what he described have actually happened?" Put another way, "Where there are problems, can a reasonable answer be found?" Tolkien often did that, treating difficulties as if they were discrepancies in ancient historical records.

With this book, I release the fruits of my labor to the world, quite aware that, as the pioneering study, it has at least its share of imperfections. Anyone who thinks they have found a mistake is encouraged to contact me through the Internet web site referenced on the copyright page. Anyone with the proper expertise who would like to see editions brought out in other languages should contact me also.

Finally, there is only one reason why a book like this is possible. Tolkien spent untold hours getting the chronology of his tale just right, making charts and calendars describing where each person was on each day. In my writing, I had none of that to consult. Instead, the chronology was recreated, one detail at a time, from the story on which it is based. In the end, I was left awed the wealth of detail that underlies the narrative and is unseen by most readers. Tolkien's account isn't perfect and there are a few discrepancies that I discuss. But few books this long could survive this level of scrutiny and come out as well. For that, each of us should be grateful.

MICHAEL W. PERRY, SEATTLE, WASHINGTON, U.S.A.
ON J. R. R. TOLKIEN'S 'ELEVENTY-FIRST' BIRTHDAY
FRIDAY, JANUARY 3, 2003

1

Dating and Chronology

Understanding Tolkien's Calendar

At first glance, the dates you see in this book will seem familiar. There are the usual twelve months of our calendar along with seven days in each week. But if you look more closely, you'll find something surprising. All the months have exactly thirty days, no more and no less. Even February has 30 days. No Hobbit child needed to learn the rhyme about "Thirty days hath September . . ."

Like Tolkien's great tale, the dates in this book are based on a Shire calendar that is different from our own in several clever ways. By itself, the thirty-day months would have created a problem. A solar year is a little over 365 days long. A calendar that just has 12 times 30 or 360 days will slip out of synchronization with the sun by five days each year. In about 30 years, January will be in summer and July in winter. Such a calendar would no longer tell the seasons or give hints about when to plant a garden. No sensible Hobbit would want to become confused about the proper time to plant potatoes.

To correct that, Tolkien's Hobbits did something clever. Most years in their calendar add five additional days that aren't a part of any month. In leap year (which came every four years in a year evenly divisible by four) they add a sixth day. The added days come during Yuletide and Lithedays.

Yuletide. Two of those days come in winter and are much like our Christmas. They are called 1 Yule and 2 Yule. The two days are next to each other, but 1 Yule comes at the end of the year just after December 30, while 2 Yule comes at the start of the year just before January 1.

Lithedays. The other two days come in summer. 1 Lithe comes just after June 30, and 2 Lithe comes just before July 1. Between them is Midyear's Day. (In leap years Overlithe comes after Midyear's Day.)

Midyear's Day. The cleverest part of the Shire calendar is Midyear's Day. Not only is it not a part of any month, it is not a day of the week either. (The same is true of Overlithe in leap years.) Why do that? Because in most calendars every day of the year is also a day of the week. Since 365 divided by 7 gives 52 with one day left over, that means each year the days of the week slip by one day (except leap years, when they slip two

In this book, we follow Tolkien's lead and modernize calendar months to their current names. Of course, the actual names in the Shire calendar were different. Tolkien took many of them from an ancient English calendar. February, for instance, was *Solmath* in the Shire calendar and *Solmonath* in the ancient English one. May was *Thrimidge* and *Thrimilchi* respectively. June and July were *Forelithe* and *Afterlithe* in the Shire calendar, while both were *Litha* in the ancient English one. August was *Wedmath* and *Weodmonath*. September was *Halimath* and *Halegmonath*. October was *Winterfilth* and *Winterfylleth*. November was *Blotmath* and *Blotmonath*. In addition, the ancient English began their year on December 25 and, whether by design or accident, January 1 in Tolkien's Shire calendar does appear to correspond to December 25 in our modern calendar. See: Albert S. Cook and Chauncey B. Tinker, ed. *Select Translations from Old English Prose* (Cambridge: Harvard University Press, 1935), 231. I am indebted to Lisa Star for this insight.

According to Tolkien, Lithe comes from the Old English names for June and July. Yule, he said, has no relationship to today's Christmas but was a Danish and Germanic term for an ancient winter festival. For more, see Tolkien's "Guide to the Names in the Lord of the Rings" in *A Tolkien Compass,* Jard Lobdell, ed. (La Salle, IL: Open Court, 1975), 199–201.

Tolkien knew in modern calendars the summer solstice is June 21 and the winter solstice is December 21. But when he developed his calendar, he may have thought of old English calendars that celebrated those events on June 24 and December 25. Similarly, March 25 is the traditional first day of Spring as well as "Lady Day," celebrating the Catholic Feast of the Annunciation. In the Shire calendar the travelers left Rivendell on December 25, the Ring was destroyed on March 25, and the White Tree was discovered on June 24. Other links between major events and special days in Christian calendar may exist. For instance, Gandalf returns to life on February 14, St. Valentine's Day, although any other parallel between the gruff old bachelor and a holiday for romantic love is unlikely.

days). By simply declaring Midyear's Day not a day of the week, the Hobbits got rid of that pesky problem. Now without exception each day of the year comes on the same day of the week. January 1, for instance, always comes on Sunday.

This means that Hobbits did not have to spend money on a new calendar each year. Except for a slight difference in leap years, the calendar is always the same. At the end of this chapter we have a Shire calendar adapted to look like one of our own. Use it whenever you like. It's good for every year in Tolkien's story.

Linking to Our Calendar

The Shire calendar works marvelously for Hobbits, but it causes problems when we need to covert dates in it to dates in our modern calendar. The first problem is simple. To synchronize two calendars, we need to find a day in one calendar that is the same as a day in the other. Unfortunately, when Tolkien described the Shire calendar in Appendix D of *The Return of the King,* he was less than clear. To a casual reader he seems to give three pairs of matching dates that cannot be reconciled with each other. We'll look at each.

Match 1: Ten Days Difference on Midyear's Day. Tolkien's first match came when he noted that Hobbits intended for Midyear's Day to come as close as possible to the summer solstice, which comes in our modern calendar on June 21 (or June 22). That, he noted, gives about a ten day difference between the two calendars at the end of June with the Shire Calendar ahead of ours.

Match 2: Eight Days Difference on New Year's Day. In the same paragraph as Match 1, Tolkien said that our New Year's Day roughly corresponded to the Shire's January 9, giving an eight day difference at the start of the year, again with the Shire calendar ahead.

Match 3: Two Days Difference on March 25. The last match comes when Tolkien links March 25 (when the Ring was destroyed) to March 27 in our calendar. That gives a two day difference, but this time our modern calendar is ahead.

Unfortunately, there is no way these differences can be reconciled. If Match 2 is right, then Midyear's Day in the Shire calendar comes on June 24 in our modern calendar rather than on June 21 as Match 1 claims. Again if Match 2 is right, then March 25 in the Shire calendar is March 19 in the modern calendar according to Match 2 but March 27 in Match 3. Those same differences appear no matter which matches you compare. Only one of the three can be right.

In this book, we have gone with Match 2. If you read carefully what Tolkien said in Appendix D, the link he established between the Shire's January 9 and our January 1 is the most precise. For the other two, he seems to have had some other purpose in mind.

With Match 1, Tolkien pointed out that the Hobbits tried to get Midyear's Day as close to the summer solstice as possible. It turns out that the closest they could get without major complications was at the end of their June, three days after the actual summer solstice. For easy-going Hobbits that was close enough.

There is an even better reason for rejecting Match 3. When Tolkien linked March 25 in the Shire calendar to our March 27, he was pointing out that *even if* the two calendars began on the same day, the differences in the length of months and the added days in the Shire calendar would make dates different throughout the year. He was not saying that March 25 in the Shire matches March 27 in our calendar.

The second problem linking the two calendars is a matter of arithmetic. For each day in the Shire calendar, the corresponding day in the modern calendar has to be calculated month by month, taking into account the different length of the months in each and the added days in the Shire calendar. Though laborious, solving this problem is straightforward. All that is needed is a starting point, a day in one calendar known to correspond to a day in the other calendar. This book assumes that January 9 in the Shire calendar is January 1 in our calendar and calculates everything from there.

Leap years create a problem of their own. Even if the Shire leap year and our own come in the same year, our added day comes at the end of February while the Shire's comes at the end of June. Fortunately that doesn't affect any significant event in this book. Almost all the action takes place in 1418–1419 and neither was a leap year, although 1420 was. Century years such as 1400 are not leap years.

Lunar Calendar

Why do we need to discover how to convert between the Shire calendar and our own? All the events in this story are given as Shire dates. What use is a calendar that, from Tolkien's perspective, wasn't invented for several thousand years later? There are two reasons.

1. Seasons. The first reason is the changing of the seasons. If the Shire calendar runs about six to eight days ahead of our own, as it seems to do, then we need to take that into account as we read. The seasons will change about a week later in Shire dating than they do in our own. The difference also affects the rising and setting times of the sun.

2. Moon. The second reason concerns the moon. Since the moon plays a critical role in Tolkien's story, aiding or hindering night travel, it would help to know more about what it is doing on any given night. To do that, this chronology converts Tolkien's occasional mention of the moon's behavior into precise statements about the moon's phase and times of rising and setting throughout much of the story, including numerous places where Tolkien does not mention the moon.

At first glance, that seems easy. There are computer programs that calculate such things in an instant. Unfortunately those programs work with our modern calendar rather than the Shire's. To use them, we absolutely must have modern dating. Given modern dates, we can then look for matches between the moon's phase as given in *The Lord of the Rings* and some modern year. Once we have a lunar calendar in

Here are terms Tolkien used about the moon: A *waxing* moon is one growing brighter as it changes from new to full. A *waning* moon is one growing dimmer between full and new. A *crescent* moon has less than half its visible surface illuminated. A *gibbous* moon has more than half its visible surface illuminated.

In a 1971 interview on BBC radio, Tolkien said that the moons and sunsets in *The Lord of the Rings* were "worked out according to what they were in this part of the world in 1942." Since the main part of the story comes in two different years, we take his remark to mean that he used a calendar covering the latter part of 1941 and the first part of 1942.

synchronization with those known dates, all the phases of the moon for the rest of the tale—new, first quarter, full and last quarter—fall into place.

At that point, things get interesting. It turns out that the matching years for the most action-packed part of this story are 1941 (for the Shire's 1418) and 1942 (for 1419). No other set of years from the mid-1930s to late 1940s matches as well. That fits perfectly with reports that Tolkien consulted a 1941–42 lunar calendar as he wrote. It also confirms our choice of Match 2 to link the two calendars. If Tolkien penciled Shire dates onto a pair of lunar calendars for 1941 and 1942 and used them as a reference, he was assuming Match 2—that the Shire's January 9 was our January 1. It makes sense that, if he were going to link the two calendars, he would begin marking with January 1 on a modern calendar rather than in late March or June.

For those who are interested, where appropriate in this book the modern date is given in smaller type alongside the Shire date and just below a count of the number of days in Frodo's travels. Those who want to follow a different matching scheme can make the proper adjustment there. In the end, the match you choose doesn't affect the accuracy of the lunar phases, since they are directly linked to Tolkien's own remarks with only an occasional minor difference.

Keep in mind, however, that there be instances when the times Tolkien assumed for the moon's rising and setting differ from those given here. Christopher Tolkien mentions in his father's notes a February 6 when the full moon rose at 9:20 p.m. and set at 6:30 a.m. the following morning. Based on the five day difference, this is the full moon of February 1, 1942. (In Tolkien's final Shire-based chronology, this becomes the important full moon of March 8.) A search of locations from Stockholm to Narobi turned up no location with times of rising and setting even remotely close to those Tolkien gives. Even more important, the times seem unlikely for a full moon, which rises in the east as the sun sets in the west. It is possible, however, that by the time the text became final, Tolkien was using a more accurate lunar calendar and that kind of error was removed.

There are other differences between the Shire calendar and our own. First, we should not forget that the Hobbits speak their own language and have their own names for months and days of the week. If you are interested, Tolkien gives them in Appendix D. To make life easier for us, Tolkien replaced their names with modern equivalents.

Second, Hobbits treat their days of the week differently than we do. At noon, Friday becomes a holiday much like our Sunday. That means Saturday is the first day of their work week and is like our Monday. In this story, that matters little. The Hobbits are in too much danger to pay attention to holidays.

Remember too that there are a few cases in this chronology where the evidence wasn't quite clear and judgments had to be made about when

There's partial confirmation of this. Christopher Tolkien notes that in one time-scheme his father wrote that the moons followed 1941–42 plus six (changed to five) days. That made the full moon of January 2, 1942 the full moon of January 7 in his calendar. Subsequent changes altered the scheme that had the Shire calendar five days ahead of modern one, but the link to the 1941–42 lunar calendar seems to have remained. See the end of *The Treason of Isengard* (Boston: Houghton Mifflin, 1989), Ch. 17, "The Great River."

The War of the Ring (Boston: Houghton Mifflin, 1990), Pt. 2, Ch. 4, "Of Herbs and Stewed Rabbits," near the end of the chapter. For dates when Tolkien gets the moon wrong, see the comments for March 8, 10 and 24, 1419. See also "Tolkien's Writing Interrupted" at the end of Chapter 14 and "Tolkien's Chronology in Shelob's Lair" at the end of Chapter 15 for evidence that Tolkien was tired and getting little sleep when those parts of the narrative were written.

In the Shire calendar that follows, notice that special days (such as the two days of Yule) tend to come on a Friday or Saturday,

Untangling Tolkien

something happened. In such cases, I explain the reason why in a note. Feel free to differ.

Anyone who studies this book will probably come to the same conclusion I have—that Tolkien went to great effort to get the little details in his story just right. In few cases, however, Tolkien's own writings seem to disagree about dating a particular event. As Tolkien himself would have done, I have weighed the evidence and reached a conclusion as to which is is correct. I have tried to note those cases and give reasons for my choices.

We begin the detailed chronology that follows with the year 1601 in the Third Age of Middle-earth. (The various ages are explained in the next chapter.) Because that is the year of the first Hobbit settlement in the Shire, it became Year 1 in the Shire calendar. In this book, we will use Shire dating for two reasons. First, since the day-to-day dating in *The Lord of the Rings* follows the Shire calendar, for consistency sake so should the years. Second, the more ancient seeming Shire dating—which for most events will be in the 1400s—does a far better job of conveying the sense that this is something that happened long ago than dating in the 3000s.

Converting between the two dating systems is easy. Simply *add* 1600 to a Shire year to get the corresponding Third Age year or *subtract* 1600 from a Third Age year to get the Shire year.

Other features in this book are fairly obvious. Chapter divisions correspond to major events such as the war against Saruman. Within chapters, division is by date, so everything that happens on the same year or day is listed together. Underneath some dates, the status of the moon is listed, usually when the moon's phase changes.

See "Phases of the Moon" at the end of Chapter 6 for the dates of the moon's phases during the War of the Ring.

In the sidebar alongside most dates are two numbers. Typically, the topmost is a count of days to or from September 23, 1418, the day Frodo and his friends left Bag End. Days before that date are labeled "Before" and count down to their departure. Days on and after that date are just labeled "Day." Those numbers should make it easy to count the days between two events by simple addition or subtraction. Also, for events that took place years in the past, the number of years to 1418 is often given as the "Years Before."

If you are calculating how long something took by subtracting the number of one date from that of another, remember to *add one* to the total. For example, the period from Day 10 to Day 12 is three days rather than two.

On each day, events are grouped into subheadings by those involved. When a group splits or joins others, a new subheading is created. A small, italicized right-justified heading tells where the group is at all times. As they travel, that changes. The sidebar lists where the events being described are in Tolkien's writings. Additional commentary has been placed either in the main body or the sidebar. In addition, where a date had to be calculated or estimated, that is noted in a small, centered subheading.

Finally, on the next three pages of this chapter is a Shire calendar arranged to look like our modern calendar. Taking into account Overlithe at the end of June for leap years, it is good for any year in Tolkien's story.

Journeys and stays are counted in a centered subhead that says something like, "Day 1 of 3 in Moria." That raises a question about how partial days of travel should be counted. When Tolkien included a count in his narrative, I usually followed it to avoid confusion. Elsewhere, the count is what seemed most useful for readers.

Shire Calendar—Good in All Years

January (Afteryule)

Saturday	Sunday	Monday	Tuesday	Wednesday	Thursday	Friday
2 Yule	1	2	3	4	5	6
7	8	9	10	11	12	13
14	15	16	17	18	19	20
21	22	23	24	25	26	27
28	29	30				

February (Solmath)

Saturday	Sunday	Monday	Tuesday	Wednesday	Thursday	Friday
			1	2	3	4
5	6	7	8	9	10	11
12	13	14	15	16	17	18
19	20	21	22	23	24	25
26	27	28	29	30		

March (Rethe)

Saturday	Sunday	Monday	Tuesday	Wednesday	Thursday	Friday
					1	2
3	4	5	6	7	8	9
10	11	12	13	14	15	16
17	18	19	20	21	22	23
24	25	26	27	28	29	30

April (Astron)

Saturday	Sunday	Monday	Tuesday	Wednesday	Thursday	Friday
1	2	3	4	5	6	7
8	9	10	11	12	13	14
15	16	17	18	19	20	21
22	23	24	25	26	27	28
29	30					

May (Thrimidge)

Saturday	Sunday	Monday	Tuesday	Wednesday	Thursday	Friday
		1	2	3	4	5
6	7	8	9	10	11	12
13	14	15	16	17	18	19
20	21	22	23	24	25	26
27	28	29	30			

June (Forelithe)

Saturday	Sunday	Monday	Tuesday	Wednesday	Thursday	Friday
				1	2	3
4	5	6	7	8	9	10
11	12	13	14	15	16	17
18	19	20	21	22	23	24
25	26	27	28	29	30	1 Lithe

> Midyear's Day—*Every year, not a day of the week*
> Overlithe—*Leap years, not a day of the week*

July (Afterlithe)

Saturday	Sunday	Monday	Tuesday	Wednesday	Thursday	Friday
2 Lithe	1	2	3	4	5	6
7	8	9	10	11	12	13
14	15	16	17	18	19	20
21	22	23	24	25	26	27
28	29	30				

August (Wedmath)

Saturday	Sunday	Monday	Tuesday	Wednesday	Thursday	Friday
			1	2	3	4
5	6	7	8	9	10	11
12	13	14	15	16	17	18
19	20	21	22	23	24	25
26	27	28	29	30		

September (Halimath)

Saturday	Sunday	Monday	Tuesday	Wednesday	Thursday	Friday
					1	2
3	4	5	6	7	8	9
10	11	12	13	14	15	16
17	18	19	20	21	22	23
24	25	26	27	28	29	30

October (Winterfilth)

Saturday	Sunday	Monday	Tuesday	Wednesday	Thursday	Friday
1	2	3	4	5	6	7
8	9	10	11	12	13	14
15	16	17	18	19	20	21
22	23	24	25	26	27	28
29	30					

November (Blotmath)

Saturday	Sunday	Monday	Tuesday	Wednesday	Thursday	Friday
		1	2	3	4	5
6	7	8	9	10	11	12
13	14	15	16	17	18	19
20	21	22	23	24	25	26
27	28	29	30			

December (Foreyule)

Saturday	Sunday	Monday	Tuesday	Wednesday	Thursday	Friday
				1	2	3
4	5	6	7	8	9	10
11	12	13	14	15	16	17
18	19	20	21	22	23	24
25	26	27	28	29	30	1 Yule

Starting with Saturday, the actual Shire names for the days of the week were:
Sterday, Sunday, Monday, Trewsday, Hevensday, Mersday, and Highday.
Hevensday was also called Hensday. Highday afternoon was a holiday.

UNTANGLING TOLKIEN

CHAPTER

2

A Brief Background

Beginning to 859

Before the Creation to the Watchful Peace

C. S. Lewis said it best. *The Hobbit* was "a fragment torn from the author's huge myth and adapted for children," but with *The Fellowship of the Ring,* Tolkien gave us all that vastness, "in their true dimensions like themselves." "You can hardly put your foot down," he noted, "without stirring the dust of history." In this chapter, we look at that history.

In the beginning, there was the One, corresponding to the One God of Jews and Christians. He created the Guardians of the World or *Valar* to rule a world to be called Middle-earth. The Valar, in turn, are much like the archangels of the Bible. The Valar did not live in Over-heaven with the One, but in the Undying Lands of the Uttermost West, which was originally within sight of Middle-earth and just to its west across a sea.

First Age—572 Years

The creation of Middle-earth began the First Age, which Elves call the Elder Days. Nothing the One created was evil, but the presence of freedom created the potential for evil to enter Middle-earth. That came when a Valar named Melchar rebelled against the established order, acquiring the new name of Morgoth. Foremost among his evil deeds was the stealing of three Great Jewels or *Silmarilli,* a story recounted in Tolkien's *The Silmarillion.*

One of those who followed Morgoth was Sauron, a name that means "abominable." He is part of a race of beings called the Maiar. Though spiritual beings, they can assume a beautiful physical appearance, as will Sauron in the Second Age.

The First Age ended with the defeat of Morgoth by the Hosts of Valar. Morgoth was cast into outer darkness, never to trouble Middle-earth again. That occurred some 6460 years before the main events in this story. The main link between that age and the present story is Sauron.

See *C. S. Lewis,* Lesley Walmsley, ed., 520, 521. This is the book review published in the August 14, 1954 issue of *Time and Tide.*

Tolkien's Middle-earth history is in his *The Letters of J. R. R. Tolkien,* Humphrey Carpenter, ed. (Boston: Houghton Mifflin, 1981), No. 131, 153, 156 and 212. Henceforth, this will be *Letters.* The reference is to the letter number and not a page number.

For this history of the three ages, I am indebted to J. E. A. Tyler's *The New Tolkien Companion.* The most complete history of the First Age is in *The Silmarillion* (New York: Ballantine, 1977). Although it was not published until four years after his death, Tolkien was writing this book as early as 1916. *Letters,* No. 294. There is also material about the First Age in Part 1 of *Unfinished Tales* (Boston: Houghton Mifflin, 1980). For an easy-to-read history, see "The First Age" in Karen Fonstad's *The Atlas of Middle-earth,* (Boston: Houghton Mifflin, 1991).

Second Age—3441 Years

Tolkien apparently borrowed "Mordor" from *Beowulf*, where *morthor* is an Anglo-Saxon for murder, punishment, torment or misery. See Lin Carter, *Tolkien: A Look Behind the Lord of the Rings* (New York: Ballantine, 1969) 182. In a 1971 interview on BBC radio, Tolkien told the interviewer he didn't "feel any guilt complex" about the time his fictional tale took away from his scholarly work because, "There's quite a bit of linguistic wisdom in it."

Hints of the horrors of the Dark Years are at the beginning of *The Silmarillion*, Ch. 19, "Of Beren and Lúthien."

For Númenor's history, see *The Return of the King*, Bk. 6, Ap. A, I, "Númenoran Kings." Tolkien refers to the parallels with Atlantis in *Letters*, No. 227. For Second Age history, see Part 2 of *Unfinished Tales*. For a summary, see "The Second Age" in Karen Fonstad's *The Atlas of Middle-earth.* See also *Letters*, No. 131.

The "Last Alliance" implies that the future will never require another such alliance, much as World War I was to be the "war to end all wars." It is clear that, by the time of *The Lord of the Rings*, Elrond, who fought in this war, no longer believed that war and evil can be so easily rooted out of Middle-earth.

Unfortunately, Sauron was not destroyed with Morgoth. He went into a deep sleep, awaking some five-hundred years into the Second Age. Realizing his opponents were powerful, he moved slowly and carefully. Some 1000 years into the Second Age he established a fortress called Mordor in a wilderness blasted by a volcano named Mount Doom.

Still not powerful enough to take on his foes directly, Sauron used deceit and treachery, seeking to beguile and charm others into giving up a part of their power. Some Elves saw through his deception, but others did not. Though the latter's assistance, Sauron was able to forge the Great Rings (also known as the Rings of Power). There were three rings for the Elves, seven for the Dwarves and nine for men. In secrecy, he created the One Ring with the power to rule the others. All these rings share a common trait. They delay the effects of time, giving long life to those who wear them. We see that in the long lives of Gollum and Bilbo.

When the Elves found out about the One Ring, and the danger it posed, they finally understood Sauron and became his undying foes. But their power was now so weakened, that Sauron was able to conquer and rule as a tyrant over much of Middle-earth for almost 2,000 years. That time became known as the Accursed or Dark Years.

The first threat to Sauron's rule came from Númenoreans, men who lived on an island called Númenor just east of the Undying Lands. Long lived and powerful, in 3261 of the Second Age they landed in Middle-earth and defeated Sauron, making him their prisoner. But Sauron proved more clever than they. Returning to his deceitful ways, he persuaded their king to sail against the Undying Lands in pursuit of eternal life. In response to that 3319 rebellion, the Valar turned to the One, who swallowed up the island of the Númenor in a great flood (like Atlantis). Only a few of its inhabitants escaped, but they included talented men that the Valar allowed to form the Kingdom of Gondor. Aragorn is descended from those men, hence his great ability and long life.

For what he had done, Sauron lost his physical body. No longer could he appear in an appealing form and deceive Elves and men. Unfortunately, he remained as a spirit who could be visualized as a lidless eye surrounded by fire. (That's how Frodo will see him.) Quietly building up his forces in Mordor, Sauron waited until 3429 in the Second Age to strike at the Kingdom of Gondor. The next year Elves and men formed a Last Alliance to defeat him. They accomplished that eleven years later in 3441, bringing an end to the Second Age. Both Sauron and the One Ring provide a link between the Second Age and our story.

Third Age—3019 Years

After Sauron's defeat, Isildur, King of Gondor, took possession of the One Ring. Rather than destroy it at nearby Mount Doom as some advised, he kept it for himself and his heirs. Two years later he lost it when he was attacked by Orcs and attempted to escape by swimming across the Anduin River. The One Ring slipped from his finger and disappeared into the river. Now visible, he was killed by Orcs.

Anticipating the danger that Sauron posed as long as the Ring existed, in the early years of the Third Age the Valar sent five of their number, called *Istari* or Wizards, to Middle-earth. These five are much like angels but with human bodies resembling old men. They are subject to pain, suffering and hunger like mortals and can even fall into evil—as happens to Saruman. If they die, they can also be restored to life, as with Gandalf. They are forbidden to reveal their true identities or use their full power. Their primary role is to guide people and encourage resistance to Sauron. When Sauron is destroyed, their role in Middle-earth will be over.

In the Third Age, Sauron slept for some 1050 years. When he awoke, he was too weak to take Mordor away from a still powerful Gondor. Instead, he secretly built Dol Guldur on a hilltop in Greenwood. As his power grew, Greenwood acquired a bad reputation and was renamed Mirkwood. Concealing his identity, Sauron became known as the Necromancer (and is mentioned by that name in *The Hobbit*), although some correctly suspected he was Sauron returned.

Unable to attack the still powerful Gondor to his south, Sauron turned to the Nazgûl—nine men who wore the Nine Rings made for men and were now totally subservient to his will. He worked through them and various wild tribes to destroy the northern kingdom of Arnor west of the Misty Mountains. That is why during this story much of that region is a vast, unpopulated wilderness and why those portions that are populated (such as the Shire) have no king to protect them. As we see in the chronology that follows, when Gondor becomes weak, Sauron is able to return to Mordor.

During this period, Sauron tried to keep his foes doubtful of his existence and, when that was no longer possible, divided about how he should be opposed. Because so much of Sauron's power had been placed in the One Ring, regaining it lay at the heart of his plan to put Middle-earth under his brutal rule yet again. Given how much weaker his foes had become during the Third Age, it is possible that these new Dark Years might endure for years beyond counting.

That, in brief, is the chilling historical background Tolkien created for *The Lord of the Rings*. The freedom of all the peoples of Middle-earth will rest in the hands of a few amiable and almost simple-minded Hobbits from an obscure farming community called the Shire.

There is more about the Third Age and useful background to *The Lord of the Rings* in Parts III and IV of *Unfinished Tales* as well in Appendix A of *The Return of the King*. See also *Letters,* No. 131.

Norse myths often include a Wizard-like figure, typically an old man who wanders about with a gray beard, weather-worn cloak and staff. See *Tolkien: A Look Behind the Lord of the Rings,* 194. For the origin of Tolkien's own Wizards, see *Letters,* No. 144. See also No. 131.

Mirkwood (as *Myrkwood*) appears 17 times in the ancient Icelandic saga, *The Elder Edda.* As in *The Hobbit,* it is a gloomy place with strange, magical powers. See *Tolkien: A Look Behind the Lord of the Rings,* 169.

In a January 1971 interview on BBC Radio 4, Tolkien told the interviewer, Dennis Gerrolt, that *The Hobbit* began as a separate story, but as soon as Bilbo went out "into the world" his story "got sucked" up into the "immense sagas" Tolkien had been working on for many years.

In that same 1971 interview, Tolkien explained that for a story as complex as this one, "you must work to a map, otherwise you can never make a map of it afterward." There is more about the Third Age and excellent maps in "The Third Age," *The Atlas of Middle-earth* by Karen Fonstad, talented cartographer.

Year 1—Shire Founded

Hobbits—Settling the Shire

Shire

- First Shire settlements established by immigrants from Bree.
- This becomes the first year in the Shire calendar.

Tolkien's English Connection

Tolkien wrote primarily for English readers like himself. Tom Shippey points out that Tolkien deliberately made the Shire's two founders, Marcho and Blancho, similar to the mythical founders of England, who were "two brothers called 'Horse'—Hengest and Horsa." In fact. "all four words are Old English words for the same animal."

Like most gifted writers, Tolkien borrowed heavily from the past, showing talent in what he selected. In his case, that meant names, themes, plots and even literary style were taken almost wholesale from the ancient languages and literature of Northern Europe. For those who understand that, his writings are filled with allusions, puns and insider jokes.

The England of history *is* much like the Shire. For great Mediterranean civilizations such as Rome, primitive England mattered little—just like the Shire. But the existence of both will later prove of critical importance, England in the war against Hitler, happening as Tolkien wrote, and the Shire in the War of the Ring. Tolkien denied that his story was an allegory—Sauron does not stand for either Hitler or Stalin. But he agreed that there were principles behind the war against Sauron that could be applied in any war against great evils. To that extent, he admitted, the story could be treated allegorically or at least used allegorical language.

For the next 1418 years—roughly the period of time from when England was a minor Roman colony until its rise to world power—the Shire will be so little noticed that most inhabitants of Middle-earth are unaware of its existence. In fact, the invisibility of the Shire becomes a critical factor in the unfolding story.

Although not an island, the Shire's countryside and climate are much like the England of Tolkien's childhood. But to make the plot more interesting, the Shire cannot rest safely behind a potent barrier such as the English Channel. As a result, Middle-earth's geography is roughly that of western Europe with the Shire in France and Mordor in Germany. Its rich complexity—from forests and mountains to grasslands and volcanos—resembles New Zealand without the latter's close proximity to the sea.

Readers who see Hobbits as diminutive humans are correct. Since Hobbits, Elves and humans are closely enough related to marry and have children (as with Aragorn's marriage to Arwen), they can be thought of as one large, extended race with differing lifespans, abilities and personalities.

The Fellowship of the Ring, "Prologue" and *The Return of the King,* Bk. 6, Ap. B, "The Tale of Years."

Tom Shippey, *J. R. R. Tolkien, Author of the Century* (Boston: Houghton Mifflin Co., 2000), 60. See also David Day, *The Hobbit Companion,* (New York: Metro-Books, 1997), 22f. There is an excellent map of the Shire in the regional maps section of *The Atlas of Middle-earth.*

Tolkien does mention allegory in a favorable sense is in *Letters,* No. 109 and 131, but both letters went to publishers he was hoping to interest in the book. Tolkien intended for Hobbiton to be at the same latitude as Oxford. *Letters,* No. 294. For more on Hobbits, see the Prologue to *The Fellowship of the Ring* and the first chapter of *The Hobbit.* In the former, Tolkien hints that the Hobbit migration from the upper Anduin River (Gollum's home) to west of the mountains may have come because of Sauron's growing power in Mirkwood. If so, then virtually all memory of that had faded away by the time of *The Hobbit.* Karen Fonstad describes their movements in "Migrations of Hobbits," *The Atlas of Middle-earth.*

See Tolkien's entry for First-born in *Tolkien Compass,* 166. Also see *Letters,* No. 131.

Years 35 to 40—Great Plague

Gondor and the Shire

Rohan, Gondor, the Shire and elsewhere

- In winter of 35–36, the Great Plague begins among the Rhovanion.
- It spreads south to Gondor and west of the Misty mountains.
- In the Shire it is called the Dark Plague.

Ancient Plagues

In the *Unfinished Tales* reference in the sidebar, Tolkien said that the plague spread most quickly in winter when both men and horses were housed in close quarters. In modern terms, that indicates either an insect like a flea or respiratory droplets spread the disease. Since the ancient societies Tolkien was describing were unlikely to understand that, Tolkien did not resolve the issue. His point of view was almost always that of his characters and their era.

Typically, those fleeing a plague carry it to other cities. Over time, the plague weakens as more and more people acquire immunity, but the economic and social harm can linger for generations. Tolkien's knowledge of ancient history was considerable, and he took that into account in crafting his tale. Some two hundred years later, attacks by Wainriders out of the east will further weaken the already crippled Gondor, leaving it less able to guard Mordor from Sauron.

The Return of the King, Bk. 6, Ap. B, "The Tale of Years," *Unfinished Tales,* Pt. 3, Ch. II, "Cirion and Eorl and the Friendship of Gondor and Rohan," the Prologue to *The Fellowship of the Ring* and *The Return of the King,* Appendix A, I, (iii). The Rhovanion are the ancestors to Rohan. For the plague's impact, see "The Great Plague" in *The Atlas of Middle-earth.*

The plague weakened as it spread. See *The Return of the King,* Bk. 6, Ap. A, I, (iii) and (iv). Section (iv) describes the Wainriders.

Years 374 to 375—Battle of Fornost

Elves, Men and Hobbits

Fornost

- The Lord of the Nazgûl attacks the Northern Kingdom.
- He captures its chief fortress at Fornost.
- He is defeated in the Battle of Fornost.

Gondor's Slow Decline

During this period, Tolkien is transitioning from the situation at the beginning of the Third Age, when Sauron was defeated and his allies scattered and weak, to that at the end of the age when Sauron seems all-powerful. At this point, Gondor was still too strong to be directly attacked, but by making war on the Northern Kingdom, the Lord of the Nazgûl thought he could weaken its allies. When he is defeated, the same Glorfindel who assists the Hobbits in their flight to Rivendell over a thousand years later appears to be the one who forces him to flee. Glorfindel then correctly prophesies that the Lord of the Nazgûl's eventual destruction, if it happens, will not come from the actions of a man. That is what happens on March 15, 1419.

The Fellowship of the Ring, "Prologue." Fuller details are in *The Return of the King,* Appendix A, I, (iii) and (iv). There is confusion in the sources as to the exact year when these long-ago events occurred, 374 or 375. Gondor and Rivendell participate in this war.

Karen Fonstad has a good description of this period of warfare in "Wainriders and Angmar," *The Atlas of Middle-earth.* Tolkien often added realism to his tales by giving characters several names. At this time the Lord of the Nazgûl is known as the Witch-lord of Angmar, Angmar being a region that included the Ettenmoors north of Rivendell.

For some reason, Tolkien placed this war remarkably close to the Shire. Fornost is on the North Road (later known as the Greenway) about 100 miles north of Bree. With war so close, it is easy to suspect that many Hobbits went into hiding, probably in the Shire's many woods. (Less than four centuries after the Shire's founding, their population may have still been small.) Their concealment was apparently successful. In 1418 the Lord of the Nazgûl does not remember their presence during this war when he begins his desperate search for 'halflings.' Hobbit tradition claims that the Shire sent archers to the Battle of Fornost, where they may have died. By the time of the main events described in *The Lord of the Rings,* it is called Deadmen's Dike, perhaps because the eroded earthwork defenses resembled a dike. Tolkien, whose expertise included how language changes over time, would understand how place names develop.

This step in Tolkien's transition from good being the stronger to evil being the stronger is successful. Though the Lord of the Nazgûl is defeated, the Northern Kingdom is not restored. The loss of life and property has been too great. Its demise, however, has little impact on life in the Shire. Hobbits had always run their little land as they pleased, so they simply continue to do so. Tolkien, who liked government to be small and unintrusive, may be giving us one of its benefits here. A central government that does little is little missed when it is gone.

For more on Tolkien beliefs about government and his opposition to a single, uniform, global culture, see John G. West, *"The Lord of the Rings* as a Defense of Western Civilization," in *Celebrating Middle-earth,* (Seattle: Inkling, 2002), 21f.

1038 Years Before

Year 380—Nazgûl in Mordor

Nazgûl

Mordor

The Return of the King, Bk. 6, Ap. A, I (iv) and Bk. 6, Ap. B, "The Tale of Years."

• The Lord of the Nazgûl occupies Mordor with eight other Nazgûl.

A Problem Avoided

Here Tolkien demonstrates how long festering problems can grow until they become almost unsolvable. In 380, the Nazgûl, mere lieutentants to a now vanished Sauron, may seem a small problem, something not worth launching a preemptive war to eliminate. But in 870 years (1250) Gandalf will prove that Sauron still exists. Then they will become very dangerous indeed. But by then it will be too late to attack them.

Dúnedain

Eriador the Northern Kingdom

The Return of the King, Bk. 6, Ap. A, I (iii) and Bk. 6, Ap. B, "The Tale of Years."

• The Dúnedain live in secrecy.

Strider's Roots

Tolkien often laid the groundwork for later events far in the past. For centuries, few will know of the existence of the Dúnedain, the former rulers of the Northern Kingdom, but it is from them that Strider (Aragorn II) will come as the sixteenth generation of wanderers. Tolkien provided no clear picture of how such a long tradition of unrewarded sacrifice could be maintained. He probably regarded them as knights without castles, and the knightly tradition did endure for centuries in Europe.

For a brief history of the Dúnedain, see *The Return of the King,* Bk. 6, Ap. A, I, (iv), "Eriador, Arnor, and the Heirs of Isilbur." Also see "Kingdoms of the Dúnedain," in Karen Fonstad, *The Atlas of Middle-earth*

Dwarves

Moria

- A Balrog appears in Moria, killing Durin VI.
- Nain I takes charge, and the Dwarves defend upper Moria.

Mysterious Balrogs and Dwarf Names

Tolkien provided no detailed description of Balrogs. Like Sauron, their past is shrouded in mystery. We do know that they were powerful creatures of fire who fought for Morgoth during the First Age. This one is a survivor (perhaps the only one). The ever-scheming Sauron may have a role in its appearance.

Tolkien took his Dwarf names from ancient sources. One named Durin appears in sagas about Hervör and Heithrek as well as a later tale about King Heidrek the Wise.

The Fellowship of the Ring, Bk. 2, Ch. 6, "Lothlórien," *The Return of the King,* Bk. 6, Ap. A, III, "Durin's Folk," and Bk. 6, Ap. B, "The Tale of Years." For Tolkien's brief remarks on Balrogs, see *Letters,* No. 144.

See *Tolkien: A Look Behind the Lord of the Rings,* 170.

Year 381—Dwarves Flee Moria

1037 Years

Dwarves

Moria and Lórien

- Náin I is killed and the Dwarves must leave Moria.
- Elves in nearby Lórien are driven south.

Weakening of Dwarves and the Rise of Orcs

Much as with Gondor, to set the stage for the rise of Sauron, Tolkien must weaken the power of Dwarves. The flight of the Dwarves from Moria leaves it undefended. In 498 years (880), Sauron will send Orcs to occupy its caves. The long delay may mean that, with the Balrog present, there was little chance the Dwarves could successfully retake Moria.

The Fellowship of the Ring, Bk. 2, Ch. 6, "Lothlórien" and *The Return of the King,* Bk. 6, Ap. A, III, "Durin's Folk," and Bk. 6, Ap. B, "The Tale of Years." Tolkien comments on his incorrect plural for Dwarf, Dwarves, in *Letters,* No. 17, 138 and 236.

Derivation of Orc

Tolkien took the term "Orc" from *Beowulf.* In a translation with the Old English term placed in square brackets, the relevant passage is:

Of Cain awoke all that woeful breed,
Etins [eotenas] and elves [ylfe] and evil-spirits [orcneas],
as well as the giants [gigantas] that warred with God
weary while: but their wage was paid them!

J. R. R. Tolkien in *Tolkien Compass,* 171.

1019 Years Before

Year 399—Lonely Mountain Founded

Thráin I

Lonely Mountain

The Return of the King, Bk. 6, Ap. A, III, "Durin's Folk," and Bk. 6, Ap. B, "The Tale of Years." The Lonely Mountain is described in *The Hobbit* at the start of Ch. 10, "A Warm Welcome."

- Thráin I begins the Dwarf kingdom at the Lonely Mountain.

Lonely Mountain, a Historical Exception

Tolkien had a good sense of history and knew that even broad historical trends have exceptions. The Dwarves may have lost Moria, but only twelve years later they establish another kingdom, Erebor, also well positioned to threaten Sauron. The Lonely Mountain stood alone on a wide plain with no other mountains nearby. That made it the best defensive position in a region some six hundred miles north of Mordor.

In 771 years (1170), Smaug the dragon will drive the Dwarves from the Lonely Mountain. In 942 years (1341), the fortress and its dragon play a major role in the adventures of Bilbo, as described in *The Hobbit*. It will also be the location for one of the multi-day battles in the War of the Ring. (See the entries for March 15, 17 and 27, 1419.) All this illustrates the amazing complexity of the world Tolkien created.

1018 Years Before

Year 400—Minas Ithil Attacked

Nazgûl

Minas Morgul

The Return of the King, Bk. 6, Ap. A, I, (iv), "Gondor and the Heirs of Anárion" and Bk. 6, Ap. B, "The Tale of Years."

- Minas Ithil is attacked by the Nazgûl.

Shelob Not a Guard

Tolkien often repeats plots with variations. The Nazgûl attack comes through Cirith Ungol. Perhaps, much like when Frodo and Sam will use Cirith Ungol to enter Mordor, the defenders of Minas Ithil trusted too much in Shelob's ability to keep others from passing through her tunnels. Shelob is a predator in search of food. She is not a guard.

1016 Years Before

Year 402—Minas Ithil Falls

Nazgûl

Minas Morgul

The Return of the King, Bk. 6, Ap. A, I, (iv), "Gondor and the Heirs of Anárion" and Bk. 6, Ap. B, "The Tale of Years." For a historical parallel, think of the late 1930s and early 1940s when refugees fled Nazi domination.

- Minas Ithil and its *palantír* are taken by the Nazgûl.

Ithilien Weakens

Again Tolkien describes a group weakening before the rising power of Sauron. As a result, the population of fertile Ithilien falls as people moved away. As that happened, Minas Ithil was renamed Minas Morgul or 'Tower of Sorcery." A thousand years later, Sauron will use the *palantír* he took from the city to manipulate Saruman and deceive Denethor II.

450—Gondor Under Stewards

Eärnur and Mardil with the Lord of the Nazgûl

Gondor and Minas Morgul

- King Eärnur disappears fighting the Lord of the Nazgûl.
- Stewardship of Gondor begins under Mardil.

Childless Eärnur

Tolkien is sometimes criticized, not very fairly, as a champion of war. Here he points out that a passion for nothing but war is irresponsible. Eärnur loved fighting so much that he did not marry and thus had no son or daughter when he disappeared. With no clear heir, all those with a claim to the throne were afraid to assert it, fearing civil war. That almost thousand-year-old uncertainty about whose heir had the right to be king may be why so many proofs of Aragorn's right to rule will be given, including victory in battle and the power to heal.

The Return of the King, Bk. 6, Ap. A, I, (iv), "Gondor and the Heirs of Anárion" and Bk. 6, Ap. B, "The Tale of Years."

Years 460 to 463—Watchful Peace Begins

Wizards, Sauron and the Nazgûl

Dol Guldur and Minas Morgul

- In 463, Gandalf investigates the Necromancer at Dol Guldur.
- Sauron moves East to avoid detection.
- Nazgûl cause no trouble, beginning 400 years of Watchful Peace.

The Mind of Sauron

With his focus almost exclusively on Hobbits, Tolkien tells us little about what went on the mind of Sauron. But imaginative readers can make an informed guess based on hints in Tolkien's writings. It is likely that soon after Sauron awoke, he began to suspect his foes had not destroyed the Ring. His very existence suggested it still existed, and his growing power added confirmation. Since his foes give no evidence they possess the Ring, logic suggests it had been lost. Moving carefully, he might find it without motivating them to launch a competing search.

Unfinished Tales, Pt. 3, Ch. III, "The Quest of Erebor" and *The Return of the King*, Bk. 6, Ap. B, "The Tale of Years."

Dol Guldur means "Hill of Darkness." For more on Sauron's history, see *Unfinished Tales*, Pt. 2 Ch. IV, "The History of Galadriel and Celeborn," particularly Notes 7f. See also Gandalf's remarks in *The Fellowship of the Ring*, Bk. 2, Ch. 2, "The Council of Elrond."

840—Gollum Born

Date Estimated

Anduin River Valley

- Gollum is born in a Hobbit fishing village.

Birth Estimated

This date is merely an estimate based on the immaturity of Gollum's behavior when the Ring is found about 863. Hobbits grow up slowly.

This estimate makes him, when the Ring was found, five years younger than Pippin was when he left with Frodo.

The Watchful Peace will continue through 859.

Tolkien's Heros

For Tolkien's remarks on the Wizards, see *Unfinished Tales,* Pt. 4, Ch. II, "The Istari." See also *Letters,* No. 131 and 144.

Tolkien's heros are never idealized. They make mistakes and can even turn from good to evil, as with Saruman and, for a time, Boromir. That is especially true of Tolkien's Wizards. Their wisdom and power have definite limits. They can and do make mistakes. For some 900 years, they are suspicious of a new evil growing in southern Mirkwood's Dol Guldur. For a time, they think it might be a Nazgûl. By 460, some suspect Sauron has returned. But in spite of that, they fail to act. This makes them procrastinators on a monumental scale.

In an October 5, 1938 speech on the now much criticized Munich agreement, Winston Churchill said: "I have watched this famous island descending incontinently, frecklessly, the stairway which leads to disaster. It is a fine broad stairway at the beginning, but after a bit the carpet ends. A little farther on there are only flagstones, and a little farther on still these break beneath your feet."

Although Tolkien expressed distaste when people drew detailed parallels between his story and events taking place at the time he was writing, it is easy to spot historical similarities. From about 1933, when Hitler took power in Germany, until World War II began in September of 1939, the political leaders of Britain and France procrastinated. They preferred to see Adolf Hitler as a Necromancer-like leader who could be appeased by letting him take over German-speaking territories such as the Rhineland, Austria and the Sudetenland. Until he attacked Poland, they failed to realize that he had a Sauron-like thirst for power and intended to dominate all Europe. Only a few spoke out with Gandalf-like warnings of danger. Chief among those was Winston Churchill, whose warnings came almost too late.

See *Letters,* No. 53 and 96. In the background to Tolkien's December 9, 1943 letter is Churchill's September 6, 1943 Harvard speech praising Basic English and suggesting that the U.S. and U.K. "spread our common language ever more widely throughout the globe."

Of course, this does not mean that Tolkien liked Churchill. He seems to have loathed the future Prime Minister as a member of what he called Britain's ruling "Theyocracy," as well as for advocating an empire that wanted all the world to speak English and adopt a similar culture. He did, however, approve of Churchill's condemnation of the little-reported persecution of Catholics by leftists in war-torn Spain.

In 1937, hoping to help Tolkien publicize *The Hobbit,* C. S. Lewis wrote to the *Times Literary Supplement,* claiming expertise in children's stories and offering to review *The Hobbit.* The result illustrates the old adage that 'no good deed goes unpunished.' He unhappily found himself being asked to review children's stories that did not interest him. See *Letters,* No. 14 for May 28, 1937.

More about the Inklings

Those wanting to know more about the Inklings, the informal writers group to which Tolkien belonged, can turn to the entry on "Inklings" by Diana Glyer in *The C. S. Lewis Readers' Encyclopedia* or read the following:

- Carpenter, Humphrey, *The Inklings,* (Boston: Houghton Mifflin, 1978).
- GoodKnight, Glen, "The Social History of the Inklings, J. R. R. Tolkien, C. S. Lewis, Charles Williams, 1939–1945," *Mythlore* 2 (Winter 1970), 7–9.
- Pearce, Joseph, *Tolkien, Man and Myth* (San Francisco: Ignatius Press, 1998).
- Reilly, R. J., *Romantic Religion: A Study of Barfield, Lewis, Williams and Tolkien,* (Athens, GA: University of Georgia Press, 1971).

3

Growing Conflict

860 to 1340

Watchful Peace ends to the treachery of Sauron

In her marvelous atlas of Middle-earth, Karen Fonstad summarized the period we are in, noting: "troubles increased until virtually all the known lands were affected in some way. Much of that evil was due, directly or indirectly, to Sauron. In spite of the loss of the One Ring, his strength and influence grew until even the weather was affected. At times the forces of good were able to counter Sauron's advances, but always those that had been defeated were soon replaced." During these dark times, Gandalf cannot persuade his fellow Wizards to act, even as Sauron grows more dangerous. Haste may make waste, but procrastination can be fatal.

Karen Fonstad, *The Atlas of Middle-Earth,* "Deepening Difficulties" in "The Third Age."

Year 860—Watchful Peace Ends

558 Years Before

Sauron

Dol Guldur

• Sauron moves back to Dol Guldur from the East.

Unfinished Tales, Pt. 3, Ch. III, "The Quest of Erebor" and *The Return of the King,* Bk. 6, Ap. B, "The Tale of Years."

Single-minded Evil

Historically, evil has often been more single-minded than good. In the early stages of a conflict, evil finds it easy to attract followers by promising power and rich spoils. Only when evil begins to threaten personal freedom, do good people act. That difference is illustrated by the long struggle between Sauron and the Wizards.

The Lord of the Rings was conceived during the 1930s, when the attraction of evil was all too evident. Totalitarian governments, whether fascist or communist, seemed the wave of the future. Some said that only they could impose the stern disciple required to shake off political chaos and economic depression. Fortunately, the presence of German troops just across the channel united the British, and Pearl Harbor gave Americans the will to fight. In a similar fashion, Sauron's growing power will eventually give Elves, Dwarves, Hobbits and even Ents and Wild Men a single-minded determination to unite and protect their lives and freedoms.

Few modern books have as been successful at making evil both real and unattractive as *The Lord of the Rings*. For a discussion of Tolkien's ideas about the nature of evil, see Peter Kreeft's "Wartime Wisdom" in *Celebrating Middle-earth,* 31f.

In his 1936 *While England Slept,* Winston Churchill summarized England's failure to stop Hitler with these grim words: "Decided only to be undecided, resolved to be irresolute, adamant for drift, solid for fluidity, all-powerful to be impotent." His remarks are an apt summary of the behavior of Tolkien's White Councils.

The Four White Councils

First
863 SR
Prob. Lórien

> Q: What to do about the Necromancer?
> A: Nothing Done.

Second
1251 SR
Rivendell

> Q: Attack the Necromancer?
> A: Nothing Done.

Third
1341 SR
Prob. Lórien

> Q: Attack the Necromancer?
> A: Yes, but too late.

Fourth
1353 SR
Unknown

> Q: What to do about Sauron?
> A: Nothing Done.

555 Years Before

Year 863—First White Council

White Council

Probably Lórien

- Lady Galadriel calls the first White Council.
- The Council cannot agree on what to do about the Necromancer.

Saruman's Seduction Begins

The Silmarillion, "Of the Rings of Power and the Third Age," *The Fellowship of the Ring,* Bk. 2, Ch. 7, "The Mirror of Galadriel" and *The Return of the King,* Bk. 6, Ap. B, "The Tale of Years." The White Council is also called the Council of the Wise. There was a similar council in the Second Age, see *Unfinished Tales,* Pt. 2, Ch. IV, "The History of Galadriel and Celeborn," Note 10.

Tolkien introduces yet more trouble, although at this point the danger is only potential. Saruman has begun to study the Rings of Power. Readers may suspect his interest in the Rings is because he concluded that, if Sauron really was recovering power as the Necromancer, then the One Ring has not been destroyed. In time Saruman becomes the Council's expert on Great Rings. Given Tolkien's Christian beliefs, Saruman may be in the story to remind us of the dangerous seductiveness of knowledge.

Gollum with Déagol—Ring Found

Date Approximate

Gladden Fields

- Déagol discovers the One Ring while fishing in the Anduin River.
- Sméagol kills his friend Déagol to get the Ring.
- He uses the Ring to spy on his fishing village.
- His odd ways earn him the nickname Gollum.

Mysterious Gollum

Tolkien made Gollum one of the most intriguing characters in the story. But he provides us with only a few clues to events in Gollum's life. Gandalf will give Frodo some details shortly after learning it from Gollum himself. (See April 12–13, 1418.)

The Silmarillion, "Of the Rings of Power and the Third Age," *The Fellowship of the Ring,* Bk. 2, Ch. 2, "The Council of Elrond" and *The Return of the King,* Bk. 6, Ap. B, "The Tale of Years."

The Fellowship of the Ring, Bk. 1, Ch. 2, "The Shadow of the Past." Additional details are in a manuscript in *The Treason of Isengard,* Ch. 2, "The Fourth Phase (1)."

Year 870—Ring Goes Underground

548 Years Before

Gollum

Date Approximate

Gladden Fields and the Misty Mountains

- Disliked by neighbors, Gollum leaves his Hobbit fishing village.
- He hides in a cave within the Misty Mountains.

Taking the Long View

As befits an expert in ancient literature, Tolkien thought in centuries. Having possessed the Ring for 478 years, in 1341 Gollum will lose it at precisely the right moment for Bilbo to find it. After such a long time, having the right person at the right time and place illustrates how Tolkien slips providence into his story. Someone is working behind the scenes to counter Sauron's evil schemes. Good is not without hope.

The Silmarillion, "Of the Rings of Power and the Third Age" and *The Return of the King,* Bk. 6, Ap. B, "The Tale of Years."

It is interesting that, while most Shire Hobbits fear boating, these made their living by fishing. Providence is discuss in "More than Chance" at the end of Chapter 14.

Year 880—Orcs to Moria

538 Years Before

Sauron and Orcs

Date Approximate

Moria

- Sauron sends Orcs to Moria.

Orcs and Sauron's Growing Power

In Tolkien's created history, Moria was abandoned by the Dwarves in 381, which was 499 years earlier. During the intervening years, only the Balrog kept Dwarves away. To illustrate Sauron's growing power, Tolkien now introduces Orcs into Moria. They prevent the Dwarves from

The Return of the King, Bk. 6, Ap. B, "The Tale of Years."

returning and keep this route through the mountains from being reopened, adding drama to travel in *The Hobbit* and *The Lord of the Rings*. Tolkien is tightening the noose around Middle-earth.

Tolkien also has evil active elsewhere. Probably with encouragement from Sauron, the Orcs build fortresses inside the Misty Mountains to control the mountain passes. This splits Sauron's enemies west of the mountains from those to its east. That situation will still exist 461 years later in 1341 when Bilbo crosses the Misty Mountains with Dwarves (*The Hobbit*) and 539 years later in 1419, when Frodo travels through Moria with Gandalf (*The Lord of the Rings*). Tolkien intends for this long unsolved problem to demonstrate how weak and divided Sauron's foes have become and how desperate the struggle that follows will be.

For more about Orcs and their possible origin, see Note 5 in *Unfinished Tales*, Pt. 4, Ch. 1, "The Drúedain." Some might question what Tolkien intended for these Orcs to eat underground. No mention is made of vast mushroom farms, so we can only assume they left the caves at night and hunted.

Years 1140 to 1147—Battle of Greenfields

Eriador, Bullroarer and the Hobbits

278–271 Years Before
8 Years

Shire

The Fellowship of the Ring, "Prologue," *The Return of the King, The Return of the King*, Bk. 6, Ap. A, I (iii), Bk. 6, Ap. B, "The Tale of Years" and *The Return of the King*, Bk. 6, Ch. 8, "The Scouring of the Shire." Bandobras is called "Bullroarer"

- In 1140 the Orcs attack Eriador from the Misty Mountains.
- In 1147 Bandobras Took defeats Orcs at the Battle of Greenfields.

The (Almost) Peaceful Shire

If the Shire is England, as Tolkien suggests, then this invasion is much like the Norman Conquest of 1066, the last time England was successfully invaded and on a date not that distant from 1140. Norman rule lasted until 1154, a date only seven years removed from the Battle of Greenfields. During the first 1418 years of Shire history, this will be the only battle to be fought within the borders of the Shire. The second will come 279 years later (near the end of Tolkien's story) with the small Battle of Bywater on November 3, 1419. Tolkien's Shire is a most peaceful place.

Karen Fonstad has excellent descriptions of these wars in *The Atlas of Middle-earth.*

Tolkien placed numerous battles across the rest of Middle-earth during this period, far too many to list in this chronology. These attacks are the first in what Tolkien intends to be a difficult two centuries for the foes of Sauron. During a time when so much of the news is bad, he adds two small events that prove of critical importance. In 1250 Gandalf will acquire a map and key from a dying Dwarf, and in 1290 a Hobbit named Bilbo will be born in the Shire.

Years 1158 to 1159—Long Winter

Gondor and Rohan

260–259 Years Before
2 Years

Rohan and Gondor

The Return of the King, Bk. 6, Ap. B, "The Tale of Years."

- Rohan is defeated by attacks from its east and west.
- Harad and Corsairs attack Gondor.

Calamity upon Calamity

Tolkien pours yet more calamities on the free peoples. Under attack at the same time, Rohan and Gondor cannot aid each other. As if Tolkien had not already done enough to make life miserable, both attacks are followed by the horrors of the Long Winter and, in a little over a decade (1170), by the arrival of Smaug the Dragon, bringing an end to the Dwarf kingdom on the Lonely Mountain. Except for the Dragon, the events he describes resemble the fall of the Roman Empire to barbarians, bringing a Medieval Europe troubled by famine, plague and climatic change.

For the ties between Gondor and Rohan, see *Unfinished Tales,* Pt. 3, Ch. II, "Cirion and Eorl and the Friendship of Gondor and Rohan." The next Corsair attack on Gondor will be that on March 8, 1419, during the War of the Ring. Both force a two-front war on the free peoples.

Gandalf and the Hobbits—Days of Dearth

Shire

• Gandalf helps Hobbits survive the brutal winter.

Unfinished Tales, Pt. III, Ch. III, "The Quest of Erebor," *The Fellowship of the Ring,* "Prologue," and *The Return of the King,* Bk. 6, Ap. B, "The Tale of Years."

Gandalf Observes Hobbit Kindness

Tolkien needed a rationale for the great trust Gandalf later places in Hobbit resourcefulness. (Their easy-going, day-to-day lives are not impressive.) He found it in the Long Winter. After the War of the Ring, Tolkien has Gandalf describe how impressed he was with the courage and compassion Hobbits displayed during this long, cold winter, as so many of them were dying of cold and starvation. At that time he reached the conclusion that their one great lack was a forgetfulness about the past which kept them from understanding the world outside their little home, and the possibility that they might play a major role in it.

Tolkien often uses the word "pity" for Hobbit-like kindness. Today the term has a negative connotation, hinting at a contempt that is thought to lie beneath the surface of otherwise helpful behavior. When you read "pity" in Tolkien, think of a compassion for those in unfortunate circumstances, compassion which recognizes that roles could easily be reversed.

Tolkien described Hobbits, including their hairy feet and three-foot height, in 1938. See *Letters,* No. 27.

As a linguist, Tolkien knew that different groups often give different names to the same event. Hobbits called this the Days of Dearth and dated it from 1158 to 1160. In this isolated farming community, the death of hundreds of Hobbits meant the loss of their skills and a slow recovery. Gandalf's presence in the little Shire rather than with the strategically more important Rohan and Gondor suggests Tolkien was hinting that the seemingly gruff Wizard often acted more from compassion than cold calculation. In fact, his whole mission to Middle-earth was probably inspired by concern for its inhabitants.

In a 1954 letter, Tolkien noted that Middle-earth was merely an old English expression for the world in which we live. *Letters,* No. 151.

Some 182 years later (in 1341), Tolkien will have Gandalf's observations about Hobbit character resurface. To give Hobbits a greater sense of world history and their potential role in it, Gandalf will choose Bilbo for a small adventure that proves far more important than he intended. The greater sense of history Hobbits develop during the War of the Ring will continue long afterward, as Tolkien notes at the end of the Prologue to *The Fellowship of the Ring.*

Tolkien described Gandalf as an angel with a human body. He was limited in knowledge and capable of feeling pain, weariness and fear. *Letters,* No. 156 and *Unfinished Tales,* Pt. 4, Ch. 2, "The Istari."

Saruman—Acquires Isengard

Isengard

Unfinished Tales, Pt. 3, Ch. V, "The Battle of the Fords of Isen" and *The Return of the King*, Bk. 6, Ap. B, "The Tale of Years." Those who find the names Sauron and Saruman confusingly similar might note that the one ending in "man" is the man-like Wizard.

- In 1159 Rohan gives Isengard to Saruman.

Rohan's Great Blunder

Tolkien did not allow any of the free peoples to escape their share of the blame for the dangers that will soon loom over Middle-earth. Even heroic Rohan blunders. If Tolkien had departed from his characteristic 'don't tell why' style and allowed Rohan to explain their reasoning, the transfer of Isengard to Saruman would have been easy to explain. With its resources strained by war and famine, the gift allows Rohan to concentrate on guarding the Fords of Isen. Look at a map and you'll see why. Anyone invading from the west (Dunland or Orcs from the Misty Mountains) can easily bypass Isengard. Only with great difficulty can they bypass the fords. There is another factor that is more cultural than economic. Rohan's military power rested in light calvary, and its men preferred to fight on horseback rather than behind stone walls. If Rohan's trust in Saruman had been justified, they would have made a good choice.

Tolkien derived Isengard from *isen*, an old English word for iron and *gard*, a Germanic word for enclosure. See *A Tolkien Compass*, 187.

No one in Rohan asks where Saruman, who has no nation or people of his own, will acquire the money, troops and supplies to fortify Isengard. If we use our imagination, we can see that Tolkien provided an answer. Some 49 years earlier Dunland been at war with Rohan. Knowing the resentment the people of Dunland still retain for Rohan, Saruman will turn to them and the Orcs for assistance. Rohan has given the fortress to a friend of their traditional foes.

248 Years Before

Year 1170—Smaug Attacks

Dwarves and Smaug the Dragon

Lonely Mountain and Dale

The Return of the King, Bk. 6, Ap. B, "The Tale of Years." For Thorin's account of the Dragon's attack, see *The Hobbit*, Ch. 1, "An Unexpected Party." In a 1938 letter, Tolkien said that Smaug comes from a German verb, *Smugan*, meaning to squeeze through a hole, making the name a linguistic jest. *Letters*, No. 25.

- Smaug the Dragon occupies the Lonely Mountain.
- He burns Dale, a town of men not far away.

No Defense from Air Attack

Trench combat in World War I gave Tolkien a feel for what warfare was like. Watching German planes fly overhead, he had seen that walls are no barrier to an airborne foe. That is why the Lonely Mountain has no defense against a flying Dragon. The Dwarves, including Thráin II and his son Thorin II, are forced to flee. (Thorin is only 24 years old.) After living for a time in Dunland, in 1202 they settle in the southern end of the Blue Mountains (Ered Luin), over 200 miles west and a little north of the Shire and near Grey Havens. In 171 years their desire to reclaim lost gold will spark the events of *The Hobbit*. For Tolkien, even Dwarvish greed can serve a good purpose.

Years 1193 to 1199

225–219 Years Before
7 Years

Misty Mountains and Wilderland

Dwarves

- The Dwarves attack Orc settlements, destroying them.

War of Dwarves and Orcs

Tolkien's Dwarves know how to get even. They begin this bloody war to revenge the killing of Thrór by the Orcs of Moria in 1190.

The Return of the King, Bk. 6, Ap. A, III, "Durin's Folk" and Ap. B, "The Tale of Years."

Years 1241 to 1245—Thráin II Disappears

177–173 Years Before
5 Years

Thráin II

Mirkwood and Dol Guldur

- In 1241 Thráin II attempts a return to the Lonely Mountain.
- In 1245 he is kidnapped by Sauron and taken to Dol Guldur.

Revenge on Smaug

According to Gandalf, Thráin left for the Lonely Mountain on April 21, 1241. Thorin's journey begins almost precisely a century later.

The Return of the King, Bk. 6, Ap. B, "The Tale of Years" and Bk. 6, Ap. A, III, "Durin's Folk."

The Hobbit, Ch. 1, "An Unexpected Party." The timing illustrates all too well that Tolkien's dwarves never forget a grievance.

Gandalf

Moria

- Gandalf passes through Moria searching for Thráin II.

Gandalf in Moria

Moria has been abandoned by Dwarves for 864 years (since 381) and occupied by Sauron's Orcs for 365 years (since 880). Entering Moria placed Gandalf in territory long held by his enemies. His route through Moria this time is from east to west, the opposite direction from that he will take 174 years later on January 13, 1419.

The Fellowship of the Ring, Bk. 2, Ch. 4, "A Journey in the Dark."

Year 1250—Gandalf in Dol Guldur

168 Years Before

Gandalf with Thráin II

Dol Guldur, Mirkwood and Rivendell

- Gandalf discovers the Necromancer is Sauron.
- He finds a dying Dwarf in prison and gets a key and map from him.
- Gandalf tells Elrond that Sauron is looking for the One Ring.

A Discrepancy in the Narrative

Tolkien's tale almost always rings true. This is a rare exception. At this time Gandalf does not realize that this dying Dwarf is Thráin II or that the key and map are for the secret entrance to the Lonely Mountain, a map he will later give to Thorin, Thráin's son, in 1341. It is difficult to explain how Gandalf could have devoted so much effort to finding Thráin II in

The Silmarillion, "Of the Rings of Power and the Third Age," *The Return of the King*, Bk. 6, Ap. B, "The Tale of Years," *The Hobbit*, Ch. 1, "An Unexpected Party," *Unfinished Tales*, Pt. III, Ch. III, "The Quest of Erebor" and *The Fellowship of the Ring*, Bk. 2, Ch. 2, "The Council of Elrond."

1245, and yet five years later not even suspect that he was meeting the Dwarf in Dol Guldur, only a short distance from where the Dwarf had disappeared. It is also hard to explain why the well-traveled Gandalf did not immediately recognize a map of the Lonely Mountain.

Tolkien does better making later events hang together. Gandalf tells Elrond that Sauron is looking for Isildur's heirs. That may explain why, when Aragorn is born 81 years later in 1331, Elrond keeps his identity a secret. Sauron must not know about the young Aragorn, a potential foe.

The death of Aragorn's father may also be linked to Sauron. See the commentary for 1331 and 1333.

167 Years Before

Year 1251—Second White Council

White Council—Sauron Undisturbed

Rivendell

The Silmarillion, "Of the Rings of Power and the Third Age," *The Return of the King,* Bk. 6, Ap. B, "The Tale of Years" and *Unfinished Tales,* Pt. III, Ch. IV, "The Hunt for the Ring." Tolkien was looking for a publisher for his as-yet unfinished *The Silmarillion* as early as 1937, forty years before it was published. See *Letters,* No. 19 for December 16, 1937.

- The Second White Council meets.
- Gandalf wants to attack Sauron. Saruman does not. Saruman wins.

Impulsive or Procrastinating

Tolkien gave names and personalities to three of the five Wizards at this conference. Gandalf is the most aggressive, while Radagast is cautious to a fault, as he demonstrates when he flees at the mere possibility that Black Riders might be about (see Midyear's Day, 1418). If we assume the remaining two Wizards are more like Radagast than Gandalf, the Council's procrastination makes sense. Forced to choose between a Gandalf who wants action and a Saruman with good reasons for waiting, the Council follows Saruman. Literature imitates life. The White Council resembles the ineffective League of Nations of the 1930s.

Near the end of Unfinished Tales, Pt. III, Ch. IV, "The Hunt for the Ring," there is an interesting account of how Saruman regarded Gandalf's interest in pipe smoking and Hobbits.

At this point, Tolkien adds treason to the woes of the free peoples. Saruman wants the Ring for himself and believes that, if Sauron is left undisturbed, the Ring is more likely to resurface. In great secrecy, he begins his own search for the Ring around Gladden Fields.

In *The Silmarillion,* Tolkien writes that Saruman said the Ring rolled down the Anduin to the sea at this council. "The Tales of Years" claims he used the argument at the Fourth White Council. The most obvious solution is that Saruman made the same claim on both occasions.

166 Years Before

Year 1252—White Tree Dies

White Tree

Minas Tirith

The Return of the King, Bk. 6, Ap. B, "The Tale of Years" and Bk. 6, Ch. 5, "The Steward and the King."

- The White Tree dies at Minas Tirith.

Tolkien and the White Tree

Tolkien loved trees and used every opportunity to work them into his stories. The White Tree is a descendant of Teleperion, the Eldest of Trees, and is a symbol of the royal line of Gondor. With no seed, the dead tree is left in place. Its replacement will sprout in the wild some 160 years later (about 1412) and be transplanted to the city by Aragorn in 1419.

Year 1279—Gimli Born

139 Years Before

Gimli

Probably the Blue Mountains

• Gimli is born to Glóin.

The Return of the King, Bk. 6, Ap. A, "Annals of the Kings and Rulers."

Gimli's Life-to-be

Tolkien's Dwarves provide much of the continuity between *The Hobbit* and *The Lord of the Rings.* Glóin will be part of Thorin's expedition with Bilbo 62 years later in 1341. After that he becomes important enough that, with his son Gimli, he is sent to take the message about Sauron's search for Bilbo's Ring to Rivendell in 1418. Finally Gimli will travel with Frodo as one of the Nine Companions and the representative of the Dwarves.

The Hobbit, Ch. 1, "An Unexpected Party and *The Fellowship of the Ring,* Bk. 2, Ch. 2, "The Council of Elrond."

Thursday, September 22, 1290—Bilbo Born

September 15
128 Years Before

Bilbo

Probably Bag End, Hobbiton, Shire

• Bilbo Baggins is born.

The Return of the King, Bk. 6, Ap. B, "The Tale of Years."

Bilbo's Family Tree

Like many Englishmen of his day, Tolkien was fascinated by family trees. Bilbo was the son of Bungo Baggins and Belladonna Took, giving him ancestors in the adventurous Took family and the stable Baggins—a mixture Gandalf will later find attractive. Bungo, the stable one, builds the marvelous Bag End home where Bilbo will live. Belladonna, the more adventurous one, has a reputation for being odd and is a daughter of Gerontius Took ('Old Took'), who is a friend of Gandalf. In *The Hobbit,* Tolkien will portray the two traditions warring within Bilbo, one urging him to seek adventure, the other preferring to stay home.

For Bilbo's two family trees, see those for "Baggins of Hobbiton" and "Took of Great Smials" in *The Return of the King,* Bk. 6, Ap. C, "Family Trees," as well as *The Hobbit,* Ch. 1, "An Unexpected Party." For Baggins' family history, see *Letters,* No. 214. You can find an interesting discussion of the meaning of "Bag End" and other Tolkien expressions in Chapter XII of David Day's *The Hobbit Companion.* For more on the Took family tree, see the start of Chapter 5.

Bilbo's Parents

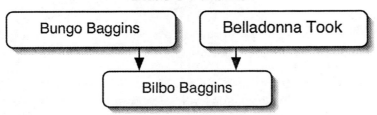

117 Years Before

Year 1301—Ithilien Depopulated

People of Ithilien

Ithilien in Gondor

The Return of the King, Bk. 6, Ap. A, "Annals of the Kings and Rulers." Frodo's travels through Ithilien are in *The Two Towers*, Bk. 4, Chapters 4 to 7. The 1354 date for the last exodus is from *The Return of the King*, Ap. B, "The Tale of Years."

- Attacks from Mordor drive out most of Ithilien's population.
- Gondor builds Henneth Annûn as a hidden refuge.

Henneth Annûn

Again, Tolkien is preparing his tale far in advance. Henneth Annûn allows Gondor to keep soldiers secretly stationed in Ithilien to observe and harass Mordor. A few people remain in Ithilien for 53 more years, until 1354, when an eruption of Mount Doom sends them fleeing across the Anduin River. This final flight from Ithilien under darkened skies may give Sauron the idea of using darkness with his attack on Minas Tirith (March 10, 1419). Frodo and Sam will visit both the region and Henneth Annûn in 118 years starting on March 7, 1419.

107 Years Before

Year 1311—The Fell Winter

Shire Hobbits

Shire

The Fellowship of the Ring, Bk. 1, Ch. 11, "A Knife in the Dark" and *The Return of the King*, Bk. 6, Ap. B, "The Tale of Years." The wolves were driven into inhabited areas because the great cold had killed their usual prey.

- Rivers freeze over and white wolves attack Shire settlements.
- Hobbits are called to action by the Horn-call of Buckland.

Sheltered Shire

Even as Tolkien builds up a sense of danger, he allows the Shire to retain a false sense of security. In 107 years on September 29, 1418, Fatty Bolger will sound the Horn-call for the first time since this wolf invasion. Only two crises in over a century hint at how sheltered life in the Shire is.

98 to 97 Years Before

Year 1320 to 1321—Old Took Dies

Gerontius 'Old' Took

Shire

The Hobbit, Ch. 1, "An Unexpected Party" and *The Return of the King*, Bk. 6, Ap. B, "The Tale of Years." For Bilbo's remarks on Old Took's long life, see *The Return of the King*, Bk. 6, Ch. 6, "Many Partings" and Bk. 6, Ch. 9, "The Grey Havens."

- In 1320 Gerontius 'Old Took' dies at the age of 130.

Old Took and a Long Life

Death is a constant theme in Tolkien's writings. Near the end of his life, Bilbo wishes to live longer than Old Took and become the longest-lived Hobbit. A century from now in 1421, when he passes through the Shire on his way to Grey Havens, he talks of doing just that. It is easy to suspect that Tolkien himself wished for a long and full life much like Bilbo's, with the last years filled with comfort, widespread respect, the loving attention of a few close friends, no worries, and a dabbling in languages and literature that did not interfere with frequent naps and good meals.

Bilbo and Gandalf

Bag End, Shire

- In 1321 Gandalf visits the Shire, noticing the young Bilbo.

Noticing Bilbo

In *Unfinished Tales,* Tolkien has Gandalf closely observing the 31-year-old Bilbo and becoming impressed with his reputation for curiosity. Since Bilbo does not remember what Gandalf looked like when they meet again twenty years from now in 1341, it is likely that he paid less attention to the Wizard than to his fireworks.

The Hobbit, Ch. 1, "An Unexpected Party," *The Return of the King,* Bk. 6, Ap. B, "The Tale of Years." and *Unfinished Tales,* Pt. 3, Ch. 3, "The Quest of Erebor," near the start.

Thursday, March 1, 1331—Aragorn Born

February 23
87 Years Before

Aragorn and Elrond

Rivendell

- Aragorn II (Strider) is born.

Aragorn's Long Life

Aragorn's family is extraordinarily long-lived. At sixty, his father Arathorn II probably has the vigor of a man in his early twenties. Aragorn will turn eighty-eight as the War of the Ring begins. Gilraen, Aragorn's mother, was born in 1307 and was 24 years old when Aragorn was born.

The Silmarillion, "Of the Rings of Power and the Third Age," *The Return of the King,* Bk. 6, Ap. A, "Annals of the Kings and Rulers," Sec. I, v, "Here Follows a Part of the Tale of Aragorn and Arwen" (beginning) and Bk. 6, Ap. B, "The Tale of Years."

Aragorn's Parents

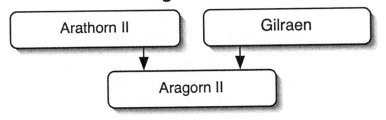

1333—Aragorn's Father Killed

85 Years Before

Uncertain, perhaps in Misty Mountains east of Rivendell

- In 1333 Aragorn's father, Arathorn II, is killed battling Orcs.

Aragorn's Childhood

Tolkien is finely crafting his narrative. Arathorn's death battling Orcs may be the result of Sauron's scheme to get rid of competitors. Notice how close he came to being successful. If Arathorn had been killed a mere three years earlier, Aragorn would have never been born. (Tolkien comments on that in "Here Follows a Part of the Tale of Aragorn and Arwen.") Afterward, Elrond becomes Aragorn's foster father, much like Tolkien's own acquisition of a guardian after the death of his parents. But Aragorn faced dangers that never troubled Tolkien. In 1250, 81 years

The Silmarillion, "Of the Rings of Power and the Third Age," *The Return of the King,* Bk. 6, Ap. A, "Annals of the Kings and Rulers," Sec. I, v, "Here Follows a Part of the Tale of Aragorn and Arwen" (beginning) and Bk. 6, Ap. B, "The Tale of Years."

earlier, Gandalf had warned Elrond that Sauron was trying to kill all the heirs of Isildur. To protect Aragorn, Elrond hides his true identity. Folk tales follow a similar theme when a prince or princess is reared in secrecy as protection from a murderous usuper to the throne.

79 Years Before

Year 1339—Saruman Searches for the Ring

Saruman

Anduin valley

- Saruman discovers Sauron is looking along the Anduin for the Ring.

Saruman's Treachery

The picture Tolkien paints grows darker. Saruman treachery is almost complete. He will say nothing about this important discovery at the critical Third White Council that meets in August of 1341.

Blending the Northern with the Mediterranean

The Silmarillion, "Of the Rings of Power and the Third Age" and *The Return of the King,* Bk. 6, Ap. B, "The Tale of Years." Sauron's search is not that far from Isengard, so from this point on Saruman remains close to Isengard and strengthens its defenses.

Letters, No. 294. For Hannah Arendt's remarks, see her *The Origins of Totalitarianism,* 172–73. For the link between her ideas and Tolkien's, see "The Ring and Totalitarianism" at the end of Chapter 16. For Tolkien's views of Nazism see, "Tolkien and 'Lunatic' Aryan Myths" and "Black and White in Tolkien" at the end of Chapter 18. By substituting "species" for "race," "Nordic" ideas on racial decay can be blended almost seamlessly with later Darwinian ideas about the survival of the fittest.

Although Tolkien was fascinated by the languages of Northern Europe, he also had "a particular love for the Latin language, and among its descendants for Spanish." *Letters,* No. 294.

Tolkien hinted at how "Nordic" tales became linked with racism in a 1968 letter in which he associated his dislike for the word "Nordic," with "racialist theories" of "French origin." He is referring to Count Arthur de Gobineau's 1853, *Essai sur l'Inégalité des Races Humaines.* As Hannah Arendt noted, Gobineau's basic idea was "that the fall of civilizations is due to the degeneration of races and the decay of races is due to a mixture of blood" with inferior races. At first his ideas were poorly received because, "the liberal optimism of the victorious bourgeois wanted a new edition of the might-right theory" (Social Darwinism), rather than pessimism about "inevitable decay." It took half a century for that optimism to fade, and it took the huge death toll of World War I to make pessimism fashionable. Because Gobineau's master race was Germanic, his ideas, echoed by others, would prove particularly attractive in Germany. Unlike France, Germany had to explain a lost war. They did that by blaming another 'race' that was mixing with Germans—the Jews.

Tolkien went on to point out that *The Lord of the Rings* concludes with a Gondorian empire centered on Minas Tirith that is "far more like the re-establishment of an effective Holy Roman Empire with its seat in Rome than anything that would be devised by a Nordic." Tolkien's ideal "Northern" culture (his favored term) was to be tempered by ideas passed from Mediterranean civilizations through the Judeo-Christian religion. It is not "Nordic" in any Gobineau sense.

4

A Chance Encounter

1341 to 1355

Gandalf meets Thorin to the Fourth White Council

Covers 15 Years
77 to 63 Years Before

As writer David Day notes, Tolkien's famous children's tale began "on a certain fateful summer afternoon in Oxfordshire in 1930." Tolkien was correcting school papers, when he came upon a blank page. In a flash of inspiration, he scribbled, "In a hole in the ground there lived a Hobbit." "Names," Tolkien would later say, always generate a story in my mind. Eventually I thought I'd better find out what Hobbits were like." What he discovered became *The Hobbit,* and out of its success grew the larger tale about the Ring that Bilbo found. In this chapter we take a chronological look at events in the former tale that affect the later story.

David Day, *The Hobbit Companion*, 10. The basic text of *The Hobbit* (except for the last chapters) existed as early as 1932, when it was read by Tolkien's friend C. S. Lewis. See *Letters*, No. 9. For the origin of *The Hobbit* see *Letters*, No. 163.

Some events that follow existed only in manuscripts during Tolkien's life. We include them because they shed light on how he may have intended to fill gaps in his story.

Thursday, March 15, 1341—Meeting in Bree

March 9
77 Years Before

Gandalf and Thorin

Bree

- Thorin and Gandalf meet in Bree.
- They decide to reestablish the Dwarf kingdom at Lonely Mountain.
- Thorin invites Gandalf to his Blue Mountain home.
- Gandalf accepts, and the two leave Bree.

The Return of the King, Bk. 6, Bk. 6, Ap. A, "Annals of the Kings and Rulers," Sec. II, "Durin's Folk" and *Unfinished Tales*, Pt. III, Ch. III, "The Quest of Erebor."

Dwarf Greed Contrasted with Wizard Planning

Keep in mind the different traits Tolkien gave Dwarves and Wizards. In this tale, Thorin and Gandalf are both true to their characters. Thorin was eastbound, probably on business. His eagerness to get rid of the dragon is linked to his desire to reclaim family gold. Dwarves are very materialistic. In contrast, Gandalf is serving a higher cause. His strategy includes the cultivation of key friendships. He is bound for the Shire for a rest that probably includes a visit with Frodo. He has not visited the Shire since the year after Old Took's death in 1320, over two decades earlier.

Tolkien offered differing accounts about where the two met, near Bree or at the inn in Bree. The issue might be settled by claiming they saw each other approaching the village but did not talk until they arrived at the inn.

Tolkien would have hated a Disney-like cartoon adaptation of *The Hobbit*. In 1937, he wrote of his "heartfelt loathing" for "anything from or influenced by the Disney studios." See *Letters*, No. 13 and 234.

To understand what Tolkien was doing as a writer, we must look at how he shaped his imagined history. The free people of Middle-earth are growing weaker with each generation and live in isolated enclaves surrounded by unpopulated wildernesses. Those east of the Misty Mountains are separated from those to the west by Orcs in the mountains. The greatest danger is the growing power of Sauron in Mirkwood. From there he poses a military threat to the Elves of Mirkwood and Lórien. However, if the Dwarf Kingdom at the Lonely Mountain could be reestablished and united with the men of Dale, bringing prosperity and a growing population to both, it would counter Sauron's expansion. That is exactly what happens 78 years later in March of 1419 during the war with Sauron. Although Tolkien's Gandalf cannot foresee the results of each step he takes, there is a practical reason behind most of them.

A greater distance, longer delays with Thorin, or more time spent getting across the Gulf of Lune merely increase Gandalf's per-day travel distance without making major changes in arrival and departure dates. It is unlikely that Gandalf's cart would create problems when he leaves with Bilbo. In an agricultural society like the Shire, it would be easy to find a farmer who would board a horse in exchange for the use of both horse and cart.

Tolkien did not provide a precise record of Gandalf's travels between March 16 and April 24, 1341. But it is possible to make assumptions. The distance from Bree to Thorin's halls in the Blue Mountains was over 350 miles, and the distance from there back to Bag End was over 250 miles. Since Gandalf traveled once from Bree to the Blue Mountains and three times to or from Bag End, he traveled over 1100 miles in 39 days. Assuming Gandalf spent two days with Thorin in the Blue Mountains on his first visit, one day visiting the Shire, and yet another day pressuring Thorin to use Bilbo on their expedition, that leaves 35 days for travel and means Gandalf averaged some 32 miles a day. The speed that would require (perhaps four miles per hour) suggests Gandalf should be seen as traveling by horse-drawn cart. Since Thorin, like most Dwarves, probably hated riding on horseback, a cart would allow the two to travel together.

Some of the dates that follow are calculated.

March 10–19
10 Days

Friday, March 16 to Sunday, March 25, 1341

Gandalf and Thorin

Dates Calculated

Through the Shire to Blue Mountains

Unfinished Tales, Pt. III, Ch. III, "The Quest of Erebor." This chapter also explains the link between *The Hobbit* and *The Lord of the Rings*.

- Gandalf and Thorin travel through the Shire from March 17 to 20.
- They continue to the Blue Mountains along the Great East Road.

Gandalf's United We Stand

Here Tolkien has Gandalf thinking strategically. If the free peoples remain as divided and contemptuous of one another as Thorin is toward Hobbits, they stand little chance against the might of Sauron. The seeds of the alliance that will form 77 years later at the Council of Elrond may have been sown in Gandalf's mind during this journey. To find what Tolkien would call an 'application' of these events, we need only turn to Europe in the 1930s, when a divided continent did not unite to resist Hitler.

Monday, March 26 to Thursday, March 29, 1341

March 20–23
4 Days

Gandalf and Thorin
Dates Calculated

Blue Mountains

- About March 26, Gandalf and Thorin reach Thorin's home.
- Thorin tells Gandalf of his plan to march against the dragon.
- Gandalf calls the plan unrealistic and leaves for the Shire (March 29).

Self-centeredness as Strength

Tolkien is making a subtle observation about human society though the Dwarves. Their self-centeredness is both their weakness and their strength. That attitude makes it difficult to get them to serve any cause but their own. But as we will see, it also means that they will not be interested when Sauron proposes an alliance with them in 1417. Evil and good both call on us to put aside petty interests and serve a greater cause. The difference lies in the means and ends of that cause.

Unfinished Tales, Pt. III, Ch. III, "The Quest of Erebor." Travel from Bree to the Blue Mountains takes some 11 days. Travel between the Blue Mountains and Hobbiton takes 8 or 9 days. At the end of this story, Frodo takes 8 days to reach Grey Havens, not far from the Blue Mountains. Sam, Merry and Pippin, eager to return to family and friends, take seven days to return to the Shire.

Thursday, April 6, 1341—Bilbo Away

March 30

Gandalf
Date Calculated

Hobbiton, Shire

- Gandalf reaches Hobbiton to see Bilbo, who is not home.
- A neighbor tells Gandalf that Bilbo may be looking for Elves.

Amazing Discovery

According to the *Unfinished Tales* reference, before leaving Bag End on April 5, Bilbo hinted to a neighbor that he was traveling in the hope of meeting Elves. For Elves, April 6 in the Shire calendar is either New Year's Day or the day before or after it (depending on the point in the 12-year leap-year cycle of the Elves), so it is likely Bilbo had gone hiking in the hope of encountering Elves celebrating in some meadow. That would lead Gandalf to assume (wrongly) that Bilbo longed for adventure.

Keep in mind what Tolkien is trying to do with the ancestry and lifestyle he has provided for Bilbo. Gandalf is looking for a Hobbit as unusual as Old Took. The news he hears about Bilbo seems good. The Hobbit is considered odd by his neighbors. He has remained a bachelor, leaving him free to depart on a moment's notice. (Tolkien took a husband's responsibilities to wife and family seriously.) Probably after spending less than a day in Hobbiton, Gandalf departs for the Blue Mountains again. He now has a scheme to recover the Lonely Mountain and perhaps teach Dwarves and Hobbits to cooperate.

The Return of the King, Bk. 6, Bk. 6, Ap. A, "Annals of the Kings and Rulers" and *Unfinished Tales,* Pt. III, Ch. III, "The Quest of Erebor." Dwarves going to and from the Blue Mountains would pass a few miles from Bag End on the Great East Road.

April 8

Saturday, April 15, 1341—Gandalf with Thorin

Gandalf and Thorin
Date Calculated

Blue Mountains

Unfinished Tales, Pt. III, Ch. III, "The Quest of Erebor" and *The Return of the King*, Bk. 6, Ap. A, "Annals of the Kings and Rulers." The Dwarves fear of the dragon is in *The Hobbit*, Ch. 12, "Inside Information." Bilbo's theft of the Arkenstone is in Ch. 13, "Not at Home," and his clever use of it to end a foolish war is in Ch. 16, "A Thief in the Night." Balin's courage is shown again when he leads the return to Moria in 1389.

- Gandalf tells Thorin to use a Hobbit to sneak up on the dragon.
- Thorin claims Hobbits are cowards but finally agrees to include Bilbo.

Making Fun of Hobbits

Tolkien has both Gandalf and Thorin malign Hobbit character. Gandalf hints that Bilbo is a professional burglar, while Thorin believes a Hobbit is too cowardly to get near a dragon. In *The Hobbit,* Tolkien gives both ideas a unique twist. He exposes the Dwarfs as less-than-brave. When it comes time to enter the Dragon's lair, only Balin accompanies him down the tunnel. Nor were the Dwarves happy to discover that, when need demanded, the burglar they hired could steal from them, as Bilbo does with the Arkenstone.

April 10

Saturday, April 17, 1341—Leave for the Shire

Gandalf and Thorin with Dwarves
Date Calculated

Blue Mountains

Unfinished Tales, Pt. III, Ch. III, "The Quest of Erebor" and *The Return of the King*, Bk. 6, Ap. A, "Annals of the Kings and Rulers."

- Gandalf and the Dwarves leave for the Shire.

Gandalf's Persuasive Powers

Perhaps as readers we can think this chronology a bit beyond what Tolkien wrote. To make sure Thorin did not change his mind about including Bilbo in the expedition, Gandalf probably traveled with the Dwarves until they reach the borders of the Shire. Then he may have raced ahead for Hobbiton to meet with Bilbo and persuade him to join the adventure, arriving a day ahead of the Dwarves. What Gandalf is trying to do—persuade Dwarves to go into business with a Hobbit and persuade a Hobbit to go on an adventure—is not easily accomplished.

See Gandalf's remarks in *The Hobbit*, Ch. 1, "An Unexpected Party." Gandalf's many trips back and forth demonstrate he has more on his mind than enriching a few Dwarves.

Don't forget another characteristic of Tolkien's Dwarves—they do not forget even the small details of grudges. Thráin II left the Blue Mountains on his ill-fated journey to the Lonely Mountain on April 21, 1241. Thorin's journey begins on almost the same day exactly a century later. (Since April 21 in the Shire calendar is always a Friday, Gandalf may be referring to the date in a Dwarf calendar.)

Chronology in The Hobbit

Tolkien was still learning to handle complex tales when he wrote *The Hobbit*. The dating in it is not as precise as that in *The Lord of the Rings*, particularly the excruciatingly slow pace that Bilbo and the Dwarves seem to travel. At times averaging only four to six miles a day, they seem to be crawling to the Lonely Mountain on their hands and knees.

For these chronological problems, see "Introduction" in "The Hobbit" section of Karen Fonstad's *The Atlas of Middle-earth.*

**At this point, the narrative of *The Hobbit* begins.
We only give events in it that are important to the story of the Ring.**

Tuesday, April 25, 1341—Gandalf meets Bilbo

April 18

Bilbo and Gandalf

Bag End, Hobbiton

- Gandalf visits Bilbo, but finds him uninterested in adventure.
- Bilbo invites Gandalf to tea the next day.

Gandalf's Haste

Tolkien worked flaws into all his characters. Gandalf has a problem with haste. Laboring under a heavy load, his mistakes often result from acting too quickly. From what others said, he assumed Bilbo longs for adventure. Instead, he discovers Bilbo has grown comfortable and lazy.

Unfinished Tales, Pt. III, Ch. III, "The Quest of Erebor" and *The Hobbit,* Ch. 1, "An Unexpected Party." *The Hobbit* came out September 21, 1937. By Christmas, demand was so great that a second printing was rushed through. *Letters,* No. 15 and 20.

Wednesday, April 26, 1341—Bilbo meets Thorin

April 19

Bilbo, Gandalf and Thorin with the Other Dwarves

Bag End, Hobbiton

- Bilbo finds 13 Dwarves arriving at his door followed by Gandalf.
- Gandalf tells the Dwarves he has a map and key to a secret entrance.
- Gandalf forces the Dwarves to take Bilbo.

Secret Tunnel

Tolkien set the stage for this ninety-one years earlier (in 1250), when Gandalf slipped into Dol Guldur, Sauron's fortress in Mirkwood. There he found a dying Dwarf and got a map and key from him. Marked on the map was a secret entrance to the Lonely Mountain. Therein lies a problem. Tolkien gives us no explanation why this secret tunnel was unknown to Thorin as a young man but visible as a tunnel entrance to Smaug. Perhaps the entrance was concealed behind stonework that was destroyed when the dragon took over the mountain. At any rate, knowing about the entrance inside did not tell Thorin where its external entrance was. For that he needed Gandalf's map and key. To get that, he must take Bilbo along. From the Dwarves perspective, Gandalf drives a hard bargain.

Unfinished Tales, Pt. III, Ch. III, "The Quest of Erebor" and *The Hobbit,* Ch. 1, "An Unexpected Party."

For Thorin's account of the dragon's attack and his flight, see *The Hobbit,* Ch. 1, "An Unexpected Party." In early drafts, Bilbo was named Bingo. For more details, see the index to *The Return of the Shadow* (London: Unwin Hyman, 1988).

Thursday, April 27, 1341—Adventure Begins

Bilbo, Gandalf and Thorin with the Other Dwarves

Shire

The Hobbit, Ch. 1, "An Unexpected Party" and Ch. 2, "Roast Mutton."

- Bilbo sleeps badly and wakes up late.
- Gandalf rushes Bilbo off with the Dwarves and follows later.

Comic Relief

The Hobbit is usually considered a children's story. For Tolkien's views about such literature, see *Letters,* No. 215.

A scene like this would go over well in a cleverly done movie. In a matter of moments, Gandalf could be shown rushing an unwilling Bilbo off, totally unprepared, on a great adventure. It would echo all the times we have been rushed into doing something we don't like.

Thursday, July 19, 1341—Finding the Ring

Bilbo, Gandalf and the Dwarves

Date Calculated

Goblin cave, Misty Mountains

The Hobbit, Ch. 5, "Riddles in the Dark" and *The Fellowship of the Ring*, "Prologue."

- All the travelers but Gandalf are captured by Goblins (Orcs).
- Gandalf frees them, and all but Bilbo escape from the cave.
- Bilbo finds a Ring, meets Gollum, and escapes from the cave.

Bilbo's Account Altered

For how Frodo learned the true story about how Bilbo got the Ring, see: *The Fellowship of the Ring*, Bk. 1, Ch. 1, "A Long Expected Party." For Tolkien's belief that the original story describing how Bilbo got the Ring had to be changed, see *Letters,* No. 109. In *The Fellowship of the Ring*, Bk. 1, Ch. 2, "The Shadow of the Past," Gandalf describes his long-held suspicions about the Ring. For Tolkien's changes to the text of *The Hobbit,* see Bonnie-jean Christensen's article "Gollum's Character Transformation in *The Hobbit*" in *A Tolkien Compass*, 9f.

Given long life by the Ring, at this time Gollum has had it for some 478 years. If he was born about 840 as estimated, he is now about 500 years old. He has spent almost all of those years underground, and the Ring has been the only thing of importance in his dreary life. It is not surprising he calls it his "precious." Tolkien clearly wants us to pity Gollum.

Chapter 5, "Riddles in the Dark" in *The Hobbit* has the most detailed description of how Bilbo acquired the Ring from Gollum, but there is also a summary in the Prologue to *The Fellowship of the Ring*. In the latter Tolkien says Bilbo originally offered a different explanation for how he got the Ring, one in which Gollum offered to give it to him in exchange for winning a riddling contest. That account actually appeared in early editions of *The Hobbit* and was altered to its present form in later editions by Tolkien. In the tale as retold, Gandalf is disturbed to find that the normally honest Hobbit would lie and that increases his suspicions about the Ring. The day after Bilbo's birthday party, Frodo tells Gandalf that he knows Bilbo gave two descriptions of how he got the Ring. With these additions and modifications, Tolkien is trying to get rid of the narrative problem created by early editions of *The Hobbit* and perhaps even turn the differing stories to his advantage.

August 1341—Third White Council

White Council and Sauron

Probably Lórien

- The Third White Council meets.
- Gandalf persuades the Council to drive Sauron out of Mirkwood.
- Sauron flees to the East.

The Ring's Mistake

At this Council, Tolkien's great hero, Gandalf, makes a mistake, but one with unexpectedly good results. Gandalf wants to force Sauron away before the Dark Lord grows too great to defeat. Saruman wants to prevent Sauron from looking for the Ring along the Anduin River. In all probability Sauron flees east rather than risk a confrontation he is not yet powerful enough to win. Yet the result is that, shortly after the Ring emerges from underground for the first time in almost 500 years, Sauron is far away. If you believe that the Ring was trying to get back to its master, this is the point where that plan went astray.

Tolkien does not tell us where this White Council met. In *The Hobbit* (Ch. 7, "Queer Lodgings"), Gandalf heads west when he leaves Bilbo and the Dwarves at the entrance to Mirkwood, and says he will be returning the horse and ponies to Beorn, who is to the northwest. Whether he intends to go to Rivendell or Lórien next, returning to Beorn's is out of his way. The weight of evidence suggests Lórien. It is nearer to Mirkwood than Rivendell and thus a better place from which to launch an attack. It is also a shorter trip for Saruman, whose role in driving Sauron out is stressed by Gandalf at the Council of Elrond. Also, if the Council were about to meet in Rivendell, we would expect Tolkien to make some mention of that while the travelers were there. Finally, what Bilbo overhears when they return to Rivendell the following spring ("Gandalf had been to a Great Council"), implies the Council met elsewhere.

The Silmarillion, "Of the Rings of Power and the Third Age," *The Return of the King,* Bk. 6, Ap. B, "The Tale of Years," *The Hobbit,* Ch. 19, "The Last Stage" and *The Fellowship of the Ring,* Bk. 2, Ch. 2, "The Council of Elrond." In the last, Gandalf said Elrond knew they were moving against Sauron too late. For more details, see *Unfinished Tales,* Pt. 3, Ch. 3, "The Quest of Erebor,"

Gandalf's effort to retain Beorn's trust proves useful. Almost 77 years later, in the spring of 1418, Gandalf seems to have borrowed another horse from the Beornings in his race to the Shire to confirm that Frodo's Ring was the One Ring. The remarks Bilbo overheard are in *The Hobbit,* Ch. 19, "The Last Stage."

Monday, May 1, 1342—Rivendell Reached

April 24
76 Years Before

Bilbo, Elrond and Gandalf

Rivendell

- Journeying back to the Shire, Gandalf and Bilbo reach Rivendell.

A Children's Tale

Tolkien was wise enough to know that a children's tale like *The Hobbit.* must have a happy ending. From Rivendell on, the narrative brightens. The one dark cloud are the lawyers of Grubb, Grubb, and Burrowes, who are selling off Bilbo's Bag End possessions as he arrives. Dragons may be killed, Tolkien may be hinting, but some evils will remain.

The Return of the King, Bk. 6, Ap. B, "The Tale of Years" and *The Hobbit,* Ch. 19, "The Last Stage." In a "Guide to the Names in *The Lord of the Rings,*" Tolkien said that Bag End was "the local name for my aunt's farm in Worcestershire." See *A Tolkien Compass,* 160.

June 14

Wednesday, June 22, 1342—Mad Baggins

Bilbo

Bag End, Hobbiton

The Hobbit, Ch. 19, "The Last Stage" and *The Return of the King,* Bk. 6, Ap. B, "The Tale of Years." For Tolkien's references to the legal profession and wills see Nicholas J. Perry, "Hobbit Law?" *Minas Tirith Evening Star* (Spring 1998), 11-12. By June of 1938, the American edition of *The Hobbit* had sold 300,000 copies. *Letters,* No. 28. Sales that great created pressure for another book about Hobbits, resulting a long sixteen years later in the first volume of *The Lord of the Rings.* It is an interesting example of a children's story inadvertently inspiring adult fiction.

• Bilbo reaches the Shire and finds his home is being sold.

Mad Baggins Influences Young Hobbits

At this point, Tolkien must weaken the Hobbit prejudice against adventure, and Bilbo provides him with an opening. Bilbo's travels give him a reputation for being eccentric, and some even call him "Mad Baggins." But the same Bilbo who once denounced adventures, doesn't seem to mind. Through his influence, Frodo will acquire a thirst for adventure and, through Frodo, so will the three young Hobbits who play important roles in *The Lord of the Rings.*

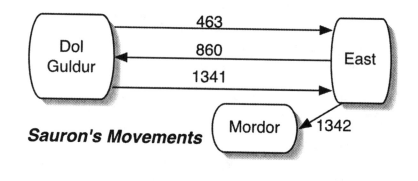

Sauron's Movements

Year 1342—Sauron in Mordor

Sauron

Mordor

The Return of the King, Bk. 6, Ap. B, "The Tale of Years." For Gollum's capture near Mordor and the problem with its dating, see the events and commentary for 1417.

• Secretly, Sauron leaves the East and occupies Mordor.

Coincidence or Planning?

Developing a chronology for Tolkien's work raises questions about whether he planned for certain things to happen, or if the result is mere coincidence. The relationship between the Ring and Mordor is one such incident. Before Sauron reoccupied Mordor, it would have been easy for whoever got the Ring to destroy it. That may have even been on Sauron's mind as he considered moving into Mordor. Did Tolkien consider that possibility and have Sauron act accordingly? Making the matter more complicated is the fact that, until he captures Gollum about three-quarters of a century later, Sauron did not know the Ring had been found by Gollum and refound by Bilbo.

Year 1344—Gollum Searches for the Ring

Gollum

Leaving the Misty Mountains

- Gollum begins to hunt for the Ring.
- He follows Bilbo's trail through Mirkwood to Dale.
- At Dale he discovers Bilbo's identity and home.

Mysterious Gollum

Tolkien wrote little about Gollum's movements during this time. Unsociable and suspicious, Gollum tells others little of what he has done and, under the influence of the Ring, what he says is often lies. As a result, we have only isolated fragments from his life.

The Fellowship of the Ring, Bk. 1, Ch. 2, "The Shadow of the Past" and *The Return of the King,* Bk. 6, Ap. B, "The Tale of Years." Gollum can no longer make himself invisible, but Dale is built over the water, so he could listen from pilings beneath the city without being seen.

Year 1349—Visiting Bag End

Balin, Bilbo and Gandalf

Bag End, Hobbiton

- Balin and Gandalf come to Bag End to see Bilbo.

Balin and Moria

Tolkien gave no reason for Balin's presence on this trip. But even at this early date, Balin may have been visiting the Dwarves of the Blue Mountains to gather support for rebuilding the Dwarf colony at Moria. At this time, eight years after the death of the dragon, the restoration at Lonely Mountain would have been going well. Moria would be the next project that would come to the minds of almost every Dwarf. In exactly forty years (1389), Balin will lead an ill-fated return to Moria. Gandalf, eager as always to strengthen the free peoples and open routes through the mountains, may have encouraged Balin in those plans. Alas, only Tolkien could have told us about that.

The Return of the King, Bk. 6, Ap. B, "The Tale of Years" and *The Hobbit,* Ch. 19, "The Last Stage." For a Dwarvish view of the return to Moria, see Glóin's remarks in *The Fellowship of the Ring,* Bk. 2, Ch. 2, "The Council of Elrond."

Year 1351—Dark Tower Rebuilt

Sauron with the Nazgûl

Mordor and Dol Guldur

- Sauron starts repairing the fortress at Barad-dûr.
- Three Nazgûl (later two) occupy Dol Guldur.

Defeat and Victory

In Tolkien's writings, defeat often proves more enduring than victory. In this case, the pessimistic Elrond is proved right and Gandalf wrong. A decade after being expelled from Mirkwood, Sauron rules in both Mordor and southern Mirkwood. Everything is growing worse.

The Silmarillion, "Of the Rings of Power and the Third Age," *The Return of the King,* Bk. 6, Ap. B, "The Tale of Years" and *Unfinished Tales,* Pt. 1, Ch. IV, Note 1.

"The Tale of Years" says that Sauron began to rebuild Barad-dûr this year. *The Silmarillion* seems to suggest it was completed the year of the Fourth White Council in 1353. This chronology assumes the rebuilding took about three years, beginning in 1351 and completed in 1353.

Arwen's Parents

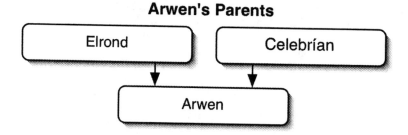

Aragorn, Arwen and Elrond—Meeting Arwen

Rivendell

The Return of the King, Bk. 6, Ap. A, I, (v), "Here Follows a Part of the Tale of Aragorn and Arwen" (beginning) and Bk. 6, Ap. B, "The Tale of Years."

In a 1938 letter, Tolkien said his tales about Hobbits were not consciously based on any book other than his own *The Silmarillion. Letters,* No. 25.

Tolkien's remarks about the importance of the romance between Aragorn and Arwen are in his *Letters,* No. 181. For Tolkien's views on romance and the relationship of the two sexes, see *Letters,* No. 43 and 49.

Aragorn and Arwen are also distantly related. See Chart II in *The Silmarillion,* "Of the Rings of Power and the Third Age."

- Elrond tells Aragorn that he is a king.
- The next day, Aragorn and Arwen meet for the first time.
- Aragorn falls in love with Arwen.

A Hobbit-centered Tale

Tolkien began *The Lord of the Rings* as a sequel to *The Hobbit,* and that made the tale very Hobbit-centered. In the main narrative, we get background for Bilbo and Frodo, but almost nothing about Aragorn. Tolkien knew his tale was complicated enough. Adding a parallel narrative about Aragorn's earlier life might strain it to the breaking point.

That is why the romance that develops between Aragorn and Arwen is hidden in appendices and half-written manuscripts. In a 1956 letter Tolkien said that, while the romance between the two is essential to the story, it is not in the narrative because it could not be worked into a tale centered almost exclusively on Hobbits. But since this book is chronology rather than a narrative, a different standard applies. A look at their romance sheds light on issues that Tolkien never put into words.

First, at this point there are reasons a marriage between the two seems unlikely. Arwen is 2710 years old and, although she appears as a beautiful maiden, she has a wealth of knowledge and experience built up over many centuries. Aragorn is a mere lad of twenty, less than one-tenth of one percent of her age. If Arwen really were a woman of about twenty as she appears, Aragorn would be a week-old baby.

Second, a look at ensuing years in this chronology shows that Tolkien expected Aragorn to show extraordinary patience. For the next 29 years (until 1380), he will be part of the struggle against Sauron, often working alone in the wilderness or in remote regions of the East and South. During that long labor he has no assurance that he will ever marry Arwen. How many other young men could endure a 29-year wait?

Even as a young man, the Aragorn that Tolkien created shows a remarkable mastery of time. Compared to Gandalf, whose impatience sometimes leads to mistakes, Aragorn can wait patiently for the proper moment. But when that time arrives, he can act quickly and decisively, as he does with his sudden choice to take the Paths of the Dead.

For Aragorn's quick response in a crisis, see the chain of events beginning on March 6, 1419.

Gollum's Travels

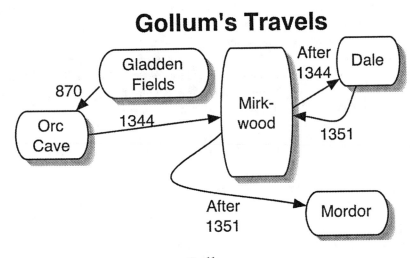

Gollum

Mirkwood to Mordor

- Returning through Mirkwood, Gollum is drawn to Mordor.

Gollum's Surprising Turn

One of the most surprising turn of events Tolkien created comes when Gollum has crossed *west* through Mirkwood, obviously headed for the Shire, but then turns *east* for Mordor. Why did he do that? Tolkien gives no clear answer (although he hints Gollum may have hoped Sauron would help him get revenge on Bilbo). For seven years Gollum has been searching for the Ring. In the Shire, he could have used his talent for stealth to locate Bilbo. Bilbo's adventures would have been at least as talked about in the Shire as they had been in Dale, and overheard conversations would have pointed him to Bag End. At that time he could have easily taken the Ring from an unsuspecting and unguarded Bilbo.

Instead, Tolkien has Gollum travel to Mordor for no sensible reason. Growing up in an isolated Hobbit village and living alone underground for almost 500 years, he may not have understood the risk he took. But hardship and danger would have soon taught him otherwise. The only explanation is that the Ring had gotten such a hold on him that he was obeying its desire to inform Sauron of its discovery.

The Fellowship of the Ring, Bk. 1, Ch. 2, "The Shadow of the Past" and *The Return of the King,* Bk. 6, Ap. B, "The Tale of Years."

Given his love for fish and his knowledge of paths in the Dead Marshes, Gollum may have lived most of the years until his capture near there. See the commentary for February 1, 1418 and March 4, 1419.

Year 1353—Fourth White Council

White Council

Location uncertain, perhaps Rivendell

- The Fourth White Council meets.
- At the meeting, Saruman insists the Ring will never be found.

Council as a League of Nations

Sauron's return to Mordor (1342) and the rebuilding of the towers of Barad-dûr (1351-53) trigger the last meeting of the White Council. Why didn't Tolkien schedule more meetings in the sixty-five years between this meeting and the Council of Elrond? He gives no reason, but we can find one in the frustration of Gandalf and Elrond. The Council had become what the League of Nations was during the 1930s, an ineffective deliberative body. Dealing with it was a waste of time.

Saruman

Isengard, Bree and the Shire

- Saruman builds up Isengard and spies on Gandalf.
- He secretly visits Bree and the Shire, establishing spies in each.

Shire as a Food Source

During this part of Tolkien's narrative, it is important to keep in mind what each character knows and doesn't know. As yet, Saruman knows nothing about Bilbo's discovery of the Ring and can't understand Gandalf's interest in Hobbits. We can only speculate about why Saruman is drawn to the Shire from slim clues Tolkien left behind.

At this time, Saruman is concentrating on building up a military force at Isengard. He needs food for a large army without arousing the suspicions of nearby Rohan. Though it is over 500 miles away, the Shire may be the closest agricultural settlement he can draw upon.

As we see later, Tolkien seems to have made one of Saruman's early Shire contacts with the greedy Sackville-Baggins family, at this time ruled over by Otho, then 43 years old, and Lobelia. We do know that in 1417–18 Saruman will secretly funnel money to their son, Lotho (1364–1419) to buy land in the Shire, so he can grow food for shipment to Isengard.

Of course, there are logistic problems with transporting food this far. Taken overland by animals, the animals might eat more grain than they can pull over such a distance. Having pastures along the way is one solution, but that would require detailed preparation. Perhaps it's best to let this point slide, particularly since Tolkien never worked this story into the narrative of *The Lord of the Rings*.

The Silmarillion, "Of the Rings of Power and the Third Age," *The Fellowship of the Ring,* Bk. 1, Ch. 2, "The Shadow of the Past" and *The Return of the King,* Bk. 6, Ap. B, "The Tale of Years." If we assume the first three councils were at Lórien, Rivendell and Lórien respectively, then this one may have continued the pattern and met at Rivendell.

For Saruman's secret visit to the Shire, see *Unfinished Tales,* Pt. 3, Ch. 4, "The Hunt for the Ring," Sec. iii. The 1353 date is from *The Return of the King,* Ap. B, "The Tale of Years," but building up these contacts in the Shire may have taken several years.

Sauron controls trade to the east and south, forcing Saruman west and north.

For more details on the Saruman and Sackville-Baggins connection, see the descriptions of events in Bree and the Shire for late 1418 and early 1419.

5

Time of Preparation

1356 to 1416

*Aragorn and Gandalf meeting
to the search for Gollum*

Covers 61 Years
62–2 Years Before

In Tolkien's great tale, evil is bound together by the power of rings. The Nazgûl, wearing the Nine Rings, must obey Sauron, creator of the One Ring. Sauron, if he gets the One Ring, will be able to force all Middle-earth to obey him. In contrast, Sauron's opponents are united by freely chosen ties of family and friendship. In this chapter, we examine how Tolkien formed those relationships and worked them into his story.

A Part of Old Took's Family Tree

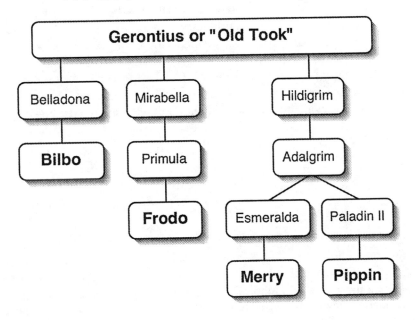

Old Took and his Descendants

Old Took died in 1320 at the age of 130. You can find a detailed family tree in "Took of Great Smials," within *The Return of the King*, Ap. C, "Family Trees." There Pippin is listed as Peregrin I and Merry as Meriadoc. Tolkien said that after Bilbo's departure, Frodo found most of his friends among Old Took's descendants, as the chart on the previous page illustrates. See the beginning of *The Fellowship of the Ring*, Bk. 1, Ch. 2, "The Shadow of the Past."

Tolkien was a bit taken with one member of the illustrious Took family—Gerontius Took, better known as "Old Took" for the advanced age to which he lived. No less than four of the five most important Hobbits in this story are his direct descendants. On the previous page is a portion of the Took family tree to illustrate that point. Notice that Bilbo is two generations removed from Old Took; Frodo is three generations removed; and both Merry and Pippin, through different parents, are four generations removed. Notice too that *all* the family links for Bilbo and Frodo were women, and that four of the seven links in all were women. Not shown here is the fact that still another Hobbit, Fredegar "Fatty" Bolger is also a fourth generation descendant of Old Took through yet another branch in that prolific family tree. Old Took had no less twelve sons and daughters, an amazing total that is only exceeded in this story by Sam and Rose's thirteen children. For Tolkien, however, Old Took's greatest legacy to Middle-earth will be the role his descendants play in the tale of the Ring. In this chapter we cover their births.

62 Years Before

Year 1356—Aragorn Meets Gandalf

Aragorn and Gandalf

Location unknown, perhaps Rivendell

The Two Towers, Bk. 3, Ch. 2, "The Riders of Rohan" and *The Return of the King*, Bk. 6, Ap. B, "The Tale of Years."

• Aragorn and Gandalf meet for the first time.

Tolkien's Male-bonding Friendship

Here, Tolkien utilizes a classic literary motif—a friendship between a ambitious young man and an experienced older man. Aragorn is a mere lad of 25, while Gandalf has been living in Middle-earth for some 2,000 years. During the years that follow, Tolkien provides Aragorn with experiences that help him mature. To give but one, he will sharpen his military skills serving both Rohan and Gondor under assumed names.

50 Years Before
September 15

Thursday, September 22, 1368—Frodo Born

Frodo Baggins

Buckland

The Return of the King, Bk. 6, Ap. B, "The Tale of Years."

To see how shocked Hobbits were 21 years after these deaths, see *The Fellowship of the King*, Ch. 1, "A Long-expected Party."

• Frodo Baggins is born.

Preparing Frodo

Frodo is the only child of Drogo Baggins and Primula (formerly Brandybuck). Although it will be painful, Tolkien is preparing him to become a most unusual Hobbit. When he is twelve, his parents are killed in a boating accident. Most Hobbits fear being on the water, so being drown is a embarrassing mark of eccentricity.

Frodo's Parents

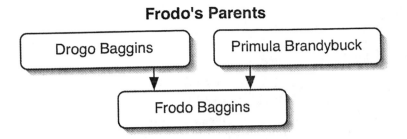

Drogo Baggins

Primula Brandybuck

Frodo Baggins

Year 1378—Boromir Born

40 Years Before

Boromir

Probably Minas Tirith

- Boromir is born as the first son of the Denthor II, Steward of Gondor.

The Return of the King, Bk. 6, Ap. B, "The Tale of Years." The second son, Faramir, will be born in five years (1383).

The Stewards of Gondor

For a lengthy history of the Stewards of Gondor, see *The Return of the King,* Bk. 6, Ap. A, "Annals of the Kings and Rulers," under "The Stewards."

Year 1380—Aragorn and Arwen Engaged

38 Years Before

Aragorn and Arwen with Galadriel

Lórien

- Aragorn (now 49) is exhausted from spying on Mordor.
- Lady Galadriel lets him enter Lórien to rest.
- Arwen falls in love with a more mature Aragorn.
- In the evening of Midsummer's day, they get engaged at Cerin Amroth.

The Return of the King, Bk. 6, Ap. A, "Annals of the Kings and Rulers" Pt. V and Bk. 6, Ap. B, "The Tale of Years." Aragorn recalls this in *The Fellowship of the Ring,* Bk. 2, Ch. 6, "Lothlórien."

Tolkien's Romantic Friendship

Tolkien put little romance into his tale and much of what is there was buried in appendices or quickly passing events. Here, he repeats a theme he explored earlier in the tragedy-filled romance between the (human) Beren and the (Elvish) Lúthien. For Arwen the cost of romance will be high. To marry him, she must take on human mortality and be separated from her father for untold years. When news of their plan to marry reaches Elrond in Rivendell, he is understandably grief-stricken. Even Elves, the most 'blessed' people in Middle-earth, have lives that include sorrow. Rather than offer happiness, their long lives multiply the opportunities to see great labors come to nothing and have centuries-old relationships come to an end. Those wanting Tolkien-like stories with more romance might try William Morris, especially his 1899 *The Roots of the Mountains*.

For more on Arwen, see *The Fellowship of the Ring,* Bk. 2, Ch. 1, "Many Meetings." For a description of Beren's romance see "Travels of Beren and Lúthien" in Karen Fonstad's *The Atlas of Middle-earth.* Aragorn will not return to Lórien until January of 1419.

Gollum

Date Approximate

Cirith Ungol, Mordor

The Two Towers, Bk. 4, Ch. 9, "Shelob's Lair" and The Return of the King, Bk. 6, Ap. B, "The Tale of Years." Cirith Ungol means "Spider's Pass." For Tolkien's remarks on Shelob, see Letters, No. 144.

• Gollum and Shelob become friends

Tolkien's Strange Friendship

The friendship that Tolkien established between Gandalf and Aragorn is the familiar bond between men focused on a great task. Tolkien contrasts that with a much odder one between Gollum and Shelob. The pair have much in common. Both prefer to live underground, shunning light. Both show little discernment in what they eat. Gollum would have eaten his fellow Hobbit, Bilbo, as easily as he ate fish. Like Gandalf, Shelob is ancient, while, like Aragorn, Gollum is inexperienced (though not young), making their relationship unequal. Of course, Aragorn's great respect for Gandalf is far healthier psychologically than Gollum's near-worship of the spider Shelob.

Thirty-nine years later, Tolkien will have Gollum exploit this relationship in his effort to get the Ring back without directly violating an oath. As in many ancient societies, breaking an oath in Tolkien's Middle-earth is fraught with dire consequences.

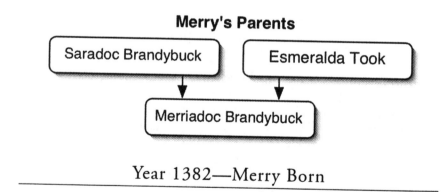

Merry's Parents

Saradoc Brandybuck   Esmeralda Took

Merriadoc Brandybuck

36 Years Before

Year 1382—Merry Born

Merry Brandybuck

Buckland

The Return of the King, Bk. 6, Ap. C, "Family Trees." For Merry's family tree, see "Brandybuck of Buckland." For a brief family history, see the opening to The Fellowship of the Ring, Bk. 1, Ch. 5, "A Conspiracy Unmasked."

• Meriadoc ("Merry") Brandybuck is born.

Tolkien's Family Friendships

Tolkien created friendships based on family links. Merry is Peregrin ("Pippin") Took's cousin and Frodo Baggins' second cousin. Three of the four main Hobbits in Tolkien's tale are thus relatives, hinting at the importance Tolkien placed on family ties and the sense of responsibility they create.

UNTANGLING TOLKIEN

Year 1383—Sam and Faramir Born

35 Years Before

Sam Gamgee

Probably Hobbiton

- Samwise Gamgee is born.

Tolkien's Work Friendships

Tolkien's Sam is the second youngest of the six children of Hamfast ("the Gaffer") Gamgee and Bell (formerly Goodchild). His family lacks the social prestige of the other three Hobbits who will leave the Shire together some four decades from now. Some critics sneer at that, as if a happy employer/employee relationship were the moral equivalent of a slave who has become so dehumanized that he loves his slavery. That is hardly the case with the friendship between Frodo and Sam. It is difficult to believe that Tolkien's tale would have been more 'realistic' had Sam continually gripped about how stupid Frodo was and looked for every opportunity to steal from him. Cynicism isn't a virtue.

The Return of the King, Bk. 6, Ap. B, "The Tale of Years." For Sam's family tree on his father's side, see "The Longfather Tree of Master Samwise" in Bk. 6, Ap. C, "Family Trees." Tolkien mentions the origin of Sam's name in *Letters*, No. 72. In No. 93, he says that Sam is more interesting than Frodo because he is a "genuine Hobbit," while Frodo must be "highminded." In No. 246, Tolkien describes Sam's "lovable and laughable" personality. In his "Guide to the Names in *The Lord of the Rings*," Tolkien said that Gamgee is an old-fashioned word for cotton-wool. See *A Tolkien Compass*, 166.

Sam's Parents

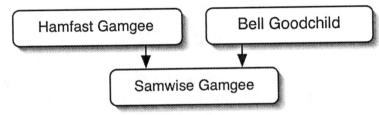

Hamfast Gamgee   Bell Goodchild

Samwise Gamgee

Faramir

Probably Minas Tirith

- Faramir is born as the second and last son of Denethor II.

Sibling Rivalry

Since Tolkien was a father, he was under no illusion that, as important as family loyalties are, brothers and sisters often become fierce rivals for their parents respect and affection. In this case the rivalry will be between Boromir, the first son (born in 1378), and Faramir, the second.

The Return of the King, Bk. 6, Ap. B, "The Tale of Years."

For more on Faramir's family background, see *Letters*, No. 244.

Year 1389—Frodo Adopted

29 Years Before

Bilbo and Frodo

Bag End, Hobbiton

- Bilbo adopts Frodo as his heir and brings him to Bag End.

The Fellowship of the Ring, Bk. 1, Ch. 1, "A Long-expected Party."

A Part of the Baggins Family Tree

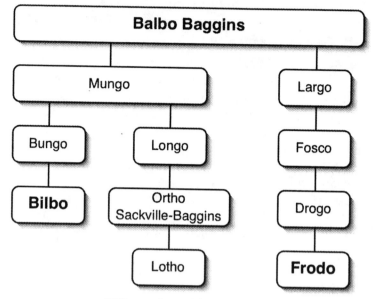

Bilbo and Frodo's Family Ties

For Bilbo and Frodo's hikes together, see *The Fellowship of the Ring*, Bk. 2, Ch. 1, "Many Meetings."

Tolkien's Hobbits mature late. Frodo is 21 and has been a orphan for 9 years. He will not come of age and be recognized as an adult until he is 33 (at Bilbo's 1401 birthday party). From the perspective of Shire society, he is still an adolescent. Bilbo is now 99 and thus quite advanced in years. Yet in spite of his age, he is able to enjoy hiking the Shire with Frodo.

For Frodo's two family trees, see those for the "Baggins of Hobbiton" and "Took of Great Smials" in *The Return of the King*, Bk. 6, Ap. C, "Family Trees." Notice that all of the first names listed above (and many others given by Tolkien) end in "o." It seems to be a family tradition.

To understand why Bilbo's adoption of Frodo made the Sackville-Baggins so mad, we need only look at a portion the family tree Tolkien created. The Sackville-Baggins share a common grandfather with Bilbo (Mungo), while Bilbo's more distant link to Frodo is through a great-grandfather, Balbo Baggins. Stated another way, three relatives separate Bilbo from Ortho, while six separate Bilbo from Frodo.

Balin with Dwarves

Moria

The Fellowship of the Ring, Ch. 2, "The Council of Elrond" and *The Return of the King*, Bk. 6, Ap. B, "The Tale of Years." For a Dwarvish perspective on the return to Moria, see Glóin's remarks in *The Fellowship of the King*, Bk. 2, Ch. 2, "The Council of Elrond."

• Balin refounds the colony at Moria.

Tolkien's Cross-racial Friendships

Here Tolkien uses a character from *The Hobbit* to establish one of the links between the twelve Dwarves who traveled with Bilbo and the events of *The Lord of the Rings*. Cooperation between races (or peoples) is such an important part of his story, we assume Tolkien deliberately included it in his story plan.

Year 1390—Pippin Born

28 Years Before

Pippin Took

Tuckborough

- Peregrin I ("Pippin") Took is born,

The Circle of Friends is Complete

With the birth of Pippin, Tolkien has given us the last of the four Hobbits who will join the Fellowship of the Ring. Like almost all Tolkien's Hobbits, Pippin's life in rooted in others. He is the youngest of the four children of Paladin II Took and Eglantine (formerly Banks). He will be the youngest of the four Hobbit travelers in this story.

The Return of the King, Bk. 6, Ap. C, "Family Trees." For Pippin's family tree, see "Took of Great Smials." For some interesting Took family history, see *Letters,* No. 214.

Pippin's Parents

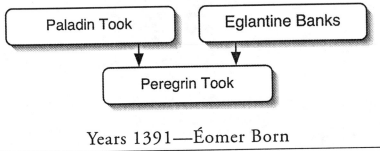

Years 1391—Éomer Born

27 Years Before

Éomer

Rohan

- Éomer, the only son of Éomund, is born.

Éomer's Family Background

For Éomer's family history see *The Return of the King,* Bk. 6, Ap. A, "Annals of the Kings and Rulers" under "The Kings of the Mark: Third Line."

The Return of the King, Bk. 6, Ap. A, "Annals of the Kings and Rulers" and Bk. 6, Ap. B, "The Tale of Years."

Wednesday, November 10, 1394—Balin Dies

24 Years Before
November 2

Balin Son of Fundin

Dimrill Dale near Moria

- Balin is killed at Dimrill Dale by an Orc.

Strong Leadership

Tolkien may be teaching us something about the importance of strong leadership. Shortly after Balin's death, the Dwarf colony he was trying to refound collapses. The fall was apparently sudden and total. Until Gandalf and his companions pass through Moria twenty-five years later on January 15, 1419, Dwarves will know little about how Balin died or Moria fell.

The Fellowship of the Ring, Bk. 2, Ch. 5, "The Bridge of Khazad-dûm and *The Return of the King,* Bk. 6, Ap. B, "The Tale of Years." This November date is taken from a record kept by Dwarves and may refer to a date in their calendar rather than that of the Shire.

1395—Éowyn Born

Éowyn

Rohan, Probably Edoras

The Return of the King, Bk. 6, Ap. A, "Annals of the Kings and Rulers" and Bk. 6, Ap. B, "The Tale of Years." For Éowyn-like characters, read of Sun-beam and Bow-may in *The Roots of the Mountains* by William Morris.

• Éowyn, daughter of Éomund and sister of Éomer, is born.

Tolkien's Brave Women

Tolkien is often criticized for not putting more women into his story. The great bravery of Éowyn shows in battle at Minas Tirith on March 15, 1419 more than compensates for that. We could just as easily fault Tolkien for not including more Elves (only four play major roles), Ents (only two), or Dwarves (only one).

Year 1400—Party Plans

Bilbo, Dwarves and Men of Dale

The Lonely Mountain and Dale

The Fellowship of the Ring, Bk. 1, Ch. 1, "A Long Expected Party."

• Bilbo orders birthday gifts for his big 1401 birthday party.

Dwarves and Men

Though the gifts were Dwarf-made, Tolkien had Bilbo order from both the Lonely Mountain and the men of Dale. He may have wanted to avoid offending either, or the Dwarves my have found it more profitable to concentrate on manufacturing and leave most sales to men. The journey is long, either over the mountains or through the Gap of Rohan. But in honor of the famous Bilbo, Dwarves will deliver these presents themselves.

Bilbo and Merry

Probably near Hobbiton

The Fellowship of the Ring, Bk. 1, Ch. 5, "A Conspiracy Unmasked."

• Merry sees Bilbo use the Ring to hide from the Sackville-Baggins.

The Conspiracy Begins

Great deeds can begin with small events. Tolkien may have intended for this brief incident with Bilbo (when Merry was about 18) to be the catalysis for what, 18 years later, becomes a conspiracy among Frodo's friends to spy out his secrets and go with him when he leaves the Shire.

Saruman

Isengard

The Return of the King, Bk. 6, Ap. B, "The Tale of Years." Aragorn described the role of Rangers in *The Fellowship of the Ring,* Bk. 2, Ch. 2, "The Council of Elrond."

• Saruman uses the *palantír* of Orthanc and is seduced by Sauron.
• His spies tell him Rangers are protecting the Shire.

Saruman's Blindness

Tolkien's transformation of Saruman from good to evil is now virtually complete. The guards that Gandalf placed around the Shire raise a question Tolkien does not seemed to have answered. Why didn't Saruman, whose every thought turned to the Ring, get more suspicious about these guards? Two answers suggest themselves.

First, those who fall into evil often see themselves as 'realists' about power. Saruman would have sneered at Gandalf's kindly protection of Hobbits as mere folly, having no practical reason.

Second, Saruman's obsession with power made it difficult for him to imagine how Gandalf could allow anyone else—much less a Hobbit—to possess the Ring. That would explain why he did not realize until too late that a Hobbit had the Ring.

Origins of The Lord of the Rings

In the preceding chapters, we have shown the complicated foundation of imaginary history that Tolkien laid for his carefully crafted tale. We have now reached a critical point. We are at the point when Tolkien chose to begin the narrative of *The Lord of the Rings*.

Initially, the choice of this particular time came by accident. With the success of *The Hobbit,* Tolkien's publisher was eager for a sequel and Tolkien, with a large family to support, was eager for added income. When his publisher declined an opportunity to publish the loosely organized collection of tales that would many years later become *The Silmarillion,* Tolkien turned his attention to creating another amusing tale about Hobbits. Both he and his publisher expected it to be a children's story with enough depth to be appreciated by adults.

The new story is set sixty years after the end of the events in the earlier book. *The Hobbit* had begun with "An Unexpected Party" involving Dwarves on a quest for gold. As Tolkien struggled to get a sense of direction for the new narrative, the 'Unexpected Party' of the first book became "A Long-Expected Party" of the second, again with Bilbo setting off on a journey with Dwarves. At this point, the narrative lacked clear direction. Though the idea seems odd to us now, Tolkien could have just as easily followed the elderly Bilbo as he tottered about the wilderness, having adventures much like those in *The Hobbit.* Or, if Bilbo had become too old to face much excitement, he might have found a replacement in the much-younger Frodo. In the end, he chose the second path, but with a journey far more serious than Bilbo's. In the process the tale became darker and more adult. Despite this fumbling beginning, Tolkien's final narrative seems so realistic many readers have trouble imagining it could have taken any other form.

Tolkien's preference for using the titles of his six books (rather than the publisher's three volumes) is discussed by Richard C. West, "The Interlaced Structure of *The Lord of the Rings*" in *A Tolkien Compass,* 82f. For a list of those titles and how they changed over time, see "Tolkien's Outline of the Book" at the end of Chapter 20.

In a October 1937 letter, Tolkien noted that, as a sequel to *The Hobbit,* one reader wanted "fuller details about Gandalf and the Necromancer." But Tolkien found that "too dark" for children (or at least what most parents wanted for children). Tolkien, however, went on to write that "A safe fairy-land is untrue to all worlds." *Letters,* No. 17.

Tolkien's narrative in *The Lord of the Rings* begins here with the first volume, *The Fellowship of the Ring,* and first book, "The First Journey."
There will be numerous flashbacks to earlier events.

Thursday, September 1, 1401—Party Talk

17 Years Before
August 25

Bilbo

Date Estimated

Hobbiton and Bywater

The Fellowship of the Ring, Bk. 1, Ch. 1, "A Long Expected Party."

- Bilbo's upcoming birthday party is discussed.

Eleventy-one

Bilbo was born in 1290, so this will be his eleventy-first birthday, a quaint Hobbit term Tolkien coined for the number 111. His adventures in *The Hobbit* took place sixty years earlier in 1341 and 1342. Frodo will turn 33 today and become an adult in Hobbit society.

August 27

Saturday, September 3, 1401

Bilbo

Date Estimated

Bag End

The Fellowship of the Ring, Bk. 1, Ch. 1, "A Long Expected Party." Tolkien mentioned having just written this chapter and thus started *The Lord of the Rings* in a December 19, 1937 letter. See *Letters,* No. 20.

- Rumors circulate that Bilbo's party will include fireworks.

Tolkien's Low-tech Shire

Given Tolkien's dislike of noisy, polluting machinery, the Shire—his idealized society—could have little that resembled a factory. Even manufacturing as simple as fireworks was not done locally and thus fireworks displays were rare and eagerly anticipated. For Bilbo's party Gandalf will provide a show not seen since Old Took died over eighty years before (in 1320) at the exceptionally old age of 130.

September 2

Friday, September 9, 1401—Dwarves Arrive

Bilbo and Dwarves

Date Estimated

Hobbiton

The Fellowship of the Ring, Bk. 1, Ch. 1, "A Long Expected Party." Typically a foot taller than Hobbits, these Dwarves stand out in the little community.

- Dwarves arrive in wagons heavily loaded with packages.

Dwarves as Industrialists

Some of these Dwarves may have come from the Dwarf settlement in the nearby Blue Mountains, but Tolkien had Bilbo ordering presents from the distant Lonely Mountain and Dale the year before. Dwarves are famous for their metal-working skills, but it is the beauty of their products rather than their usefulness that is praised. Through them, Tolkien conceded the necessity of at least some manufacturing, although in *The Lord of the Rings* none of the major characters will admire a factory for its usefulness like they do the beauty of forests or caves.

Friday, September 16, 1401—Gandalf Arrives

Bilbo, Frodo and Gandalf

Bag End, Hobbiton

- On a cart loaded with fireworks, Gandalf arrives at Bilbo's home.
- Gandalf and Bilbo discuss a joke Bilbo will play at his party.

Bilbo and Frodo

Tolkien frustrates Gandalf by having Bilbo not understand the danger that lies in possessing the Ring. He will frustrate Gandalf yet again by having Frodo adopt a similar attitude to the Wizard's warnings in the spring of 1418, when the Hobbit needs to leave the Shire quickly. Having little experience with raw evil, both Hobbits make life difficult for Gandalf, who might be called the Hasty and Quick Tempered Wizard.

The Fellowship of the Ring, Bk. 1, Ch. 1, "A Long Expected Party." *The Fellowship of the Ring* was first published in the U.K. on July 29, 1954 and in the U.S. almost three months later on October 21, 1954. *Letters*, No. 148 and "Notes on the Text" at the beginning of recent editions of *The Lord of the Rings*.

Saturday, September 17, 1401

Bilbo, Frodo and Gandalf

Date Estimated

Bag End, Hobbiton

- More carts arrive at Bilbo's house.
- During the week, food and other items are ordered.

The Fellowship of the Ring, Bk. 1, Ch. 1, "A Long Expected Party."

Monday, September 19, 1401—Tents Go Up

Bilbo and Frodo

Date Estimated

Bag End, Hobbiton

- Tents go up in a field near Bilbo's front door.

Renting Tents in the Shire

It's difficult to imagine how a community as simple and agricultural as the Shire could support a business that rents circus-sized tents capable of seating almost 150 diners. In Tolkien's day someone could rent such things from a nearby English city. But the Shire has no industrialized cities. Tolkien's Shire is not only like the rural England of his childhood, it implies the existence of something he doesn't mention as present—the large and often useful urban centers of late Victorian England. Here we must assume the tent came from Michel Delving, though it is probably no larger than a typical market town for a farming community.

The Fellowship of the Ring, Bk. 1, Ch. 1, "A Long Expected Party."

September 14

Wednesday, September 21, 1401—Party Worries

Bilbo and Frodo

Bag End, Hobbiton

- The weather turns cloudy and some worry the party will be canceled.

Rain and Tents

Perhaps fearing rain, Bilbo rented tents, including a large one for 144 special guests. Tolkien's Hobbits know how to party. Even with tents, rain would have made the party far less pleasant and the fireworks impossible.

The Fellowship of the Ring, Bk. 1, Ch. 1, "A Long Expected Party." For Tolkien's lengthy remarks about Hobbit birthday customs, see Letters, No. 214.

September 15

Thursday, September 22, 1401—The Birthday Party

Bilbo, Frodo and Gandalf

Bag End, Hobbiton

- At the end of a speech, Bilbo uses the Ring to disappear.
- With Gandalf's assistance Bilbo leaves the Ring for Frodo.
- Bilbo leaves with three Dwarves.

Leaving the Ring Behind

Good sense would suggest that the Ring would have been safer with Bilbo in Rivendell where it could be protected by the Elves rather than in the loosely guarded Shire. But Tolkien did give reasons why Gandalf wanted it left behind with Frodo. First, Bilbo's original plans were rather vague, little more than a wish to see mountains and wilderness again. Gandalf needed the Ring where he could find it. Second, since the Ring's hold on its owner increases over time, it was far better to provide a new owner who was not as bound to it, particularly someone like Frodo who had not sought it.

Bilbo retained a longing for the Ring. When he meets Frodo at Rivendell over seventeen years later (October 24, 1418), he mentions wanting to go back to the Shire to get it, but being prevented by Elrond and Gandalf. Both the latter believed that possession of the Ring should not being determined by the will of Hobbits, Elves or men. An unseen Providence had placed it in Frodo's hands and that must be respected.

The Fellowship of the Ring, Bk. 1, Ch. 1, "A Long Expected Party."

Gandalf later said the Bilbo was the first possessor of the Ring to give it up voluntarily. See *The Fellowship of the Ring, Bk. 2, Ch. 2, "The Shadow of the Past."* Later, Sam gives the Ring back to Frodo on March 14, 1489. See *The Return of the King, Bk. 6, Ch. 1, "The Tower of Cirith Ungol."*

The Fellowship of the Ring, Bk. 2, Ch. 1, "Many Meetings."

September 16

Friday, September 23, 1401

Frodo and Gandalf

Bag End, Hobbiton

- Gandalf warns Frodo to use the Ring little and leaves.

The Fellowship of the Ring, Bk. 1, Ch. 1, "A Long Expected Party."

Aragorn and Gandalf with the Rangers

Shire and elsewhere

- Increasingly, Gandalf believes Bilbo's Ring is the One Ring.
- The number of Rangers guarding the Shire is doubled.
- Gandalf and Aragorn begin a 17-year search for Gollum.

A Serious Blunder

Tolkien has Gandalf and Aragorn make a serious blunder. They assume only Gollum can tell them enough about the Ring to establish its identity. Later, probably in 1417, Gandalf realizes that the Ring itself may reveal enough to establish its identity and journeys to Minas Tirith to study the history of the Great Rings.

The Fellowship of the Ring, Bk. 2, Ch. 2, "The Council of Elrond" and *The Return of the King,* Bk. 6, Ap. B, "The Tale of Years." At the Council of Elrond, Gandalf seems to say that it was at this time he first told Aragorn his fears concerning the Ring.

November 1401—Bilbo at Rivendell

Bilbo with Three Dwarves

Date Estimated

Rivendell

- Bilbo arrives at Rivendell.

Bilbo Reaches Rivendell

Later Frodo, leaving the day after his own birthday party and traveling hurriedly, took until October 20 to reach Rivendell. Since Bilbo describes his own journey as leisurely, it is almost certain he could not have arrived until November, even if he kept to roads. On the other hand, while Bilbo is an exceptionable Hobbit, despite his love of adventure he retains a Hobbit's love for 'homely' comfort. So it is reasonable to assume he reached Rivendell as the winter cold set in. For Frodo and the others traveling west from Rivendell in 1419, the golden fall ended and the weather turned bad the last week in October, hurrying them on to Bree. Something similar could have happened to Bilbo traveling the opposite direction in 1401.

See Frodo's conversation with Bilbo in *The Fellowship of the Ring,* Bk. 2, Ch. 1, "Many Meetings." Some may wonder why, in the 17 years between Bilbo's arrival at Rivendell and that of Frodo, Bilbo couldn't have gotten Gandalf or a traveling Elf band to deliver a letter describing his safe arrival. But that would remove much of the mystery from this story. Like any good writer, Tolkien knew that what does not happen can often be as important as what does.

Spring 1402—Bilbo at Dale

16 Years Before

Bilbo with Three Dwarves

Date Estimated

Rivendell to Dale on the Old Forest Road

- Bilbo travels from Rivendell to the Dale.

Bilbo's Companions

Though Tolkien gives these Dwarves no names, it is likely that Bilbo's three companions are either Dwarves from the Lonely Mountain who had brought goods to Bilbo's birthday party or Dwarves from the Blue

See Frodo's conversation with Bilbo in *The Fellowship of the Ring,* Bk. 2, Ch. 1, "Many Meetings."

Mountains with business to conduct at the Lonely Mountain. Whatever the reason for their journey, it seems reasonable to assume that, traveling with a Frodo who is 111 years old, they spent the winter in hospitable Rivendell and take on the difficult mountain passes in the late spring. Bilbo would understand well the dangers of the Misty Mountains.

Fall of 1402—Bilbo Returns to Rivendell

Bilbo with Elrond

Date Estimated

Dale to Rivendell on the Old Forest Road

The Fellowship of the Ring, Bk. 2, Ch. 1, "Many Meetings" and The Return of the King, Bk. 6, Ap. B, "The Tale of Years."

- After visiting the Dale, Bilbo returns to Rivendell to live.

Bilbo's Stay in Rivendell

Again Tolkien provides only sketchy details. Given his great age, it is likely that Bilbo had companions for his return, perhaps even Elves, though none are mentioned. Since the journey is long and this visit to be his last to the Dale, it is likely that Bilbo stayed through the summer.

Nothing is said about the reason for Elrond's generosity in providing for Bilbo's retirement. But with Sauron's growing power, Gandalf may have encouraged him to protect the Ring-finder. During his travels Bilbo apparently said nothing to Dwarves about giving the Ring to Frodo, since in 1417 they assume it is with him at Rivendell.

Éomund, Éomer and Éowyn

Rohan

The Return of the King, Bk. 6, Ap. A, "Annals of the Kings and Rulers," under "The Kings of the Mark: Third Line." Éomund is now a Marshal of the Mark.

- Éomund is ambushed by Orcs and killed at Emyn Muil.
- His wife Théodwyn dies leaving two children, Éomer and Éowyn.
- King Théoden adopts his sister's children as his own.

Tolkien and Death

Tolkien is laying the foundation for events sixteen years in the future. King Théoden's own wife had died in childbirth, and he never remarried. Théodred, his only child, will die in battle on February 25, 1419.

We should never forget that Tolkien was born before antibiotics. He understands better than we ever can that vast stretch of time when death from childbirth or wounds in war was all too common. Though only a century removed from us, the younger Tolkien lived far closer to ancient times than we do today. To understand life thousand of years before, he only had to remove from his mind pictures of trains, steamships, printing presses and the telegraph. We have to remove much more. Our lives are filled with technologies that did not exist when Tolkien was a child and they cloud and clutter our vision of the past.

Years 1404 to 1408—Watching Frodo

Frodo and Gandalf

Bag End, Hobbiton

- Gandalf returns in 1404, looks at Frodo, and leaves.
- Gandalf makes many overnight stays over the next four years.

Gandalf's Absence

After his autumn of 1408 visit, Gandalf will remain absent until April 12, 1417, almost nine years later. If asked, Tolkien would have probably said he was busy with many activities, including the pursuit of Gollum. Given the importance Gandalf attached to this mysterious Ring, he would not have neglected Bilbo. It makes sense to assume that from 1404 to 1408, Gandalf was active west of the Misty mountains and could easily visit the Shire. From 1409 to 1418, he seems to have shifted his activities to more distant regions, perhaps east of the Misty Mountains. Those activities would have included the search for Gollum.

The Fellowship of the Ring, Bk. 1, Ch. 2, "The Shadow of the Past." Gandalf wants to see if Frodo's aging is being delayed by the Ring as was Bilbo's. That indicates that it is one of the Great Rings.

Year 1409 and After—Arwen to Rivendell

Arwen and Elrond

Lórien to Rivendell

- Elrond has his daughter Arwen move to Rivendell.

Arwen's Move

Tolkien gives no reason for this move, but one possibility is that, with the growing power of Sauron and travel becoming increasingly unsafe, Elrond preferred to have his only daughter close to him.

The Return of the King, Bk. 6, Ap. B, "The Tale of Years."

Aragorn, Arwen and Elrond

Date Approximate

Rivendell

- Aragorn comes to Rivendell
- Elrond tells Aragorn that Arwen will only marry the King of Gondor.
- Aragorn returns to his struggle against Sauron.

A Love Story: Aragorn and Arwen

In "The Tale of Aragorn and Arwen," the date of this meeting between Aragorn and Elrond is unclear, but it seems to come shortly after Arwen returns to Rivendell. Perhaps Arwen sent word to Aragorn of her move.

The Return of the King, Bk. 6, Ap. A, "Annals of the Kings and Rulers" Pt. I, v, "Here Follows a Part of the Tale of Aragorn and Arwen" and Bk. 6, Ap. B, "The Tale of Years."

Aragorn and Gandalf and Gollum

Anduin, Mirkwood, Rhovanion and Mordor

- Over the next eight years, Aragorn and Gandalf search for Gollum.

The Return of the King, Bk. 6, Ap. B, "The Tale of Years."

Sauron, Gandalf and Gollum

At the time the Great Rings were created, Sauron was able to deceive many by appearing beautiful and noble. For a history of Sauron and the Ring, see the last chapter in *The Silmarillion,* "Of the Rings of Power and the Third Age." For more about Gandalf's search for Gollum and his effort to discover whether Bilbo's Ring is the One Ring, see *Unfinished Tales,* Pt. III, Ch. IV, "The Hunt for the Ring."

Six Years Before

Spring of 1412—White Tree Sprouts

White Tree of Gondor

Date Calculated

Mount Mindolluin above Minas Tirith

- A White Tree sprouts on Mount Mindolluin.

The White Tree

The Return of the King, Bk. 6, Ch. 5, "The Steward and the King." Aragorn said the tree appeared to be *less* than seven years old, so the actual sprouting may have been in 1413 or 1414.

According to Tolkien, this White Tree descended from Teleprion, the Eldest of Trees and is the official symbol of the Kings of Gondor. Seven years later (1419) it will be found by Aragorn and replanted in Minas Tirith.

Elrond refers to the White Tree and its withering at the Council of Elrond. See *The Fellowship of the Ring,* Bk. 2, Ch. 2, "The Council of Elrond."

The last White Tree in Minas Tirith had died 160 years earlier in 1252 without leaving a seed to be planted, so the seed for this tree must have been planted far in the past. (Gandalf hints that may have been during the Second Age over three thousand years earlier.) The long-delayed but timely sprouting of this tree is another indication that more is going on in this story than is seen.

3–2 Years Before

1415 to 1416

Gollum with Sauron

Date Estimated

Roads north of Morannon that run into Mordor

- Sometime between 1409 and 1417 Gollum is captured by Sauron.

Gollum's Capture

The range of years is from *The Return of the King,* Bk. 6, Ap. B, "The Tale of Years." In *The Two Towers,* Bk. 4, Ch. 2, "The Passage of the Marshes" Gollum claimed his imprisonment came a long time before 1418, but his honesty is always questionable. Any time in Sauron's prisons would seem long.

The date of Gollum's capture seems to have been long enough before 1417, that Sauron could conclude he could get no more by torture and might benefit from letting Gollum escape and be followed. On the other hand, the imprisonment did not last long enough for Gollum's health to be broken. (Thráin II, a sturdy dwarf, lasted only five years, 1240 to 1245, in Dol Guldur.) One or two years in prison is perhaps as good a guess as any, dating the capture to perhaps 1415 or 1416. If Sauron treated him better than other prisoners, however, he could have been captured several years before that.

6

Searching for the Shire

1417 to Late August 1418

Covers 20 Months

*Gollum's capture by Sauron
to Black Riders searching the Anduin Valley*

In an article in *The National Post*, a Canadian newspaper, the well-known Tolkien literary biographer, Tom Shippey, said of Tolkien:

> For much of his life he was haunted by the fear of never finishing anything—the theme of one of his few short stories, "Leaf by Niggle." In "The Notion Club Papers," not published until 20 years after his death, he imagines his own work as a manuscript discovered on a dusty shelf sometime far in the future, incomprehensible and anonymous.

Tom Shippey, "Tolkien Teaches Us To Take Courage," *National Post*, (January 6, 2003). Shippey is the author of *J. R. R. Tolkien: Author of the Century.*

Tolkien's fear of not finishing may be why his best known hero, an unimpressive, middle-aged Hobbit bachelor named Frodo Baggins, makes his mark on history by finishing the long and difficult task that was thrust upon him against his wishes. This chapter looks at how that task began.

Year 1417—Gollum Escapes

1 Year Before

Gollum with Sauron

Barad-dûr and Cirith Ungol

- Gollum has been tortured and questioned by Sauron at Barad-dûr.
- He escapes through Cirith Ungol.

Lying to Sauron

To create a sense of drama, Tolkien must turn Sauron's attention to the Hobbit who possesses the Ring and yet not permit him to discover where the Ring is too quickly. He does that by having Gollum tell a critical lie—that the Shire from which the Baggins who stole the Ring came was near Gollum's own home on the banks of the Anduin River (that is, east of the Misty Mountains rather than west).

Tolkien did not give us a date for Gollum's capture by Sauron. If Sauron allowed Gollum to escape, as Tolkien hints, then his escape would only come after Sauron was certain he had extracted all the information he

The Fellowship of the Ring, Bk. 1, Ch. 2, "The Shadow of the Past," Bk. 2, Ch. 2, "The Council of Elrond" and *Unfinished Tales*, Pt. III, Ch. IV, "The Hunt for the Ring." Gollum briefly describes his capture in *The Two Towers*, Bk. 4, Ch. 2, "The Passage of the Marshes" and his escape in Bk. 4, Ch. 3, "The Black Gate is Closed."

Unfinished Tales, Pt. III, Ch. IV, "The Hunt for the Ring."

could get by deprivation and torture. That suggests he was held captive for a year or longer. Here we date the capture to 1415 or 1416.

Tolkien also left readers uncertain when Gollum escaped from Mordor. "The Tale of Years" gives the year as 1417. At the Black Gate of Mordor on March 5, 1419, Gollum told Frodo and Sam that his escape took place years earlier, which suggests a date no later than 1416. However, at that time Gollum was lying to conceal how much he knew about the passage through Cirith Ungol.

When the Orcs take Frodo's unconscious body away, Shagrat also puts Gollum's escape years before, so it is possible that Gollum escaped much earlier, but for some strange reason remained close to Mordor. See *The Two Towers*, Bk. 4, Ch. 10, "The Choices of Master Samwise."

Since Gollum escaped Mordor intent on finding the Ring and had no reason to remain near its terrors, it is likely he escaped in late 1417. The physical harm he received under Sauron and the need to find food in a barren waste in winter then slowed his flight long enough for Aragorn to capture him in the Dead Marshes on the date assumed here, February 1, 1418. Although that date is difficult to reconcile with some remarks and may be controversial, it fits beautifully with the overall drama of the narrative.

The Two Towers, Bk. 4, Ch. 1, "The Taming of Sméagol." Gollum also tells Frodo and Sam he was captured by Sauron on the well-patrolled road to Mordor north of the Dead Marshes.

Finally, when Gollum was captured by Frodo and Sam on the edge of the Dead Marshes, he claimed that an accident led to his coming near Mordor and being captured by Sauron. That is probably his self-obsessed way of saying that getting caught was not a part of his scheme.

Éomer

Rohan

The Return of the King, Bk. 6, Ap. A, "Annals of the Kings and Rulers." See under "The Kings of the Mark: Third Line."

- Éomer becomes a Marshal of the Mark and patrols his father's area.

Éomer the Leader

Tolkien made Éomer like his father, Éomund, who was killed fighting Orcs in 1402. He is an aggressive and independent-minded leader. In two years, he will play a critical role in Merry and Pippin's escape from Orcs.

Dáin II, Gimli and Glóin

Lonely Mountain

The Fellowship of the Ring, Bk. 2, Ch. 2, "The Council of Elrond."

- A messenger from Sauron comes to the Dwarves about October.
- Sauron wants to know where the Hobbit with the Ring lives.
- Sauron's messenger returns twice, once in 1418.

Warning Bilbo

For a history of the Dwarves and a family tree of their rulers, see *The Return of the King*, Bk. 6, Ap. A, "Annals of the Kings and Rulers," Sec. III, "Durin's Folk."

In *The Hobbit*, Tolkien's Bilbo was reluctant to discuss his magic Ring. He behaves much the same in this sequel. Though Bilbo traveled extensively with Dwarves, visiting the Dale (and perhaps the Lonely Mountain) about 1402, he apparently said nothing about giving the Ring to Frodo.

Gandalf with Denethor II

Minas Tirith

- Gandalf goes to Minas Tirith to study Ring history.
- He finds a scroll written by Isildur that describes the Ring.
- He is apparently in Minas Tirith until early 1418.

The Ring's History

For a history of Sauron and the Ring, see the last chapter in *The Silmarillion,* "Of the Rings of Power and the Third Age." For more about Gandalf's search for Gollum and his effort to discover whether Bilbo's Ring is the One Ring, see *Unfinished Tales,* Pt. III, Ch. IV, "The Hunt for the Ring." For Elrond's eyewitness account of what Isildur did with the Ring, see *The Fellowship of the Ring,* Bk. 2, Ch. 2, "The Council of Elrond," near the beginning of the chapter. For how the Ring was lost, see *Unfinished Tales,* Pt. 3, Ch. I, "The Disaster of the Gladden Fields."

Unfinished Tales, Pt. III, Ch. IV, "The Hunt for the Ring," *The Fellowship of the Ring,* Bk. 2, Ch. 2, "The Council of Elrond" and *The Return of the King,* Bk. 6, Ap. B, "The Tale of Years." Saruman had also studied Ring lore in Minas Tirith.

Tuesday, February 1 to Wednesday, March 21, 1418

235–191 Days Before
January 23–March 15
45 Days

The wary Gollum may have put too much trust in darkness. On February 1, the winter sun set about 5:30 p.m. and the moon, a waning crescent only about 30% illuminated, will not rise until after 4:30 a.m. He expects to have over 9 hours of total darkness to increase the distance between himself and the horrors of Mordor.

Aragorn with Gollum

Dead Marshes to Mirkwood

- On February 1, Aragorn captures Gollum in the Dead Marshes.
- He brings Gollum to the Elves in Mirkwood on March 21.

Dating Gollum's Capture by Aragorn

Tolkien left confusion about when this capture occurred. "The Tale of Years" dates it to 1417. "The Hunt for the Ring" in *Unfinished Tales* gives the date as February 1, with no year given. Gandalf's account at the Council of Elrond gives no date but offers hints. When Gandalf first heard the news, he assumes (rightly) that Aragorn was still with Gollum. That would be unlikely if capture had occurred a year earlier. Given how intensely Aragorn and Gandalf had searched for Gollum over the past eight years and the extreme importance of the news that Sauron now knew the Ring was found, it seems unlikely that Aragorn would have taken Gollum to the Mirkwood Elves in March of 1417, and done so little that Gandalf did not get the news for a full year. In addition, the tightly knit and rapidly moving sequence of events that follow the capture fit far better with the February 1, 1418 date assumed here than with the 1417 date Tolkien gives in "The Tale of Years."

Unfinished Tales, Pt. III, Ch. IV, "The Hunt for the Ring," *The Fellowship of the Ring,* Bk. 2, Ch. 2, "The Council of Elrond," and *The Return of the King,* Bk. 6, Ap. B, "The Tale of Years." Given how well Gollum knows the Dead Marshes and how difficult the maze of swampy ground is for anyone who did not know it, Sauron's spies may not have been able track him there. That would make him overconfident and vulnerable to capture by Aragorn. Taking him to Mirkwood, Aragorn covered 900 miles in 45 days, averaging with his captive a grueling 20 miles a day.

The March 5 remark is from *The Two Towers,* Bk. 4. Ch. 3, "The Black Gate is Closed." Keep in mind that Gollum has been living in a dayless, seasonless and yearless cave for over five hundred years. That will affect his ability to describe time.

In many ways, this problem resembles that Tolkien faced with the first edition of *The Hobbit,* where Gollum freely gave the Ring to Frodo. That clashed with the plot of *The Lord of the Rings* and had to change. In similar fashion, the fast-paced drama of Gollum's capture by Aragorn and Gandalf's race, first to Mirkwood and then to the Shire, clashes with Tolkien's earlier writing, which indifferently placed Gollum's escape from Sauron and capture by Aragorn two or more years in the past. Given the opportunity, Tolkien might have come up with a solution to this chronological problem.

Unfortunately, both the 1417 and 1418 dates for Gollum's capture by Aragorn face another problem. They clash with a remark Frodo makes to Gollum on March 5, 1419, when he says that Aragorn had captured Gollum "some years ago." Tolkien's 1417 date for the capture was only a few weeks over two years before, and the date used in this book is just over a year in the past. Neither fits with a "some years" remark, and it seems unlikely that, when Gandalf came to Frodo at Bag End to tell him about the Ring, he would not tell him when Gollum was captured.

One alternative would be for Aragorn to capture Gollum in 1417 and for Gandalf to arrive to question him soon afterward with that questioning going on for just over a year. When Gollum finally breaks, Gandalf has all the evidence he needs to establish the Ring's identity. But that dating runs headlong into an almost insurmountable problem. Gandalf *already* knew enough from his research at Minas Tirith to test the Ring and see if it was the One Ring. It seems unlikely that, with that sort of knowledge, Gandalf would tarry a year in dark Mirkwood listening the Gollum hiss and whine. While it may be true that Gandalf needed Gollum's account to know just how much Sauron knew, the fact that Sauron had captured Gollum and tortured him should have been sufficient to tell Gandalf that Frodo needed to be warned very quickly.

So, all in all, a March 1, 1418 date for Gollum's capture fits best with what Tolkien's characters are doing, however it may clash with isolated bits of information and scraps of conversation.

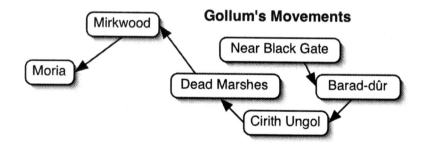

Gollum's Movements

Early to Mid-March of 1418—To Mirkwood

Gandalf

Date Estimated

Lórien to Mirkwood

Unfinished Tales, Pt. III, Ch. IV, "The Hunt for the Ring" and *The Fellowship of the Ring,* Bk. 1, Ch. 2, "The Shadow of the Past."

- Elves in Lórien tell Gandalf of Gollum's capture.
- Gandalf leaves for Thranduil's Caverns in Mirkwood.

Gandalf and Gollum's Capture

Since Gandalf reaches Thranduil's Caverns, 400 miles from Lórien, only two days after Aragorn, it seems almost certain that, as Aragorn traveled north from the Dead Marshes, he found a way to send word of the capture to Lórien, a little over 200 miles to his west. If Gandalf was able to gallop for Mirkwood as rapidly as he is later able to reach the Shire, he probably received word of Gollum's capture in mid-March. If he must travel on foot, then he must leave Lórien by early March. Aragorn probably passed east of Lórien in mid-February, so even on foot the news could have reach Lórien by early March.

Notice how providential the timing is. If this news had not arrived until after Gandalf had left Lórien for the Shire, Gollum would not have been questioned by Gandalf, if at all, until later. As a result, Frodo would not have been as well-warned of danger as he was. Gandalf and Aragorn would have not met until later, and the Shire might not have been as well guarded by Rangers when the Black Riders arrive in late September. Much hinged on Gandalf getting this news in time.

This suggests that in these manuscripts Tolkien was wrestling with what could have become an interesting tale, one that was unfortunately never completed.

Friday, March 23 to Wednesday, March 28, 1418

183–178 Days Before
March 17–22
6 Days

Aragorn and Gandalf with Gollum

Northeastern Mirkwood

- Gandalf reaches Thranduil's Caverns on March 23.
- Questioning Gollum, Gandalf concludes the Ring is the One Ring.
- Gandalf discovers Sauron knows the Ring is found.

Unfinished Tales, Pt. III, Ch. IV, "The Hunt for the Ring" and *The Fellowship of the Ring,* Bk. 1, Ch. 2, "The Shadow of the Past."

Delay in Mirkwood

Tolkien often placed his characters in situations where they must alter their plans based on changed circumstances. Here he has Gandalf headed for the Shire to examine the Ring based on what he learned at Minas Tirith. Gollum's capture introduces a delay in that trip, but what he learns from Gollum makes the journey to Bag End even more important.

Thursday, March 29 to Tuesday, April 11, 1418

177–165 Days Before
March 23–April 4
13 Days

Gandalf and Aragorn

Day 1 to 13 of 14 to the Shire

Mirkwood and Carrock

- On March 29, Gandalf and Aragorn leave Mirkwood for the Shire.
- At Carrock they get horses, probably from the Beornings.

Unfinished Tales, Pt. III, Ch. IV, "The Hunt for the Ring."

Managing Characters

Few authors manage their characters and plot as well as Tolkien. In 1341 (77 years earlier) Gandalf had been careful to return a borrowed horse and ponies to Beorn to keep his trust. Now he reaps the benefit of that care by acquiring desperately needed horses for himself and Aragorn.

The Fellowship of the Ring, Bk. 1, Ch. 10, "Strider." Gandalf's return of Beorn's horses is in *The Hobbit,* Ch. 7, "Queer Lodgings."

Gandalf travels 800 miles in 14 days, averaging almost 60 miles a day over a route that includes primitive trails and a mountain range.

From what Aragorn (as Strider) tells the Hobbits in Bree just after they meet, Aragorn accompanied Gandalf on this trip, perhaps stopping east of the Shire (about April 11) to ensure it is well-protected by his Rangers. Before parting, they probably schedule their May 1 meeting at Sarn Ford.

To add to the mystery, at this time across the Shire rumors of strange events cause even the most reclusive Hobbits to sense things are changing on the outside. Sam's participation in the discussion at *The Green Dragon* may have stimulated his curiosity and encouraged him to eavesdrop on the April 13 conversation between Gandalf and Frodo. Tolkien dates that discussion to early April, but in the narrative itself he may be hinting that it took place on April 11, the night before Gandalf's arrival.

*164 Days Before
April 5*

Wednesday, April 12, 1418—Gandalf in the Shire

Frodo and Gandalf

Day 14 of 14 to the Shire

Bag End, Hobbiton

The Fellowship of the Ring, Bk. 1, Ch. 2, "The Shadow of the Past" and Unfinished Tales, Pt. III, Ch. IV, "The Hunt for the Ring." For more on Tolkien's use of light and darkness, see "Black and White in Tolkien" at the end of Chapter 18.

• In evening Gandalf reaches Frodo and they talk.

Night and Day, Darkness and Light

Tolkien now weaves mystery and suspense into a narrative that up to this point has had nothing more adventurous than a birthday party. He has Gandalf end their conversation by warning that some things are best left to daylight. Evil in Tolkien is often linked to darkness and good to light.

*163 Days Before
April 6*

Thursday, April 13, 1418—Ring Talk

Frodo, Gandalf and Sam

Frodo's Study at Bag End, Hobbiton

The Fellowship of the Ring, Bk. 1, Ch. 2, "The Shadow of the Past."

It has been 77 years since Bilbo's adventure and the discovery of the Ring. Frodo and Gandalf have not seen each other since the fall of 1408, over nine years earlier.

• In the morning, Gandalf and Frodo talk further about the Ring.
• They discover Sam listening outside the window.

Tolkien's Hints and his New Story

In his writings Tolkien constantly dropped hints about the future. In this conversation between Gandalf and Frodo, he offers two significant hints. He has Gandalf tell Frodo that Gollum should be pitied because he may have a crucial role to play. He also has Frodo demonstrate an inability to toss the Ring into an ordinary fire. If he cannot do that while well-fed, rested, and safe in the Shire, how will an exhausted Frodo find the strength to thrown it into the Crack of Doom?

Readers often sense that the first chapter of *The Lord of the Rings* is less dark and serious than the rest of the book, and that the book really begins with the second chapter. That's because Tolkien intended to write a sequel to *The Hobbit,* but found himself drawn into a far different tale. The literary transition comes during this conversation between Gandalf and Frodo. Tolkien even put his plot transformation in Frodo's mouth. To fight boredom, Frodo had planned to leave on a adventure much like Bilbo's (the original sequel to *Hobbit*). He now realizes he must face danger of a different sort (the new tale). At that point Tolkien's writing was transformed from children's story into a complex adult work of fiction.

Late April, 1418—Gandalf's Warning

Frodo and Gandalf

Date Approximate

Bag End, Hobbiton

- Gandalf warns Frodo he must leave quietly and soon.
- Frodo decides to leave with Sam in late September.
- Gandalf suggests they head for Rivendell.

What Did Sauron Know?

Here Tolkien created tension between the need for speed and secrecy. Too quick a departure by the long-settled Hobbit would attract attention. Too long a wait increases the danger from Sauron. Though it was written over three decades earlier, at this point Tolkien's plot also suggests two questions that were often raised during President Nixon's Watergate scandal—"What did the President know and when did he know it?" Here we must ask, "What did Sauron know about the Ring and when did he know it?" From Gollum, Sauron has learned that the Ring is possessed by someone named 'Baggins' in a place called the 'Shire.' But he has no idea where the Shire is located. The deceptions of Gollum and Saruman have led him astray and the Ranger's shield around the Shire protects it from Sauron's roving spies.

This limit in Sauron's knowledge allows Tolkien to create a crisis. Sauron's need to know is so great that he is forced to turn to his greatest weapon, the Black Riders. Only they can penetrate the defense Gandalf and Aragorn have created around the Ring. But Tolkien made Sauron pay dearly for that move. The terror Nazgûl create by their presence (even when invisible) is so great that they cannot travel in secrecy. In an effort to conceal that, Sauron launches his war against Gondor earlier than planned. He acts in haste rather than continue to build up his strength.

Sauron and the Nazgûl

Mordor

- From spies, Sauron learns that Gollum has been captured.
- Sauron fears his scheme to retake the Ring will be blocked.

The Fellowship of the Ring, Bk. 1, Ch. 3, "Three is Company." Tolkien completed this chapter by early March of 1938. *Letters,* No. 26. For those who think that, despite Tolkien's protests to the contrary, his tale has unconscious links to contemporary events, at the time Tolkien was writing of the threat Sauron posed to the Shire, Hitler was threatening to annex Austria by force.

The detail and realism of these stories is not accidental. Tolkien wrote that he intended to create an "imaginary" history of our own world. He stressed he was not writing about "imaginary worlds (such as Fairyland) or unseen worlds (as Heaven and Hell)." *Letters,* No. 183.

Unfinished Tales, Pt. III, Ch. IV, "The Hunt for the Ring."

Many Names

In the Victorian England into which Tolkien was born, important people often had several names and titles. Tolkien's imaginary history followed a similar pattern. At this time the Lord of the Nazgûl and six his lieutenants live in Minas Morgul at the western entrance to Mordor. The second in command, Khamûl, lives at Dol Guldur in southern Mirkwood with another Nazgûl who serves as his messenger. That makes a total of nine Nazgûl, corresponding to the nine rings made for man. They have several names, including Ringwraiths and Nazgûl. When clothed in black and on horseback, they are known as Black Riders. To avoid confusion, in this book their names will be used much as they are in Tolkien's account.

Sauron is probably using the Nazgûl at Dol Guldur to spy on the Elves of Mirkwood, and he may get news of Gollum's capture and imprisonment from them.

145 Days Before
April 24

Monday, May 1, 1418—Gandalf and Aragorn Meet

Gandalf and Aragorn

Sarn Ford on Brandywine River southeast of Shire

- Gandalf and Aragorn meet at Sarn Ford.
- Gandalf tells Aragorn that Frodo will leave at the end of September.

Aragorn's Movements

The Fellowship of the Ring, Bk. 1, Ch. 10, "Strider" and Bk. 1, Ch. 9, "At the Sign of the Prancing Pony." Aragorn's business probably took him north or west. If he had gone east or south, he would have picked up news of the terror earlier. Sarn Ford means 'stony ford.' See *A Tolkien Compass,* 190.

Tolkien kept his narrative centered on Hobbits, so we often know little about the movements of other major characters. In the spring, Aragorn came west with Gandalf to guard the Shire. Afterward, he visits Bree, probably for supplies and rest. Knowing Gandalf is watching over Frodo, Aragorn leaves on other business, probably shortly after this meeting, and will not be around when news of the Nazgûl and their wave of terror arrives in late June or early July. (When Gandalf stays overnight at *The Prancing Pony* on Midyear's Day, he leaves no letter for Aragorn, suggesting he knows Aragorn has already gone.) Aragorn will return some time before Frodo's scheduled departure (perhaps early September) and be alarmed to hear of a missing Gandalf and rumors about Black Riders.

Early Summer, 1418—Frodo Sells Bag End

Frodo and Gandalf

Date Approximate

Bag End, Hobbiton

The Fellowship of the Ring, Bk. 1, Ch. 3, "Three is Company."

- Frodo buys a small house in Crickhollow.
- Frodo sells Bag End to the Sackville-Baggins.

A Quiet Departure

For more on Lotho's ties to Saruman, see the comments for Bree and the Shire at the end of 1418.

Tolkien needs a clever scheme to allow Frodo to slip off for Rivendell without attracting attention. Since the Sackville-Baggins have wanted Bag End for a long time, their purchase will surprise no one and, as Tolkien notes, buying a Crickhollow house puts Frodo on the Rivendell side of the Shire, making it easy to slip away.

Tolkien may have intended for this Bag End purchase to be linked to the secret business ties between Saruman and Lotho Sackville-Baggins. We do know that Tolkien had Lotho using Saruman's money to quietly buy up Shire farms, so their produce could feed Saruman's army at Isengard. We can speculate that Lotho saw Bag End—located near the center of the Shire and close to the Great East Road—as a central location from which to run this operation

In modern terms, this made Bag End the corporate headquarters for a future Sackville-Baggins 'empire.' Of course, we know that empire became the victim of a less-than-friendly 'corporate takeover' by Saruman. Tolkien only hinted at that subplot in his published works, but he may have been commenting on something he could see around him, the takeover of small, quaint English family farms by large and highly efficient agri-businesses.

> The parallel between *Sackville* and *Baggins* are obvious and admitted by Tolkien in *Tolkien Compass*, 160. There's also a pun between Bag End (a cul-de-sac) and Baggins.

> John Steinbeck described the human impact of the loss of family farms in the American Midwest in *The Grapes of Wrath*. His book came out in 1939, at the very time Tolkien was writing *The Lord of the Rings*.

Mid-June, 1418—The Dream

Boromir and Faramir

Date Estimated

Osgiliath

- Faramir has a dream several times.
- His brother, Boromir, has the same dream once.

> *The Fellowship of the Ring*, Bk. 2, Ch. 2, "The Council of Elrond."

Dreams that Hide

Tolkien knew that in ancient tales dreams often hide more than they reveal. That's certainly true of this dream. Though useful for getting Boromir to Rivendell, it leaves ambiguous who will win the coming war. Did the fact that Faramir received it several times and Boromir only once mean the former was expected to go? Since Boromir is the one who responded, we will never know. There is another chilling possibility to consider. Boromir never had a real opportunity to take the Ring from Frodo. If their roles had been reversed and Boromir been with Frodo at Henneth Annûn, he could have taken the Ring away quite easily.

> Elrond summarized the history of Gondor and Osgiliath at the Council of Elrond. See *The Fellowship of the Ring*, Bk. 2, Ch. 2, "The Council of Elrond." For more on dreams see Michael N. Stanton, *Hobbits, Elves and Wizards* (New York: Palgrave Macmillan, 2001), 166f.

Monday, June 20, 1418—Battle of Osgiliath

On the day of this attack, the moon is three days past full. It rises just after midnight the next day.

> 96 Days Before
> June 12

Boromir and Faramir

Ruins of Osgiliath

The Return of the King, Bk. 6, Ap. B, "The Tale of Years," *The Fellowship of the Ring*, Bk. 2, Ch. 2, "The Council of Elrond" and *Unfinished Tales*, Bk. 3, Ch. IV, "The Hunt for the Ring." Gondor continues to hold the west side of the river, probably because Sauron halts his attack. For Boromir's role in Gondor retaining the west bank of the river see the remarks of Beregond in *The Return of the King*, Bk. 5, Ch. 1, "Minas Tirith."

- Sauron's forces attack the Anduin bridges at Osgiliath.
- Boromir and Faramir defend the east end of the last bridge.
- Only Boromir, Faramir and two others make it across the river.

The Decline of Gondor and the Defense of Rome

By placing the first battle in the War of the Ring at Osgiliath, Tolkien illustrated how far Gondor has declined. The once great city is now in ruins. From Boromir's remarks at the Council of Elrond, it appears that in the city's heyday, it had many bridges spanning the river. Now the last remaining bridge must be destroyed to prevent its use by Sauron.

Boromir's account is similar to the classic Roman tale of "Horatius at the Bridge." In it, the fate of Rome, still a city rather than an empire, hinges on a small band of men led by Horatius holding a wooden bridge over the Tiber River against a surprise attack by a Etruscan army until the bridge can be destroyed. Horatius orders most of his men to cross the river and chop away the bridge's foundations while he and three others defend the far side. As the bridge is about to collapse and be swept away by the current, the men on the safe shore call for the remaining four to flee while there is yet time. At that point, the Etruscans launch a calvary attack. Horatius orders his remaining three men to flee across the bridge, while he alone stands, defending the city of Rome. After the bridge is gone, he backs slowly into the water, his face to his foes. A Etruscan dart blinds his left eye, but he swims safely across the river. Before the battle, he made remarks that reflect the attitude of the warriors of Gondor and Rohan.

> To every man upon this earth
> Death comes soon or late.
> And how can man die better
> Than facing fearful odds,
> For the ashes of his fathers
> And the temple of his Gods?

Nazgûl—Crossing the Anduin

Day 1 of 92 Searching for the Shire

Osgiliath

Unfinished Tales, Pt. III, Ch. IV, "The Hunt for the Ring."

- Invisible and on foot, seven Nazgûl slip across the bridge.
- With the Nazgûl across, Sauron halts his attack.

A Nazgûl Weakness, True or False?

For the Nazgûl weakness see, *Unfinished Tales*, Pt. III, Ch. IV, "The Hunt for the Ring." under (ii) "Other Versions of the Story."

In literature, a super hero or a powerful evil figure is often given a secret weakness. Tolkien seems to have toyed with the idea of doing that with the Nazgûl. Except for their Lord, they were not to be able to cross water except over bridges or in the most desperate circumstances. That might explain why, in their pursuit of Frodo, they prefer to stay on roads (which have bridges). It may also explain why it took them so long to recover from being swept away at the Ford of Bruinen—the roughly two-and-a-half months from October 20 to the January 8 sighting of a flying Nazgûl. Finally, it explains why Sauron had to create this mock attack to get them across the wide Anduin at a point where there is a bridge.

Late June, 1418—Gandalf Leaves the Shire

Frodo and Gandalf

Bag End, Hobbiton

- Gandalf leaves at dawn to gather news south of the Shire.
- He promises to travel to Rivendell with Frodo and Sam.

The Fellowship of the Ring, Bk. 1, Ch. 3, "Three is Company."

Gandalf

South of Shire

- Gandalf gets news from refugees coming up from the South.
- He hears of war, defeat in Gondor, and a great terror.

The Fellowship of the Ring, Bk. 2, Ch. 2, "The Council of Elrond."

News of Trouble

Even before Gandalf arrived, Tolkien described Dwarves traveling through the Shire along the Great East Road and bringing news of growing evil in Mordor. Perhaps Gandalf, hiding in Bag End, occasionally slipped out and went to the Great East Road at Bywater to talk to these travelers. But many of those from Rohan and Gondor who were going north on the Greenway would bypass Bree and Bywater by crossing the Sarn Ford and intercepting the Great East Road in the western Shire. To talk with them, Gandalf needed to either go south or west. If he went south, he could also talk with those of a suspicious sort that Aragorn's Rangers and the Shire's "bounders" were refusing to let into the Shire. He chose south.

The Fellowship of the Ring, Bk. 1, Ch. 2, "The Shadow of the Past" near the beginning of the chapter. Elsewhere, Tolkien wrote that Gandalf's role as a Wizard was to advise and motivate others to resist Sauron rather than do the work himself. See: *Letters*, No. 156.

Gollum—Escape from Wood Elves

Mirkwood

- Elves let Gollum climb a tree that stands all alone.
- One day, he refuses to come down and that night Orcs attack.
- Elves discover Gollum gone and follow his trail toward Dol Guldur.

The Return of the King, Bk. 6, Ap. B, "The Tale of Years" and *The Fellowship of the Ring*, Bk. 2, Ch. 2, "The Council of Elrond."

Gollum's Movement

Again, the Hobbit-centered Tolkien leaves many of Gollum's movements uncertain. Gollum seems to have either eluded or escaped from the Orcs. We know he flees west to live in the tunnels of Moria, perhaps in the autumn as the weather grows colder. Fear of the flying Nazgûl may be another reason he hides underground.

Tolkien may have placed in Gollum's mind an intention to travel through Moria to the Shire and take the Ring. If that were true, then Tolkien stops him with a single doorway. The West-gate that Gollum must

Unfinished Tales, Pt. III, Ch. IV, "The Hunt for the Ring." Living in underground Moria and perhaps preying on Orcs, Gollum is returning to his old way of life.

take out of Moria requires the strength of two to open. He has no allies and is too weak to push it open himself. He will not be heard from again until the travelers enter Moria in mid-January of 1419.

Dating Gollum's Escape from the Elves

"The Tale of Years" dates Gollum's escape from the Elves to the time of the attack on Osgiliath (June 20). But at the Council of Elrond, Legolas said it came on a moonless night. Since the battle was only three days after a full moon, Gollum's escape may have been in late June. The moon was new on Midyear's Day, two days after the end of the month, but the date need not be that late. On June 28 a waning crescent moon did not rise until after 3 a.m., giving the Orcs plenty of time to attack and disappear into the depths of Mirkwood. Of course, since the night was also described as starless, it is possible that the moonlessness resulted from dark clouds. But it seems unlikely that clouds could totally obscure a nearly full moon.

Sam remarks that the moon was not visible in Lórien (probably because nothing so constantly changing would be permitted there), does not apply to Mirkwood, whose 'magic' was of a different sort. Sam's remark is in *The Fellowship of the Ring,* Bk. 2, Ch. 9, "The Great River."

84 Days Before
June 24

Midyear's Day, 1418—Gandalf's Letter

The moon is new on this date. As he leaves, Gandalf will have no moonlight to assist his ride to Isengard.

Gandalf and Radagast

On the Greenway near Bree

- Seeking more news, Gandalf goes north on the Greenway.
- Near Bree he meets Radagast the Brown with a message from Saruman.
- Gandalf asks Radagast to send news to him at Orthanc.

Two Wizards that Failed

Tolkien sent five Wizards to Middle-earth. About two we know almost nothing and two of the remaining three are less than impressive. Here Tolkien provides us with insight into the characters of the two failures. He does not say that Radagast is a coward, but he allows the Wizard to demonstrate that by his deeds. Radagast is so frightened he can barely deliver Saruman's brief message to Gandalf. He was, however, not a complete failure. By telling the birds to bring messages to Gandalf at Orthanc, Tolkien was hinting that in war even frightened non-combatants are useful.

Tolkien's Saruman is as deceptive as Radagast is cowardly. If Tolkien consulted his notes, he knew that the Nazgûl were not yet riding on horseback as Black Riders and will not be until July 17, The Nazgûl are west of the Anduin, but they will be searching its upper waters. They will be nowhere near the Shire. By exaggerating the danger, Saruman is taking advantage of Gandalf's impulsiveness.

The Fellowship of the Ring, Bk. 2, Ch. 2, "The Council of Elrond" and Bk. 2, Ch. 3, "The Ring Goes South."

Perhaps the most detailed information about the Wizards is in a 1954 Tolkien essay published in *Unfinished Tales,* Pt. 4, Ch. II, "The Istari." Istari is the name for Gandalf's order of Wizards.

Saruman may have intelligence about the Black Rider's future plans, possibly through his *palantír.* He may even be mistaking a vision of the future for present events.

Gandalf

The Prancing Pony, Bree

- Gandalf spends the night at *The Prancing Pony*.
- He writes a note that Butterbur is to deliver to Frodo.
- In the note, he tells Frodo to leave for Rivendell immediately.

The Fellowship of the Ring, Bk. 2, Ch. 2, "The Council of Elrond" and Bk. 1, Ch. 10, "Strider."

Telling Saruman

At this point, we can test the plausibility of Tolkien's plot. Some inner good sense may have kept Gandalf from mentioning his suspicions about the Ring to Saruman. If so, it is good that he heeded it. Given the secret contacts Saruman established in the Shire some 65 years earlier in 1353 (possibly with the Sackville-Baggins relatives of Bilbo and Frodo), Saruman would have been able to send men to attack Bilbo (until 1401) or Frodo (after 1401) and take away the Ring. Concealed as ordinary travelers or traders, his men could have slipped past the Rangers and Hobbits guarding the Shire.

2 Lithe, 1418—Gandalf to Isengard

83 Days Before
June 25

Gandalf

Day 1 of 11 to Isengard

Bree

- At dawn, Gandalf leaves for Isengard.

Gandalf's Haste

Again, Tolkien has Gandalf's haste create problems. At the Council of Elrond, Gandalf will admit that leaving without personally warning Frodo was a grave mistake. His trip down, though hurried, is not as fast as his return. He will take 11 days to reach Isengard. Returning a greater distance in September on Shadowfax will take 6 days to reach Sarn Ford.

The Fellowship of the Ring, Bk. 2, Ch. 2, "The Council of Elrond." It is unlikely that Gandalf met Rangers on his trip to Isengard, since they would have gotten word to Aragorn about the Nazgûl and Gandalf's departure.

Sunday, July 1, 1418—Nazgûl Hunt

82 Days Before
June 26f.

Nazgûl

Day 15 of 92 Searching for the Shire

Anórien northward to the Wold

- On July 1, the Nazgûl begin searching northward for the Shire.

Preferring Darkness

The delay from June 20 to July 1 is odd. Perhaps Tolkien has the Nazgûl wait for dark nights and a reduction in the number of Gondor troops before beginning their search for the Ring.

Unfinished Tales, Pt. III, Ch. IV, "The Hunt for the Ring." The New Moon is now two days old.

Wednesday, July 4, 1418—Boromir Leaves

Boromir, Denethor II and Faramir

Day 1 of 110 Boromir to Rivendell

Minas Tirith

- Earlier, the brothers ask their father Denethor II to explain their dream.
- He tells them Imladris is an old name for the Elves under Elrond.
- Today, Boromir leaves Minas Tirith to find Elrond.

Another Jacob and Esau

The Fellowship of the Ring, Bk. 2, Ch. 2, "The Council of Elrond," The Return of the King, Bk. 5, Ch. 4, "The Siege of Gondor," and Bk. 6, Ap. B, "The Tale of Years." Boromir is about 40 years old and Faramir is 35. Their father is 88. For the conflict between Jacob and Esau, see Genesis 25:19f. Pippin will make Boromir's journey in the opposite direction and by a different route in 76 days, traveling roughly 45 of those days.

Tolkien knew conflicts between brothers can be like that between the biblical Jacob and Esau. Here Boromir, the elder, has his father's favor and Faramir, five years younger, does not. As a result, Boromir is able to take the journey. Not knowing the way, Boromir will take 110 days to reach Rivendell, not arriving until October 24. Later, Denethor demonstrates his bitterness that Boromir died on this journey rather than Faramir. See Faramir's report to his father on the evening of March 10, 1419 in *The Return on the King*, Bk. 5, Ch. 4, "The Siege of Gondor."

Gandalf Leaves the Shire

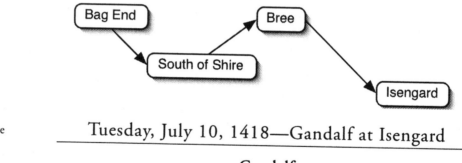

Tuesday, July 10, 1418—Gandalf at Isengard

Gandalf

Day 11 of 11 to Isengard

Orthanc, Isengard

- Gandalf reaches Isengard late in the evening.
- Saruman wants Gandalf to tell him who has the Ring.
- Gandalf refuses and is imprisoned in Orthanc.

Tolkien's Orthanc

The Fellowship of the Ring, Bk. 2, Ch. 2, "The Council of Elrond" and The Return of the King, Bk. 6, Ap. B, "The Tale of Years."

Through the White Council and his secret trade dealings, Saruman already knows where the Shire is and has spies there.

As part of his rich and varied landscape, Tolkien made Orthanc an impregnable five-hundred-foot tower located inside the walls of Isengard. It was built long before by Gondor. Sixty-five years earlier Saruman persuaded the Steward of Rohan to give him Isengard and the keys to the tower. For Rohan, that proves a near-fatal mistake. Gandalf will be a prisoner there for two and a half months. He can only hope Frodo got his letter and left the Shire.

If you visit Washington, D.C., you can see a stone tower almost identical in height to Orthanc and similarly constructed. The Washington Monument is 500 feet from ground level to the observation level and has a total height of 555 feet. At its base, the monument is 55 feet wide and has walls 15 feet thick. At the observation level, the walls are only 18 inches thick. Exactly 36,491 marble stones were used in its construction and, if you choose to walk to the top, you ascend 896 steps. Work on the Washington Monument began on July 4, 1848, but construction halted at the 152-foot level in 1858 and did not begin again until 1878. It was completed in 1888 and extensively remodeled between 1998 and 2000.

The Washington Monument was modeled on an Egyptian obelisk. Orthanc, which means "Mount Fang," seems to have been intended to look like the tooth of a fearsome predator, perhaps for the psychological effect.

Tuesday, July 17, 1418—Nazgûl on Horseback

66 Days Before
July 12

Nazgûl or Black Riders

Day 31 of 92 Searching for the Shire, Date Approximate

On the Anduin above Sarn Gebir

- The Lord of the Nazgûl and six lieutenants reach the Anduin River.
- Abandoning secrecy, they acquire horses and clothing.
- They travel north looking for the Shire.

Unfinished Tales, Pt. III, Ch. IV, "The Hunt for the Ring."

Nazgûl or Black Riders?

Tolkien's use of "Black Riders" to describe the Nazgûl on horseback is unambiguous. But he did not give the Nazgûl's flying beasts a name, so there is some confusion when he uses the term. Does it mean the Ringwraiths, their beasts, or the two together?

In a 1945 letter Tolkien called the beasts "Nazgûl-birds" *Letters,* No. 100.

In what follows, the Nazgûl are called the Black Riders.

Sunday, July 22, 1418 and After—Black Riders Meet

61 Days Before
July 17

The moon is one day past last quarter and rapidly waning.
This gives the Black Riders the dark nights
in which they prefer to operate.

Black Riders

Day 36 of 92 Searching for the Shire

Upper Anduin River Valley

- The Lord of the Black Riders and six lieutenants meet at the Field of Celebrant with two Black Riders from Dol Guldur.
- They discover the Shire is not near Gladden Fields.
- They do not return to the Wold until September.

Unfinished Tales, Pt. III, Ch. IV, "The Hunt for the Ring."

A Crucial Delay

Unfinished Tales, Pt. III, Ch. IV, "The Hunt for the Ring." Hobbits have three stocks. Gollum was of Stoor stock, which once lived in the upper Anduin. Most Shire Hobbits are Harfoot stock, though some of the leading families are Fallohide. Some information about Hobbits is in the Prologue to *The Fellowship of the Ring.*

Tolkien's manuscripts disagree about what the Black Riders did in the upper Anduin. In one, the settlements of Gollum's ancestors are found deserted and lifeless. In another, the Black Riders find a few small settlements and kill or scatter their inhabitants. The Shire is too well-populated for such treatment, but this harsh treatment illustrates how brutally Sauron would have treated the Shire had he won the War of the Ring. The time they waste in this search will prove critical to Frodo's escape.

Late July to Early August, 1418—Boromir in Rohan

Boromir

Day 27 of 110 (August 1) Boromir to Rivendell, Date Estimated

Rohan (perhaps Edoras) to the Fords of Isen

The Fellowship of the Ring, Bk. 2, Ch. 8, "Farewell to Lórien" and *The Two Towers,* Bk. 3, Ch. 2, "The Riders of Rohan."

- Boromir passes through Rohan and is loaned a horse.
- He crosses the Fords of Isen.

Boromir in Rohan

Tolkien provided only two specific dates for Boromir's long journey—July 4 when it began at Minas Tirith and October 24 when it ended at Rivendell. For the rest, we must depend on clues. Boromir is the oldest son of Gondor's Steward. It is difficult to imagine Tolkien having him travel to Edoras by any means except horse. Boromir could make that journey in a week, but there are hints it took longer. On February 16, 1419, just before the travelers leave Lórien, Boromir mentions passing through Rohan but gives no date. When Éomer first meets Aragorn, Gimli and Legolas on February 30, 1419, he mentions Boromir passing through Rohan and acquiring a horse without giving a date. Why would Boromir leave Minas Tirith with a horse but need another at Edoras? The most likely possibility is that something happened to the first horse on the journey north. That suggests the journey to Edoras took longer than a week and may have taken as long as the sixteen days it took the cart carrying King Théoden's body to make the journey.

If that were so, Boromir might have arrived at Edoras about July 20. A little over a week asking those learned in ancient lore about Imdalis, would have him leaving Rohan by early August. By his own account, he crossed the Fords of Isen, passed westward through the Gap of Rohan a few days later, and turned north, probably taking the same Old South Road (Greenway) north that Gandalf will pass over in late September.

Boromir's visit to Rohan may explain how Tolkien intended for Saruman to find out about the dream. On his first encounter with Aragorn, Éomer already knows about Boromir's dream. If he knew, then the well-placed Gríma certainly knew and would have passed the news to Saruman by early September at the latest.

Obsessed by the Ring, Saruman would realize that "Isildur's Bane" in the dream was the Ring and conclude, logically but wrongly, that the Ring was now at Rivendell. That would explain why in manuscripts Tolkien toyed with the idea of having Saruman tell the Black Riders where the Shire is about September 18. Sending them to the Shire would misdirect their quest while appearing to cooperate with Sauron.

Saruman had little reason to pass this news on to Gandalf. If he had, Gandalf would have been more confident that the Hobbits would arrive safely in Rivendell.

Late August of 1418—Boromir at Tharbad

Boromir

Day 56 of 110 (August 30) Boromir to Rivendell, Date Estimated
Crossing the Greyflood at Tharbad

- Boromir looses his horse crossing the Greyflood at Tharbad.
- He continues on foot, while the horse returns unaided to Rohan.

Boromir's Journey North

Tolkien gave no date for this disastrous crossing of the Greyflood. Boromir could have easily made the roughly 350 mile journey from the Fords of Isen to Tharbad on the Old South Road to Tharbad in a couple of weeks since Gandalf, a little later and in a much greater hurry on Shadowfax, covers that same distance in less than five days. This late August date is only an estimate and is driven by the need to stretch out Boromir's journey as long as possible.

From Tharbad north, attaching a plausible chronology to Boromir's movements becomes even more difficult. At Tharbad he is two months and some 350 miles from Rivendell. He could have stayed on the Old South Road until it intersects the Great East Road in Bree, but that seems unlikely. If Tolkien had intended for him to travel that way, we would expect him to have also slipped some hint of his passage through Bree into the narrative. Boromir would have been an outsider asking strange questions about how to find the mysterious Elvish colony.

A Bree route would give Tolkien other problems. As Boromir passed near the Shire, he might have encountered Aragorn's Rangers and entered the story at that point. Even more important, if we place him on the Great East Road bound for Rivendell at the same time as Aragorn and the Hobbits, we have trouble explaining why Boromir makes no mention of encountering the Black Riders who were racing up and down the Road.

That suggests Tolkien intended for Boromir to travel northeast from Tharbad, living off the land and struggling on foot through an unpopulated wilderness. The difficulty of the terrain, the need to hunt for food, and the fact that he has no idea where Rivendell is would explain why he averages only seven miles a day.

The Fellowship of the Ring, Bk. 2, Ch. 8, "Farewell to Lórien." Boromir did not describe this part of his journey to the Council of Elrond. Notice that Boromir does not seem to be careful with horses. Since Rohan probably offered the best winter pasture, the horse probably returned there before the end of 1418.

Rather than finding Rivendell, Boromir may have been found by it. Though Elves normally avoid contact with men, the search Elrond initiated for the Hobbits may have led to Boromir, blundering though the wilderness, being questioned by Elves and taken to Rivendell, arriving on October 24, just barely in time for the Council. Though Boromir's behavior is a mixture of good and bad, his arrival is as providentially timed and arranged as that of the other travelers.

Phases of the Moon

These changes vary depending on where the observer is on earth and where the moon is in a 19-year cycle. In the northern hemisphere, the line of light or shadow always moves across the moon's surface from right to left.

The modern dates from which these Shire dates were derived comes from U.S. Naval Observatory data for 1941–1942.

The lunar cycle repeats every 29.5 days. If you think of the sun and moon racing one another across the sky, then the moon is the slower one, falling behind about 13 degrees or roughly an hour a night. When the moon is new, it rises (almost invisible) with the sun at dawn and sets at sunset. At first quarter it has fallen back, rising at noon and setting at midnight. At full moon it rises at sunset and sets at dawn. Finally, the last quarter moon rises at midnight and sets at noon.

The chart below lists the phases of the moon during the most active portion of Tolkien's narrative, that from September of 1418 to October of 1419. The dates are those in the Shire Calendar. Notice the full moon of March 9, which is given as March 8 in Tolkien's text.

The Phases of the Moon During the War of the Ring

New	First Quarter	Full	Last Quarter
1418			
August 28	September 5	September 12	September 20
September 28	October 4	October 12	October 20
October 27	November 4	November 12	November 20
November 27	December 3	December 11	December 19
December 26			
1419			
	January 2	January 10	January 18
January 24	February 2	February 9	February 16
February 23	March 1	March 9	March 15
March 22	April 1	April 8	April 15
April 22	April 30	May 7	May 14
May 22	May 30	June 7	June 13
June 21	June 29	July 3	July 10
July 18	July 26	August 2	August 9
August 18	August 25	September 2	September 9
September 17	September 24	October 1	October 9
October 17	October 23	November 1	November 9

CHAPTER

7

Hiking to Crickhollow

Early September to September 25, 1418

Aragorn's return to the Hobbits at Crickhollow

Few authors have created a 'historical' backdrop as detailed and complex as Tolkien's. For hundreds of years, Gandalf and a few allies have been locked in spiritual conflict with Sauron. During that time most inhabitants of Middle-earth have been unaware that defeat could place them under the most terrible of tyrannies. No group is less aware of that struggle than Hobbits. That is about to change.

Tolkien describe the literary appeal of this change in a speech, noting: "Stores that are actually concerned primarily with 'fairies,' that is with creatures that might also in modern English be called 'Elves,' are relatively rare, and as a rule not very interesting. Most good 'fairy stories' are about the adventures of men in the Perilous Realm or upon its shadowy marches." We need only change "men" to "Hobbits" to understand what Tolkien did with his popular tale.

The quote is from Tolkien's "On Fairy-Stories," originally given as the 1938 Andrew Lang Lecture at the University of St. Andrews and published in The Tolkien Reader *(Ballantine, 1966), 27f.*

Early September, 1418—Aragorn Returns

*The moon reaches its first quarter on September 5
and is full on September 12.*

Aragorn
Date Estimated

East of the Shire

- Aragorn returns to the Shire borders to guard Frodo's departure.
- From Elves, he hears of Black Riders and Gandalf's disappearance.

The Fellowship of the Ring, Bk. 1, Ch. 10, "Strider." Strider said he returned to guard the Shire "many days" earlier rather than many weeks. Early September is perhaps the latest his return can be dated.

Aragorn and Frodo

Tolkien's failure to have Gandalf introduce Aragorn to Frodo serves its purpose here. If Aragorn had shown up at Bag End and tried persuade Frodo to flee, Frodo might not trust him, confusing the plot. If he did trust him, the drama of the flight to Crickhollow and Bree would be lost.

Dáin II, Glóin and Gimli
Date Estimated

Lonely Mountain

The Fellowship of the Ring,
Bk. 2, Ch. 2, "The Council of
Elrond." Isolated on far-away
Lonely Mountain, Dáin II
does not know about all that
is happening. He merely
wants Elrond's advice. For
Bilbo and Gandalf's return,
see *The Hobbit,* Ch. 18, "The
Return Journey" and Ch. 19,
"The Last Stage." Also see
Karen Fonstad's chronology
in the "Introduction" to "The
Hobbit" section of *The Atlas
of Middle-earth.*

- Dáin II Ironfoot sends Glóin and Gimli to Rivendell.

The Dwarves' Journey to Rivendell

This date is merely an estimate. It provides the Dwarves with almost two months to reach Rivendell, a journey they undoubtedly made as quickly as possible. In *The Hobbit,* Bilbo and Gandalf seemed to have spent about two months on the Road returning from the Lonely Mountain to Rivendell, though they spend part of the winter with Beorn and go around rather than through Mirkwood. (Given the growing power of Sauron, Glóin and Gimli may have also avoided Mirkwood.) Remarks at the Council of Elrond suggest that most participants had recently arrived. No one arrives too late, an indication than an unseen providence was at work bringing them there.

Many of the descriptions of events that follow exist only in draft manuscripts, so some chronological and other difficulties are to be expected.

Mid-September, 1418—Black Riders to Isengard

Black Riders
Day 89 of 92 (September 15) Searching for the Shire, Date Estimated

Wold in Anduin Valley to Isengard

Unfinished Tales, Pt. III, Ch.
IV, "The Hunt for the Ring."

- The Black Riders return from the Wold after looking for the Shire.
- Sauron decides Saruman knows where the Ring is.
- He orders the Black Riders to Isengard, spreading terror in Rohan.

Sauron's Growing Desperation

The increasing openness with which Sauron uses his Black Riders hints at his growing desperation to find the Ring. He is ending a centuries-old policy of not creating a sense of danger great enough to unite his foes. Hitler's invasion of Poland and Japan's surprise attack on Pearl Harbor had a similar effect, though neither had happened at the time Tolkien was writing this portion of his narrative.

5 Days Before
September 11

Sunday, September 18, 1418—Gandalf Escapes

This evening the moon is six days past full and rose about 11 p.m., so Orthanc is easily spotted by Gwaihir. The moon shines the rest of the night, making it easy to navigate to Edoras.

Gandalf

Orthanc to Edoras

- In the early hours of the night Gwaihir comes to Orthanc.
- He takes Gandalf to Edoras, 120 miles away.

Providence in Tolkien

When all seems darkest, Tolkien often slips in a little old-fashioned divine providence. Providence describes how God quietly intervenes in the world to provide assistance or guidance when most needed. Here everything appears natural. Since Radagast the Brown is not in Saruman's conspiracy, he has done as Gandalf requested and asked birds to bring reports of Black Riders to Orthanc.

The eagle may have borne Gandalf only to the outskirts of the city, since Gandalf does not enter it until the next day. Gwaihir may fear an arrow in mistake from the soldiers on the city wall.

The Fellowship of the Ring, Bk. 2, Ch. 2, "The Council of Elrond."

Gwaihir also tells Gandalf of Gollum's escape. See the beginning of *The Fellowship of the Ring,* Bk. 2, Ch. 3, "The Ring Goes South." For the sake of the story, we might assume Gandalf came out on the tower peak to look on the moon as it rose about 11 p.m. and shortly after that Gwaihir arrived.

Saruman and the Black Riders

Day 92 of 92 Searching for the Shire, Date Uncertain

Isengard

- The Black Riders arrive at Isengard and question Saruman.
- Saruman claims only Gandalf knows where the Shire is.
- They go after Gandalf.

A Differing Tolkien Manuscript

Because Tolkien did not work these details into a final published story, there is no authoritative version of what was happening to the Black Riders at this time. In one Tolkien manuscript, it is Saruman who tells the Black Riders the location of the Shire. Claiming to have just forced the information from Gandalf, he says it is 600 miles to the northwest. Saruman might have done this because he assumed (based on news about Faramir's dream) that the Ring is now safe in Rivendell. That may also explain why, although he has secret contacts in the Shire and knows the Ring was there, he makes no effort to get the Ring. He thinks, incorrectly, that the Ring has already left. He may even believe Bilbo carried the Ring with him to Rivendell years earlier.

Unfinished Tales, Pt. III, Ch. IV, "The Hunt for the Ring" and *The Return of the King,* Bk. 6, Ap. B, "The Tale of Years." The "Tale of Years" only says that the Black Riders cross the Fords of Isen on this day. For more details on dating their arrival at Isengard, see "The Fast-Riding Black Rider Problem" on September 22, 1418.

Monday, September 19, 1418—Shire Located

4 Days Before
September 12

Gandalf

Edoras, Rohan

- Dressed as a beggar, Gandalf arrives at Edoras but cannot see the king.

Gandalf's Delays

Gandalf experiences delay getting in to see Théoden and yet more delay taming Shadowfax. Tolkien did not let Gandalf's dramatic escape relieve

The Return of the King, Bk. 6, Ap. B, "The Tale of Years." No reason is given why Gandalf was dressed as a beggar. It is not the best way to gain an audience with a king.

the tension created when he forced an inexperienced Frodo to act without Gandalf's guidance.

Black Riders with Gríma

Day 1 of 4 in their Ride to the Shire, Date Uncertain

South of Isengard

Unfinished Tales, Pt. III, Ch. IV, "The Hunt for the Ring." Gríma is also called "Worm-tongue," an apt name.

- The Black Riders capture Gríma, who is rushing to Isengard.
- They force Gríma to tell them where the Shire is.
- The Lord of the Black Riders divides his lieutenants into four pairs.
- All begin a frantic ride to the Shire.

Providence in Reverse

The Black Riders could take the time to question travelers because in those troubled times few would be traveling south or east into danger and those who were are likely to be working for either Saruman or Sauron.

There is a balance in Tolkien's writings. Evil benefits from fortunate timing almost as often as good. According to Tolkien manuscripts, along the way, the Black Riders capture two of Saruman's agents. One is carrying maps of the Shire that prove invaluable. They take the maps and send the servant to Bree as a spy. (He is the squint-eyed southerner from Dunland.) This servant may tell them that, if they are looking for a Baggins, they should go to Hobbiton. That is almost fatal for Frodo.

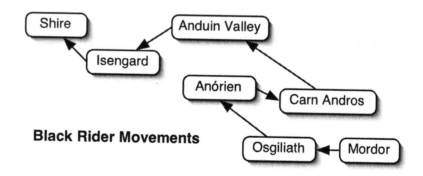

Black Rider Movements

3 Days Before September 13

Tuesday, September 20, 1418—Shadowfax Given

The last quarter moon sets in the west-northwest about three in the afternoon.

Fatty, Folco, Frodo, Merry, Pippin and Sam

Bag End, Hobbiton

The Fellowship of the Ring, Bk. 1, Ch. 3, "Three is Company."

- Friends arrive to help Frodo move to Crickhollow.
- Two covered carts leave for Buckland with household items.

Frodo's Five Friends

Along with the neighborly Sam, the friends helping Frodo with this move are Fredegar (Fatty) Bolger, Folco Boffin, Pippin Took and Merry Brandybuck. Folco soon disappears from the story, and Fatty will play only a brief but important role.

Gandalf

Day 1 of 3 in Taming

Edoras, Rohan

- Théoden offers Gandalf any horse in exchange for leaving quickly.
- Gandalf takes Shadowfax but must tame him.

The Return of the King, Bk. 6, Ap. B, "The Tale of Years."

The Origin of Shadowfax

Tolkien linked the name "Shadowfax" to an expression he created from Old English by combining *Sceadu* (shadow) with *fax* (mane). This suggests that Shadowfax had the light grey color of a shadow. At night, such a color would look almost white.

J. R. R. Tolkien, *Tolkien Compass*, 172.

Wednesday, September 21, 1418—Frodo Waits

2 Days Before September 14

Frodo

Bag End, Hobbiton

- Frodo spends the day waiting for Gandalf.

The Fellowship of the Ring, Bk. 1, Ch. 3, "Three is Company."

Gandalf

Day 2 of 3 in Taming

Plains of Rohan

- Gandalf tries to win Shadowfax's trust, but the horse flees.

The Return of the King, Bk. 6, Ap. B, "The Tale of Years."

Taming Shadowfax

The three critical days Tolkien has Gandalf spend chasing and taming Shadowfax suggest that he intended for the Wizard to attach great importance to the horse's abilities. For this particular journey, Gandalf might have been better off leaving immediately on a less capable horse.

Thursday, September 22, 1418—Frodo's Birthday

1 Day Before September 15

Fatty, Folco, Frodo, Merry, Pippin and Sam

Bag End, Hobbiton

- In the evening Frodo has a birthday party for himself and friends.

The Fellowship of the Ring, Bk. 1, Ch. 3, "Three is Company."

Different Parties and Different Times

Bilbo's own going away party 17 years earlier was much larger and livelier. With this small and somber party, Tolkien hints at dark times.

Gandalf

Day 3 of 3 in Taming

Plains of Rohan

- Gandalf catches up with Shadowfax and seeks the horse's trust.

The Return of the King, Bk. 6, Ap. B, "The Tale of Years."

Thursday, September 22, 1418—Frodo's Birthday

Black Riders with the Rangers
Day 4 of 4 in their Ride to the Shire

Sarn Ford, Southeast of the Shire

Unfinished Tales, Pt. III, Ch. IV, "The Hunt for the Ring" and *The Return of the King*, Bk. 6, Ap. B, "The Tale of Years."

- About sunset, the first Black Riders arrive at Sarn Ford.
- Some Rangers flee north to warn Aragorn and are killed or driven away.
- Other Rangers hold the Ford until dark.

The Black Riders average 150 miles a day on their journey. Racing for the Shire on Shadowfax, Gandalf averages about 100 miles a day.

The Fast-riding Black Rider Problem

Two Tolkien manuscripts say that the Black Riders arrived at Isengard two days after Gandalf escaped while only one says they came on the same day as the escape. But the earlier dating adopted here allows much needed time for the Black Riders to get to the Shire (roughly 600 miles away) at sunset on September 22, after only four days of riding. In comparison, in July Gandalf, also on horseback and in a hurry, took eleven days to make that same journey. Following after the Black Riders, Gandalf will take six days to reach Sarn Ford on Shadowfax, though he may have had to cover a greater distance.

Sauron's horse stealing is described by Éomer in *The Two Towers*, Bk. 3, Ch. 2, "The Riders of Rohan." For more about Gondor's errand-riders, who could average about 13 miles per hour with often-replaced horses, see "Gondor's Pony Express" at the end of Chapter 14.

Though nothing is said in any text, to make this ride plausible we must assume Sauron has agents or collaborators along the route to supply fresh horses. (That would explain why Tolkien had Sauron stealing Rohan's black horses.) Perhaps it is also true that the disembodied Black Riders did not need to stop to sleep or eat, and that they drove their horses more ruthlessly than Gandalf ever would. With replacement horses, the Black Riders could ride around the clock and need to average only a little over 7 miles per hour during the roughly 82 hours available to them. In contrast, if one set of horses is ridden 12 hours a day, resting the remainder of the day, those horses must average 15 miles per hour over 600 miles of often rough roads. That seems impossible.

Aragorn with the Rangers

Great East Road near Bree

Unfinished Tales, Pt. III, Ch. IV, "The Hunt for the Ring."

- Aragorn is standing watch on the Great East Road near Bree.

Rangers as Unsung Heroes

The popular prejudice against Rangers is seen in *The Fellowship of the Ring*, Bk. 1, Ch. 10, "Strider."

The Rangers of the North (or Dúnedain) are Tolkien's unsung heros. For centuries they have guarded places such as the Shire from bandits and Orcs. Though little noticed by most readers, their sacrifice at Sarn Ford plays a crucial role in Frodo's escape. But for them, the Black Riders might have reached Bag End in time to capture Frodo and the Ring.

As Sauron grew in power, these Rangers had to operate in secrecy, lest he realize they are a potent foe and hunt them down. But secrecy has a price. Local inhabitants often suspect them (including Aragorn) of being robbers and outlaws.

Friday, September 23, 1418—Shire Invaded

Fatty, Frodo, Folco, Merry, Pippin and Sam

Bag End, Hobbiton

- Merry and Fatty leave with the last cart of luggage for Crickhollow.
- After lunch, Folco Boffin returns home.

The Fellowship of the Ring, Bk. 1, Ch. 3, "Three is Company."

Frodo as a Hiker

The hike planned for this evening is not unusual. Recovering at Rivendell, Tolkien has Frodo recall his youthful hikes with Bilbo. Tolkien also wrote that after Bilbo left seventeen years earlier, Frodo often hiked the Shire with Merry and Pippin as well as alone. Tolkien notes that, contrary to the usual Hobbit tendency to settle down, as Frodo approached 50 he longed for longer journeys and more adventure—even as he hiked less and fell out of shape. It is easy to suspect that the gruff Gaffer discouraged Sam from joining them, preferring to keep his son working.

The Fellowship of the Ring, Bk. 2, Ch. 1, "Many Meetings" as well as the beginning of Bk. 1, Ch. 1, "The Shadow of the Past."

Gandalf leaves for the Shire on the same day Frodo leaves Bag End.

Frodo, Pippin and Sam

Day 1 of 3 in their Hike to Crickhollow

Bag End and traveling through Tookland

- After dark they leave for Green Hill Country and hike three hours.
- They eat supper in a birch grove and hike until midnight.
- After covering 18 miles, they camp in a fir grove.

Tolkien as a Hiker

Tolkien gives a lot of detail here because he loved hiking. In 1944, he wrote his son Christopher, stationed with the Royal Air Force in South Africa, that the "autumn wanderlust" had hit him, and he wanted to take to the road with a pack on his back. *Letters,* No. 81.

The Fellowship of the Ring, Bk. 1, Ch. 3, "Three is Company." Friday afternoon starts the Hobbit weekend, so leaving then attracts less attention. At this time, Sam told Rose he would be back in the spring. See *The Return of the King,* Bk. 6, Ch. 8, "The Scouring of the Shire."

Gandalf

Day 1 of 7 in his Race to the Shire

Leaving Rohan

- Gandalf leaves for the Shire on Shadowfax.

Gandalf Pursuit

At the Council of Elrond, Tolkien has Gandalf claim to have gained on the Black Riders over several days of his race for the Shire. That appears to be a mistake. By Tolkien's own chronology in "The Tale of Years," four of the Black Riders enter the Shire before dawn on September 23, the same day (and presumably later than dawn) that Gandalf finally tames Shadowfax and first rides for the Shire. Gandalf may be trying to rationalize the time he spent taming Shadowfax.

The Return of the King, Bk. 6, Ap. B, "The Tale of Years." From the plains of Rohan, the Shire is over 600 miles away.

Black Riders—Entering the Shire

Day 1 of 28 Pursuing Frodo

Shire and Greenway

Unfinished Tales, Pt. III, Ch. IV, "The Hunt for the Ring" and *The Return of the King,* Bk. 6, Ap. B, "The Tale of Years." Andrath is a narrow valley on the Greenway south of Bree. In her *The Atlas of Middle-earth,* Karen Fonstad suggested it was located where the hills of the Barrow-downs intersect the Greenway.

- Before sunrise, four Black Riders enter the Shire.
- Four others drive the Rangers up the Greenway.
- The Lord of Nazgûl sets up a base at Andrath.

Nazgûl and Barrow-wights

Some Tolkien manuscripts suggest the Lord of the Nazgûl stirred up the Old Forest and Barrow-wights. Both will pose a grave threat to the escaping Hobbits. While the Hobbits are in the Shire, their greatest threat will come from Khamûl, the Lord of Dol Guldur. Next to the Lord of the Nazgûl himself, Khamûl is the most aware of the presence of the Ring. It is he who pursues them closely—speaking to the Gaffer at Hobbiton, following them on the Stock road, and almost catching them at Bucklebury Ferry. Fortunately, his abilities are weakened by daylight.

Day 2
September 17

Saturday, September 24, 1418—Hiking

There is no moon tonight. The waning crescent of the moon sets about 6 p.m. The new moon is in four days. The dark nights add to the danger the Hobbits face from Black Riders.

Frodo, Pippin and Sam

Day 2 of 3 in the Hike to Crickhollow

Green Hill Country

The Fellowship of the Ring, Bk. 1, Ch. 3, "Three is Company" and *Unfinished Tales,* Pt. II, Ch. IV, "The Hunt for the Ring." On Weathertop, Strider describes how Black Riders sense people. See *The Fellowship of the Ring,* Bk. 1, Ch. 11, "A Knife in the Dark," near the end of the chapter. For more about how the four Hobbits grow in ability and character, see "The Testing of Hobbits" at the end of Chapter 11.

- They begin hiking just after 10 a.m.
- In early afternoon, Sam hears hooves, so they hide in the woods.
- A Black Rider approaches, sniffs and goes on.
- Sam tells Frodo about the black-clad stranger the night before.

Fortunate Instinct

Tolkien was a romantic in the literary sense, which meant that he believed intuition was at least as valuable a guide to life as logic and reason. Until this point in the narrative, his Hobbits have been naive, not taking seriously Gandalf's warnings. Here what Tolkien called a "feeling" and a "sudden desire," leads them to hide from a danger they were not really expecting. Only after escaping the first Black Rider on a hunch, do they learn to think and plan their way out of danger.

Woody End and the Stock Road toward Woodhall

The leader of these high Elves is Gildor Inglorion, who is related to the Elves of Rivendell.

- Just after sundown, Frodo hears hooves, so they hide.
- A Black Rider stops and creeps toward them.
- Elves arrive singing, and the Black Rider leaves.
- Told about Black Riders, the Elves let the Hobbits travel with them.

Safety in Horses

One key to the Hobbit's safety is that the Black Riders are using horses. The hooves give warning and the difficulty of taking horses through thick brush and down steep hillsides provides an escape route.

Hills above Woodhall

- Elves and Hobbits hike to the hills above Woodhall to feast.
- Frodo talks with Gildor and then sleeps.

Despite a late start, they hike an impressive 28 miles today.

Elf Messages

These Elves are eastbound, so Tolkien has them pass word of the Hobbits' plight to Tom Bombadil, Aragorn and the Elves of Rivendell. Each gets to help the fleeing Hobbits. These Elves will soon leave Middle-earth and are becoming detached from it. That may be why Tolkien did not have them accompany the Hobbits all the way to Rivendell.

For an early history of Elves, see *The Silmarillion*, Ch. 3, "On the Coming of the Elves and the Captivity of Melkor." When the Elves tell Aragorn of their meeting with Frodo, they do not know if Frodo has left Crickhollow safely. See *The Fellowship of the Ring*, Bk. 1, Ch. 10, "Strider."

Black Riders

Day 2 of 28 Pursuing Frodo, Date Estimated

Bree and Greenway south of Bree

- The Nazgûl Captain hides along the Greenway south of Bree.
- Two Black Riders go into the Bree.

Flight to Rivendell

The question of how much Sauron knows applies here. The four who enter the Shire are searching for "Baggins," the name Sauron tortured from Gollum. (See the Black Rider's conversation with the Gaffer in Ch. 3, "Three is Company.") The Nazgûl Captain and the two who visit Bree assume 'Baggins' will flee east to Rivendell. Faramir's dream and logic suggest that for Rivendell is the closest refugee safe from Black Riders.

The Fellowship of the Ring, Bk. 2, Ch. 2, "The Council of Elrond." Gandalf gives this description of the movements of the Black Riders at the Council of Elrond on October 25.

Gandalf

Day 2 of 7 in his Race to the Shire

Isen River

- Gandalf reaches the Isen River, 500 miles from the Shire.

The Return of the King, Bk. 6, Ap. B, "The Tale of Years."

Sunday, September 25, 1418—Crickhollow

Day 3
September 18

Frodo, Pippin and Sam with Farmer Maggot

Day 3 of 3 in the Hike to Crickhollow

Hiking to Bucklebury Ferry

- The three Hobbits cut cross-country to Bucklebury Ferry.
- They see a Black Rider behind them and drift too far south.
- Farmer Maggot offers to feed them and take them to the ferry.

The Fellowship of the Ring, Bk. 1, Ch. 4, "A Short Cut to Mushrooms." Frodo and Sam will hear a similar cry to that heard today in Emyn Muil on February 29, 1419.

The Mysterious Farmer Maggot

The Fellowship of the Ring, Bk. 1, Ch. 7, "In the House of Tom Bombadil," near the end.

Tolkien made Farmer Maggot a most unusual Hobbit. Later, Tom Bombadil hints that the farmer has contacts with both him and the Elves—almost unheard of behavior for a Hobbit.

Frodo, Merry, Pippin and Sam with Maggot

Bucklebury Ferry

The Fellowship of the Ring, Bk. 1, Ch. 4, "A Short Cut to Mushrooms" and also Bk. 1, Ch. 5, "A Conspiracy Unmasked." The ferry is about five miles from the farm.

- After dark, they leave for the ferry and meet Merry.
- The four Hobbits cross the Brandywine on the ferry.
- As Merry ties the boat up, Sam catches sight of a Black Rider.

Black Rider in the Dark

This Dark Rider must be barely visible by lamp light since the sliver of a moon set several hours earlier. The close timing of their escape and the effectiveness of a river barrier illustrate Tolkien's subtle use of providence, as does the fact that the Black Rider arrives soon enough to be seen rather than a few minutes later. That warns them not to delay in Crickhollow. The Black Riders will attack the Crickhollow cottage in four days on the evening of September 29.

Fatty, Frodo, Merry, Pippin and Sam

Crickhollow house

The Fellowship of the Ring, Bk. 1, Ch. 5, "A Conspiracy Unmasked."

- Merry rides ahead while the others hike to Crickhollow.
- Frodo discovers his friends have been watching him.
- They agree they must travel through the Old Forest.

Tolkien's Practical Hobbits

Fatty Bolger is a relative of Frodo. For his family history, see the entry for Fredegar in "Took of the Great Smials," Bk. 6, Ap. C, "Family Trees, *The Return of the King.*

One delight of Tolkien's Hobbits is their down-to-earth practicality. Frodo's friends have prepared carefully for this trip, including ponies. Fatty Bolger will stay behind to make the cottage appear as if Frodo were still there. All that is very sensible. Frodo hasn't thought matters through nearly as well as his friends.

Gandalf

Day 3 of 7 in His Race to the Shire, Location Calculated

Entering Dunland

No text records where Gandalf is today. This location assumes he covers about 100 miles per day. He is about 400 miles from Hobbiton.

- Gandalf enters Dunland.

Tolkien's Hillbillies

The Dunlendings are Tolkien's hillbillies. Isolated and culturally backward, they hate the proud horsemen of Rohan, so it is unlikely that Gandalf, riding a horse out of Rohan, received assistance from them. In all likelihood, Tolkien assumed he rode through on the Old South Road, purchasing food and allowing Shadowfax to rest and feed as necessary.

CHAPTER

8

Flight to Bree

September 26 to 29, 1418

Entering the Old Forest to arrival at Bree

The safe and idyllic Shire that Tolkien labored so hard to create and that many Tolkien fans love so dearly is no more. The author has sent the forces of Sauron into its very heart. The Hobbits must flee for their lives.

Tolkien now takes us on a journey back in time. The Old Forest represents an evil from the First Age, clinging precariously to existence like some near-extinct species in an isolated mountain valley. In much the same way, the Great Barrows is deeply rooted in the evil of the Second Age. Yet the modern evil that the four Hobbits face is so great that these ancient evils are to be preferred. Never before, Tolkien is hinting, has Middle-earth faced a terror quite like this.

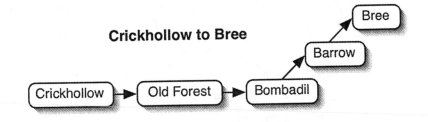

Monday, September 26, 1418—Old Forest

The sun rises about 6:30. The new moon is two days away and what little moon there is sets at 7 p.m., so the nights are dark.

Fatty, Frodo, Merry, Pippin and Sam

Day 1 of 4 to Bree

Crickhollow to the Hedge

• Leaving at six a.m., an hour later they reach the border hedge.

The Fellowship of the Ring, Bk. 1, Ch. 6, "The Old Forest."

Frodo, Merry, Pippin and Sam with Tom Bombadil

Old Forest to the River Withywindle

The Fellowship of the Ring, Bk. 1, Ch. 6, "The Old Forest." Tom and Goldberry seem to be exceptions to Tolkien's claim that the book has no allegories.

- Frodo, Sam, Merry and Pippin enter the Old Forest.
- In late afternoon they reach the River Withywindle and rest.
- Old Man Willow attacks Frodo, Pippin and Merry.
- Sam frees Frodo and Tom Bombadil frees Pippin and Merry.
- Tom takes them home.

More on Tom Bombadil

Letters, No. 19 and 144. See also The Treason of Isengard, Ch. 12, "Treebeard."

In 1937, Tolkien said that Tom Bombadil represented the spirit of the Oxford and Berkshire countrysides. Later he decided that Tom was best left an enigma. In draft manuscripts, Treebeard talks about the Old Forest and Tom Bombadil.

Frodo, Merry, Pippin, Sam, Tom Bombadil and Goldberry

Tom Bombadil's Home

The Fellowship of the Ring, Bk. 1, Ch. 7, "In the House of Tom Bombadil." Tolkien had reached this chapter by late August, 1938, noting to his publisher that "it is no bedtime story." Letters, No. 33. Later, Gandalf pointed out that Frodo's dream was "late in coming." See: The Fellowship of the Ring, Bk. 2, Ch. 2, "The Council of Elrond." Tolkien said Goldberry stood for the seasonal changes along rivers in the fall. Letters, No. 210. For Goldberry as a Celtic river goddess, see Leslie Ellen Jones, Myth and Middle-earth (Cold Spring Press: Cold Spring Harbor, NY, 2002), 52f.

- The four Hobbits meet Tom's wife, Goldberry.
- Frodo dreams of a man carried by an eagle and galloping in the East.

Delayed Dream

In literature, dreams often anticipate the future. Here Tolkien gave Frodo a dream describing what had already happened. An eagle had taken Gandalf away from Orthanc eight days earlier (September 18), and the Black Riders have been on horseback since July 17, over two months earlier. They began riding for the Shire perhaps a week earlier on September 19.

Gandalf's Movements

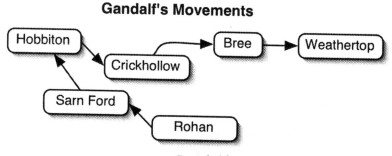

Gandalf

Day 4 of 7 in His Race to the Shire, Location Calculated

Central Dunland

At the day's end, Gandalf is some 300 miles from Bag End.

- Gandalf passes through central Dunland.

Gandalf's Long Ride

Gandalf's location was calculated based on the average distance he covers each day, some 100 miles.

Black Riders

Day 4 of 28 Pursuing Frodo

Bree

- A Black Rider enters Bree from the north, then one from the south.
- The two go to the *The Prancing Pony* and ask about "Baggins."
- They frighten a gatekeeper into spying for them.

The Fellowship of the Ring, Bk. 1, Ch. 10, "Strider."

A Spy for Sauron

Both Strider and Barliman describe the Black Riders and their visit to Bree. For the Black Rider's conversation with the gatekeeper, see *The Treason of Isengard,* Ch. 3, "The Fourth Phase (2)."

Aragorn

Bree

- Aragorn observes the Black Riders talking to the gatekeeper.

The Fellowship of the Ring, Bk. 1, Ch. 10, "Strider."

Aragorn's Distrust

This observation explains why Aragorn (as Strider) slips over the gate when he enters Bree behind the Hobbits on September 29. He knows Harry Goatleaf, the gatekeeper, is not to be trusted.

Tuesday, September 27, 1418—Rest and Rain

Day 5
September 20

Frodo, Merry, Pippin, Sam, Tom Bombadil and Goldberry

Day 2 of 4 to Bree

Tom Bombadil's Home

- Because it is raining, the Hobbits decide not to travel.
- Tom asks for the Ring, puts it on, and does not disappear.
- Tom gives them a song that will bring him if they get into trouble.

The Fellowship of the Ring, Bk. 1, Ch. 8, "In the House of Tom Bombadil." Goldberry is a character in the Medieval romance, *Havelock the Dane.*

One of a Kind Tom Bombadil

Interested in creating a world so complex and varied that it seems as real as our own, Tolkien was not afraid to place in Middle-earth people who don't quite fit in. Tom Bombadil is one such person. He is a survivor from the far distant past. At the Council of Elrond, Gandalf explains why the Ring did not make Tom invisible or hide Frodo from him.

See *The Fellowship of the Ring,* Bk. 2, Ch. II, "The Council of Elrond." For a delightful poem about Tom, read "The Adventures of Tom Bombadil," a part of *The Tolkien Reader.*

Gandalf

Day 5 of 7 in his Race to the Shire

Greyflood

- Gandalf reaches the Greyflood River (also know as the Gwathlo).

The Return of the King, Bk. 6, Ap. B, "The Tale of Years."

Fording the Greyflood

Gandalf probably crosses the river at a ford near the long-deserted town of Thrabad. At that point, he is some 200 miles south of the Shire.

Day 6
September 21
Autumn Equinox

Wednesday, September 28, 1418—Leaving Tom

A barely visible new moon sets in the west about 8 p.m. In the modern calendar, today is the Autumn Equinox, when day and night are of almost equal length. After today, the nights will be longer than the days.

Frodo, Merry, Pippin, Sam, Tom Bombadil and Goldberry

Day 3 of 4 to Bree

Leaving Tom Bombadil's Home

- After breakfast, the Hobbits leave and meet Goldberry.

Frodo's Dream of a Green Land

The Fellowship of the Ring, Bk. 1, Ch. 8, "Fog on the Barrow-downs."

Letters, No. 91 and C. S. Lewis, Ch. 2, "The Island." in *The Pilgrim's Regress*. Tolkien wanted his tale treated as ancient history, while Lewis was clearly writing allegory. For why Tolkien as a philologist disliked allegory, see Leslie Jones, *Myth & Middle Earth*, 44.

In a 1944 letter, Tolkien said the "far green country" Frodo dreams about while at Tom Bombadil's house was a vision of where he would go when he sailed from Grey Havens. Compare that to the "green wood" and distant island that C. S. Lewis had his main character dream of before his great journey in *Pilgrim's Regress* (first published in 1933). For much more on what Tolkien and Lewis intended to do with their writings, see "Tolkien and Lewis" at the end of Chapter 9.

Frodo, Merry, Pippin and Sam

Crossing the Barrow-downs

The Fellowship of the Ring, Bk. 1, Ch. 8, "Fog on the Barrow-downs." Is it significant that the Hobbits leave Tom (with his close links to nature) on the first day of Autumn in our modern calendar? Probably not, but it is an interesting coincidence. The Hobbits also begin their desperate flight just five days before Fall begins and leave Rivendell four days before the start of Winter. Finally, the Ring is destroyed two days before Spring. For some reason, major events in the tale do come near the changing of seasons.

- The Hobbits head north toward the Great East Road.
- They wander east, stop for lunch and fall asleep.
- They awake at sunset and start for the road.
- They become separated from each other in a fog.
- Frodo blacks out.

Evil Spirits Not Evil People

Though a devout Catholic, Tolkien seems to have found the dead that Aragorn summons on the Path of the Dead (March 8, 1419), so useful to his plot that he allowed the pagan beliefs connected with them to slip into his story. The same is not true of Barrow-wights. They are not evil people whose spirits live on like ghosts in a haunted house. They are evil spirits who merely animate the bodies of the dead. That is why Tom Bombadil can have fond memories of the woman whose brooch he finds in a Barrow. She had no connection to the evil that is now present. When Tom cleansed the Barrow, he was serving as an exorcist and helping those long-dead friends. Something similar may be true of the faces that Frodo, Sam and Gollum see in the Dead Marshes on March 1, 1419. If Sam is right, they are evil spirits animating reflections that merely resemble the long-dead.

Gandalf
Day 6 of 7 in his Race to the Shire
Sarn Ford

- Gandalf crosses the Sarn Ford on the Brandywine River.

The Return of the King, Bk. 6, Ap. B, "The Tale of Years." Gandalf is now about 100 miles from Bag End.

Gandalf's Pursuit

The Black Riders reached the Sarn Ford on the evening of September 22, so Gandalf was some six days behind them at that point. At first glance, that seems to make it impossible for him to catch up. However, Gandalf gets a chance to close the gap when the Black Riders fail to capture the Hobbits in the Shire and do not pursue them into the Old Forest, Gandalf began a week behind the Hobbits, but by the time he reaches Bree, he is only a few hours behind them.

Thursday, September 29, 1418—Barrow to Bree

Day 7
September 22

Frodo, Merry, Pippin, Sam and Tom Bombadil
Day 4 of 4 to Bree
Barrow-downs to Great East Road

- Shortly after sunrise Frodo wakes, a captive of a Barrow-wight.
- Frodo protects Sam, Pippin and Merry from an arm with a sword.
- Frodo sings Tom's song and they are rescued.
- Tom takes them to Great East Road just as the sun sets.
- He suggests they stay at *The Prancing Pony*.

The Fellowship of the Ring, Bk. 1, Ch. 8, "Fog on the Barrow-downs." This may be the barrow of the last prince of Cardolan, dead over 1600 years. See *The Return of the King*, Appendix A, I, (iii).

Tom's Detachment

Since Tom can eliminate a Barrow-wight with a mere song, why didn't Tolkien have him clean out all the barrows and rid Middle-earth of the trouble they cause? To do that, Tolkien would have had to portray Tom acting against the personality he was given. Gandalf rights wrongs, while Tom accepts life as it comes. He may help with specific situations that thrust themselves into his life, but as Gandalf later warns, he is an untrustworthy ally in a long struggle. Tolkien cannot do more with Tom because, as an author, he must remain true to his characters. Given Tom's close links to nature, Tolkien may also be suggesting that in the great struggles between good and evil, nature and its forces (such as the weather) will be neutral and are thus untrustworthy allies. See "Tolkien's Natural World" at the end of this chapter.

See *The Fellowship of the Ring*, Bk. 2, Ch. 2, "The Council of Elrond." Strider overhears the conversation when they reach the road, but for some reason doesn't reveal himself, suggesting that he and Tom have never met. *The Fellowship of the Ring*, Bk. 1, Ch. 10, "Strider."

Frodo, Merry, Pippin, Sam and Butterbur with Strider
Bree

- When they arrive after dark, a gatekeeper questions the Hobbits.
- Someone slips over the gate and disappears into the shadows.
- Barliman gives the Hobbits rooms.

The Fellowship of the Ring, Bk. 1, Ch. 9, "At the Sign of The Prancing Pony."

Thursday, September 29, 1418—Barrow to Bree

For Goatleaf's recruitment by Black Riders, see *The Treason of Isengard*, Ch. 3, "The Fourth Phase (2)." For Strider slipping over the gate, see *The Fellowship of the Ring*, B. 1, Ch. 10, "Strider."

The Fellowship of the Ring, Bk. 1, Ch. 9, "At the Sign of The Prancing Pony" and Bk. 1, Ch. 10, "Strider." The horses and horns in Frodo's dream are happening that very night.

In early drafts, Strider was a Hobbit named Trotter. See the index for *The Return of the Shadow*. Tolkien made major changes in Gandalf's movements during this time. See the first four chapters of *The Treason of Isengard*. In drafts, Gandalf did give Strider a letter of introduction to show the Hobbits. See *The Treason of Isengard*, Ch. 4, "Of Hamilcar, Gandalf, and Saruman." Gandalf's mention of Aragorn is in *The Fellowship of the Ring*, Bk. 1, Ch. 2, "The Shadow of the Past."

The Fellowship of the Ring, Bk. 1, Ch. 11, "A Knife in the Dark." Tolkien was working on a draft of this chapter in October of 1938. *Letters*, No. 34.

This is the first time the Horn-call of Buckland has been sounded since 1311, which was 107 years earlier. Except in hot pursuit, the Black Riders confine themselves to highways, where they can move quickly on horseback. Fatty is also called Fredegar.

Tolkien in the Details

Here Tolkien is in control of details that few readers notice. As we learn elsewhere, the gatekeeper is Harry Goatleaf, a spy for Sauron. The person who slips over the gate is Strider, who has followed the Hobbits since they joined the Great East Road.

Frodo, Merry, Pippin, Sam, Strider and Butterbur

The Prancing Pony, Bree

- Frodo sings, falls, puts on the Ring, and disappears.
- Strider warns of danger and offers to protect them.
- Butterbur gives them Gandalf's letter, written on Midyear's Day.
- Merry arrives and tells them he has seen a Black Rider.
- Frodo dreams of horses and blowing horns.

Strider and Gandalf

Tolkien gives no reason why Gandalf did not introduce Strider to Butterbur (perhaps when they passed near Bree the previous April), so the innkeeper would not be suspicious of him. The most likely explanation is that his role in guarding the Shire had to be concealed even from a well-meaning but talkative Butterbur. Revealing the special protection that Rangers were providing might draw Sauron's attention and result in a confrontation the Rangers could not win. Gandalf did, however, mention Strider as Aragorn to Frodo in passing when he talked about the Ring on April 13, 1418. But when Frodo reads Gandalf's letter, which equates Strider with Aragorn, he gives no indication of remembering the earlier conversation.

Fatty with the Black Riders

Day 7 of 28 Pursuing Frodo

Crickhollow, Buckland

- That evening, Fatty Bolger sees shadows creeping toward the cottage.
- Black Riders smash down the door.
- Fatty sounds the Horn-call of Buckland.
- The Black Riders leave by the North-gate.

Movements of the Black Riders

Fatty's role playing was quite effective. It has been four days since a Black Rider saw the Hobbits cross on the ferry into Buckland. Some of that time was spent locating Frodo's new home and some preparing for their attack. Since the four Hobbits were gone by sunrise the next morning, the Black Riders have wasted four days. If only one of those had been available, five Black Riders might been in Bree this evening rather than two. In that case, the attack at the inn could have been much more aggressive, and Frodo and the Ring might have been taken.

Gandalf with the Gaffer

Day 7 of 7 in his Race to the Shire

Bag End, Hobbiton

- Gandalf visits the Gaffer in Hobbiton.
- He hears of Frodo's departure and the Black Rider's visit.

The Fellowship of the Ring, Bk. 2, Ch. 2, "The Council of Elrond" and *The Return of the King,* Bk. 6, Ap. B, "The Tale of Years."

Explaining Gandalf

Since Gandalf knew that, if Frodo had stuck to his original schedule, he would be in Crickhollow or Bree by now, why didn't Tolkien have him go to either of those places first? Going to Crickhollow was obviously a bad idea. If Frodo were about to leave or had just left, that would draw attention to his departure. Gandalf wanted to avoid that at all costs. If Gandalf had gone to Bree, he would have arrived before the Hobbits and been waiting for them there, spoiling much of the adventure that takes place between Bree and Rivendell.

Tolkien's Natural World

There's no mistaking the love that Tolkien has for the Shire. Much of the horror we experience reading about the Black Riders comes from a realization that even his idyllic Shire is no longer safe from Sauron. A love for nature in general and for trees in particular also fills his writings. Some of his best narratives revolve around moving descriptions of mountains, forests and grasslands. But it is important to realize that his view of nature differs from some attitudes common today. Tolkien's love for nature is closely tied to his love for Hobbits, Elves, Ents, men and even Dwarves— the free peoples of Middle-earth.

In a 1972 letter to the *Daily Telegraph,* Tolkien described Middle-earth's forests, see *Letters,* No. 339.

Tolkien's natural world is intrinsically people-centered. It needs people to guide its growth, much like a garden needs a gardener or sheep need a shepherd. The Shire is a marvelous place because pastures, forests, Hobbits and wild animals live in harmony, with none an enemy of the others. The same is true of the Elf-created beauty of Lórien. You also see this with non-living nature, when Gimli describes how his people would, with the greatest of care, improve the Glittering Caves of Helm's Deep.

That ideal does not exist everywhere. Later, as the travelers drift down the Anduin River, there is a contrast between the Orc-infested wastelands to their left and the beautiful human-inhabited grasslands of Rohan on their right. When the Orcs take their captives across Rohan, they are at war with the lands over which they are traveling—something that is not true of the riders of Rohan. For Sauron and his kind, nature exists to be exploited or ignored. It is not something to be appreciated or nurtured.

For a discussion of Tolkien's view of nature that does not taken into account shepherding and sees it as contradictory beyond hope of reconciliation, read Verlyn Flieger, "Taking the Part of Trees: Eco-Conflict in Middle-earth," in *J. R. R. Tolkien and His Literary Resonances,* George Clark and Daniel Timmons, ed. (Westport: Greenwood, 2000), 147f.

Nature's need to be lovingly shepherded by people comes through most clearly when the Hobbits leave the Shire and enter the Old Forest—an 'old growth' forest where people have never lived. There nature is at war with

For Tolkien's remarks on Tom Bombadil and Old Man Willow, see *Letters,* No. 153.

people, while malice and hatred dominate the thoughts of trees. True, Tom Bombadil is a shepherd of sorts. But he is too lighthearted to take the job seriously, displaying no interest in reforming trees or turning Old Man Willow from his evil ways. He is satisfied merely to rescue and entertain the Hobbits. He displays little of the tender love the Ents have for the trees of Fangorn. To a lesser extent, the same is true of the wood Elves of Mirkwood, who (in *The Hobbit*) prefer partying to countering the dark influence of the Necromancer to their south. As a result, there is little beauty in glum Mirkwood.

Tolkien's marvelous knack for describing woods and wilderness is like that of William Morris, a talented nineteenth century artist and writer who influenced Tolkien's writing style. Two of Morris' best tales, *The House of the Wolfings* and *The Roots of the Mountains,* have been republished in one volume as *More to William Morris.* The first tale concerns a Rohan-like people's defense of their freedom against a Roman invasion. The second has the same people fighting hundreds of years later against an attack by ruthless Huns. The technological sophistication and power of the first foe resembles Sauron, and the barbarism and cruelty of the second is roughly similar to Orcs.

The pattern repeats when Tolkien describes places where people no longer live. They have either become evil (the Barrow-downs and the Dead Marshes) or are depressingly somber and inhospitable (the depopulated lands around Weathertop). At worse, the absence of people puts nature under evil. At best, it creates the dreariness of Tolkien's wilderness journeys, which contrast markedly with the joys of populated places such as Rivendell or Lórien. Perhaps the only exception is recently depopulated but lovely Ithilien, where Gondor's influence still lingers despite its proximity to foul Mordor.

Similarities exist between Tolkien's views about nature and those in the first three chapters of the Biblical Genesis. There man is placed in a wooded garden and expected to care for it and name its animals much as a kind shepherd might name his sheep. But that was soon followed by what theologians call the 'Fall of Man.' Adam and Eve exploited nature, misusing the garden they had been given by taking from the only tree whose fruit was forbidden to them. Their disobedience resulted in a conflict with nature much like that we see in Tolkien between the Old Forest and Hobbits. The natural world is now flawed and often hostile. The soil will grow "thorns and thistles," and food comes only through "painful toil." What Genesis describes as a curse is personified in Tolkien as the hatred of trees for all those who cut and burn. For both, nature is flawed and in as much need of redemption as humanity.

So as you read Tolkien's loving account of the natural world and sense his particular love for trees, recall that his is a world in which, if they so chose, people and nature can live in harmony. Even more important, his is a world in which people are neither the inherent enemies of nature nor are they mere minor actors with roles far less important than those assigned to forces of nature such as wildfires or volcanic eruptions. Tolkien believed we have a special responsibility *over* nature as shepherds (much like the Ents have for trees), one that calls on us to enhance its richness and increase its beauty. Without downplaying our flaws, he did not see us as a disease inflicted upon an otherwise innocent natural world. Nor did he romanticize nature as something wise and good in itself apart from our assistance.

9

Journey to Rivendell

September 30 to October 20, 1418

Leaving Bree to arrival at Rivendell

Much of the power in Tolkien's epic lies in the great emotional range it spans, from the simple happiness of Shire life to the violent clash of vast armies. We are now entering what is perhaps the most discouraging period in that tale. The three days it took to reach Crickhollow and the four days to Bree were driven a terror of the Black Riders, the Old Forest and the Barrow-wright that left little time for reflection. In contrast the three weeks of slogging through the wilderness to Rivendell will allow the four Hobbits many hours for discouraging thought, broken by only two brief moments of terror on Weathertop and at the Ford of Bruinen totaling perhaps five minutes. Michael Stanton summarized their plight when he remarked that "the unspoken theme of Book 1 is discouragement." He goes on to say:

> There is a sense—and we sense it long before Gandalf's letter makes it plain—that everything has been left too late, and that the forces of evil have gained far too much strength and momentum.

Michael N. Stanton, *Hobbits, Elves and Wizards,* 31.

Friday, September 30, 1418—Leaving Bree

Day 8
September 23

The moon is two days past new. It rises about 10 a.m. and sets a little after nine in the evening. In the days ahead, it will give a little more light and stay in the sky a bit longer each evening.

Frodo, Merry, Pippin, Sam and Strider

Day 1 of 21 to Rivendell

Bree to Western Chetwood

- The Hobbits' unoccupied bedroom is attacked by Black Riders.
- Black Riders steal the horses and ponies in the inn's stable.
- The travelers buy a pony and leave Bree at 10 a.m.
- They take a trail that goes north through Chetwood Forest.

The Fellowship of the Ring, Bk. 1, Ch. 11, "A Knife in the Dark." For how Butterbur responds to their return see *The Return of the King,* Bk. 6, Ch. 7, "Homeward Bound."

No Safe Place

First the Shire is invaded and now an inn in Bree, Tolkien is making clear that the safe, idyllic times these Hobbits have known is now past. No place is safe from the long arm of Sauron.

Gandalf—Crickhollow to Bree

Crickhollow and Bree

The Fellowship of the Ring, Bk. 2, Ch. 2, "The Council of Elrond" and The Return of the King, Bk. 6, Ap. B, "The Tale of Years." For Tolkien's effort to explain Gandalf's absence during this period, see The Treason of Isengard, Ch. 1, "Gandalf's Delay."

- Gandalf visits Frodo's Crickhollow cottage.
- In the evening he arrives in Bree.

Hasty Gandalf

Tolkien often has Gandalf act in haste. The Wizard does not stay long enough in Crickhollow to discover that no Hobbits were captured by Black Riders, making his desperate pursuit unnecessary. Fortunately, this time no harm comes from his haste.

Saturday, October 1, 1418—Chetwood

Day 9
September 24

Frodo, Merry, Pippin, Sam and Strider

Day 2 of 21 to Rivendell

Eastern Chetwood

The Fellowship of the Ring, Bk. 1, Ch. 11, "A Knife in the Dark." Many of the distances given here are derived from maps and charts in The Atlas of Middle-earth.

- Strider and the Hobbits travel east through Chetwood.

Wilderness Travel

During this part of their journey, Strider and the Hobbits will average about 16 miles a day, a rapid pace for wilderness travel on foot.

Black Riders

Day 9 of 28 Pursuing Frodo

Bree

The Fellowship of the Ring, Bk. 2, Ch. 2, "The Council of Elrond."

- At least five Black Riders come from the west.
- They smash through Bree and head south on the Greenway.

Black Riders in Pursuit

As Tolkien refined his story, he gave a greater role to the Black Riders, using them to provide a sense of danger that could not be created by the always-distant Sauron. These Black Riders had been searching for the Hobbits in the Shire and watching for them along the Great East Road to Bree. They are now in hot pursuit, keeping as usual to the roads.

By having them ride through Bree rather than around it, Tolkien demonstrated their contempt for the village's peaceful inhabitants. Good men such as Gandalf and Strider, however fierce and stern they may be in battle, are able appreciate simple and peaceful folk like those in Bree. Evil men cannot. They equate peacefulness with weakness. In the end that arrogance will be their undoing. They will underestimate their foes.

Gandalf

Day 1 of 18 to Rivendell

Great East Road

- Before dawn, Gandalf exits Bree, following the Black Riders.

Friendship between Gandalf and Aragorn

Tolkien placed the first meeting between Gandalf and Strider (as Aragorn) 62 years earlier in 1356. Scattered through his writings are hints that the two often worked together on projects such as their search for Gollum. As a result, Tolkien can assume that each understands the other well. Gandalf knows Strider will not stay on the Great East Road, and that it would be difficult to find him on wilderness trails. So he gallops for the one place he might intercept them, Weathertop. He will reach it before sundown on his third day out of Bree. Strider is thinking similarly. Although he has no idea where Gandalf might be, he knows his friend well enough to also think of Weathertop.

The Fellowship of the Ring, Bk. 2, Ch. 2, "The Council of Elrond" and *The Return of the King*, Bk. 6, Ap. B, "The Tale of Years."

Sunday, October 2, 1418—Midgewater

Day 10
September 25

Frodo, Merry, Pippin, Sam and Strider

Day 3 of 21 to Rivendell

Western Midgewater Marshes

- The travelers enter a wilderness leading to the Midgewater Marshes.
- The ground becomes wetter and they are attacked by insects.

No Illusions

For all his love of nature, Tolkien had no illusions about what an unpopulated wilderness could be like. What we now romantically call a "wetland," he considered a miserable, bug-infested swamp. Those who have hiked through swamps, particularly in warm climates, are likely to agree with him.

The Fellowship of the Ring, Bk. 1, Ch. 11, "A Knife in the Dark."

Monday, October 3, 1418—Battle on Weathertop

Day 11
September 26

Frodo, Merry, Pippin, Sam and Strider

Day 4 of 21 to Rivendell

Eastern Midgewater Marshes

- Strider and the Hobbits travel through the Midgewater Marshes.
- That night, Strider and Frodo see lightning-like flashes to their east.

The Fellowship of the Ring, Bk. 1, Ch. 11, "A Knife in the Dark."

Gandalf with the Black Riders

Day 3 of 18 to Rivendell (Gandalf)
Day 11 of 28 in Pursuit of Frodo (Black Riders)

Weathertop

- Before sunset, Gandalf reaches Weathertop and finds Black Riders.
- After dark they battle on the hilltop.

The Weathertop Post Office

Nineteenth-century whaling captains often knew of remote islands where crews might meet and outbound ships leave mail to be picked up by homebound ships. Weathertop, where both Strider and Gandalf are headed, seems to have been used for similar purposes.

The Fellowship of the Ring,
Bk. 2, Ch. 2, "The Council of
Elrond" and The Return of the
King, Bk. 6, Ap. B, "The Tale
of Years." Strider mentions
Weathertop as a meeting
place in *The Fellowship of the*
Ring, Bk. 1, Ch. 10, "Strider."

Day 12
September 27

Tuesday, October 4, 1418—Gandalf Flees

A first quarter moon rises in the east-southeast about three in the afternoon and sets in the west-southwest after midnight.

Frodo, Merry, Pippin, Sam and Strider
Day 5 of 21 to Rivendell

Approaching the Weather Hills from the West

- The travelers leave the marshes for higher ground and see the hills.

The Fellowship of the Ring,
Bk. 1, Ch. 11, "A Knife in the
Dark."

A first and last quarter moons
offer only about nine percent
of the light of a full moon, so
the real increase in night-time
brightness comes in the days
ahead as the moon changes
from first quarter to full.

Creating Suspense

Tolkien may be deliberately leading the Hobbits into grave danger to heighten the suspense. There is little practical reason for Strider to take the Hobbits to Weathertop. The chance of meeting Gandalf there is more than balanced by the danger of meeting Black Riders. It would have been far safer to avoid the mountain and cross the road quickly and secretly.

Gandalf with the Black Riders
Day 4 of 18 to Rivendell (Gandalf)
Day 12 of 28 Pursuing Frodo (Black Riders)

North of Weathertop

- At sunrise, Gandalf escapes north, chased by four Black Riders.

The Fellowship of the Ring,
Bk. 2, Ch. 2, "The Council of
Elrond." For more details, see
The Treason of Isengard, Ch.
4, "Of Hamilcar, Gandalf,
and Saruman." This is one of
the few times that Black Riders leave the roads. Gandalf
may deliberately make it possible to pursue him on horseback to make sure these four
Black Riders follow him for
at least one or two days,
before abandoning Shadow-
fax and fleeing on foot.

Adapting to Circumstances

Tolkien's characters cannot foresee the future, but some show an ability to adapt quickly. Often Gandalf and Strider make one set of plans, but find circumstances forcing them down a different path. Gandalf had hoped to join the travelers at Weathertop. He ended up getting four of the nine Black Riders to chase him, weakening the attack two days later.

After escaping from the Black Riders, Gandalf takes a roundabout route, arriving in Rivendell two weeks later on October 18. Along the way, Gandalf releases Shadowfax, who finds his own way back to Rohan, arriving over four months later on February 23.

Wednesday, October 5, 1418—Weather Hills

Frodo, Merry, Pippin, Sam and Strider

Day 6 of 21 to Rivendell

Weather Hills

- At nightfall, the travelers camp at the foot of the Weather Hills.

The Fellowship of the Ring, Bk. 1, Ch. 11, "A Knife in the Dark."

Weathertop's Destruction and Decay

The watchtower on top of Weathertop was destroyed in war over 1600 years earlier. The fortifications decayed and the region became depopulated with the end of the North Kingdom over a thousand years earlier. That is why Tolkien places nothing but stone ruins on and around the mountain.

For more details, see *The Return of the King,* Ap. A, I, (iii), "Eriador, Arnor, and the Heirs of Isildur."

Thursday, October 6, 1418—Reaching Weathertop

Frodo, Merry, Pippin, Sam and Strider with Black Riders

Day 7 of 21 to Rivendell (Hobbits)
Day 14 of 28 Pursuing Frodo (Black Riders)

Weathertop

- The travelers reach Weathertop.
- From its top, Strider, Frodo and Sam see five Black Riders.
- After dark, Black Riders attack their camp.
- Frodo slips on the Ring, is struck by a knife, and collapses.

The Fellowship of the Ring, Bk. 1, Ch. 11, "A Knife in the Dark."

The Time of the Attack

We can determine the approximate time of the Black Rider attack from the fact that the moon is described as just rising above the mountain as it begins. On this day, the moon was two days past first quarter and rose about 4:30 p.m. in the east–southeast. But the Hobbits are in a sheltered dell on west side, so it was much later before it rose above Weathertop. It will set in the west-southwest about 2:30 a.m. Those rising and setting times mean that the moon is at its highest point about 9:30 p.m., a little south of directly overhead, so the attack may have come an hour or two before that, perhaps at 8:30.

The relatively early hour of the attack explains why Strider had so much time to search for *Athelas* leaves and the setting time explains why it is so dark later in the night. Given this accuracy of detail, it is easy to suspect that Tolkien had lunar calendars on his desk as he wrote this chapter. Since he wrote this section in early 1939, he may have rewritten it later, using newly acquired lunar calendars for 1941 and 1942.

The sun travels across the sky at fifteen degrees an hour. Because of its rotation around the earth, the moon travels across the sky a little slower, falling behind the sun a little each day and creating the phases of the moon.

For more on Tolkien's use of a lunar calendar, see Chapter 1, "Dating and Chronology," "Phases of the Moon" at the end of Chapter 6, and "Tolkien's Writing Interrupted" at the end of Chapter 14.

Friday, October 7, 1418—Frodo Wounded

Friday, October 7, 1418—Frodo Wounded

Frodo, Merry, Pippin, Sam and Strider
Day 8 of 21 to Rivendell, Day 1 of 14 from Weathertop

West side of Weathertop to Lone-lands

The Fellowship of the Ring, Bk. 1, Ch. 12, "Flight to the Ford." Tolkien reached this chapter by early February 1939. He had written 300 pages of manuscript and estimated it would take another 200 pages to finish. He judged badly. In the published version some 800 pages of narrative follow. Instead of 60 percent of the book, he had completed only 25 percent. This is obviously a story that 'grew in the telling.' *Letters*, No. 35.

- Strider finds *Athelas* leaves and treats the wounded Frodo.
- They cross the Great East Road and enter the Lone-lands.

Creating Tension

At this point in his narrative, Tolkien had a choice. He could have kept the travelers on the Great East Road. On it they could have reached Rivendell before Frodo's wound got serious. But they would have also had to face five (and soon nine) Black Riders. Since they barely survived the first attack, it is difficult to imagine how they could manage a second.

Instead, Tolkien has them leave the road for the trackless Lone-lands to its south. As usual, he assumes the Black Riders will not follow them off road. Frodo's worsening illness will provide dramatic tension for what would otherwise be a dreary journey.

Saturday, October 8 to Wednesday, October 12, 1418

The nights are becoming more brightly lit, even when the moon is hidden by clouds. On October 12th, a full moon rises in the east just before 8 p.m. and sets in the west the next morning about 9 a.m.

Frodo, Merry, Pippin, Sam and Strider
Days 9 to 13 of 21 to Rivendell, Day 2 to 6 of 14 from Weathertop

Lone-lands to approaching the Last Bridge

The Fellowship of the Ring, Bk. 1, Ch. 12, "Flight to the Ford." With the pony carrying Frodo, they average a respectable 20 miles per day.

- From October 8 to 11, the travelers plod east.
- Near sunset on October 11, they turn northeast toward the Last Bridge.
- On October 12, they see the Great East Road.

Comparing Travel Times

Tolkien had both Gandalf and the Hobbits take 14 days to reach Rivendell from Weathertop. Gandalf traveled further and faster, while the Hobbits were delayed by Frodo's injury. Tolkien seems to have assumed the two factors balanced one another.

Glorfindel with Black Riders
Day 1 to 5 of 8 on Patrol (Glorfindel)
Oct. 11: Day 19 of 28 Pursuing Frodo (Black Riders)

Great East Road

- On October 9, Glorfindel leaves Rivendell.
- On October 11, he drives three Black Riders from the Last Bridge.
- He leaves a jewel to show the bridge is safe.

The Fellowship of the Ring, Bk. 1, Ch. 12, "Flight to the Ford."

Hobbit versus Elf Communication

Although Tolkien may not have been aware of it, as an author he offers an interesting contrast between Hobbits and Elves. Hobbits do have a Shire-wide mail system, but there seems to have been no organized way to get mail from a Bree Hobbit to a Shire Hobbit. When Gandalf needed to get a letter from Bree to Hobbiton, he is forced to ask Butterbur to find a messenger. On the other hand, Tolkien provided Elves with excellent (though informal) long-distance communication. The Elves that the Hobbits met a little over two weeks earlier on the evening of September 24 had sent word about the little party threatened by Black Riders. Hearing the news, Elrond sends Elves to their rescue including Glorfindel.

Thursday, October 13, 1418—Last Bridge

Day 21
October 6

Frodo, Merry, Pippin, Sam and Strider

Day 14 of 21 to Rivendell, Day 7 of 14 from Weathertop

Last Bridge

- In the morning, they reach the Last Bridge.
- They find Glorfindel's jewel and cross the bridge.

The Fellowship of the Ring, Bk. 1, Ch. 12, "Flight to the Ford." Glorfindel had driven the Black Riders from the Last Bridge two days earlier.

The Last Bridge

This bridge is last in a double sense. It is the last (furthest downstream) bridge on the Mitheithel River (also called the River Hoarwell) and also the last (eastmost) bridge on the Great East Road. From that point on, the river is too wide to bridge and must be crossed at fords.

Western Trollshaws

- Just past the bridge, the travelers leave the road and turn north.

Strider's Wanderings

Tolkien provided Strider with 67 years (since 1351) of wandering about Middle-earth. But even he will have trouble finding their way in the heavily wooded and rocky wilderness they have entered. Keep in mind that in this distant past there are no compasses.

Friday, October 14, 1418—Frodo Weakens

Day 22
October 7

Frodo, Merry, Pippin, Sam and Strider

Day 15 of 21 to Rivendell, Day 8 of 14 from Weathertop

Western Trollshaws

The Fellowship of the Ring,
Bk. 1, Ch. 12, "Flight to the Ford."

• The rugged terrain slows their pace to 5–10 miles a day.

A Deadly Bind

Tolkien has placed the travelers in a deadly bind. The greater their delay in reaching Rivendell, the more Frodo weakens, and the more he weakens, the slower they must travel.

Day 23
October 8

Saturday, October 15, 1418—Rain and Misery

Frodo, Merry, Pippin, Sam and Strider
Day 16 of 21 to Rivendell, Day 9 of 14 from Weathertop

Western Trollshaws

The Fellowship of the Ring,
Bk. 1, Ch. 12, "Flight to the Ford."

• Rain leaves them unable to build a fire.

Tolkien Outdoors

The realism in Tolkien's writings leaves the impression that he was an experienced wilderness traveler. Though he did hike, like many Englishmen of his generation he preferred day hikes with nights spent at comfortable inns around a roaring fire. His grim experience of what it is like to be out-of-doors in all sorts of weather must have come from serving in the trenches of World War I.

Day 24
October 9

Sunday, October 16

Frodo, Merry, Pippin, Sam and Strider
Day 17 of 21 to Rivendell, Day 10 of 14 from Weathertop

Trollshaws

The Fellowship of the Ring,
Bk. 1, Ch. 12, "Flight to the Ford."

• They spend the night in a cave with little protection from the rain.

Glorfindel—Last Bridge
Day 7 of 8 on Patrol

Last Bridge

The Fellowship of the Ring,
Bk. 1, Ch. 12, "Flight to the Ford."

• Glorfindel finds the travelers' footprints on the Last Bridge.

Footprints and Black Riders

Why didn't the Hobbits, so desperate to avoid discovery by the Black Riders, erase their footprints? Because unlike dust, which can be swept smooth, it is almost impossible to create something that resembles the smooth, unfootprinted mud that follows a rain. The erasure would have been as least as obvious as the footprints themselves. All their footprints revealed was their number, and the Black Riders already knew that from their spies in Bree.

Monday, October 17, 1418

Frodo, Merry, Pippin, Sam and Strider

Day 18 of 21 to Rivendell, Day 11 of 14 from Weathertop

Approaching the Ford of Bruinen

- They travel southeast toward the Ford of Bruinen.

Ford of Bruinen

There's less magic in Tolkien's tale than many might expect in a story with Wizards and Elves. The Ford is a rare example of magic that is actually useful. The river does the only thing it can do to stop those who invade Rivendell, it floods. This Elvish use of nature parallels Sauron's use of a snowstorm to block Redhorn Gate to the travelers on January 11, 1419. For Tolkien, though often beautiful, nature is morally neutral and thus can be used for good or evil.

The Fellowship of the Ring, Bk. 1, Ch. 12, "Flight to the Ford." For Tolkien's view of nature, see "Tolkien's Natural World" at the end of Chapter 8.

Tuesday, October 18, 1418—Finding Trolls

Frodo, Merry, Pippin, Sam and Strider

Day 19 of 21 to Rivendell, Day 12 of 14 from Weathertop

Returning to the Great East Road

- They discover the trolls that Gandalf tricked into stone long before.
- Just before sundown they join the Great East Road.

A Difficult Choice

Having extracted all the drama he can from wilderness travel, Tolkien creates a new dilemma. The travelers can continue to hike through the wilderness and Frodo will die, or they can travel on the Great East Road and risk the Black Riders. Tolkien has them take the road.

The Fellowship of the Ring, Bk. 1, Ch. 12, "Flight to the Ford." For the story of Gandalf and the trolls see *The Hobbit*, Ch. 2, "Roast Mutton." It is set 77 years earlier in 1341.

Frodo, Merry, Pippin, Sam and Strider with Glorfindel

Great East Road

- As it gets dark, Glorfindel arrives from the west.
- Frodo is put on Glorfindel's horse and they hike through the night.

Providential Help

Without the timely arrival of Glorfindel on horseback, the mission would have failed. At their present pace, Frodo would not have survived to reach Rivendell and, more important, without Glorfindel's horse, he would not have made it across the Ford of Bruinen. Ponder for a moment the thought of Frodo trying to outrace the Black Riders on Sam the pony, and you get a picture of how things might have been.

There is another question we might raise. Given Frodo's desperate situation, why didn't Glorfindel place him on his horse and ride rapidly for Rivendell? The most obvious reason is that would have made the plot less

The Fellowship of the Ring, Bk. 1, Ch. 12, "Flight to the Ford."

The Sindarin language that Strider speaks to Glorfindel when they meet is similar to Middle Welch, but the differences can be comic. As Leslie Jones notes, in Welch Strider's greeting resembles, "It's not a drunken Dúnadan! It's a blacksmith!" See *Myth & Middle-earth*, 42.

dramatic. But it is also true that when a group has faced hardship and danger together, they often become so bonded to each other they think in "all or none" terms—either all of them make it or none. This is exactly how Frodo feels when, on this day, he protests that he will not get on Glorfindel's horse, if that means "leaving my friends behind in danger."

Gandalf
Day 18 of 18 to Rivendell

Rivendell

The Return of the King, Bk. 6, Ap. B, "The Tale of Years."

• Gandalf arrives at Rivendell.

Gandalf's Hardiness
Tolkien only gives the barest details about this two-week journey, but what he says makes it clear that, despite his appearance of age, Gandalf is quite hardy. Mostly on foot, he traveled up the Hoarwell River, through the Ettenmoors and south through the Coldfells.

Day 27
October 12

Wednesday, October 19, 1418—Race for the Ford

Frodo, Merry, Pippin, Sam and Strider with Glorfindel
Day 20 of 21 to Rivendell, Day 13 of 14 from Weathertop

To the Ford of Bruinen

The Fellowship of the Ring, Bk. 1, Ch. 12, "Flight to the Ford."

• At dawn they rest for a few hours.
• During the day they cover 20 miles, then rest overnight.

Perhaps if you are killed by a Balrog, you may not stay dead—an interesting thought.

Glorfindel Killed
Although there is some debate, this Glorfindel is apparently the same one who defeated the Lord of the Nazgûl over a thousand years earlier at the Battle of Fornost in 374/375. There are, however, accounts which suggest he later died in a battle with a Balrog. If so, then his restoration to life parallels that of Gandalf.

Day 28
October 13

Thursday, October 20, 1418—Ford of Bruinen

A last quarter moon sets in the west-northwest just after three in the afternoon.

Frodo, Merry, Pippin, Sam and Strider with Glorfindel and the Black Riders
Day 21 of 21 to Rivendell, Day 14 of 14 from Weathertop
Day 28 of 28 Pursuing Frodo (Black Riders)

Ford of Bruinen to Rivendell

The Fellowship of the Ring, Bk. 1, Ch. 12, "Flight to the Ford" and Bk. 2, Ch. 1, "Many Meetings."

• They hike all day.
• At the Ford in late afternoon, five Black Riders appear behind them.
• Glorfindel orders his horse to take Frodo across the Ford.

- Four Black Riders appear in front of Frodo, but he crosses safely.
- Glorfindel and Strider drive the Black Riders into the flooded river.
- Frodo is rushed to Rivendell.

The Fellowship of the Ring, Bk. 2, Ch. 1, "Many Meetings."

Elvish Guards at the Ford of Bruinen?

Other than Glorfindel, Tolkien does not mention any Elves at the Ford. But it is likely that some were present, perhaps hiding in the bushes on the high eastern bank. One reason is that their presence makes good military sense. The river's ability to flood when needed is only useful if someone is there to make sure it happens and report back to Rivendell. The other is hinted in Gandalf's account to Frodo, when the latter comes out of his coma on October 24. It seems that Elves (plural) took the almost dead Frodo to Rivendell. Since a horse and pony were available and Frodo a mere Hobbit, it makes no sense for the others to race to Rivendell and ask Elves to come back to transport Frodo. It seems plausible that Tolkien assumed other Elves were already at the Ford, perhaps with fast horses hidden nearby for messengers. It is they, perhaps with Glorfindel's assistance, who rush the almost dead Frodo to Rivendell. The other weary travelers follow as fast as they can. Since they are no longer in danger, Frodo's refusal to leave them behind no longer applies.

Looking Back

When he reaches Rivendell, Frodo will have been ill with his wound for 14 days. It has been 21 days since he left Bree, 25 days since he left the Shire, and exactly four weeks since he left Bag End, unaware of the dangers he faced. Tolkien has packed a lot of excitement into that month.

The Significance of the Ring

Tolkien often deplored those who tried to make what he had written into an allegory in which each character and event exists merely to stand for something else. The only difference between Middle-earth history and our own, he stressed, was that those who lived in Middle-earth were inside an invented history. Within that history, they are as real as you or I.

That said, Tolkien was aware that parallels did exist between their history and ours, much as parallels exist within our own history. Some historians, for instance, compare Napoleon's attempt to conquer Europe with Hitler's. Both were real, so neither is an allegory for the other, and yet there are ways they are alike. If Hitler had been less arrogant, he would have learned from Napoleon the folly of fighting the Russian winter.

Tolkien regarded the One Ring much the same way. In the Third Age of Middle-earth, the Ring and its terrible power were all too real. But historical parallels to the Ring can be found in our own society. Some things around us have powers that are every bit as evil as the Ring. Those who would use them are like those who seek the Ring. Whether their

Letters, No. 109, 131, 136, 203, 226, 297 and 309. Some connect Tolkien's Ring with other tales, especially that by Richard Wagner. But in *Myth and Middle-earth,* Leslie Jones says that Tolkien's sources were "too diffuse to be pinned down to a single myth," and how he handled those sources "too idiosyncratic" to make comparisons relevant (page 16).

Letters, No. 81, 109 and 186.

initial intentions are good or evil, in the end the power they acquire will corrupt them.

In his letters, Tolkien pointed to examples of this. For instance, he loathed social planners, organizers and regimenters of all sorts. He harshly criticized those for whom freedom meant nothing more than being dominated by those who spoke the same language, as if that made a difference. He hated scientific materialism for what it made of people. He hated the two socialisms then at war—Hitler's National Socialism and Stalin's international socialism. Even those great evils, he believed, should not be met by matching their power with a similarly coercive power. In short, the Ring should not be used to defeat Sauron.

Letters, No. 66, 81, 96 and 109.

In today's context, you might say that Tolkien believed that the strength of a nation rests in the character and wisdom of its people, rather than in its Ring-like wealth and technological prowess. That is why the Council of Elrond chose to send nine lightly armed volunteers, including four small Hobbits, against the great might and vast armies of Sauron. In the end, Tolkien is telling us, the struggle between good and evil will not settled by which side has the most power or by which regiments its people the most ruthlessly. It will be won by those who place the greatest reliance on ordinary virtues such as friendship, kindness, courage and honesty.

In the 1930s, it was common for those who championed large and intrusive governmental solutions for social ills to downplay the role of personal character, individual responsibility and voluntary mutual assistance. They believed that their systems would remove the need for such old-fashioned ideas. Tolkien clearly disagreed.

Tolkien and Lewis

It is easy to suspect that when Tolkien imagined the relaxed and intellectually stimulating atmosphere at Rivendell, he thought of his own relationship with a small group of Oxford writers who called themselves the Inklings and met on Tuesday mornings at the *Eagle and Child* pub and on Thursday evenings in C. S. Lewis' rooms at Magdalen College, Oxford. Tolkien described the group's name as "a pleasantly ingenious pun in its way, suggesting people with vague or half-formed intimations and ideas plus those who dabble in ink."

Tolkien described how the Inklings began as an undergraduate club in *Letters,* No. 298. He praised the encouragement Lewis gave him in No. 227. For a brief biography of Lewis, see that by John Bremer at the front of *The C. S. Lewis Readers' Encyclopedia.* The *Eagle and Child* is nicknamed the "Bird and Baby."

The Thursday evening meetings had a practical purpose. As Warren Lewis (brother of C. S.) explained, "When half a dozen or so had arrived, tea would be produced, and then when pipes were well alight Jack [C. S. Lewis] would say, 'Well, has nobody got anything to read us?' Out would come a manuscript, and we would settle down to sit in judgment upon it." It was there that Tolkien first read drafts for *The Lord of the Rings,* a chapter at a time. This gathering of Inklings was very much like Bilbo reading his poetry at Rivendell and listening as Elves gave friendly comments as to its merit. For someone like Tolkien, a life filled with warm friendship, good food, and stimulating conversation was the best of all worlds.

The Partnership between Tolkien and Lewis

In 1938, Tolkien wrote of an agreement with Lewis. Both would write books of the sort then called "Thrillers." Lewis would write a "space-journey," and Tolkien would write a "time-journey." The quicker Lewis soon fulfilled his half of the bargain by writing his science fiction trilogy. The detail-obsessed Tolkien took far longer with *The Lord of the Rings.*

Although Lewis and Tolkien had different writing styles, they shared many interests. The popular Narnia series of children's stories by Lewis creates a world as magical as Tolkien's Middle-earth. The science fiction trilogy that Lewis wrote—*Out of the Silent Planet, Perelandra,* and *That Hideous Strength*—has visits to a Mars and Venus as exotic as anything in Tolkien, as well as an England facing an emerging dictatorship almost as terrifying as that of Sauron. For daring to criticize bad science in his third book, Lewis was labeled anti-scientific, much as Tolkien's hostility to some machinery has led others to brand him a reactionary.

If you read Lewis' trilogy, remember that the first two books are not typical tales of space adventure. They are science fiction as it might have been written during the Middle Ages or Renaissance, the literary periods that were his speciality. The last book in the series, *That Hideous Strength,* is an anti-utopian novel roughly similar to Aldous Huxley's *Brave New World,* but set in a present-day university town.

Allegory, History and True Myth

Perhaps the greatest influence Tolkien had on C. S. Lewis is one that sheds light on Tolkien's oft-repeated claim that *The Lord of the Rings* was "invented history" rather than allegory.

During the 1920s, Lewis moved gradually from a cynical atheism to a theism in which he conceded, almost against his will, that God existed. As he described it, "In the Trinity Term of 1929, I gave in, and admitted that God was God, and knelt and prayed; perhaps, that night, the most dejected and reluctant convert in all England." But Theism is not Christianity. A great lover of Pagan mythology, Lewis was troubled because the central story of Christianity, God's coming to earth in Jesus, was such a common mythical theme. How could it be both myth and true?

The answer came on the evening of September 19, 1931, when Lewis talked until the early morning hours with Tolkien and Hugo Dyson. Tolkien told him that all truth came from God, and that pagan tales preserved fragments of that truth, however distorted. The difference was that with Jesus myth had stepped into history and that real event had been described in the Bible. Traveling with his brother a little over a week later, Lewis made the final step: "When we set out I did not believe that Jesus Christ is the Son of God, and when we reached the zoo I did." For both Tolkien and Lewis, Christianity was true because the events it described actually happened. It was also myth because behind those historical events

Letters, No. 24. In No. 159 Tolkien quoted Lewis saying that to get books the two like, "we shall have to write them ourselves."

Tolkien discussed his debt to Lewis in *Letters,* No. 227. He mentions that "Numinor" in Lewis' writings was consciously borrowed from Tolkien's "Númenor." At that time, Lewis had only heard Tolkien's tales read out loud. He notes other words that Lewis may have borrowed from him in *Letters,* No. 276.

Lewis described the cosmology behind his stories in *The Discarded Image* (Cambridge: Cambridge University Press, 1968), 92f. In Lewis' trilogy, Ransom resembles Tolkien. Joseph Pearce, *Tolkien, Man and Myth* (San Francisco: Ignatitus, 1998), 70.

For some of the similarities Lewis saw between the Christian and the Pagan see "Religion without Dogma" and "Is Theism Important" in *God in the Dock.* For differences, see his articles: "The Grand Miracle" and "Is Theology Poetry" in *C. S. Lewis* (Lesley Walmsley, ed.).

For more on this theme, see Tolkien's *Letters,* No. 89, 131 and 153. Henry Victor "Hugo" Dyson, (1896–1975) was at that time a lecturer at the University of Reading. He later came to Merton College, Oxford and became a member of the Inklings.

Tolkien's 1956 remark is in *Letters*, No. 192. See also "Never Absent and Never Named" at the end of Chapter 19. For Lewis' views about how myth influences our thinking, see "The Funeral of a Great Myth" in *C. S. Lewis* (Lesley Walmsley, ed.), 22f.

See *Pilgrim's Regress*, Bk. 8. Ch. "History's Words." For more on what Lewis meant by a map and its usefulness, see Bk. IV, Ch. 1, "Making and Begetting," in his *Mere Christianity*. See also "Myth Became Fact" in *C. S. Lewis* (Lesley Walmsley, ed.), 138f.

In Lewis' terms, Tolkien gives us pictures of the spiritual without a map, hence the virtual absence of religion. The difficulty Lewis had reaching a modern audience with *Pilgrim's Regress* may partly explain why Tolkien was so determined his tale not be regarded as an allegory. Paul's remarks are in Acts 17: 16–34.

These remarks are from Lewis' review of *The Fellowship of the Ring* published in the August 14, 1954 issue of *Time and Tide* and republished in *C. S. Lewis*, 521.

For the quote, see the start of C. S. Lewis, *Mere Christianity*, Bk 4, Ch. 1, "Making and Begetting."

lay answers to ultimate questions about the meaning human existence. Tolkien and Lewis called this powerful combination "true myth."

Along with that came an idea about what the art of writing meant. Tolkien's term for the process was "sub-creation." With his tales he was imitating, ever so feebly in literature, what God did on a much larger scale in history. God created true myth. Tolkien was creating myth that, while not strictly true, was intended to have the ring of truth, hence his obsession with detail and accuracy. That's also why in a 1956 letter he could describe God as the "Writer of the Story." For both Tolkien and Lewis, God is the ultimate author of all stories, whether imagined or real.

Lewis tried to get this concept of "true myth" across to a wider audience through allegory. In his 1933 *Pilgrim's Regress* he described how the Pagans got pictures of a much desired island (heaven) from the Landlord (God), but routinely got lost because they had no map (Bible). The map, Lewis said, came only through the Shepherds (Jews). "The truth is," Lewis wrote, "that a Shepherd is only half a man, and a Pagan is only half a man, so that neither people was well without the other, nor could either be healed until the Landlord's Son came into the country."

The distinction Lewis made between Pagan and Jew may answer an important question—to what extent are Tolkien's religious beliefs in *The Lord of the Rings*? Remember that Middle-earth was an ancient Pagan society. Tolkien could have offered readers the answers that Paganism provided—the grimness of Northern religions or the squabbling gods of Greeks and Romans. But rather than give answers he considered wrong, he excluded almost all references to religion. All that remains are the allusions Pagan religions made to a distant 'High God' who created the world and guided human destinies from afar. The Apostle Paul referred to that when he told Athenians that they worshiped an "unknown God."

Lewis understood what Tolkien was doing and told readers that in his friend's great tale, "we are reading myth, not allegory." That, he stressed, means that there are "no pointers to a specifically theological, or political, or psychological application. A myth points, for each reader, to the realm where he lives most. It is a master key, use it on whatever door you like."

Of course, therein lies a problem. A master key is all you need if you simply want to explore a vast building, roaming from room to room in joyful abandon. But when you've grown hungry and need to find the kitchen, a map of the sort the Jews provided Pagans can be very handy. Lewis said as much when he wrote: "As long as you are content with walks on the beach, your own glimpses are far more fun than looking at a map. But the map is going to be more use than walks on the beach if you want to get to America."

10

Rivendell to Lórien

October 21, 1418 to February 14, 1419

Treating Frodo to rest at Lórien and Gandalf reviving

Tom Shippey has pointed that Tolkien was an unusual writer: "An experienced professional author writing to make a living and with a good sense of potential markets . . . would have known not to stop the action dead with a 15,000-word account of a confused committee meeting, which is 'The Council of Elrond.'"

Fortunately for us, Tolkien knew better. As readers, we can enjoy a "committee meeting" that—contrary to the rules for proper writing—really does hold our attention. We examine that meeting and its aftermath in this chapter.

Tom Shippey, "Tolkien Teaches Us To Take Courage," *National Post,* (January 6, 2003). Shippey knows Tolkien is a marvelous writer and has even praised him as the "author of the century."

Friday, October 21 to Sunday, October 23, 1418

Day 29–31
October 14–16
3 Days

Frodo, Gandalf, Merry, Pippin, Sam and Strider

Day 1 to 3 of 64 at Rivendell

Last Homely House, Rivendell

- From October 21 to 23, Frodo lies in a coma at Rivendell.
- On the evening of October 23, Elrond cures Frodo's illness.

British Homeliness

Tolkien's name for Rivendell—the Last Homely House—illustrates just how English he is. For the English, "homely" means a pleasant place to relax and enjoy the company of others. In a 1971 BBC interview, Tolkien would profess a fondness for what the interviewer called, "those homely things of life that the Shire embodies: the home and pipe and fire and bed—the homely virtues." When one visitor sneered at the Tolkien home for not being stylish according to the fashion of the times, he failed to grasp the importance Tolkien placed on comfort. Look at how he described Bag End at the start of *The Hobbit*—lots of storage and no stairs. In a similar fashion, Rivendell will live up to its name and provide a cozy winter refugee from Sauron.

The Fellowship of the Ring, Bk. 2, Ch. 1, "Many Meetings."

Although Elrond plays a critical role in this tale, in the narrative of *The Lord of the Rings* we are told almost nothing about him. For his long history, see the indices to *The Silmarillion* and *Unfinished Tales.*

Monday, October 24, 1418—Awake in Rivendell

Frodo, Gandalf, Merry, Pippin, Sam and Strider
Day 4 of 64 at Rivendell

Last Homely House, Rivendell

The Fellowship of the Ring, Bk. 2, Ch. 1, "Many Meetings." For Tolkien's reasons for loving Rivendell, see "Tolkien and Lewis" at the end of Chapter 9.

- At ten in the morning Frodo awakes.
- A feast that evening celebrates Frodo's recovery.
- The four Hobbits meet Bilbo.

Bilbo as a Poet

Tolkien provided a background for the poem about Eärendel that Bilbo recites this evening. See *The Treason of Isengard*, Ch. 5, "Bilbo's Song at Rivendell."

Aragorn, Elladan and Elrohir with Others

From the Wild to Rivendell

The Fellowship of the Ring, Bk. 1. Ch. 1, "Many Meetings."

Glorfindel's mention of Elves being sent out is in *The Fellowship of the Ring*, Bk. 1, Ch. 12, "Flight to the Ford." Fifteen days round-trip would have allowed them travel south about halfway to Hollin Ridge. Later the nine travelers take 15 days to reach the ridge.

- Elladan and Elrohir return and report to Aragorn and others.

Elladan and Elrohir

Elladan and Elrohir were Elrond's twin sons. Tolkien did not tell us what they reported, but it must have concerned the Black Riders. The fact that their arrival was unexpected suggests that they were not returning from a quick reconnaissance following the events at the Ford, but that they had left earlier. When Elrond heard of the plight of Frodo and his friends, he had sent his most powerful Elves to the north, south and west, including Glorfindel, who went west. Elladan and Elronir may have left at the same time. Intelligence about any forces Sauron had to the south would be especially valuable. Glorfindel left Rivendell on October 9, so if these two left at the same time, they would have been gone for 15 days.

Boromir

Day 110 of 110 Days Boromir to Rivendell

Rivendell

The Return of the King, Bk. 6, Ap. B, "The Tale of Years" and The Fellowship of the Ring, Bk. 2, Ch. 2, "The Council of Elrond." Born in 1378, Boromir turns forty this year.

- That evening, Boromir reaches Rivendell.

Boromir's Journey

Tolkien seems to have assumed that Boromir arrived too late or too tired to participate in the feast the Hobbits attended. Like other journeys that do not involve Hobbits, Tolkien told us little about Boromir's travels, but he says enough to make clear that it was long and difficult. Boromir left Minas Tirith 110 days earlier on July 4, knowing little about where he was going. In this chronology, we estimate that he reached Rohan in the latter half of July and left around the end of the month, traveling through the Gap of Rohan and heading north to the fords at Tharbad where he lost the horse Rohan had loaned him, perhaps in late August.

Tolkien also left uncertain when Boromir arrived at Rivendell. "The Tale of Years" has him arriving after dark on October 24. At the Council the next morning, Elrond says he arrived in the early morning light, apparently on the 25th. This chronology assumes Elrond was referring to the time he first saw Boromir rather than when Boromir actually arrived.

From this point on, Strider will be referred to as Aragorn, and the Black Riders become the Nazgûl.

Tuesday, October 25, 1418—Council of Elrond

Day 33
October 18

The new moon will come in three days and winter approaches.

Aragorn, Boromir, Elrond, Frodo, Gandalf, Glóin, Merry, Pippin and Sam with Others

Day 5 of 64 at Rivendell

Council of Elrond, Rivendell

- In early morning, the Council of Elrond meets.
- Glóin tells about a messenger from Mordor looking for a Ring.
- Elrond gives a history of Sauron and the Rings of Power.

The Fellowship of the Ring, Bk. 2, Ch. 2, "The Council of Elrond."

Other Councils

The text leaves an impression that this Council has met before, but no mention is made of those occasions. It was similar in purpose to the Four White Councils, at least one of which was held in Rivendell (the second in 1251). Perhaps the distinction rests on where the decision-making authority rests. While the White Councils were held so the Wise could decide on a common course of action, the Council of Elrond seeks advice from Elrond. That is clearly why both Glóin and Boromir came.

For Elrond's family tree, see Charts I and III in *The Silmarillion,* "Of the Rings of Power and the Third Age."

Council of Elrond, Rivendell

- Boromir describes how he came to Rivendell.
- Bilbo explains in detail how he acquired the Ring.
- Frodo describes his journey to Rivendell.

Galdor of Grey Havens

Few readers probably pay much attention to the presence of Galdor, who represents the Elves at Grey Havens. Since Legolas came from Mirkwood, that means that, of all the Elf colonies who play a role in this tale, only Lórien is not represented at the Council. Why Galadriel, whose ability to see from afar is second to none, did not send a representative is not explained, but dramatic reasons suggest one reason why. If an Elf from Lórien were present, it would be difficult for Tolkien to keep him from joining the party as it goes south. With such a person included, the mystery and awe surrounding their arrival in Lórien would have been seriously weakened.

The Fellowship of the Ring, Bk. 2, Ch. 2, "The Council of Elrond." For more about the family tensions in Boromir's departure from Minas Tirith, see the exchange between Denethor and Faramir in *The Return of the King,* Bk. 5, Ch. 4, "The Siege of Gondor."

Council of Elrond, Rivendell

The Fellowship of the Ring,
Bk. 2, Ch. 2, "The Council of
Elrond."

- Gandalf gives the Ring's history and Saruman's deception.
- Aragorn tells of the capture of Gollum.
- Legolas describes Gollum's escape.
- As their leader, Elrond says the Ring must be destroyed.

Making the Great Rings

For a brief but excellent history of the making of the Great Rings (including the role of the Elves), see "Advent of the Dark Years" in Karen Fonstad's *The Atlas of Middle-earth*. Note especially her remarks that Sauron found it easier to seduce men to his side than Elves. Note too that the defeat of Sauron depended on an alliance with Númenor, a military advantage the free peoples no longer possess. Now they must fight alone.

Council of Elrond, Rivendell

- Boromir wants them to use the Ring but is opposed.
- At noon, Frodo volunteers to take the Ring to Mordor.
- Elrond advises sending Frodo and Sam with others.

The Elves' Great Sacrifice

See for instance *Letters*, No.
183. For Elrond's remarks,
see *The Fellowship of the
Ring*, Bk. 2, Ch. 2, "The
Council of Elrond." For Gandalf's remarks, see *The War
of the Ring*, Pt. 3, Ch. XII,
"The Last Debate."

Tolkien described the dangers the Ring posed for the Elves, stressing the great sacrifice that Elrond and the other Elves accept at this Council. For Elves, victory over Sauron means leaving Middle-earth. (Those are the departures at the end of this tale.) Tolkien put similar ideas in the mouths of others. At the Council, Elrond expressed a fear that the end of the One Ring means that the power of the Elves, linked to their three rings, will fade. Finally, from a different perspective Gandalf feared the Ring's ability to corrupt anyone—Elves included—who took it up.

According to Tolkien, the
name Rivendell has nothing
to do with a river. Its meaning
is "deep dale of the cleft," a
reference to its location
below the surrounding landscape. See *A Tolkien Compass*, 190.

Unlike Dwarves, Hobbits, or humans, the Elves have no 'good' solution to the problems posed by the Ring. If they take up the Ring, it will corrupt them, making them as evil as Sauron. If they do nothing, Sauron will get the Ring, and even they cannot long stand against its power. Even the destruction of the Ring offers no lasting peace. If they try to remain, the fading power of their three rings will introduce change and decay into their little enclaves, making life in Middle-earth intolerable for them and forcing them to leave. When they join the fight, they are choosing the *right* answer for Middle-earth, however *bad* the results are for themselves.

With the departure of the Elves, Middle-earth will lose something unique. With their ability to live many thousands of years, Elves offer a wisdom and a perspective lacking in more short-lived peoples.

Rivendell and surrounding wilderness

- On this day and the next, Elves leave to look for Black Riders.

Aragorn's Sword

The Fellowship of the Ring,
Bk. 2, Ch. 3, "The Ring Goes
South."

Aragorn joins the Elves who leave today. That answers a disturbing, though minor question. Since the travelers spend over two months at Rivendell, why did Aragorn wait until the eve of their departure to get his broken sword reforged? He delayed because he was far away in the wilderness. Of course that brings up yet another and perhaps unanswerable question. Given the dangers Aragorn routinely faced, why did he carry an almost worthless sword? For such a matter-of-fact person, he is carrying the symbolism a bit far. Perhaps Tolkien would say that he normally wore a useful sword and turned to symbolism only when Frodo and the Ring put him on the path that led to reclaiming his kingdom.

Wednesday, October 26 to Friday, December 17, 1418

Day 34–85
October 19–December 9
52 Days

Aragorn, Frodo, Gandalf, Merry, Pippin and Sam
Day 6 to 57 of 64 at Rivendell

Last Homely House, Rivendell

• In mid-December scouts return, having seen no Black Riders.

Delay at Rivendell

A two-month delay at Rivendell seems overly long. But Tolkien needed enough time for a search that would make sure the travelers will not encounter any Black Riders when they leave. Though unhorsed, some of the Black Riders might have remained near Rivendell rather than returning to Sauron to be reequipped. In a second encounter, the Black Riders would be more through. They will not assume a single knife wound will give them the Ring.

The Fellowship of the Ring, Bk. 2, Ch. 3, "The Ring Goes South." The "strange country" Elrond's sons visited was almost certainly Lórien. Celeborn's welcome to the travelers on January 17, 1419, suggests the sons carried Elrond's messages to him. See *The Fellowship of the Ring,* Bk. 2. Ch. 7, "The Mirror of Galadriel."

Saturday, December 18, 1418—Nine Chosen

Day 86
December 10

Aragorn, Boromir, Frodo, Gandalf, Gimli, Legolas, Merry, Pippin and Sam
Day 58 of 64 at Rivendell

Last Homely House, Rivendell

• The nine members of the Company of the Ring are chosen by Elrond.
• The Company will leave in one week.

The Almost-missing Pippin

For how Tolkien selected the nine, deciding not to send Pippin back to the Shire as originally planned, see *The Treason of Isengard,* Ch. 7, "The Ring Goes South." Because in Hobbit society Pippin was not yet an adult, there were doubts about sending him on such a dangerous mission. At twenty-eight, he would be looked on much like we might look at a sixteen-year-old boy. Whatever his personal maturity, he would still be seen as too young for war. That may be why Gandalf takes him under his personal protection for the ride to Minas Tirith (March 5, 1419), leaving the older Merry to ride with Théoden's men.

The Fellowship of the Ring, Bk. 2, Ch. 3, "The Ring Goes South." Gandalf's role in the selection is described near the beginning of *The Return of the King,* Bk. 5, Ch. 8, "The Houses of Healing." Hobbit adulthood comes at 33 rather than our 18 and 21.

Day 87–92
December 11–16
6 Days

Sunday, December 19 to Friday, December 24, 1418

On December 19th, a last quarter moon sets in the west just after one in the afternoon. It rises about one the next morning.

Aragorn, Boromir, Frodo, Gandalf, Gimli, Legolas, Merry, Pippin and Sam

Day 59 to 64 of 64 at Rivendell

Last Homely House, Rivendell

The Fellowship of the Ring, Bk. 2, Ch. 3, "The Ring Goes South."

Merry brags of his map study just after he and Pippin escape from the Orcs. See the end of The Two Towers, Bk. 3, Ch. 3, "The Uruk-Hai." Pippin mentions his map study when the nine travelers reach Hollin Ridge on January 8, 1419, See The Fellowship of the Ring, Bk. 2, Ch. 3, "The Ring Goes South."

• Aragorn's sword is reforged by Elvish blacksmiths.

Leaving Bilbo in the Dark

At Rivendell, Tolkien had Aragorn and Gandalf use maps and books to plan their trip without Frodo's involvement. Other than the fact that it enhances the drama when the nine separate, we know of no reason why Tolkien did not have Gandalf better prepare Frodo, teaching him more about the routes to Mordor. More limited in his knowledge than others realize, perhaps we can say that Gandalf did not anticipate Frodo and Sam having to go on by themselves. Merry, however, used some of his time at Rivendell well, wisely studying maps, as did Pippin, who nevertheless claimed he had trouble remembering what he had seen.

Day 93
December 17

Saturday, December 25, 1418—Leaving Rivendell

The travelers leave Rivendell when the nights are darkest. The next day (the 26th) is the new moon. The winter solstice, which has the shortest day in the year, will come in four days.

Aragorn, Boromir, Frodo, Gandalf, Gimli, Legolas, Merry, Pippin and Sam

Day 1 of 21 to Moria, Day 1 of 23 to Lórien

Rivendell to the Ford of Bruinen

The Fellowship of the Ring, Bk. 2, Ch. 3, "The Ring Goes South." For details about whether Tolkien intended for the mission of the nine to extend from Christmas to Easter, see "Exactly Three Months" under March 25, 1419. See also A Tolkien Compass, 201.

• In the morning Bilbo gives Frodo Sting and his *mithril* mail coat.
• After dark, they depart Rivendell and leave the Great East Road.
• They head south on trails among the hills, hiking until dawn.

A Well-timed Departure

Tolkien timed this departure well, placing it in darkest winter and near the new moon. Travel at night is particularly important at this stage since, with the Black Riders far away, Sauron's chief spies are birds. The more nights they travel in secrecy, the wider the area around Rivendell that Sauron must search. Their departure date, December 25, is Christmas in our calendar. The date when the Ring is destroyed, March 25, is near Easter and is even on a Sunday like Easter.

Late December 1418 to Early January 1419

Men and Hobbits of Bree

Date Approximate

Bree

- Near the end of the year, Bree expels strangers who are causing trouble.
- Helped by Harry Goatleaf and Bill Ferny, the strangers return.
- In a fight, three men and two Hobbits are killed.
- The strangers are driven into the wilderness.

The Return of the King, Bk. 6, Ch. 7, "Homeward Bound."

Sneaky Harry

This Harry Goatleaf is the gatekeeper who made trouble for the Hobbits when they entered Bree three months earlier on September 29.

Lotho Sackville-Baggins

Date Approximate

Shire and Isengard

- Lotho Sackville-Baggins has been exporting pipe-weed.
- With money from Saruman, he secretly bought farmland.
- The food from those farms goes to Saruman, leaving Hobbits hungry.
- Early in the new year, Lotho proclaims himself Chief.

The Return of the King, Bk. 6, Ch. 8, "The Scouring of the Shire."

Supplying Isengard

Saruman's first contact with the Shire seems to have come just after the Fourth White Council in 1353. To conceal the tobacco and food shipments from the Shire to Rohan, Tolkien had the supplies go openly down the Old South Road to Dunland. From there it was sent secretly to Isengard. In some drafts, Tolkien had Dunlanders fighting for Saruman.

Shipments: *Unfinished Tales,* Pt. 3, Ch. 4, "The Hunt for the Ring," Note 18. Dunland: *The War of the Ring,* Pt. 1, Ch. 4, "Flotsam and Jetsam."

Sunday, December 26, 1418 to Saturday, January 7, 1919

Day 94–107
December 18–31
14 Days

The waxing moon will reach its first quarter on January 2. The nights will be growing brighter.

Aragorn, Boromir, Frodo, Gandalf, Gimli, Legolas, Merry, Pippin and Sam

Day 2–15 of 21 to Moria, Day 2–15 of 23 to Lórien

Rugged lands west of the Misty Mountains

- At night, they hike south through difficult terrain.
- During the day they sleep in thickets and eat cold food.

The Fellowship of the Ring, Bk. 2, Ch. 3, "The Ring Goes South."

Distance Traveled

Over the next fourteen days, they cover about 15 miles each night.

Sunday, January 8, 1419—Hollin Ridge

Day 108
December 31

**Aragorn, Boromir, Frodo, Gandalf, Gimli,
Legolas, Merry, Pippin and Sam**

Day 16 of 21 to Moria, Day 16–21 of 23 to Lórien

Hollin Ridge

*The Fellowship of the Ring,
Bk. 2, Ch. 3, "The Ring Goes
South."*

On the other hand, since Aragorn says the crows are a species that lives near Isengard, Tolkien may be hinting that Saruman sent them. We should not forget that this complex tale has two evil leaders.

- They plan to rest at Hollin Ridge before taking on the mountain pass.
- Seeing crows, Gandalf and Aragorn decide to move east after dark.

Hollin Ridge

In a direct path, Hollin Ridge is some 135 miles south of Rivendell and cuts from east to west across their path. Sauron may regard its less wooded ridge tops as good places to spot the travelers if they are headed south, hence his use of crows on January 8 and a Nazgûl on January 9.

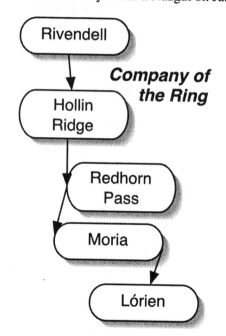

Company of the Ring

Day 109–110
January 1–2
2 Days

Monday, January 9 to Tuesday January 10, 1419

On January 10th, the full moon rises in the east-northeast about 5:30 in the afternoon and sets in the west-northwest at 9 a.m. the following day. Secrecy becomes more difficult.

**Aragorn, Boromir, Frodo, Gandalf, Gimli,
Legolas, Merry, Pippin and Sam**

Day 17–18 of 21 to Moria, Day 17–18 of 23 to Lórien

Approaching Caradhras Mountain

- Just before dawn on the 9th, they see a shadow pass overhead.
- On both days, they follow a road up to Redhorn Gate.

Nazgûl Aloft as Spies

With this fleeting shadow Tolkien introduces Sauron's secret weapon, a flying Nazgûl. He may intend for Sauron to be taking advantage of the almost full moon for his search. The route the travelers are on is, after all, a route from Rivendell to Gondor, where the main conflict will occur. While Tolkien undoubtedly intended for Sauron to never consider the possibility that his opponents might want to destroy the Ring, it is reasonable to assume that Sauron believed they might bring it closer to the battle lines to better use its power against him. Although the steps the travelers take cannot be concealed, their ultimate goal can be hidden behind one Sauron finds more plausible.

The Fellowship of the Ring, Bk. 2, Ch. 3, "The Ring Goes South."

Wednesday, January 11, 1419—Redhorn Gate

Day 111
January 3

*On this day in the modern calendar, January 3, 1892,
J. R. R. Tolkien was born in Bloemfontein, South Africa.*

Aragorn, Boromir, Frodo, Gandalf, Gimli, Legolas, Merry, Pippin and Sam

Day 19 of 21 to Moria, Day 19 of 23 to Lórien

Approaching Redhorn Gate

- In late afternoon, they set out for Caradhras and Redhorn Gate.
- Trapped by a blizzard, they halt under a cliff.

The Fellowship of the Ring, Bk. 2, Ch. 3, "The Ring Goes South."

Sauron's Schemes

If Sauron contrived this weather, it may not be because he knows precisely where the travelers are, but because he wants to force them to reveal themselves by blocking their passage. Gandalf says as much when he starts their fire.

Thursday, January 12, 1419—Warg Attack

Day 112
January 4

Aragorn, Boromir, Frodo, Gandalf, Gimli, Legolas, Merry, Pippin and Sam

Day 20 of 21 to Moria, Day 20 of 23 to Lórien

Retreating from Redhorn Gate

- Before dawn, the blizzard ends, and they force their way back down.
- Gandalf suggests they go through Moria.
- They hear Wargs howling, climb a hill, and start a fire.

The Fellowship of the Ring, Bk. 2, Ch. 3, "The Ring Goes South" and Bk. 2, Ch. 4, "A Journey in the Dark."

The Hobbit, Ch. 6, "Out of the Frying-Pan into the Fire." The West-gate to the Mines of Moria is over 15 miles from the foot of Redhorn Pass.

Another Fire, Another Cave

Tolkien also had Gandalf use fire to drive off the Wargs in *The Hobbit.* On that occasion they had just escaped an Orc-infested cave that passed through the Misty Mountains. This time they are about to enter an Orc-infested cave that also passes through the Misty Mountains. Tolkien liked to repeat plots with slight variations.

Day 113
January 5

Friday, January 13, 1419—Entering Moria

The moon, three days past full, rises a little after 8 p.m. in the east-northeast. It will offer some help against the Warg attack.

Aragorn, Boromir, Frodo, Gandalf, Gimli, Legolas, Merry, Pippin and Sam

Day 21 of 21 to Moria, Day 1 of 3 in Moria, Day 21 of 23 to Lórien

Small hilltop near Redhorn Pass

The Fellowship of the Ring, Bk. 2, Ch. 4, "A Journey in the Dark." Tolkien was working on this chapter in December of 1939. *Letters,* No. 37.

For the other Warg attack, see *The Hobbit,* Ch. 6, "Out of the Frying-Pan into the Fire."

- In the night, one Warg is killed by Legolas' arrow.
- As morning approaches, Wargs attack in mass.
- When Gandalf sets trees and Wargs aflame, the Wargs flee.

Wargs and Fire

Tolkien had a talent for keeping the behavior of his creatures consistent. Wargs resemble the werewolves of European folk tales. While ordinary wolves serve only their stomachs. Wargs can be enlisted in higher and more evil causes. In *Hobbit,* they serve the Orcs of the Misty Mountains, and in this tale they serve Sauron. In both, Gandalf fights them with fire.

Escaping to Moria

The Fellowship of the Ring, Bk. 2, Ch. 4, "A Journey in the Dark." Ten months from now on October 28, 1419, Sam will discover that Bill, a clever pony, returned safely to Bree.

- At sunset, they reach the West-door of Moria.
- Wargs and a lake creature force them into Moria.

Suspending Skepticism about Tolkien's Caves

Tolkien's underground passages are often immense and built by hand, taking advantage of natural caves. They are as long and far larger in volume than anything built by modern man. The East-gate exit the travelers are headed for is at least forty miles away.

The longest road tunnel in the world is the 15.3 mile-long Laerdal in Norway. The longest rail tunnel (to be finished in 2010) is the Swiss Gotthard at 35.3 miles. The "Chunnel" under the English Channel is 31 miles long.

What are we to make of this? Enjoying any work of fiction requires some suspension of disbelief. Asking whether Dwarves, without explosives or power tools, could have built anything this vast or where they might have put all the rocks they removed is a waste of time. The adventures in this cave more than compensate for the lack of rubble outside.

Inside the Mines of Moria

The Fellowship of the Ring, Bk. 2, Ch. 4, "A Journey in the Dark."

- After a meal and a short rest, they set out.
- Frodo hears footsteps behind them.

Necessary Stealth

Tolkien provided hundreds of years of background for a journey that takes less than three days. The Orcs have been in Moria for 539 years (since 880). That has given them a long time to improve its defenses and make the place so feared that few dare enter it. Gandalf's previous visit to Moria came in 1245, 174 years earlier, when he traveled in the opposite direction, from east to west. At that time he was looking for Thráin II, the Dwarf king who had been captured by Sauron near Mirkwood.

Some might think Gandalf's arguments for entering Moria are strained. The Orcs have had over three-quarters of a century to recover from the Battle of Five Armies (in *The Hobbit*), and the chance that Balin has survived a quarter of a century deep inside Moria are about as close to zero as anything can be. Perhaps Tolkien was hinting that, as disaster looms ahead, Gandalf's judgment has begun to slip.

Four and a half days earlier, Tolkien subtly introduced the Nazgûl into his story. Now he introduces Gollum.

Saturday, January 14, 1419—Inside Moria

Day 114
January 6

Aragorn, Boromir, Frodo, Gandalf, Gimli, Legolas, Merry, Pippin and Sam

Day 2 of 3 in Moria, Day 22 of 23 to Lórien

Deep inside Moria

- In the middle of the night, they rest.
- Pippin drops a stone down a well, angering Gandalf.
- After about twenty miles, they enter a large hall near the East-gate.
- They rest until daylight comes down shafts.

The Fellowship of the Ring, Bk. 2, Ch. 4, "A Journey in the Dark."

Moria's History

For more on the history of Moria from Tolkien's manuscripts see *The Treason of Isengard*, Ch. 7, "The Council of Elrond (2)."

Sunday, January 15, 1419—Fleeing Moria

Day 115
January 7

Aragorn, Boromir, Frodo, Gandalf, Gimli, Legolas, Merry, Pippin and Sam

Day 3 of 3 in Moria, Day 23 of 23 to Lórien

Tomb of Balin, Mines of Moria to Great Gates

- As day comes, they discover a diary recording Balin's death.
- Attacked by Orcs, they fight and flee.
- The Balrog and Gandalf tumble into the chasm of Durin's Bridge.
- The others escape out into daylight in early afternoon.

The Fellowship of the Ring, Bk. 2, Ch. 4, "A Journey in the Dark" and Bk. 2, Ch. 5, "The Bridge of Khazad-dûm."

The Death of Balin

The same Balin who accompanied Bilbo in *The Hobbit* enters the story at this point. Thirty years earlier, in 1389, Tolkien had him lead an expedition to Moria to retake the city for Dwarves. For five years (until 1394) they held part of the city until they were attacked and killed by an Orc army. When the travelers arrive, 25 years have passed since Balin's death, and yet the Dwarves know nothing about his fate.

It is easy to forget that our modern age, with its instant communication, is unusual. For most of history, every ship that sailed over the horizon and every explorer who entered blank regions on maps could disappear as utterly as did Balin. Tolkien understood that. Remember too that, had Balin's last stand taken place in a forest, the possibility of someone escaping with the news would have been far more likely than it was with everyone trapped in a cave.

We do not know how Tolkien intended for Gollum to cross the chasm. Perhaps sensing danger and anticipating the travelers' moves, he slipped ahead of them and exited first. He was, after all, an expert at living in Orc-filled caves. He also probably had several months to learn his way around Moria.

Aragorn, Boromir, Frodo, Gimli, Legolas, Merry, Pippin and Sam
Day 1 of 32 in Lórien

To Lórien

The Fellowship of the Ring, Bk. 2, Ch. 6, "Lothlórien."

- At three in the afternoon, they rest.
- They travel after dark, and Frodo hears steps behind them.
- After dark, they reach the Nimrodel River and enter Lórien.

Prior Knowledge of the Nine

The Fellowship of the Ring, Bk. 2, Ch. 3, "The Ring Goes South." It is at that December 18 conference that Merry and Pippin insist on being included in the nine.

Earlier, Tolkien mentioned in passing that when parties went out to search for the dehorsed Black Riders, Elladan and Elrohir (Elrond's twin sons) visited a mysterious place on the Silverlode River. We do not need to be brilliant literary scholars to realize that Tolkien was hinting they visited Lórien. This means they carried news of *nine* travelers that Celeborn and Galadriel reveal when *eight* travelers arrive. The fact that the sons carried news of nine travelers also meant that Elrond had decided on that number back in the fall, although who would make up their ranks was not settled until the December 18 conference.

Lórien, Lothlórien and Laurelindórenan are all names for the Golden Wood. Here we use the shortest and simplest name.

Northwestern Lórien

The waning moon is not in the sky in early evening, but it is later when an Elf sees Gollum.

- Legolas and Frodo talk with Elves.
- The others climb into trees as protection from Orcs.
- During the night, Frodo sees Gollum.

Young Tolkien in Switzerland

Letters, No. 232 and 306. The latter includes a description of the hiking trip written to his son, Michael, in 1967.

Some of the descriptions in this portion of the narrative and similar passages in *The Hobbit* build on hiking that Tolkien did "over many high passes" in Switzerland at the age of 19.

Gandalf with the Balrog
Day 1 of 11 with Balrog

Chasm beneath Durin's Bridge

- Gandalf falls into the chasm beneath Durin's Bridge.
- At the bottom, both plunge into cold water and fight.
- Gandalf chases the Balrog toward the surface.

The Two Towers, Bk. 3, Ch. 5, "The White Rider."

Moria and Mithril

Tolkien put much of his creative skill into the history of Moria, making it the greatest and most interesting of the Dwarf cities. Beneath its inhabited levels, Dwarves discovered that most valuable metal, *mithril.* But as they plunged deeper in the pursuit of more *mithril* and the wealth it brought, they unloosed an ancient terror on the world—the Balrog of Morgoth. The Dwarves were forced to flee Moria and their name for the city, Khazad-dûm ("Mansion of the Khazad"), was superseded by the Elvish Moria ("Black Pit"). In that great disaster, both peoples were guilty. Although it was Dwarvish greed which released the Balrog, it was Elvish love for beautiful *mithril* that fed Dwarvish greed.

For more on the history of Moria, see the indices to both *Unfinished Tales* and *The Silmarillion.* The Elvish name, which stands over the west entrance, apparently predates the Balrog and Orcs. Even when the city was occupied by peaceful Dwarves, Elves would consider it an awful "Black Pit" and avoid it whenever possible.

Monday, January 16, 1419—Reaching Lórien

Day 116
January 8

Aragorn, Boromir, Frodo, Gimli, Legolas, Merry, Pippin and Sam

Day 2 of 32 in Lórien

Central Lórien

- The entire party is blindfolded and led along.
- In the evening they sleep, still blindfolded, on the ground.

The Fellowship of the Ring, Bk. 2, Ch. 6, "Lothlórien." They cover some 30 miles.

Lórien's Defenses

Tolkien had reasons for the elaborate precautions he has these Elves take. Lórien's geographic defenses were weak—little more than an easily bridged river. Remember that there are no compasses in Middle-earth. In a dark wood, Orcs who are more familiar with caves than forests could easily become confused and travel in circles. Lórien depended on its deep woods to confuse foes long enough for arrows fired from hiding to destroy an attack. An enemy with a knowledge of its paths could make a lightning thrust for the capital, capturing it before an effective defense could be mounted. The fewer who know Lórien's paths, the better.

Tuesday, January 17, 1419—Cerin Amroth

Day 117
January 9

On January 18, the waning moon will reach last quarter.
Outside Lórien, the nights grow darker.

Aragorn, Boromir, Frodo, Gimli, Legolas, Merry, Pippin and Sam with Gollum

Day 3 of 32 in Lórien

The Fellowship of the Ring, Bk. 2, Ch. 6, "Lothlórien."

Central Lórien and the Silverlode

- The next morning the Company makes another march.
- Elves see Gollum fleeing down the Silverlode River.

Cerin Amroth

- They arrive at Cerin Amroth, remove blindfolds and rest.

Tolkien and Trees

Letters, No. 294.

Reflecting his great love for trees, Tolkien considered the Company's arrival at Cerin Amroth one of his favorite passages in the entire tale.

Caras Galadhon

The Fellowship of the Ring Bk. 2, Ch. 7, "The Mirror of Galadriel." This is Aragorn's first visit to Lórien since thirty-one years earlier (in 1380) when he and Arwen became engaged at Cerin Amroth.

- At sunset, the Company sets out for Caras Galadhon, the royal city.
- There they are taken to Celeborn and Galadriel.

Lórien and Shangri-la

Tolkien's isolated and idyllic Lórien resembles the Shangri-la of Frank Capra's award-winning 1937 film, *Lost Horizon,* which is in turn based on a 1933 book of the same name by James Hilton. Hidden deep in the Himalaya mountains, Shangri-la is a beautiful and peaceful land where time seems to have stopped and people live for centuries.

From a review in *Time and Tide,* October 22, 1955, republished by Lesley Walmsley in *C. S. Lewis,* 524–25.

The special light in which we view a Shangri-la or Lórien illustrates the value of myth. As C. S. Lewis noted, myth "takes all the things we know and restores to them the rich significance which has been hidden by the 'veil of familiarity.' The child enjoys his cold meat (otherwise dull to him) by pretending it is buffalo, just killed with his own bow and arrow. And the child is wise. The real meat comes back to him more savoury for having been dipped in the story; you might say that only then is it the real meat."

Any mountain will be more exciting, if we imagine that just behind it lies a Shangri-la. Any wood becomes more beautiful when it shares in the mystery of Lórien. Myth lets us see the world with new eyes. By opening us up to new truth, it can transform our lives. Tolkien's great gift was his marvelous ability to create myth.

**From January 18 until February 13, the travelers rest
and recover their strength in Lórien.**

Day 123
January 15

Monday, January 23, 1419—Fight on Zirak-zigil

Tomorrow will bring the new moon. The dark nights ahead will make the fire on the mountain even more visible. First quarter is on February 2, and the full moon is on February 9.

Gandalf with the Balrog
Day 9 of 11 with Balrog

Up the Endless Stair within Mount Zirak-zigil

- Gandalf chases the Balrog to the top of Mount Zirak-zigil.
- The two fight with fire and thunder.

Endless Stair

Although Tolkien wrote as if the Endless Stair was by then shrouded in legend, it's actually a somber part of Middle-earth history. The Dwarves of Moria built it to spiral from deep within the earth to Durin's Tower at the peak of Zirak-zigil (or Celebdil). They used it as an observation post.

The Return of the King, Bk. 6, Ap. B, "The Tale of Years" and *The Two Towers*, Bk. 3, Ch. 5, "The White Rider."

Wednesday, January 25, 1419—Balrog Killed

Day 125
January 17

Gandalf with the Balrog

Day 11 of 11 with Balrog, Day 1 of 20 with Gandalf Dead
Durin's Tower, Mount Zirak-zigil

- Gandalf throws the Balrog off Mount Zirak-zigil.
- Strange visions and death overcome Gandalf.

Lucifer's Fall

The Balrog's plunge to earth parallels that of Lucifer in the writings of the Hebrew prophet Isaiah, except that Lucifer was a creature of light who wanted to seize heaven while this is a creature of darkness who prefers the underworld. Isaiah describes Lucifer this way:

> How your have fallen from heaven, O star of the morning, son of the dawn. You have been cut down to the earth, you who have weakened the nations. But you said in your heart, I will ascend to heaven; I will raise my throne above the stars of God, and I will sit on the mount of assembly. I will ascend above the heights of the clouds; I will make myself like the Most High. Nevertheless, you will be thrust down to Sheol, to the recesses of the pit.

The Return of the King, Bk. 6, Ap. B, "The Tale of Years" and *The Two Towers*, Bk. 3, Ch. 5, "The White Rider." Gandalf will remain dead until February 14.

Isaiah 14: 12–15. "Sheol" is a Hebrew word for the place where the dead go. The parallel between Lucifer and Sauron is even stronger. Both are powerful creatures, but neither is co-equal with the God who is good. They owe their existence to God and their evil to their own choices.

Monday, February 14, 1419—Gandalf Alive

Day 144
February 6

Gandalf and Galadriel

Day 20 of 20 with Gandalf Dead
Durin's Tower, Mount Zirak-zigil

- Gandalf returns to life atop Mount Zirak-zigil.
- With the Endless Stairs blocked, he is trapped.

The Return of the King, Bk. 6, Ap. B, "The Tale of Years" and *The Two Towers*, Bk. 3, Ch. 5, "The White Rider."

Gandalf's recovery comes after being killed by Balrog. Something similar may have happened to Glorfindel. For Tolkien's belief that Gandalf's return to life was a 'defect' in the story, see *Letters*, No. 156. Notice that it comes on St. Valentine's Day.

The Gandalf Mystery

Sometime during the next three days, Tolkien had Lady Galadriel receive news of Gandalf's return to life. Since she did not mention this to the travelers, the revelation probably came after they left on the 16th. If she knew of Frodo's vision of a Wizard in white, she may have concluded that Frodo had seen a still-living Gandalf. (If Frodo's vision had been of Gandalf in the past, he would have been in grey.) She then began to look for evidence he was still alive, perhaps by sending out Gwaihir.

No Generation Gap

As often in this chronology, calculated ages are based on the year of birth, since actual birthdays are not usually known.

Frodo is well past the age when a little adventure is tolerated. But since Hobbits mature socially about a decade later than humans, Merry and Sam are bachelors not yet under pressure to marry. Pippin is even younger, and would be seen by Hobbits much like we would see a teenager. As news spread of their disappearance, some may have even considered Frodo irresponsible for taking someone that young into danger.

Tolkien's Shire appears to have no generation gap. The ages of the four Hobbits who travel varies widely, At the time they left the Shire, Frodo just turned 50. Merry is 36, and Sam is 35. At 28, Pippin is the youngest of the travelers. Fatty Bolger, who remains behind, is 38.

Frodo may take life a bit more seriously than Pippin at half his age. But they like the same music, poetry and stories as well as have ideals in common. They even see each other as close friends.

There are a number of reasons why the Shire has so little tension between generations. First, things change so slowly that both father and son grow up the same world, doing the same things for the same reasons. Differences existed, but have more to do with personality than age.

Second, no one made money exploiting differences between young and old. Children have their own games, but once someone grew up, sons live like their fathers. There wasn't one pub with one kind of music and talk for the Gaffer and another for Sam. Musicians didn't appeal to the young by denouncing parents and treating rebelliousness as a virtue. The old didn't sneer at the young and lament, "what the world was coming to."

Finally, the happiness most Hobbits find in their lives means they have no need to blame the Shire's few social ills on others, be that the "old fogies" in charge or "rebellious" youth. Displaying a common sense that really was common, Hobbits knew where society should set its limits and where it shouldn't. They took troublemakers to their borders and tossed them out without a twinge of guilt. But they were also tolerant of things that didn't matter. Sam may have met with more murmurs of approval when he married Rose than the partying Merry and Pippin. But the two were left to ride about, dressed in outlandish military outfits, with no more than a few smiles of amusement. Perhaps this stability over time and the lack of a generation gap are among the reasons why today's readers, whatever their age, are attracted to Hobbits and their peaceful little Shire.

11

Lórien to Parting

February 15 to February 26, 1419

Mirror of Galadriel until Company separates

Before the travelers leave Lórien, we should compare that Elvish country with their previous place of refuge, Rivendell. Michael Stanton does that marvelously when he writes:

> Rivendell is a house, actually—a kind of great lodge; Lothlórien is a country. Rivendell is a kind of crossroads or is at least a meeting-place, as we have seen; many were welcome there in former days. Lothlórien is secret, unvisited, closely guarded; so secluded that later the Riders of Rohan say they believe it is only a legend.

Always sensitive to the sound and meaning of words, Tolkien expressed this difference in their names. Rivendell is known as the Last Homely House, a name suggesting warmth and friendship. Lórien is the Golden Wood, a name laden with wonder and mystery.

Michael N. Stanton, *Hobbits, Elves and Wizards,* 41–42. Professor Stanton also noted, "But the major difference between Rivendell and Lothlórien is in feeling or atmosphere: 'In Rivendell there was memory of ancient things; in Lórien the ancient things still lived on.'"

Tuesday, February 15, 1419—Mirror of Galadriel

Day 145
February 7

Frodo, Sam and Galadriel

Day 31 of 32 in Lórien

Mirror of Galadriel

- At twilight, Galadriel takes Sam and Frodo to the Mirror.
- Sam sees Frodo in the future and the Shire being destroyed.
- Frodo sees a Wizard in white and Bilbo in Rivendell.
- Frodo offers Galadriel the One Ring, but she refuses.

The Fellowship of the Ring Bk. 2, Ch. 7, "The Mirror of Galadriel."

Dating the Mirror of Galadriel

In an appendix, Tolkien dated these visions to February 14, the same day that Gandalf returned to life. But it seems clear from the narrative that these visions came the evening before their departure on the 16th. This chronology follows Tolkien's narrative.

The Return of the King, Ap. B, "The Tale of Years."

Three Elf Rings

Letters, No. 144. Galadriel has not always chosen good over evil. For her history, see the references to her in the indices to *The Silmarillion* and *Unfinished Tales,* as well as *Letters,* No. 320.

In a 1954 letter, Tolkien said that the three Elf rings, which include Galadriel's Nenya, shield from the effects of time. Though not created by Sauron, they resulted from his instruction and are under the One Ring. When it is destroyed, Elves linked to it by their rings can no longer hold back the decaying effects of time and must leave Middle-earth. Without realizing it, Frodo placed before Galadriel a great temptation.

Aragorn, Boromir, Frodo, Gimli, Legolas, Merry, Pippin and Sam with Celeborn and Galadriel

Chamber of Celeborn and the Pavilion at Caras Galadhon

The Fellowship of the Ring, Bk. 2, Ch. 8, "Farewell to Lórien."

- Later in the evening, the travelers meet with Celeborn and Galadriel.
- Then they meet alone and debate what to do.
- Frodo suspects Boromir wants to use the Ring himself.

The Tempting of Boromir

The Fellowship of the Ring, Parth Galen: Bk. 2, Ch. 10, "The Breaking of the Fellowship." Council: Bk. 2, Ch. 2, "The Council of Elrond." Galadriel and Temptation: Bk. 2, Ch. 7, "The Mirror of Galadriel."

We see here why Tolkien's great tale can be read again and again. In their first reading, many are surprised when Boromir tries to take the Ring at Parth Galen. In later readings they discover that Tolkien scattered hints of the danger Boromir posed throughout the text. One came at the Council of Elrond, when Boromir opposed the idea of destroying the Ring. Another came when they first met Galadriel, and Boromir expressed doubts about her intentions. When Galadriel successfully resisted the temptation to take the Ring for herself, Tolkien was contrasting two responses to the Ring, one good (Galadriel) and one evil (Boromir).

Day 146
February 8

Wednesday, February 16—Departing Lórien

As with Rivendell, they depart Lórien as the nights grow darker. Today, a last quarter moon rises in the east-southeast about 1 a.m. and sets in the west-southwest just before noon. If necessary, this will allow them to travel in secrecy, particularly in the early evening, but the darkness also aids their enemies.

Aragorn, Boromir, Frodo, Gimli, Legolas, Merry, Pippin and Sam with Celeborn and Galadriel

Day 32 of 32 in Lórien

Pavilion, Caras Galadhon and Silverlode River

Fellowship of the Ring, Bk. 2, Ch. 8, "Farewell to Lórien." For details about the long and complex lives of Galadriel and Celeborn, see *Unfinished Tales,* Pt. 2, Ch. 4, "The History of Galadriel and Celeborn."

- In the morning they prepare to leave and Elves bring gifts.
- About noon, they hike to where the Silverlode and Anduin merge.
- They canoe up the Silverlode, meeting Celeborn and Galadriel.
- They dine on the grass and Galadriel provides gifts.

Departing Gifts

For All from the Elves

1. Three canoes, each with Elvish rope.
2. *Lembas,* Elvish travel food.
3. Cloaks that take on the color of their surroundings.

For Each from Lady Galadriel:

1. Aragorn: Sheath for his sword and a brooch.
2. Boromir: Golden belt.
3. Frodo: Phial to provide light.
4. Gimli: Strands of Galadriel's hair.
5. Legolas: Larger bow with arrows.
6. Merry and Pippin: Silver belts.
7. Sam: Small box with soil and a seed.

The brooch given Aragorn comes from Arwen. That is why it means so much to him.

Notice the contrast Tolkien set up. Every Elf gift is useful, but only three of Galadriel's nine gifts prove of value in the dangers they face. Odd as it seems, Galadriel is making sure that Boromir, Merry and Pippin leave well-dressed for a journey that may mean their death, and she sends Aragorn, Gimli, and Sam out burdened, ever so slightly, with keepsakes. Was Tolkien telling us Galadriel has a romantic, impractical bent of mind, or is she certain of victory and focusing on what will follow?

Gimli suggested his own gift. Perhaps because of the long ill-will between Elves and Dwarves, Lady Galadriel was uncertain what sort of gift Dwarves preferred.

Aragorn, Boromir, Frodo, Gimli, Legolas, Merry, Pippin and Sam

Day 1 of 10 in Voyage

Anduin River near Lórien

- They travel south down the river long after dark, paddling little.

Three Canoes

When canoeing, it is usually best to put the strongest and most expert canoeist in the rear. That's exactly what Tolkien does. The canoes travel in this order and with this seating arrangement.

Fellowship of the Ring, Bk. 2, Ch. 8, "Farewell to Lórien." Since Mordor is to the east, the west or right bank of the river is safer.

1. Aragorn, Frodo and Sam—Aragorn in rear, Sam in front.
2. Boromir, Merry and Pippin—Boromir in rear, Pippin in front.
3. Legolas and Gimli—Legolas in rear, supplies in middle.

They seem to have kept this arrangement throughout the voyage. When they enter the rapids near midnight on February 23, Sam is their lookout, sitting at the front of the lead canoe.

Of course, when exploring it is also best to distribute supplies through *all* the vessels, so the loss of one is less disastrous.

Thursday, February 17, 1419—Gandalf Rescued

Day 147
February 9

Aragorn, Boromir, Frodo, Gimli, Legolas, Merry, Pippin and Sam

Day 2 of 10 in Voyage

On the Great River

The Fellowship of the Ring, Bk. 2, Ch. 9, "The Great River."

- They rest at night on the river's west side.
- They start in early morning and drift far into the night.

Distance Traveled

For Fonstad's estimates, see her Pathways Table in "Pathways," *The Atlas of Middle-earth.* For a calculation of Boromir's drift speed, see "Boromir's Drifting Canoe" under February 29, 1419.

Karen Fonstad estimates Tolkien had them drift just over 3 miles an hour and cover 40 miles on day 2 through 4. On day 5 and 6, they paddle 55 miles a day, averaging just over 4 miles per hour. Since paddling one mile per hour seems slow, their drift speed may have been slower and their paddling speed higher, making their drift speed above Rauros Falls closer to that calculated for Boromir's funeral canoe, 2.8 miles per hour.

Gandalf and Gwaihir with Lady Galadriel

Mount Zirak-zigil to Lórien

The Return of the King, Bk. 6, Ap. B, "The Tale of Years" and *The Two Towers,* Bk. 3, Ch. 5, "The White Rider."

- Galadriel sends Gwaihir to look for Gandalf
- Gwaihir finds him on Mount Zirak-zigil and carries him to Lórien.

Rescuing Gandalf

To see how the Hobbits felt about the change in Gandalf after his return to life, see *The Two Towers,* Bk. 3, Ch. 9, "The Palantír," near the beginning of the chapter.

It has been 32 days since Gandalf fell into the chasm with the Balrog and three days since he returned to life. A mountain peak seems an unlikely place to find someone last seen disappearing into an underground chasm. But Tolkien may have assumed that Gwaihir heard reports of fire on the mountain from January 23 to 25. At Lórien, Gandalf recovers from his ordeal and is clothed in white.

Friday, February 18, 1419—Brown Lands

Day 148
February 10

Aragorn, Boromir, Frodo, Gimli, Legolas, Merry, Pippin and Sam

Day 3 of 10 in Voyage

Voyaging through the Brown Lands

The Fellowship of the Ring, Bk. 2, Ch. 9, "The Great River."

- They start early, drifting long after dark.
- During the day they enter the Brown Lands.

The Devastation of War

For Tolkien's remarks on the destruction of the Entwives' land, see *Letters,* No. 144.

The Brown Lands are the once-fertile lands cultivated by the Entwives. They were devastated in the war of the Last Alliance against Sauron over three thousands years earlier and have never recovered. Perhaps the Ents go to war against Saruman in part because they fear that he will do to their forest what Sauron did here.

Saturday, February 19, 1419—Seeing Gollum

Aragorn, Boromir, Frodo, Gimli, Legolas, Merry, Pippin and Sam

Day 4 of 10 in Voyage

Voyaging through the Brown Lands

- Near dusk Sam briefly sees Gollum.

Gollum Following

Tolkien has dropped hints the travelers are being followed by Gollum since shortly after they entered Moria on January 13, over a month earlier.

The Fellowship of the Ring, Bk. 2, Ch. 9, "The Great River." Gollum is behind Gimli's boat, the last of the three.

Sunday, February 20, 1419—Fleeing Gollum

Aragorn, Boromir, Frodo, Gimli, Legolas, Merry, Pippin and Sam

Day 5 of 10 in Voyage, Travel Time Estimated

Brown Lands to Downs

- In the early morning Frodo sees Gollum and tells Aragorn.
- They paddle all day and most of the night to escape Gollum.

Transitioning from Day to Night Travel

How did Tolkien intend for the travelers to transition from day to night travel? They could have taken the easy approach and rested all day on the 20th (after sleeping the night before) and begun their night travel on the evening of the 20th. But given Aragorn's haste to outrun Gollum, that seems unlikely. They probably paddled all day on the 20th and most of the following night. Tolkien seems to hint at this when, after being told by Frodo that Gollum is following, Aragorn says they will "try going faster tomorrow," and the next paragraph speaks of beginning night travel.

The Fellowship of the Ring, Bk. 2, Ch. 9, "The Great River."

The long time Frodo spent on watch apparently pushed his sighting of Gollum into the next day, while Aragorn seems to be using "tomorrow" in the sense of daylight beginning a new day. The travelers have one advantage over the lone Gollum. They can take turns paddling, while the others sleep.

Monday, February 21, 1419—Night Travel

Aragorn, Boromir, Frodo, Gimli, Legolas, Merry, Pippin and Sam

Day 6 of 10 in Voyage

Crossing the Downs

- They paddle at night and rest during the day, not seeing Gollum.

Sleepy Gollum

Pity sleepy Gollum. Traveling almost 24 hours without rest on the night of February 20 and 21 and all night thereafter makes it impossible for Gollum to follow *just behind* them. Unfortunately, Gollum could take a

Tolkien provided no specific description of this day. It is covered in *The Fellowship of the Ring,* Bk. 2, Ch. 9, "The Great River."

different approach—lying, asleep and awake, on a log day and night, drifting *ahead* of the travelers, and perhaps helping Orcs set a trap for the evening of February 23. Drifting full-time would cover about 62 miles a day versus 55 miles covered paddling during the night. In three days, that would put Gollum about 20 miles or 5 hours of travel time ahead, more than enough time to arrange the Orc ambush. Drifting ahead is also similar to what Tolkien had him do when the travelers entered Lórien. Then Gollum, unable to follow, guessed where they would exit and lay in wait for them. Gollum is a skilled hunter.

Day 152
February 14

Tuesday, February 22, 1419—Emyn Muil

Aragorn, Boromir, Frodo, Gimli, Legolas, Merry, Pippin and Sam
Day 7 of 10 in Voyage

Leaving the Brown Lands

There is no specific description of this day. It is covered in *The Fellowship of the Ring,* Bk. 2, Ch. 9, "The Great River." The moon became new at 10:02 a.m. (Tolkien's U.K. time) on the 23rd.

• They rest during the day and travel at night.

Mistaking the New Moon

Today, Tolkien has Sam see the new moon setting with the sun. In the early morning darkness of the 24th, Aragorn corrects Sam's mistake, telling him the moon was new on the 23rd. In a practical sense, it matters little. The moon provides no illumination either night.

Day 153
February 15

Wednesday, February 23, 1419—Orc Attack

The Orcs choose the darkest possible night for their attack. Today the moon is new, rising and setting with the sun.

Aragorn, Boromir, Frodo, Gimli, Legolas, Merry, Pippin and Sam
Day 8 of 10 in Voyage

Entering Emyn Muil

The Fellowship of the Ring, Bk. 2, Ch. 9, "The Great River."

• They travel until sunrise and rest during the day.
• Flocks of birds and an eagle cause Aragorn to suspect spies.
• They leave after sunset.

In the northern hemisphere, the last of the 'old moon' sets just before sunset and is a sliver on the left. The early new moon sets just after the sun and is a sliver on the right.

Aragorn's Haste

Tolkien has Aragorn make two mistakes. Moving with a current, it is easy to underestimate travel distances. Not realizing how far they have come, Aragorn hurries on. Given Tolkien's description of the land they are traveling through, today they seem to have paddled well into the early morning twilight, stopping only after day clearly breaks. If any of the birds they see are spies, they have foolishly revealed their location. Aragorn corrects that mistake by waiting until dark to leave, but makes another that

UNTANGLING TOLKIEN

is even worse. Because they are further down river than he thought, they are almost trapped by rapids and Orcs. As with Gandalf in Moria, Tolkien may be hinting that Aragorn's judgment has begun to slip just before disaster strikes.

Sarn Gebir Rapids

- Shortly before midnight rapids force them toward the east bank.
- They are attacked by Orcs.
- They retreat to the west bank and Legolas shoots a Nazgûl-bird.

Wednesday or Thursday?

In Appendix B of *The Return of the King,* Tolkien dated this attack to February 23. However, in the narrative he has them enter the rapids near midnight, and their long struggle upstream to the safety of the west bank probably extended these events well into early morning hours of the 24th. To avoid separating closely related events, everything is placed here.

The Fellowship of the Ring, Bk. 2, Ch. 9, "The Great River." The trap was cleverly set. The rapids not only pulled them toward the east bank, they made flight downstream impossible. Over six weeks earlier, at Hollin Ridge on January 8, the travelers saw a mysterious shadow pass overhead. This is their second sighting of a Nazgûl.

Shadowfax

Rohan

- In the evening, a wild Shadowfax returns to Rohan.

The Return of Shadowfax

Gandalf released Shadowfax in early October, almost five months earlier. Like the horse loaned to Boromir, Shadowfax returned to Rohan, a good indication how attractive its grassy plains are to horses.

The Two Towers, Bk. 3, Ch. 2, "The Riders of Rohan." The fact that the men of Rohan notice the return of Gandalf and Boromir's horses hints at their great love for the beasts.

Dead Men from the Dark Years

Date Estimated

Harrowdale Valley to the Paths of the Dead

- The dead travel the Harrowdale Valley to the Paths of the Dead.

Preparing to Meet Aragorn

Tolkien only tells us that this movement took place on a moonless night. As the night of the new moon closest to Aragorn's summons, this date, plus or minus a couple of days, is the most likely time.

The Return of the King, Bk. 5, Ch. 3, "The Muster of Rohan." In two weeks (March 8) they will meet Aragorn.

Thursday, February 24, 1419—Canoe Portage

Day 154
February 16

Aragorn, Boromir, Frodo, Gimli, Legolas, Merry, Pippin and Sam

Day 9 of 10 in Voyage

Sarn Gebir Rapids

- In the morning, Aragorn and Legolas find a portage.
- In the afternoon, they carry the boats and supplies below the rapids.
- They rest that night.

The Fellowship of the Ring, Bk. 2, Ch. 9, "The Great River." They stay awake most of a night and day to adjust back to daylight travel.

Sam's Confusion

The War of the Ring, Pt. 1, Ch. I, "The Destruction of Isengard" and the Notes at the end of Pt. 2, Ch. 1, "The Taming of Sméagol." Notice the January 31 date, a date that did not exist in the Shire calendar. At that time Tolkien must have been using a different calendar.

Sam's confusion about the moon's phase in the early morning hours of February 24 reflects changes Tolkien made as he developed and refined his story. Originally, he had intended for the passage of time on the outside to stop while they were in Lórien, so their month-long rest there would cause no delay in their journey. Christopher Tolkien gave an example of that when he noted that January 31 in his father's early drafts later becomes March 2. Though Tolkien decided not to have time stop in Lórien, Sam's remarks suggest that he still wanted Lórien to leave an impression on visitors that time passed differently within the Golden Wood. In a sense, the anti-aging effect the One Ring had on its bearer was to be paralleled by a roughly similar effect that Galadriel's Great Ring, Nenya, had on Lórien. Time still passes there, but change comes more slowly. Perhaps that is why Sam never saw the moon—the most constantly changing object in the sky—over Lórien.

Day 155
February 17

Friday, February 25, 1419—Parth Galen

Aragorn, Boromir, Frodo, Gimli, Legolas, Merry, Pippin and Sam

Day 10 of 10 in Voyage

Passing Argonath, the Pillars of the Kings to Lake Nen Hithoel

The Fellowship of the Ring, Bk. 2, Ch. 9, "The Great River."

- Just after dawn, they start out and pass the Pillars of the King.
- In early afternoon, they reach Lake Nen Hithoel.

Parth Galen

The Fellowship of the Ring, Bk. 2, Ch. 10, "The Breaking of the Fellowship."

- By dark, they reach Parth Galen and camp.

A Forced Choice

For ten days Tolkien has been building up the tension, reminding readers that at Parth Galen each of the travelers must chose between going east to Mordor or west and south to Minas Tirith. Since Frodo is committed to Mordor, we must wonder who will go with him. Asked at this point in the narrative, it is unlikely that many first-time readers would guess that Tolkien will send on an inexperienced Frodo accompanied only by the faithful but less-than-brilliant Sam. Did Tolkien really value personal loyalty over wilderness expertise? Apparently he did.

In the end circumstances overtake the travelers, and Tolkien leaves no one free to act as they wish. Boromir dies after his attempt to get the Ring forces Frodo to go on alone and Sam, true to his nature, follows Frodo. Merry and Pippin, who would not have willingly parted with Frodo, are taken west against their wills by Orcs. Despite the importance of Frodo's mission, Aragorn, Gimli and Legolas must pursue the Orcs to save their friends. Tolkien has events beyond anyone's control compel everyone's actions. Life is often like that.

Théodred

Fords of Isen

- Théodred dies fighting in the first battle at the Fords of Isen.

Saruman, Théodred and Théoden

Here, Tolkien worked details into the plot that some readers may not notice. Saruman had ordered Théodred, Théoden's only natural son, killed whatever the cost. As a result, Saruman's success at the Fords was not as great as it would have had his troops concentrated on purely military objectives. Théoden will not get the news of his son's death for two days.

Tolkien no doubt intended for Saruman's concentration on killing Théodred to break Théoden's will to fight. The untimely death of Théodred does contribute to the bitterness and depression Théoden feels when Gandalf arrives at Edoras on March 2, a week from today. It also explains his anger at the still-living Éomer, his adopted son.

The Return of the King, Bk. 6, Ap. B, "The Tale of Years" and *Unfinished Tales*, Pt. 3, Ch. 5, "The Battles of the Fords of Isen."

Saturday, February 26, 1419—Company Divides

Day 156
February 18

The moon, three days past new and about 20 percent illuminated, sets about 10 p.m. It provides Aragorn, Legolas and Gimli with little help in their pursuit of Merry and Pippin.

Aragorn, Boromir, Frodo, Gimli, Legolas, Merry, Pippin and Sam

Parth Galen

- Frodo asks for time alone to make his choice.

The Fellowship of the Ring, Bk. 2, Ch. 10, "The Breaking of the Fellowship."

Boromir and Frodo

Parth Galen

- Boromir follows Frodo and tries to take the Ring.
- Frodo puts on the Ring and flees.

The Fellowship of the Ring, Bk. 2, Ch. 10, "The Breaking of the Fellowship."

Frodo's Wisdom

Notice from Frodo's words to Boromir how much the Hobbit has learned in the little over ten months since Gandalf first told him about the Ring in mid-April of last year. No longer simply a naive and fun-loving Hobbit, Frodo knows the potential for evil that lurks in human and Hobbit heart. In contrast, Boromir has learned nothing and has no understanding of the danger the Ring poses.

Aragorn had taken over the fellowship when Gandalf's wisdom failed. Now his judgment is failing. For the first time, Frodo is displaying the good sense he will need to reach Mordor. That good sense will lead him to trust Gollum as a guide and Faramir as an ally. When his judgment fails in Shelob's Lair, it is Sam who steps in, calls for Galadriel's light, and rescues the mission. From that point on, he is Frodo's equal in good sense.

The Fellowship of the Ring, Bk. 1, Ch. 2, "The Shadow of the Past."

Frodo with Gandalf and Sauron

Seat of Seeing, Amon Hen

The Fellowship of the Ring, Bk. 2, Ch. 10, "The Breaking of the Fellowship."

- On the Seat of Seeing, Frodo sees war and the Eye of Sauron.
- Sauron calls for him.
- A voice (Gandalf's) demands he remove the Ring, which he does.

Gandalf Unrecognized

The parallel was probably unconscious. In a letter from about 1956 Tolkien wrote that the "Incarnation of God" was "infinitely greater" than any topic about which he would "dare to write." *Letters,* No. 181 (at end). In contrast, his Protestant friend, C. S. Lewis, did not hesitate to use biblical themes in his Narnia children's stories. See the discussion of "true myth" in "Tolkien and Lewis" at the end of Chapter 9.

Unconsciously, Tolkien may have been drawing parallels between the revived Gandalf and the resurrected Jesus. Here Frodo does not recognize the source of the voice in his mind as Gandalf, even though Gandalf's warning is remarkably like his last words to them as he plunged into chasm at Durin's Bridge (January 15, 1419). Later Aragorn, Gimli and Legolas will fail to recognize Gandalf when they see him in Fangorn Forest (March 1, 1419). In much the same fashion, the transformed Jesus was not at first recognized by Mary Magdalene (John 20: 14ff) or two disciples traveling to Emmaus (Luke 24: 13ff). In both case, the changes wrought by death and the preconceptions of observers distorted for a time what they saw.

Gandalf

Mount Methedras near Isengard

The Two Towers, Bk. 3, Ch. 5, "The White Rider" and *The Treason of Isengard,* Ch. 24, "The White Rider."

- He struggles with Sauron to protect the Ring.

Exhausted Gandalf

Tolkien may have intended for Gandalf's exhaustion after his struggle with Sauron to explain why he doesn't talk to Treebeard in Fangorn the next day, and why he seems so distant when he first meets Aragorn, Legolas and Gimli in Fangorn five days later on March 1. We can only guess why Tolkien placed Gandalf near Isengard, but the most obvious reason is to spy on Saruman. Given Gandalf's weakened condition, he may have been carried to Mount Methedras by Gwaihir or another eagle.

Aragorn, Boromir, Gimli, Legolas, Merry, Pippin and Sam

Parth Galen

The Fellowship of the Ring, Bk. 2, Ch. 10, "The Breaking of the Fellowship."

- Boromir returns to the group and they search for Frodo.

The Two Towers, the second volume of the three published volumes begins here with Book 3, "The Treason of Isengard."

The Two Towers Identified

For a time, Tolkien was confused about the meaning behind the title *The Two Towers*. His first cover design shows Orthanc and Minas Morgul. In an August 1953 letter he said the meaning could be "left ambiguous." Then in January of 1954, he said the towers were Orthanc and Cirith Ungol, representing Saruman and Sauron. Knowing many readers would assume the towers were Minas Tirith and Mordor, by that time he was unhappy with the name his publishers had chosen. Unfortunately, it is not authors who chose titles but publishers.

Letters, No. 140 and 143. For the cover, see Note 140 on page 444 of *Letters. The Two Towers* was first published in the U.K. on November 11, 1954 (three and a half months after the first volume) and in the U.S. on April 21, 1955 (exactly six months after the first volume).

Merry and Pippin with Boromir and Orcs

Day 1 of 4 as Captives

Parth Galen to Rohan

- Merry and Pippin are captured by Orcs and Boromir dies.
- Orcs fight and five of Sauron's Orcs are killed.
- Pippin gets a knife and cuts the rope around his hands.
- A Rohan scout sees the Orcs.

Both Evil and Good Divided

At this point Tolkien was drawing parallels between the just-exposed division among the free peoples (Boromir and Frodo) and the division between Sauron and Saruman. Uglúk commands Saruman's Orcs, while Grishnákh those of Sauron. After the fight between Orcs, Grishnákh apparently sent someone back to Mordor with news of the Hobbit capture. That will turn Sauron's suspicions toward Saruman. The results of these divisions, however, is different. The conflict between the free peoples leads Frodo and Sam to go on alone, a risky but ultimately successful venture. The conflict between Orcs allows Merry and Pippin to escape.

The Two Towers, Bk. 3, Ch. 3, "The Uruk-hai." Pippin is the cleverer of the two. He cuts his bonds, leaves footprints, and understands first why Grishnákh gropes them.

Even with his life in danger, Pippin, the youngest of the four Hobbits, remains calm and observant. His suspicion that, after this fight between Orcs, Grishnákh sent a messenger to Sauron is in *The Two Towers,* Bk. 3, Ch. 9, "Flotsam and Jetsam."

Aragorn and Boromir

Parth Galen

- Aragorn races up the hill following Frodo's tracks.
- Aragorn finds Boromir dying.
- Boromir tells Aragorn the Hobbits have been captured by Orcs.

The Two Towers, Bk. 3, Ch. 1, "The Departure of Boromir."

Lack of Communications

The eagle Aragorn saw while looking for Frodo was sent by Gandalf, but Aragorn had no way of knowing that. In this Tolkien was being true to the age he had created. Living in an era of near-instant contact, we see the obvious value of rapid communication. But the people of Middle-earth, born in when most messages traveled no faster than a horse, could not easily see that. Lórien could have arranged for eagles to maintain almost day-to-day contact with the travelers as they went south, but did not. Every culture, including our own, has blind spots.

Aragorn, Legolas and Gimli with Boromir
Day 1 of 5 in Pursuit, Day 1 of 10 Drifting (Boromir)
Lake New Hithoel and Parth Galen to western Emyn Muil

The Two Towers, Bk. 3, Ch. 1, "The Departure of Boromir."

The Two Towers, Bk. 3, Ch. 2, "The Riders of Rohan."

- They send Boromir over the falls of Rauros in a canoe.
- They discover Frodo and Sam left by canoe.
- Just before dark, they pursue Merry and Pippin.
- In stony hills, the trail becomes harder to follow.

Boromir's Fate

Despite the harm Boromir brings to the company, Tolkien retained a kindly interest in the fallen warrior, giving him a heroic death and following his body as it drifts down the Anduin. For details about his funeral canoe, see the comments for February 29 and March 5, 1419.

Frodo and Sam
Day 1 of 4 by Themselves

Eastern Emyn Muil

The Fellowship of the Ring, Bk. 2, Ch. 10, "The Breaking of the Fellowship." In an early manuscript, Sam does not find Frodo at the boats and must trail him for two days, first on his own and later by following Gollum.

- Sam finds Frodo and insists on going with him.
- Gathering up gear and supplies, they paddle to the east shore.

A Fortunate Misfortune

As unfortunate as the capture of Merry and Pippin may have seemed, it had an often unnoticed good effect. Both Sauron and Saruman's Orcs were in a position to intercept the Ring-bearer. When Merry and Pippin were captured, Orcs that Sauron had placed just east of Lake Nen Hithoel were drawn westward across Rohan, leaving the Dead Marshes approach to Mordor temporarily unguarded (or lightly guarded) at the very time Frodo and Sam use it. It is unlikely that Sauron was bothered by this brief gap in his defenses since, as Gandalf will note when he meets Aragorn, Gimli and Legolas on March 1, Sauron assumes that his foes are going to Minas Tirith to use the Ring against him.

Tolkien's Book 4, "The Journey of the Ring-bearers" begins at this point and describes events happening on the same day as those in Book 3, "The Treason of Isengard," which also began on this day.

Eastern Emyn Muil

The Two Towers, Bk. 4, Ch. 1, "The Taming of Sméagol." Tolkien was working on this chapter in early April of 1944. *Letters,* No. 58.

- Frodo and Sam travel across Emyn Muil.
- They look for a path down the near vertical cliff face to their right.

Concealing Adds Realism

In Book 3, Tolkien could have shifted his narrative between Frodo/Sam and the rest as easily as he does between Merry/Pippin and Aragorn/Gimli/Legolas. Because he waited until Book 4 to cover Frodo and Sam, readers are left knowing as little about their fate as their friends did at the time. That unconsciously heightens the sense of realism.

Faramir

Gondor

- In the afternoon, Faramir hears Boromir's horn blowing.

Missing Boromir

It has been almost eight months since Boromir left on his journey, so his father is probably expecting bad news about his fate. News of his passage through Rohan (perhaps in late July of the previous year) has almost certainly reached Minas Tirith by this time. Even news about the return of the horse he had been loaned (perhaps toward the end of 1418) may have been passed down from Rohan. As the eldest son of the Steward of Gondor, Boromir is a very important person.

The Two Towers, Bk. 4, Ch. 5, "The Window on the West." It seems reasonable to assume that the post riders kept for emergencies were used for routine dispatches between the two countries in peacetime. That would keep both man and beast in good condition.

Éomer

Rohan

- A scout tells Éomer that Orcs are crossing Rohan.

The Return of the King, Bk. 6, Ap. B, "The Tale of Years." Éomer is the son of Éomund, once Chief Marshall of the Mark. After his father's death, Théoden took Éomer into his home as a second son.

The Testing of Hobbits

At the time they separate, the nine companions, now reduced to eight, had been traveling together for 11 days since Lórien and 9 weeks since Rivendell. It has been just over 22 weeks since the four Hobbits left Bag End. Since the Hobbits spent three months resting at Rivendell and Lórien, Frodo and Sam will journey to the heart of Mordor with only 10 weeks of experience in wilderness travel, while Merry and Pippin will face the horrors of Orc captivity with that same limited experience. During those days the inner toughness Gandalf sensed in Hobbits will be fully tested.

Using all these experiences, Tolkien has taken the Hobbits through four stages. The first was their initial, childlike innocence about the dangers that surrounded them, illustrated by the first hours of their hike to Crickhollow. Pursed by Black Riders, they grew up quickly, learning that the world can be a dangerous place, and that danger must be met with courage and good sense. The second began when Strider became their teacher, disciplining them in wilderness travel and teaching them what they might not have lived long enough to learn on their own. The third came at Rivendell, when they were accepted into a team of seasoned travelers, each with talents and strength that made the whole greater than the sum of its parts. With the scattering of the Company, we begin the fourth stage, one that will test if these Hobbits have grown enough to survive their own, unaided by Wizard, Dwarf, Elf or man. (Even Gollum, Frodo and Sam's companion, is a Hobbit, however degraded he has become because of the Ring.) At the close of this story, we see hints of a fifth stage, an enduring bond that can exist long after the fighting is over and lives have taken separate paths.

We can think of these four stages as childhood, early and late adolescence, and finally adulthood. The third is an almost classic example of the "one for all and all for one" attitude some call "male bonding." The sense of responsibility it creates lies at heart of what it takes to forge a group of isolated, self-centered individuals into a team that can face danger together and risk their lives for one another in the pursuit of a great cause.

A Different Tale

Perhaps nothing provides us with a better indication that Tolkien got his tale just right, than the reaction of many readers when they are told of characters and plots that Tolkien considered but rejected. "Change that?" they react, "You can't change that. That's the way it really happened!"

Not actually. Middle-earth is, after all, a created world with an invented history. It was born in the fertile imagination of J. R. R. Tolkien, a professor at Oxford University, whose own tastes resemble those of the Hobbits he invented. It has no other existence. Tolkien fans who forget that and put "Frodo Lives" stickers on the bumpers of their cars, can't really complain if their friends consider them a bit odd.

Tell some people that Bilbo was once named Bingo and they will respond, "Bingo's a good name for a dog, but it's a silly name for the hero of a story." They are right. We are lucky Tolkien tossed it out. I remember once reading a short tale that included a hen named Tupperware. Set in modern times, that might have been acceptable. But it was in a mythical world where chickens talked and no plastic kitchenware was in sight. It was as grating as if Tolkien had put a traditional red British telephone booth outside Bywater's *Green Dragon*.

The same can be said for Trotter, a mysterious Hobbit-character that Ring readers would have first met in Bree, much like they meet Strider in the actual tale. Forgetting for a moment that Trotter is the name of a pony, there is this now-defunct character's out-of-place wooden shoes. It is not just that Tolkien originally expected us to regard this footwear as oh-so mysterious for a member of a race that usually goes barefoot. It is that *The Hobbit* has accustomed us to Hobbits who move as silently as shadows. The idea of one clomping about in wooden shoes, like a Dutch boy over the cobblestones of a children's tale, is as out of place as the grim and disciplined Strider getting drunk and sentimental that first evening at *The Prancing Pony*.

Some of Tolkien's rejected plots are a little disturbing. For a time he planned to make Treebeard and his fellow Ents as evil as Old Man Willow was in the Old Forest. At some writing-class level, that might make sense. All thinking trees, this more ideologically inclined Tolkien would be saying, hate us because we are nasty creatures who cut and burn. But without Ents, how is Saruman going to be defeated? Even with them, that was difficult. Even more important, if forests are as good a Tolkien would have us believe, how can individual trees, given personality, always be evil? Clearly, the Old Forest must the exception rather than the rule and Ents must be likeable. Treebeard also provides a kindly counterpart to the cruel Balrog. The Balrog lives unseen in a dark cave and attacks his foes with fire. Treebeard lives equally unseen in a sunny wood, but as the shepherd of trees, he hates fire more than anything else.

As Tolkien himself admitted, the Hobbits owe a little to the Snergs in E. A. Wyke-Smith's 1927 *The Marvelous Land of Snergs*. For an interview with the grandson of Wyke-Smith, see Dave Smith's article in *The People's Guide to J. R. R. Tolkien* (Cold Spring Harbor: Cold Spring Press, 2003), 158f. The book is a diverse collection of articles originally posted to the Internet site TheOneRing.Net. For Tolkien's remark, see *Letters*, No. 163.

Many discarded characters and plots are described in Christopher Tolkien's "History of Middle-earth" series. For Bingo and Trotter, see the index to *The Return of the Shadow*. Given how similar their names are, some Tolkien fans may wish he had picked a different name for either SAURon or SARUman.

Evil Ents are in *The Treason of Isengard*, Ch. 1, "Gandalf's Delay" and Ch. 4, "Of Hamilcar, Gandalf, and Saruman."

12

Captivity and Pursuit

February 27 to March 1, 1419

Hobbits captive to Entmoot

Covers 5 Days
Day 157 to 161

Michael Stanton described how Tolkien wrote of evil this way:

Such theology as *The Lord of the Rings* embodies is conventional or traditional enough, at least as it concerns the nature of evil. Evil is a falling away from good, a negation of good, an absence, rather than a positive and original force in itself. "For nothing is evil in the beginning," Elrond tells his council. Because evil is a negativity, it cannot create. It can only mock living forms, as Treebeard tells Merry and Pippin: Trolls and Orcs mock or parody Ents and Elves respectively.

Normally, Tolkien gives only fleeting glimpses of evil—Sauron is terrifying but distant, and the Black Riders depart as quickly as they come. But as the Orcs drive Merry and Pippin across the plains of Rohan, he gives us a rare, up-close look at evil's emptiness and cruelty.

Michael N. Stanton, *Hobbits, Elves and Wizards,* 163. A Notice the contrasts: A Troll is dead stone given the power of movement, while an Ent is a living tree given that same power. Orcs see nature as a thing to be crushed and live for the moment, while Elves admire nature and look at life through the lens of centuries.

Sunday, February 27, 1419—Hobbits Pursued

The moon is just four days past new and sets at 11 p.m., so it will not aid Aragorn and the others in their pursuit.

Day 157
February 19

Merry and Pippin with Orcs

Day 2 of 4 as Captives

Wall of Rohan

- During the night Pippin escapes briefly, leaving footprints.
- Before being recaptured, he drops his Elf-made brooch.
- Orcs carry the Hobbits or force them to run.

Scratched Initials

In one of Tolkien's drafts, Merry and Pippin's initials were scratched on the back of the brooch, perhaps to make clear that both are alive. Tolkien may have dropped that because it is difficult to imagine how, watched and with their hands bound, the Hobbits could have scratched their initials.

The Two Towers, Bk. 3, Ch. 3, "The Uruk-hai." Leaving footprints and a brooch is Pippin's second clever move.

The Treason of Isengard, Ch. 20, "The Riders of Rohan." The captivity is told from Pippin's perspective. At Isengard, both describe it.

Aragorn, Legolas and Gimli

Day 2 of 5 in Pursuit

Plains of Rohirrim

The Two Towers, Bk. 3, Ch. 2, "The Riders of Rohan." The dead Orcs served Sauron, while their killers served Saruman.

- They find five dead Orcs.
- Just after sunrise Legolas sees an eagle flying north.
- In the morning Aragorn finds Pippin's tracks and broach.
- After dark, they rest rather than risk losing the trail.

Stiff Pace

Motives and ends mattered to Tolkien. He praised their rapid pace, while ignoring the much more impressive pace kept up by Orcs.

Although Tolkien does not let the three catch up with the Orcs. He does move them along at a stiff pace. At the end of this day, they will have covered some 72 miles in their pursuit and 36 miles since dawn.

Frodo and Sam

Day 2 of 4 by Themselves

Eastern Emyn Muil

The Two Towers, Bk. 4, Ch. 1, "The Taming of Sméagol."

- The two search for a route down the steep cliff face.

Gandalf and Treebeard

Fangorn

The Two Towers, Bk. 3, Ch. 4, "Treebeard" and Bk. 3, Ch. 5, "The White Rider." This event is also hinted at by Pippin, when he describes Gandalf's arrival at Isengard in Bk. 3, Ch. 9, "Flotsam and Jetsam." Though friends, Gandalf and Treebeard are quite different. Gandalf is often hasty, while Treebeard never acts in haste.

- Gandalf and Treebeard see each other in Fangorn but do not talk.

Not a Snub

While it may seem odd that two old friends, who have not seen each other for a long time, would not talk, Tolkien provides an explanation when he has Gandalf meet Aragorn, Gimli and Legolas on March 1. Gandalf had much to think about and was still exhausted from his struggle with Sauron two days earlier. Being too tired or distracted to meet an old friend is a feeling most of us can understand.

Éomer

Eastfold in Rohan

The Return of the King, Bk. 6, Ap. B, "The Tale of Years."

- Éomer leaves to attack the Orcs crossing the plains of Rohan.

Éomer

For more about Éomer, see *Unfinished Tales*, Pt. 3, Ch. 5, "The Battles of the Fords of Isen."

Day 158
February 20

Monday, February 28, 1419—Orcs Surrounded

Merry and Pippin with Orcs

Day 3 of 4 as Captives

River Entwash to Fangorn Forest

The Two Towers, Bk. 3, Ch. 3, "The Uruk-hai."

- In the morning, Sauron's Orcs flee and return.
- All the Orcs race for Fangorn.

- That afternoon Rohan horsemen come up behind.
- At sunset the Orcs are surrounded on a hilltop close to the forest.

Rohan's Light Calvary

Orcs have better night vision, so fighting at night would give them an advantage. Rohan denies them that advantage and launches a daylight calvary attack. In words that were once applied to the Apaches of the American Midwest, we can say that Rohan has the "best light calvary in Middle-earth." On horseback, no one can equal them.

Aragorn, Legolas and Gimli

Day 3 of 5 in Pursuit

Approaching the Downs

- The three pursue to the northwest.
- Near the end of the day, the trail turns more north and they stop.

The Two Towers, Bk. 3, Ch. 2, "The Riders of Rohan." They have covered 100 miles in under three days.

Frodo and Sam

Day 3 of 4 by Themselves

Eastern Emyn Muil

- Frodo and Sam look for a path down the sheer cliff.
- That night they sleep in a hollow.

The Two Towers, Bk. 4, Ch. 1, "The Taming of Sméagol."

Near Disaster

Here the two Hobbits' ignorance of geography almost leads to disaster. They waste much time looking for a path down and, if Gollum had not appeared on their fourth day on their own, they might have either been captured avoiding the Dead Marshes or gotten lost in them. Since their food proves barely adequate as is, any further delay would have resulted in their collapse several days short of Mount Doom.

Tuesday, February 29, 1419—Hobbits Escape

Day 159
February 21

The crescent moon, two days before first quarter, sets around midnight. So no Orcs can slip away, Rohan probably shortens and tightens its patrol line as it goes down.

Merry and Pippin with the Orcs

Day 4 of 4 as Captives

Near Fangorn Forest

- Grishnákh, leader of Sauron's Orcs gropes for the Ring.
- He seizes both Hobbits, tries to escape Rohan's lines, and is killed.

The Two Towers, Bk. 3, Ch. 3, "The Uruk-hai." Picking up on Grishnákh's intent is Pippin's third clever move.

Michael Stanton points this out in *Hobbits, Elves and Wizards,* 53.

Presumed Dead

Notice that in Tolkien's narrative, Merry and Pippin's escape on Day 4 is described in Chapter 3, *after* readers—reading about the pursuit of Aragorn, Gimli and Legolas—were told in Chapter 2 (describing Day 5) that Hobbits were not found among Orcs and could be presumed dead. Tolkien was a gifted writer. That delay heightens our delight when we discover the Hobbits alive and free.

Merry, Pippin with Treebeard
Day 1 of 7 with Ents

Into Fangorn Forest

The Two Towers, Bk. 3, Ch. 3, "The Uruk-hai."

- Pippin unties Merry and they hide in the woods.
- At dawn the horsemen attack and no Orc survives.
- Merry and Pippin go deeper into Fangorn and meet Treebeard.

The Two Towers, Bk. 3, Ch. 4, "Treebeard." Rumors of Ents, called "Tree-men," had reached the Shire. See the conversation at *The Green Dragon* in *The Fellowship of the Ring*, Bk. 1, Ch. 2, "The Shadow of the Past."

Blinding Foes with Light

Tolkien often reuses plots. Rohan uses the rising sun to blind Orcs much like the Hobbits will use a bonfire to blind their foes in the battle against Saruman's ruffians in Bywater on November 2, 1419. Perhaps Tolkien, who fought in the trenches of World War I, bitterly remembered German attacks coming out of a rising sun.

Wellinghall in Fangorn

The Two Towers, Bk. 3, Ch. 4, "Treebeard." Wellington was deep within Fangorn at the foot of Methedras, called the Last Peak or Last Mountain because it lay at the southmost tip of the Misty Mountains just north of the Gap of Rohan. Tolkien modeled Treebeard's loud, booming voice on that of his friend C. S. Lewis. See Joseph Pearce, *Tolkien, Man and Myth*, 70.

- At sunset they reach Wellinghall, Treebeard's home.
- Treebeard tells them about Saruman cutting down trees.
- Treebeard wants to organize Ents for war.

Entwives

When he created a history for the Ents, Tolkien thought in thousands of years rather than his usual (but still impressive) hundreds. According to Treebeard, the initial separation between Ents and Entwives came during the Great Darkness at the close of the First Age, almost 6500 years earlier. After that, contact between the two was sporadic. The Ents's first unsuccessful search for their Entwives came almost 3200 years earlier during the Second Age, after the land west of the Anduin (where the Entwives lived) was destroyed during Sauron's war with Númenor. The Ents and their sorrow for their lost Entwives demonstrates that Tolkien did not intend to create a "they lived happily ever after" tale. Much of the tale's sorrow remains unresolved at its end.

Aragorn, Legolas and Gimli
Day 4 of 5 in Pursuit

Downs of Rohan

The Two Towers, Bk. 3, Ch. 2, "The Riders of Rohan."

- At 11 a.m. they reach the Downs.
- Legolas estimates the Orcs reached the forest at sundown.
- At sunset, they near the end of the Downs and rest.

Elf Superiority

This march demonstrates the physical superiority of Elves over men and Dwarves. Legolas has more stamina in this pursuit than Aragorn or Gimli as well as far better vision.

Frodo and Sam

Day 4 of 4 by Themselves

Down the Cliffs of Emyn Muil

- During the day, they look for a path down the cliffs.
- Near sunset, they follow a ravine to the cliff face.
- Frodo climbs part of the way down and becomes stranded.
- Sam uses an Elf rope to bring Frodo back up.
- Frodo lowers Sam down with the rope and follows.

The Two Towers, Bk. 4, Ch. 1, "The Taming of Sméagol."

Nazgûl Cry and Flight Path

The erie cry that Frodo and Sam hear at this time is like that they heard on September 25, 1418 during their shortcut to the Bucklebury Ferry. In both cases they believe the cries are made by Nazgûl and a cry used to communicate means there are at least two of them.

Since Sauron's Orcs intercepted the travelers six days earlier (February 23) and one of his Nazgûl flew over their heads that same night, it is likely that Tolkien meant for these Nazgûl to be spies. The distance and difficult terrain makes flying more practical than Orc patrols.

Because Sauron does not suspect the Ring is being taken to Mordor, it is unlikely the Nazgûl were searching during this portion of their flight. Instead, they are either going to where they will begin their search west of Lake Nen Hithoel, or they have been sent to investigate Rohan's attack on the Orcs that morning near Fangorn. (Remember that Sauron has a *palantír* that allows him to glimpse distant events.) In either case, if the Nazgûl received orders from Sauron at Barad-dûr and departed from there, this is the route they would take. Over the next seven days (until the Hobbits reach the Black Gate on March 5 and turn south), Frodo, Sam and Gollum will be under the flight path of these terrifying spies.

Night aerial navigation is difficult. The Nazgûl may be using a standard technique. From Mordor they fly northwest in a direction that will take them over the easily visible Anduin River at a point they know must be north of Lake Nen Hithoel. They then follow the river down to the lake, which could never be mistaken for something else. That gives them a fixed point from which to depart on the next leg of their journey. Whether they intend to fly to Fangorn, Isengard, or Edoras, the lake provides a checkpoint halfway through their night journey. Techniques such as these were routinely used before modern navigational instruments were developed.

Frodo and Sam with Gollum

Day 1 of 7 to Black Gate

Beneath the Cliffs of Emyn Muil

- The two Hobbits stop for the night beneath the cliff.
- They see Gollum creeping down the cliff and capture him.

Rock Climbing Gollum

Contrary to what Sam said, except when a rope is used, going up a cliff face is usually easier than going down, in part, because it is easier to see hand and foot holds, particularly in the dark. Gollum's strange, head-down, spider-like technique may be a risky attempt to get around that difficulty.

The Two Towers, Bk. 4, Ch. 1, "The Taming of Sméagol." Tolkien was writing this segment in early April of 1944. *Letters*, No. 59. Gollum is visible in the lingering moonlight of early evening.

Faramir with Boromir's Body

Day 4 of 10 Drifting (Boromir)

The Two Towers, Bk. 4, Ch. 5, "The Window on the West."

On the Anduin near Osgiliath

- Near midnight Faramir is near Osgiliath on the Anduin.
- He sees his brother Boromir's body drift by in an Elvish boat.

Boromir's Drifting Canoe

Boromir's arrival at the Great Sea is in *The Two Towers*, Bk. 3, Ch. 1, "The Departure of Boromir."

Tolkien seems to have calculated an appropriate time for the canoe bearing Boromir to float the roughly 225 miles from the south end of Lake Nen Hithoel to Osgiliath. Since Boromir's canoe was released about midafternoon on the February 26, the canoe traveled 9 hours that day and all of February 27, 28 and 29, for a total of about 81 hours, giving a reasonable average speed of 2.8 miles per hour. If it continued to drift at the same speed, it would have reached the Great Sea, 350 miles below Osgiliath, during the early morning darkness of March 5. That fits with Tolkien's claim that Boromir drifted out to sea under a starlit sky.

Day 160
February 22

Wednesday, February 30, 1419—Entmoot Begins

Merry and Pippin with Treebeard and Quickbeam
Day 2 of 7 with Ents, Day 1 of 3 in Entmoot

Fangorn

The Two Towers, Bk. 3, Ch. 4, "Treebeard." Derndingle is in southwest Fangorn, conveniently close to Isengard.

- Treebeard carries the Hobbits to the Entmoot at Derndingle.
- They stay with Quickbeam.

Adjusting the Chronology

The changes were made in October of 1944. *Letters*, No. 85. Quickbeam means "living or lively tree" in Old English. See *A Tolkien Compass*, 172.

Tolkien alluded to changes he made to his "dislocated chronology" to shift events one or two days later. He added a day to the Entmoot and to the journey of Frodo and Sam to Ithilien, as well as probably two days to Aragorn's pursuit.

Aragorn, Legolas and Gimli with Éomer and Rohan
Day 5 of 5 in Pursuit

Plains of Rohan

The Two Towers, Bk. 3, Ch. 2, "The Riders of Rohan." In this encounter Tolkien captures the stress warrior societies place on honor.

See *The Two Towers*, Bk. 3, Ch. 5, "The White Rider." For other conjectures, see *The Treason of Isengard*, Ch. 24, "The White Rider." For Gandal's hint, see *The Two Towers*, Bk. 3, Ch. 9, "Flotsam and Jetsam."

- Aragorn and Éomer meet Éomer and are loaned horses.
- In late afternoon, they reach the battle site and look for Hobbits.
- That night they camp next to Fangorn and see a mysterious man.

Mysterious Visitor

In genuine history, some mysteries are never resolved. In his invented history, Tolkien also left some mysteries unsolved and this mysterious visitor is one. When the travelers meet Gandalf, he tells them he was never near their camp. That means this old man may be Saruman searching the battleground for the Ring. Only that would pull him away from Isengard only three days before the war with Rohan. Later, when the travelers are reunited at Isengard, Gimli tells Merry that Gandalf hinted their visitor was the "old villain," meaning Saruman.

Frodo and Sam with Gollum

Day 2 of 7 to Black Gate

Approaching the Dead Marshes

- After the moon sets, they follow Gollum into a gully headed east.
- Just before sunrise, Gollum insists they hide.
- After dark they continue their journey in the gully.

The Two Towers, Bk. 4, Ch. 1, "The Taming of Sméagol" and Bk. 4, Ch. 2, "The Passage of the Marshes." The moon sets about 1 a.m.

Gollum and their Food Supply

Gollum spent years near Mordor, so it is quite possible that Tolkien intended for us to assume he lived in these complex marshes. A marsh is just the sort of place a creature who had grown up along a river and spent most of his life on an island in an underground lake would like. It would provide the fishes he loved and places to hide from Orc patrols. In addition, Gandalf mentions that Gollum first approached Mordor from Mirkwood to the north. If so, the Dead Marshes would be the first habitable locale near Mordor he would have reached. Finally, it was in these very marshes that Aragorn captured Gollum.

Gandalf describes the major events of Gollum's life in *The Fellowship of the Ring*, Bk. 1, Ch. 2, "The Shadow of the Past." For a discussion of Aragorn's capture, see February 1, 1418.

Tolkien is putting his two Hobbits in an increasingly desperate situation. On this day, he has Sam estimate that they have about three weeks of food left. That would last them until March 21, although the meals and food Faramir provides on March 7 and 8 will extend that a few more days. They will not reach the Crack of Doom until the 25th.

Faramir's food gift is mentioned at the beginning of *The Two Towers*, Bk. 4, Ch. 7, "Journey to the Cross-roads."

Thursday, March 1, 1419—Gandalf Returns

Day 161
February 23

A first quarter moon rises in the east-northeast about noon and sets in the west-northwest about 3 a.m. the next day.

Merry and Pippin with Quickbeam

Day 3 of 7 with Ents, Day 2 of 3 in Entmoot

Derndingle in Fangorn Forest

- The Hobbits stay at Quickbeam's house.

The Two Towers, Bk. 3, Ch. 4, "Treebeard."

Tolkien and Treebeard

Tolkien considered having Treebeard and his fellow Ents serve evil much as the trees of the Old Forest did. According to Tolkien, Ent comes from an Old English word that means giant, a reference to their large size.

Ents: *The Treason of Isengard*, Ch. 1, "Gandalf's Delay" and Ch. 4, "Of Hamilcar, Gandalf, and Saruman." Word: *Tolkien Compass*, 164–65.

Gandalf, Aragorn, Legolas, Gandalf and Gimli

Day 1 of 5 Together, Aragorn's Birthday

Fangorn Forest

- Aragorn, Legolas and Gimli find signs of the Hobbit escape.
- They search the woods and discover a Hobbit trail.
- They meet Gandalf and exchange news.
- They leave on horseback for Edoras.

The Two Towers, Bk. 3, Ch. 5, "The White Rider" and *The Treason of Isengard*, Ch. 24, "The White Rider."

Aragorn's Birthday and Shadowfax's Return

Aragorn was born in 1331, so today is his 88th birthday. He comes from a long-lived family and ages about three times more slowly than most men, so physically, he is about 30 years old. There is no mention of his birthday in the narrative, but Aragorn does mention his age to Gandalf.

Gandalf's remarks to Shadowfax imply that the two have not ridden together since the horse was released around October 4 of the previous year. This suggests that Gandalf's more recent travels—to Methedras and Fangorn—were by eagle or on foot.

They are headed for Edoras, which is about 125 miles to the south. In their conversation, Gandalf explains the Nazgûl to them. At present, Sauron is keeping the Nazgûl east of the Anduin as his secret weapon. Gandalf also tells them about Ents.

Frodo and Sam with Gollum

Day 3 of 7 to Black Gate

Dead Marshes to Noman-lands

- By sunrise, they reach the Dead Marshes.
- With the sky cloudy, Gollum will travel by day.
- When the sky clears, they hide in a thicket.
- After dark, they start out and see lights and faces in pools of water.

Battle of Dagorlad

The faces in the Dead Marshes are from the Battle of Dagorlad some three thousand years earlier. It was the greatest battle of the Second Age and pitted Sauron against the Last Alliance of Elves and men. Tolkien has Frodo take the view of Spiritualists of the late nineteen-century, claiming it is possible to have contact with the dead. Sam takes a Christian position, that the faces are an evil deception. Gollum, who thinks only of food, has no opinion either way. Later, Frodo suggests to Faramir that the faces may be a deception of Sauron.

The Two Towers, Bk. 4, Ch. 2, "The Passage of the Marshes." In these marshes exactly thirteen months earlier Aragorn captured Gollum.

For more on this battle, see "The Last Alliance" in *The Atlas of Middle-earth.* Gandalf summarizes the battle in *The Fellowship of the Ring,* Bk. 1, Ch. 2, "The Shadow of the Past." Frodo's remarks to Faramir are in *The Two Towers,* Bk. 4, Ch. 5, "The Window on the West."

After the Last Alliance won, it lay siege to Mordor. Seven years later Sauron was defeated and the Second Age ended. After their victory, Isildur cut the One Ring from Sauron's hand and kept it, refusing to listen to those who advised him to destroy it. Two years later, Isildur was attacked by Orcs at Gladden Fields. He put on the Ring and used its invisibility to escape. But the Orcs pursued him by smell. To avoid leaving a scent, Isildur dove into the Anduin River. Part of the way across, the Ring slipped from his finger, revealing him to Orc archers who killed him. Because of the role the Ring played in his death, it is called Isildur's Bane, a bane being a source of harm or misfortune.

In a 1960 letter, Tolkien said that the Dead Marshes were influenced by his experience in France "after the Battle of the Somme," but that they were more influenced by William Morris and his *The House of the Wolflings* and *The Roots of the Mountains.* *Letters,* No. 226. To avoid mistakenly calling this the "*Death* Marshes," remember that their waters contain faces of the long *dead.*

Faramir

Minas Tirith for Ithilien

- Faramir leaves Minas Tirith for Ithilien.

Faramir

Faramir will not return to Minas Tirith until March 10, the day the Darkness begins.

The Two Towers, Bk. 4, Ch. 5, "The Window on the West" and *The Return of the King,* Bk. 5, Ch. 4, "The Siege of Gondor."

A Duty to Disobey

Some Tolkien critics claim that the societies he described, with their hereditary kings and stewards, are antiquated and reactionary. The implication is that such literature is harmful to readers, who are assumed to be childlike, naive and gullible. For several reasons, that is not true.

First, his tale is set far in the past and can only be believable if is fits with what we know of the past. Electing politicians by secret ballot after feverish political campaigns conducted in the mass media would be as out of place in Middle-earth as regularly scheduled airline flights between Minas Tirith and Edoras. Good literature is true to the time and culture it describes. It doesn't try to be crassly ideological or describe circumstances as some fashionable moderns might think they should have been.

Second, Tolkien includes only enough flavor from the past to create the proper atmosphere. In some ways, his Middle-earth is better than many of its ancient models. Some ancient societies did have rigid hierarchies in which a rich nobility ruled over an almost rightless class of serfs. While there are hints that such societies exist where Mordor holds sway, the free peoples of Middle-earth do not live that way. They live in a societies that are in many ways more egalitarian than our own.

You see that when Sam slips into the Council of Elrond—the equivalent of a secret war council at the highest governmental level. Elrond smilingly teases him for doing no worse than coming without an invitation. Nothing is said about Sam being the barely literate son of a common laborer. Even more important, there is none of the concealed arrogance so common today—the kind that claims to be in touch with the rough side of life while demonstrating the opposite. The fact that Elrond, perhaps the greatest of living Elves, is associating with Hobbit country folk is not only not regarded as unusual, it's not even regarded at all. Refreshingly often in Tolkien's Middle-earth, people are rated by the content of their character—traits such as courage, kindness, and honesty—rather than by the group to which they belong. That is genuine equality.

Third, in no way does Tolkien convey the idea that those who are in charge are without flaws. Everyone in his tale makes mistakes, including Gandalf, Aragorn and the Elves. Even more important, at several points in the narrative the success of their mission hinges on a subordinate deliberately choosing to disobey. Here are examples.

Éomer's battle with the Orcs, which led to the escape of Merry and Pippin, was in disobedience of Théoden's orders. We have just read how, on February 30th, Éomer chose to disobey again and provided Aragorn, Legolas and Gimli with horses. Tolkien is clear that Éomer, the soldier, is right and Théoden, his king, is wrong. Fortunately, under the influence of Gandalf, Théoden comes to recognize Éomer's good sense.

It is worth noting, however, that Aragorn's acceptance as king includes a 'vote' by acclamation from the people he will rule. See: *The Return of the King,* Bk. 6, Ch. 5, "The Steward and the King." Today, the most unfashionable idea in the tale is probably the pleasure its characters find in smoking.

The Fellowship of the Ring, Bk. 2, Ch. 2, "The Council of Elrond." Also, the fellowship of nine includes four Hobbits because three Hobbits make clear that, whatever Elrond might order, their minds are made up. They are going with Frodo. For Tolkien, moral principles clearly outrank any 'chain of command.'

Perhaps while serving in World War I, Tolkien saw instances where, to prevent disaster, a low-level officer had to disobey orders.

Éomer's disobedience is in *The Two Towers,* Bk. 3, Ch. 2, "The Riders of Rohan" and Bk. 3, Ch. 6, "The King of the Golden Hall."

For Faramir's situation see: *The Two Towers*, Bk. 4, Ch. 6, "The Forbidden Pool." For Denethor's anger, see *The Return of the King*, Bk. 5, Ch. 4, "The Siege of Gondor."

For Beregon, see: *The Return of the King*, Bk. 5, Ch. 4, "The Siege of Gondor" and Bk. 5, Ch. 7, "The Pyre of Denethor."

There is a discussion of Webb and Wells' political and social agenda in Ch. V and VI of *The Pivot of Civilization in Historical Perspective* (Seattle: Inkling, 2001). The quote from the letter to Wells is on page 41 and comes from *The Letters of Sidney and Beatrice Webb*, vol. 2, 144.

Saruman's resemblance to Sauron is exposed by Gandalf in *The Fellowship of the Ring*, Bk. 2, Ch. 2, "The Council of Elrond." Treebeard's description of Saruman is in *The Two Towers*, Bk. 3, Ch. 4, "Treebeard." The topic of freedom in Tolkien is discussed in John G. West's *Celebrating Middle-earth*.

The poetry is from "The Charge of the Light Brigade" by Alfred Lord Tennyson (1809–1892) and concerns a calvary charge in the Crimean War. Three-fourths of the men die in an attack that was known in advance to be futile.

In a week, on March 8, there will be another rebellion. Faramir will choose to disobey his father, Denethor the Steward of Gondor, when he spares Gollum's life and allows Frodo and Sam to travel freely about Ithilien. Unfortunately, Faramir's father proves less willing to see the wisdom of that disobedience.

Then there is Beregon who, on March 15, acts in direct defiance of Denethor and in spite of those who angrily accuse him of being a traitor. His willful and open disobedience saves Faramir from the flames and for that he will be rewarded by Aragorn.

Finally, it is easy to suspect that some critics object, not to the fact that Tolkien's tale includes those who give orders, but to the sort of leaders he praises—men such as Aragorn, who rules more because of the strength of his character than for his birth. There is within Tolkien's writings a rebellion against the rule of an amoral bureaucratic elite being advocated while he was young and that remains common today.

Sidney Webb, one of the founder of Britain's Fabians, praised that sort of manipulative, dehumanizing leadership in a 1901 letter to science fiction writer H. G. Wells. In *Anticipations,* published earlier that year, Wells advocated a soon-coming world state run by an "open conspiracy of intellectuals." Webb had no problem with that. He simply wanted to have a slightly different person in charge. As he told Wells: "But all experience shows that men need organising as much as machines, or rather, much more; that the making of such arrangements and constant adjustments. . . is a professional art in itself—not consciously studied in England, but recognized in India, and deliberately studied in Germany."

Saruman advocated something chillingly similar, causing Gandalf to reply that he sounded like a messenger of Sauron. When Treebeard met Merry and Pippin, he said that Saruman had a mind like a machine.

In retrospect, Webb's praise of Germany is chilling. The willingness of Germans to obey Hitler was not born in madness. It was the direct result of many years of bureaucratic conditioning—conditioning that taught people to obey rules without question. It is those sorts of people that the four Hobbits will find in charge when they return to the Shire, people who like to make and enforce rules by the score. All that is necessary to transform Saruman's Shire into a Nazi Germany is the transformation of petty and malicious rules into hideously evil ones.

It is no exaggeration to say that the fate of Middle-earth hinged on the willingness of a few to disobey foolish or wrong orders. Contrary to some in the England into which he was born, Tolkien did *not* accept the idea—which sounds so pretty in poetry—that: "Theirs not to make reply, Theirs not to reason why, Theirs but to do and die." Those who fight in *The Lord of the Rings* know why they risk death. They fight as free men with minds and wills of their own and not as the brutalized slaves of Sauron or the cleverly manipulated machines of Wells and Webb.

The Humanity of Ancient People

There is view of humanity and its history that some have called "Whiggish," after a British political movement which considered itself at the forefront of human progress. Its followers see almost everything as a struggle between the forces of reaction (their opponents) and those of progress (themselves). A classic example of Whiggish history was Thomas Macaulay's *The History of England from the Accession of James III,* which opened by claiming that, "the history of our country during the last hundred and sixty years is eminently the history of physical, of moral, and of intellectual improvement." In contrast, the best known criticism of the Whiggish point of view is Herbert Butterfield's still-in-print 1931 *The Whig Interpretation of History.*

With so much "progress" packed into recent history, Whigs believe we can learn little from those who lived hundreds of years ago. ("Positively Medieval" comes easily to their lips, as does "turn back the clock.") An all too logical extension of that belief is the attitude that ancient people (as well as their modern 'savage' counterparts) were primitive, driven by irrational, violent and animal-like emotions. Our ancestors, in their point of view, were not fully human or much like us. G. K. Chesterton dealt a heavy blow to that attitude when he wrote:

> A priest and a boy entered sometime ago a hollow in the hills and passed into a sort of subterranean tunnel that led into a labyrinth of such sealed and secret corridors of rock. They crawled through cracks that seemed almost impassible, they crept through tunnels that might have been made for moles, they dropped into holes as hopeless as wells, they seemed to be burying themselves alive seven times over beyond the hope of resurrection. . . . What [that boy] did see at last was a cavern so far from the light of day that it might have been the legendary Domdaniel cavern that was under the floor of the sea. This secret chamber of rock, when illuminated after its long night of unnumbered ages, revealed on its walls large and sprawling outlines diversified with coloured earths; and when they followed the lines of them they recognized, across the vast void of ages, the movement and gestures of a man's hand. They were drawings or paintings of animals; and they were drawn or painted not only by a man but by an artist. . . . They showed the experimental and adventurous spirit of the artist, the spirit that does not avoid but attempts difficult things; as where the draughtsman had represented the action of the stag when he swings his head clean round and noses toward his tail. . . . In this and twenty other details it is clear that the artist had watched animals with a certain interest and presumably a certain pleasure. In that sense it would seem that he was not only an artist but a naturalist; the sort of naturalist who is really natural.

Most modern historians do not like to be called "Whiggish," since it implies that they force a particular point of view on the history they describe. But in other fields the view is more open and common.

For a classic example, think of the violent monkey scenes that open Stanley Kubrick's *2001: A Space Odyssey* and compare them to the overly suave scenes of modern space travel immediately following.

The quote is from G. K. Chesterton, *Everlasting Man,* Ch. 1, "The Man in the Cave." Although a writer and a popular journalist, Chesterton was trained as an artist and was an excellent cartoonist. He was describing the cave art discovered in France and Spain over the past century. An October 3, 2001 BBC news report noted that this art was drawn as far back as 30,000 years ago. Even more surprising is the fact that recent dating has shown that the older art is every bit as skilled as that from many thousands of years later. Helene Valladas, a scientist, noted: "Prehistorians, who have traditional interpreted the evolution of prehistoric art as a steady progression from simple to more complex representations, may have to reconsider existing theories of the origins of art."

Tolkien and C. S. Lewis referred to the claim that new ideas are better than old as "chronological snobbery." Lewis also blasted those who failed to "show *that* a man is wrong," before they explain "*why* he is wrong," an error he called Bulverism. Whigs make that error when they assume that simply pointing out that someone lived long ago is enough to prove their ideas wrong. (See the entry for "Notes on the Way" in *The C. S. Lewis Readers' Encyclopedia*.) For a discussion of the influence G. K. Chesterton may have had on Tolkien, see Joseph Pearce, *Tolkien, Man and Myth*, 160f.

Letters, No. 226. Both these William Morris tales are in *More to William Morris*. In the first, the Romans are the evil foe and in the second the Huns.

Sadly, some of the bile directed against Tolkien for setting his tale in the ancient past is the fury of a Whig, angry to see people from an age that is distant beyond all counting portrayed with talents and virtues that are rare even in our own and presumably more enlightened age. If Tolkien has done nothing more than impress on us the humanity of our distant ancestors, he has accomplished quite a bit.

Tolkien, War and Cynicism

World War I forever altered the lives of the millions of men who fought in its trenches and on its battlefields. In *The Great War and Modern Memory,* Paul Fussell said that books such as William Morris's *The Well at the World's End* had inspired those who entered the war to believe in virtues such as courage in the face of death. (Some British soldiers attacked machine-gun-infested German lines kicking a ball before them, as if what they were doing were no more than a schoolyard sport.) He went on to point out that in the horrors of the trenches some became cynical, questioning whether any sacrifice in any war was worth the cost. The result is still with us. Many modern cynics, two generations or more removed from the suffering in those trenches, now believe that all wars are meaningless and futile.

Tolkien would not have agreed. In a 1960 letter describing his own war experience he wrote: "The Dead Marshes and the approaches to the Morannon owe something to Northern France after the Battle of the Somme. They own more to William Morris and his Huns and Romans, as in *The House of the Wolflings* or *The Roots of the Mountains*." For Tolkien, if the cause was just and the foe evil, even death in battle had meaning. You see that in Rohan's brave ride to aid its southern ally and in the desperate fighting at Helm's Deep, Minas Tirith and the Black Gate. Even more important, you see it in the strength that Frodo and Sam display as they struggle toward Mount Doom across a landscape as blasted as any World War I battlefield.

13

War with Saruman

March 2 to 5, 1419

Covers 4 Days
Day 162 to 165

Motivating Théoden to the defeat of Saruman

Tolkien's talent as a writer is shown as much by what he does *not* tell us as in what he does. Sometimes, he shifts back in time to take up a different narrative thread, told as it was happening. At other times, he lets his characters simply recall what happened to them. Since that's considered a less vivid way of writing, why did Tolkien use it? Tom Shippey thinks he knows the answer.

Things like missing out the sack of Isengard perhaps provide a clue. Tolkien dropped a big action scene, yes. What he got in exchange, and what he clearly wanted to get, was a major surprise, as one plot strand—Aragorn, Legolas and Gimli, now mixed up with the Riders of Rohan—quite unexpectedly runs across the results of another—Merry and Pippin and Saruman and the Ents—although the day has already been saved for the first group by the marching wood at Helm's Deep in Rohan. None of the characters, as Tolkien wrote the story, really understands the whole of what is going on.

Not even Gandalf. In fact, the only thing they do know is that their fate will not, in the end, be determined by visible events but by a mostly invisible one: the stealthy crawl of three insignificant-looking characters into the lion's mouth of Mordor. The great ones and the heroes are continually trying to see what is happening elsewhere, through the *palantirs* and the Mirror of Galadriel and the Eye of Sauron. The attempt is repeatedly disastrous. Denethor commits suicide because of what he sees in his *palantir,* but he has read it wrong. As Gandalf says, "Even the wise cannot see all ends," and the really wise remember that.

By concealing events from us as they happen and recounting them later, Tolkien is teaching us that life must be lived in the present, even when we do not know all that is happening or will happen. We cannot see all ends, but must live our lives moment by moment, doing the very best we can with the feeble vision we have been given.

The quote is from Tom Shippey, "Tolkien Teaches Us to Take Courage" *National Post,* January 6, 2003. C. S. Lewis said much the same thing when he wrote of Shakespeare's *King Lear* (III, vi) about a character so minor, "he is merely 'First Servant.' All the other characters around him ... have fine long-term plans. They think they know how the story is going to end, and they are quite wrong. The servant has no such delusions. He has no notion how the play is going to go. But he understands the present scene. He sees an abomination (the blinding of old Gloucester) taking place. He will not stand it. His sword is out and pointed at his master's breast in a moment; then Regan [King Lear's daughter] stabs him dead from behind. That is his whole part: eight lines all told. But if it were real life and not a play, that is the part it would be best to have acted." See "The World's Last Night" in *C. S. Lewis* (Lesley Walmsley, ed.), 48–49.

Friday, March 2, 1419—Ents to War

The waxing moon is one day past first quarter. It rises in the east-northeast in the early afternoon and will set in the west-northwest about 5 a.m. tomorrow. That brings increasingly bright nights for the war and for Frodo's dangerous approach to Mordor.

Merry and Pippin with the Ents

Day 4 of 7 with Ents, Day 3 of 3 in Entmoot

Derndingle to the Outskirts of Isengard

The Two Towers, Bk. 3, Ch. 4, "Treebeard."

- In the afternoon the Ents choose war and march for Isengard.
- After sunset, the Huorns join them, and at midnight they reach Isengard.

Those Mysterious Huorns

Huorns are either Ents who have become tree-like or trees that have become Ent-like. The issue may never be unresolved.

Gandalf, Aragorn, Legolas and Gimli with Théoden

Day 2 of 5 Together, Day 1 of 4 Riding with Théoden

Edoras

The Two Towers, Bk. 3, Ch. 7, "Helm's Deep."

The Two Towers, Bk. 3, Ch. 7, "Helm's Deep." Today Saruman's armies win the Fords of Isen.

See *The Treason of Isengard,* Ch. 26, "The King of the Golden Hall." Éowyn is ordered to lead those who remain behind. The Fords of Isen are about 120 miles from Edoras.

- In the morning, they reach Edoras and enter Théoden's hall.
- Encouraged by Gandalf, Théoden agrees to attack Saruman.
- In early afternoon, Théoden leaves for the Fords of Isen.
- Long after dark, they stop.

A Romance that Was Not

Éowyn, daughter of Éomund, sister of Éomer, and Théoden's adopted daughter is 24 years old. At one point, Tolkien considered a romance between Aragorn and Éowyn that ends when she dies saving Théoden.

Frodo and Sam with Gollum

Day 4 of 7 to Black Gate, First Nazgûl Overflight

Noman-lands

The Two Towers, Bk. 4, Ch. 2, "The Passage of the Marshes."

- A Nazgûl passes overhead westbound, terrifying Gollum.
- At sunrise, they leave the Dead Marshes for Noman-lands.
- During the day they hide under a black stone.

Winged Nazgûl

In a draft, this Nazgûl is bound for Isengard. See *The War of the Ring,* Pt. 2, Ch. II, "The Passage of the Marshes." The notes at the end of that chapter discuss the various Nazgûl flights.

Tolkien may have Sauron sending Nazgûl to observe the war about to break out between Saruman and Rohan. In three days, late on March 5, another Nazgûl will pass near Isengard, causing Gandalf to conclude Sauron may act quickly once he sees Saruman has been defeated.

This is not the Hobbits' first encounter with Nazgûl. One may have passed over their heads on January 8, 1419, one attacked them on February 23, and another flew near them on February 29. For some reason, this Nazgûl seems to get no further than Lake Nen Hithoel.

Saturday, March 3, 1419—Attack on Isengard

Merry, Pippin and Treebeard with Gandalf
Day 5 of 7 with Ents, Day 1 of 2 with Ents at War

Isengard

- In the dark Ents and Hurons creep down Wizard's Vale.
- Saruman's troops march out to battle Rohan and Hurons follow.
- Ents attack and Saruman hides inside Orthanc.
- Gandalf asks for help and at midnight the Ents flood Isengard.

The Two Towers, Bk. 3, Ch. 9, "Flotsam and Jetsam." This is recounted later by Merry and Pippin. Treebeard will allow Saruman to leave Orthanc on August 15, 1419.

Shakespeare's Marching Trees

In a 1955 letter Tolkien said his account of Ents marching on Isengard came from his schoolboy "disgust" with Shakespeare's "shabby use" of an army marching with branches. He resolved to tell a tale where a wood actually marched on a fortress. Here is Shakespeare's tale.

Letters, No. 163. For Tolkien's other use of Shakespeare, see March 15, 1419. Tolkien was working on this chapter in early December of 1942. *Letters,* No. 47.

Three witches call up an apparition for Macbeth.

APPARITION: Be lion-mettled, proud and take no care who chafes, who frets, or where conspirers are; Macbeth shall never vanquish'd be until Great Birnam Wood to high Dunsinane Hill shall come against him.

MACBETH: That will never be. Who can impress the forest, bid the tree unfix his earth-bound root?

Macbeth, Act 4, Scene I.

Later at Birnam Wood an army advances on Macbeth.

MALCOLM: What wood is this before us?

MENTEITH: The wood of Birnam.

MACDUFF: Let every soldier hew him down a bough and bear't before him; thereby shall we shadow the numbers of our host, and make discovery err in report of us. . . .

Macbeth, Act 5, Scene IV.

Macbeth at his castle, Dunsinane

MACBETH: Thou com'st to use they tongue; thy story most quickly.

MESSENGER: Gracious my lord, I should report that which I say I saw, but know not how to do't.

MACBETH: Well, say sir.

MESSENGER: As I did stand my watch upon the hill, I look'd toward Birnam and anon me-thought the wood began to move.

MACBETH: Liar and slave!

MESSENGER: Let me endure your wrath, if't be not so. Within this three mile may you see it coming; I say, a moving grove.

MACBETH: I thou speak'st false, upon the next tree shalt thou hang alive, till famine cling thee. If thy speech be sooth, I care not if thou dost for me as much. I pull in resolution, and begin to doubt the equivocation of the fiend that lies like the truth, "Fear not, till Birnam wood do come to Dunsinane." And now a wood comes toward Dunsinane.

Macbeth, Act 5, Scene V.

Gandalf, Aragorn, Legolas and Gimli with Théoden

Day 3 of 5 Together, Day 2 of 4 Riding with Théoden

To the Fords of Isen and Helm's Deep

- Just after dawn, they ride for the Fords of Isen.
- A horsemen tells them the Fords fell yesterday.
- Théoden orders his men to Helm's Deep and Gandalf rides off alone.

Indefensible Edoras

Tolkien made his military tactics reasonable. Edoras is the capital of Rohan. Though fortified, it was not built to withstand a major siege, forcing Théoden to go to the much more defensible Helm's Deep.

Aragorn, Legolas and Gimli with Théoden

Dike at Helm's Deep

- Saruman's Orcs burn homes and fields.
- Théoden's men reinforce the Deeping Wall.
- The Orcs reach the Dike, driving back defenders.

Visualizing the Battle

For a map and an account of the battle see Karen Fonstad, "Helm's Deep" and "The Battle of Hornburg" in *The Atlas of Middle-earth.*

Frodo and Sam with Gollum

Day 5 of 7 to Black Gate

Noman-lands

- They travel by night.

Dating Tolkien's Writing

We often get clues about when Tolkien was writing a particular chapter from remarks in letters. On April 13, 1944, he wrote his son Christopher, who was with the Royal Air Force in South Africa, that the day before he had "brought Frodo nearly to the gate of Mordor." Though it is probably exaggerating the parallel, at the very time the Allies were preparing to invade Hitler's "Fortress Europe" with huge armies, two small Hobbits were searching for a way into Sauron's "Fortress Mordor."

Sunday, March 4, 1419—Fighting at Helm's Deep

Aragorn, Gandalf, Legolas and Gimli with Théoden

Day 4 of 5 Together, Day 3 of 4 Riding with Théoden

Helm's Deep

- Shortly after midnight, the battle begins.
- After dawn, Théoden leads a calvary attack, driving back their foes.
- Gandalf arrives with Erkenbrand and a thousand soldiers.

The Two Towers, Bk. 3, Ch. 7, "Helm's Deep." The darkness Legolas sees around Isengard is connected with Hurons who can "wrap themselves in shadow" and perhaps also to the "fires and foul fumes" that Saruman unleashes on the Ents. See Merry's remarks in *The Two Towers*, Bk. 3, Ch. 9, "Flotsam and Jetsam."

The Two Towers, Bk. 3, Ch. 7, "Helm's Deep." For the battle, see: *Unfinished Tales*, Bk. 3, Ch. 5, "The Battles of the Fords of Isen." Helm's Deep is some 30 miles from the Fords. In better days, Isengard, at the northern end of the Gap of Rohan, and Helm's Deep, to the south, defended the Gap together.

The Two Towers, Bk. 4, Ch. 2, "The Passage of the Marshes."

Letters, No. 60. Tolkien was hoping to read this new material to C. S. Lewis and Charles Williams the next day. That suggests how quickly his text could move from writing to friendly criticism. He mentions their approval in *Letters*, No. 62.

Day 164
February 26

The Two Towers, Bk. 3, Ch. 7, "Helm's Deep."

- Orcs flee into a wood of Huorns and are not seen again.

A More Complex Battle

In Tolkien's drafts, the plot for the battle for Helm's Deep was far more detailed and complicated than in the final version.

The War of the Ring, Pt. 1, Ch. II, "Helm's Deep."

Helm's Deep and to Isengard

- Théoden orders a muster at Edoras two days after the full moon.
- As the sun sets, they leave with 20 men for Isengard, 45 miles away.
- They camp about 16 miles from Isengard.

The Two Towers, Bk. 3, Ch. 8, "The Road to Isengard."

Muster at Harrowdale

The full moon is March 8, so this muster is set for March 10, six days from now. When he passes through Edoras on March 6, Gandalf will modify this order. Nazgûl are now flying over the land, so the Rohirrim should assemble in the Harrowdale Valley and light as few fires as possible. That may keep them from being spotted by Sauron's aerial spies.

Merry and Pippin—Flooding Isengard
Day 6 of 7 with Ents, Day 2 of 2 with Ents at War

Gate of Isengard

- During the night, Isengard floods.
- The Hobbits retreat to a guardhouse at the gate, and the flood recedes.

The Two Towers, Bk. 3, Ch. 9, "Flotsam and Jetsam."

Frodo and Sam with Gollum—Noman-lands
Day 6 of 7 to Black Gate, Second Nazgûl Overflight

Desolation of Marannon

- In the morning, they reach the Desolation of Marannon and rest in a pit.
- In the evening, Sam sees Gollum hunched over a sleeping Frodo.
- In the dark, they travel again, and a Nazgûl passes high above.

The Two Towers, Bk. 4, Ch. 2, "The Passage of the Marshes." This is their sixth day (in the sense of any time during a calendar day) with Gollum but, as Tolkien notes, their fifth morning.

Gollum and the Nazgûl

Though Tolkien never fully explained Gollum's fear of the Nazgûl, there is a probable cause. It is possible that earlier they spotted him from the air and were responsible for his capture and torture by Sauron. Given Gollum's long experience underground with Orcs, he probably had no trouble outsmarting often dull-witted Orcs, but he may have found it much more difficult to evade the Nazgûl.

Monday, March 5, 1419—Meeting Saruman

Day 165
February 27

Merry and Pippin with Treebeard
Day 7 of 7 with Ents

Gate of Isengard

- Gríma arrives and Treebeard forces him into the tower.
- In the morning, the Hobbits gather food and tobacco.

The Two Towers, Bk. 3, Ch. 9, "Flotsam and Jetsam."

Trade with the Shire

Aragorn finds the presence of Shire tobacco at Isengard suspicious. If he had known the full extent of the trade between the Shire and Isengard, he would have been even more worried, as the Shire's future King, about the little community's safety.

For more on Saruman's trade with the Shire see *The Return of the King*, Bk. 6, Ch. 8, "The Scouring of the Shire" and *Unfinished Tales*, Pt. III, Ch. IV, "The Hunt for the Ring," Sec. iii. Also see the entry in this book for late December 1418.

Gandalf, Aragorn, Legolas and Gimli—At Isengard

Day 5 of 5 Together, Day 4 of 4 Riding with Théoden

Gate of Isengard

The Two Towers, Bk. 3, Ch. 8, "The Road to Isengard."

- At dawn Gandalf and the others ride to Isengard, arriving after noon.
- They find Merry and Pippin and hear what happened at Isengard.

The Two Towers, Bk. 3, Ch. 9, "Flotsam and Jetsam."

- Théoden and Gandalf leave to talk with Treebeard.

Rest and Relaxation

Soldiers love their R&R—Rest and Relaxation. Here the travelers get a brief time to relax, eat and share experiences. It's easy to suspect that the Tolkien of World War I trenches sometimes enjoyed food and tobacco scrounged up much like that found by Merry and Pippin.

This relaxed meeting is one of the rare occasions when Tolkien gave the current date. For tobacco lore, see *The War of the Ring*, Pt. 1, Ch. 3, "The Road to Isengard" and the Prologue to *The Fellowship of the Ring*.

Aragorn, Gimli, Legolas, Merry and Pippin

Gate of Isengard

The Two Towers, Bk. 3, Ch. 9, "Flotsam and Jetsam."

- They eat and talk.

Aragorn, Gandalf, Gimli, Legolas, Merry and Pippin

Orthanc at Isengard

The Two Towers, Bk. 3, Ch. 10, "The Voice of Saruman." *The Return of the King*, Bk. 6, Ap. A, I, (iv), "Gondor and the Heirs of Anárion" and Bk. 6, Ap. B, "The Tale of Years."

- They go to Orthanc and talk with Saruman.
- Gandalf casts Saruman out of the Council.
- Gríma throws a *palantír* from Orthanc.
- Treebeard promises to keep Saruman confined.

Child-like Hobbits and Grumpy Gandalf

At times, Tolkien portrayed Hobbits as curious children and Gandalf as a father too tired, busy and distracted to satisfy their curiosity. If Gandalf had explained what a *palantír* was and warned of its danger, would Pippin have become so obsessed with finding out about it? We will never know.

To Camp at Dol Baran

The Two Towers, Bk. 3, Ch. 11, "The Palantír."

- At sunset, they leave Isengard, halting a few hours later.
- Pippin takes the *palantír* from a sleeping Gandalf.
- He looks into it, sees Sauron, and screams.

Sauron's Suspicions

Tolkien rarely told us *why* something happened, but he worked hard behind the scenes to make what happened seem plausible. When Sauron saw a Hobbit in the *palantír*, he had reason to suspect Saruman had captured Hobbits. Earlier in the day, Pippin claimed that on February 26 Grishnákh had sent word of their capture back to Mordor. As they flee,

Pippin explained how Sauron might know about their capture in *The Two Towers*, Bk. 3, Ch. 9, "Flotsam and Jetsam."

Gandalf, who had not heard Pippin's remark, tells Pippin he believes Sauron may have read Saruman's mind about the Hobbits as the two communicated through their *palantír*.

Dol Baran

- The *palantír* is given to Aragorn, its rightful owner.
- A Nazgûl flies overhead and Gandalf orders everyone to flee.
- Gandalf takes Pippin with him on Shadowfax.

Gandalf's Sudden Flight

To understand why Tolkien had Gandalf flee so hurriedly in the middle the night, we need to realize just how powerful a military force the Nazgûl were. They could operate much like today's elite special forces, moving in quickly by air, briefly achieving overwhelming military superiority, and flying away with captives, which could include the two Hobbits, who might be tortured and forced to reveal Frodo's secret mission. Aragorn and Gandalf stood little chance against such a force. In such a situation, flight was far wiser than a fight.

Aragorn, Gimli, Legolas and Merry with the Rohirrim

Camp at Dol Baran

- They travel with King Théoden.

Frodo and Sam with Gollum—Black Gate

Day 7 of 7 to Black Gate, Third Nazgûl Overflight

Desolation of Marannon to the Black Gate

- A Nazgûl passes westward high overhead about 1 a.m.
- Gollum will go on only after Frodo threatens him with a sword.

Black Gate

- Before dawn, they are a mile from the Black Gate.
- They see four Nazgûl overhead, and armies enter Mordor.
- Frodo decides to take Gollum's mysterious other route.

Land of Shadow

At this point, Tolkien discovered that his book was becoming much longer than he had planned. He had intended to cover in one chapter events that required the first three chapters of Book 4. He was writing the third, which he called "Gates of the Land of Shadow" and which became "The Black Gate is Closed," on April 23, 1944.

Black Gate and to the South

- They rest during day in the shade of a rock.
- After dark, they travel south parallel to the road.

Gollum's Uncertainty

Tolkien may have a reason for making Gollum seem uncertain about the alternate route. After Gollum's escape, Sauron could have closed this

The Two Towers, Bk. 3, Ch. 11, "The Palantír." These events are dated to March 5 in *The Return of the King,* Ap. B., "The Tale of Years."

Sauron acquired his *palantír* when the Nazgûl took Minas Morgul over a thousand years earlier in 402. *The Return of the King,* Bk. 6, Ap. A, I, (iv), "Gondor and the Heirs of Anárion." For more on the *palantír,* see *Unfinished Tales,* Pt. 4, Ch. 3, "The Palantíri"

The Return of the King, Bk. 5, Ch. 2, "The Passing of the Grey Company."

The Two Towers, Bk. 4, Ch. 2, "The Passage of the Marshes."

The Two Towers, Bk. 4, Ch. 3, "The Black Gate is Closed."

Letters, No. 61 for April 18, 1944.

The Two Towers, Bk. 4, Ch. 4, "Of Herbs and Stewed Rabbits."

gap in his security. But the ever-scheming Gollum also needs to appear deceptive, pretending to know less about the route than he actually does.

Boromir
Day 10 of 10 Drifting, Date Calculated

Delta of the Anduin River

• In the morning darkness, Boromir's body drifts into the Great Sea.

Tolkien and Technology

For the calculation of this date, see the Faramir entry for February 30. For the legend that Boromir's body reached the sea at night, see *The Two Towers*, Bk. 3, Ch. 1, "The Departure of Boromir."

Letters, No. 257, 332 and 154. Tolkien's attitude can be compared with that of the Amish, a religious group that adopts technology only if it assists rather than hinders relationships. For a discussion of the influence that William Blake, William Cobbett and G. K. Chesterton had on Tolkien's view of industrialization, see Joseph Pearce, *Tolkien, Man and Myth,* 160f.

Letters, No. 64 Tolkien does not seem to have given much thought to factory workers who need to live where they could afford a home and work where there were jobs.

Letters, No. 75.

Tolkien loathed the war-making machinery Saruman concealed beneath Isengard and was undoubtedly glad to see it drowned forever by the Ents. Some take that as one indication among many that Tolkien loathed all technology. The truth is a bit more complicated.

Tolkien had no objection to technology as such. In a 1964 letter he confessed to dreaming of being rich enough to afford an electric typewriter sophisticated enough to print in his invented languages. In a 1972 letter to his son Michael, he mentioned that he might buy a then-new gadget, a telephone answering machine, to screen unwanted calls. With that attitude, it is easy to believe he would have used a personal computer to lighten the tedious labor of editing and typing. Indeed, one of the faults of the Elves, he said, was that they had become "embalmers" who wanted Middle-earth to be without change or history. Gondor, he added, had a similar fault. The only thing it venerated were the tombs of its ancestors. In short, Tolkien seems to have had no problem with technology when it brought genuinely useful, human-centered improvement.

Technologies Tolkien Loathed

That said, there were technologies Tolkien loathed, and chief among them were the gasoline engine and airplane. The reasons for his dislike for the things powered by gasoline are easily explained. They were not only noisy and polluting, keeping him awake at night, the roadways they required ruined old cities like Oxford and his beloved countryside.

Explaining his dislike for airplanes requires us to step back into the late 1930s, when the story of the Ring was coming together. At that time, airplanes seemed to have few benefits. For the rich, air travel was expensive, uncomfortable and dangerous. For the rest, airplanes meant little more than the terror bombing of cities—as England would soon discover. Humanitarian uses of aircraft to transport food to the hungry and take the injured to medical care were still in the future. For someone like Tolkien, virtually the only benefit an airplane offered lay in the rapid movement of mail. In a 1944 airletter to his son Christopher in South Africa, he conceded that, offering to forgive the "Mordor-gadgets" a portion of their sins, if they would get his letter overseas more quickly.

Tolkien and H. G. Wells

Tolkien also had an intellectual reason for seeing the airplane as a tool of evil. Politically, Tolkien and a contemporary of his, the famous science fiction writer H. G. Wells, could not have been further apart. Tolkien loathed regimentation of all sorts and loved small, closely knit agricultural communities like the Shire, where there is a maximum of friendship and a minimum of bureaucracies and bothersome rules. The existence of the British empire sent him into a rage and even a Great Britain was more than he liked. He preferred to give his loyalty to a little England and let the Irish, Scotch and Welch live as they pleased.

In contrast, for most of his life H. G. Wells labored to promote a radically different vision of the future. He wanted a world state in which a small scientifically trained elite made rules that the many obeyed without question. In his less-known writings, he tried to come up with a plan that would transform that vision into reality. One of his better known schemes involved the brutal use of air power to intimidate the world's reactionary little Shires into obeying his centralized Mordor.

Without knowing what Tolkien was then writing, George Orwell captured the difference between the two in a brilliant 1941 magazine article entitled "Wells, Hitler and the World State." There he wrote:

> If one looks through nearly any books that [Wells] has written in the last forty years one finds the same idea constantly recurring: the supposed antithesis between the man of science who is working towards a planned World State and the reactionary who is trying to restore a disorderly past. In novels, utopias, essays, films, pamphlets, the antithesis crops up, always more or less the same. On the one side science, order, progress, internationalism, aeroplanes, steel, concrete, hygiene; on the other side war, nationalism, religion, monarchy, peasants, Greek professors, poets, horses.

Tolkien Compared to George Orwell and Aldous Huxley

Orwell's anti-utopian novel, *1984,* gives us a modern version of what life might have been like under Sauron. The heavily policed drabness and ugliness of England in his fictious year of 1984 is also similar to what the Shire briefly became under Saruman.

Just as interesting is a parallel to another major anti-utopia novel, Aldous Huxley's *Brave New World.* It offers a vision of the future that is far more disturbing than Orwell's. It bears some similarity—although not as great—to "The New Shadow," a sequel to *The Lord of the Rings* that Tolkien began but abandoned in disgust. Set a hundred years after the death of Aragorn in a era when people faced no real threats to their freedom, some had become decadent, dissatisfied with good and worshiping evil fantasies. Substitute sex and violent entertainment for Tolkien's occult religion and Orc-imitating, and you have Huxley's novel.

Letters, No. 53. In this area, Tolkien's political views resemble those of G. K. Chesterton, another popular Catholic writer and critic of H. G. Wells. Some have called Chesterton the father of the "small is beautiful" movement.

For Wells' air dictatorship, see his 1933 *The Shape of Things to Come* (also a 1936 film directed by William Menzies). Wells had a particular loathing for Tolkien's Catholicism, as demonstrated by his 1943 *Crux Ansata.* C. S. Lewis called this world view "Wellsianity." See *C. S. Lewis* (Lesley Walmsley, ed.), 13 and 22.

This article was first published in the August 1941 issue of *Horizon* and republished in George Orwell's *Collected Essays* (London: Secker & Warburg, 1961), 139f. Notice how accurately Orwell described Tolkien's literary world down to its horses, poets and professors of ancient languages.

Orwell's *1984* came out in 1949, modeled on the *hard totalitarianism* of the Nazi and Soviet dictatorships.

Letters, No. 256 and No. 338. Humphrey Carpenter, *J. R. R. Tolkien: A Biography,* 228. Huxley's 1932 novel is more disturbing because its *soft totalitarianism* allows people retain the illusion of freedom, particularly in its attitudes toward sex and mood-altering drugs, making them less likely to rebel.

Tolkien and Technology

Letters, No. 96 for January 30, 1945. There he referred to World War II, then drawing to a close, as the "First War of the Machines," noting that it had killed millions of people and left, "only one thing triumphant: the Machines."

Much like the Controllers in *Brave New World.* Wells wanted to control childbearing. He directed particular attention to reducing the birthrate of black people in Africa. See *The Pivot of Civilization in Historical Perspective,* Ch. 5–6.

Tolkien also placed his vision in the past rather than the future, leading some to label his books "escapist." Few of his more serious readers would agree with that judgment.

In short, Tolkien did not dislike technology as such. But he did fear that, if we are not careful, we could become the servants of our machines rather than their rulers. Put in literary terms, he feared that a Ring would be discovered with the power to shape us to its will, leaving us with the most terrible of choices. We could rule like the Nazgûl, we could become enslaved like the pitiful Gollum, or we could live in misery, hating this new age of repression much like the fearful Hobbits. The alternative to all three is to fight for freedom whatever the cost.

In this, Tolkien was hardly alone. Orwell and Huxley shared similar fears and recognized the dangers as well as benefits of technology. They described worlds dominated by omnipresent television cameras (*1984*), where babies were reduced to parentless commodities manufactured to fixed specifications in bottles (*Brave New World*). Tolkien's hatred of some machines no more makes him a neo-Luddite intent on smashing all machines than they. The depth of his vision about what our society might become for good or evil was every bit as impressive as theirs. That vision also explains why those whose world view resembles Wells, elitist and manipulative, find Tolkien's writings so infuriating.

Most important of all, in Tolkien's writings friendship, courage and loyalty enable freedom to triumph over tyranny. Neither Orwell nor Huxley were able to accomplish that great feat. In their novels freedom, defended only by an odd individual or two, loses its battle with tyranny. That makes Tolkien's achievement all the greater.

14

Preparing for War

March 6 to 9, 1419

Fleeing the Nazgûl to Rohan receives the Red Arrow

Both Tolkien and his friend, C. S. Lewis, served in the trenches of World War I. Some forty years after that war, Lewis remarked that the war with Sauron, "has the very quality of the war my generation knew. It is all here, the endless, unintelligible movement, the sinister quiet of the front when 'everything is now ready,' the flying civilians, the lively, vivid friendships, the background of something like despair and the merry foreground, and such heaven-sent windfalls as a *cache* of tobacco 'salvaged from a ruin.'"

This is from Lewis' review of the last two books in *The Lord of the Rings* as published in *Tide and Time* on October 22, 1955 and republished in Lesley Walmsley's *C. S. Lewis*, 523.

Tuesday, March 6, 1419—Scattering in the Night

Day 166
February 28

In two days the moon will be full, so these nights are brightly lit. Today the moon rises in the east-northeast about 4 p.m. and will set in the west-northwest about 6 a.m. the following day.

Gandalf and Pippin

Day 1 of 4 in Night Ride

Plains of Rohan

- During the night, Gandalf and Pippin ride southeast.
- Pippin questions Gandalf about the *palantír* and the Nazgûl.

The Two Towers, Bk. 3, Ch. 11, "The Palantír." For more about the different *palantíri*, see *Unfinished Tales*, Pt. IV, Ch. III, "The Palantíri."

**The third volume, *The Return of the King* and Book 5, "The War of the Ring,"
now begins, directing attention away from Frodo and Sam.**

Edoras

- At sunrise, Gandalf and Pippin reach Edoras.

Gandalf the Tactician

Here Tolkien displays Gandalf's skill as a military tactician. He has Gandalf tell the Rohirrim to meet in the Harrowdale Valley, rather than at

The Return of the King, Bk. 5, Ch. 1, "Minas Tirith" and Bk. 5, Ch. 3, "The Muster of Rohan."

Edoras as Théoden had ordered. By assembling in the mountains and using as few lights and fires as possible, Rohan conceals its growing strength from the Nazgûl prowling overhead. Remember that Tolkien intends for Sauron's chief weakness to be his inability to imagine that others might choose good over evil. Without evidence otherwise, Sauron will assume Rohan selfishly keeps its calvary at home rather than sending it far away to defend Minas Tirith. Gandalf intends to keep contrary evidence from him.

Edoras

The Return of the King, Bk. 5, Ch. 1, "Minas Tirith" and Bk. 5, Ch. 3, "The Muster of Rohan."

- A Nazgûl frightens Edoras.
- Gandalf and Pippin rest during the day and ride on after dark.

Hobbit Ignorance

The Return of the King was first published in the U.K. on October 20, 1955 (almost a year after the second volume) and in the U.S. on January 5, 1956 (just over 8 months after the second volume).

Carried by Shadowfax, Tolkien has Gandalf and Pippin bound for Minas Tirith, some 450 miles away. After four nights of hard riding, they will arrive about sunrise on Friday, March 9. At this point it makes sense to ask why a Hobbit, who obviously knows little about life outside the Shire, has to ask Gandalf about the dangers ahead. Why didn't Tolkien have Gandalf teach the Hobbits more about the lands they would cross and the enemies they would face? There was more than enough time during their two months at Rivendell for a class on "The World as It Really Is for Hobbits Who Have Been Sheltered Way Too Much." Why is Gandalf so secretive or, more accurately, why did Tolkien make Gandalf so uncommunicative?

Tolkien began writing Book 5 on Tuesday, October 10, 1944. *Letters,* No. 84. Two chapters in Book 4, however, seem to have been incomplete at that time. *Letters,* No. 87.

The reason is much the same as the one that drove Gandalf to ride by night to Minas Tirith. For Tolkien's Wizards, knowledge is power and strength lies in stealth. For much of their history, Gandalf and his colleagues have survived by keeping their schemes to themselves. (For example, the Dwarves and Hobbits in *The Hobbit* seem to know little of Gandalf's larger role.) Saruman carried that to excess, and it played a role in his fall into evil. But even Gandalf says little to friends unless prompted by questions or forced by events.

Fortunately, everything turns out well as Tolkien's Hobbits demonstrate a remarkable ability to learn quickly. By limiting their preparation, Tolkien makes their adaptability and growth even more impressive.

Aragorn, Gimli, Legolas, Merry and the Rohirrim

Near the Fords of Isen to Hornburg

The Return of the King, Bk. 5, Ch. 2, "The Passing of the Grey Company." Théoden's scouting party had 24 horses and 26 people, so even a small force would outnumber it. They meet 32 Rangers.

- After crossing the Fords, they meet Aragorn's Rangers.
- At sunrise, they reach Hornburg and Merry becomes Théoden's squire.
- Aragorn decides to take the Paths of the Dead.

Gifts from Afar

At several points in his tale, Tolkien assigns a critical role to gifts. Here, Elrohir brings advice from Elrond, asking that he consider the Paths of the

Dead, while Halbarad brings a royal banner and encouragement from Arwen. Both advice and banner will prove as important to Aragorn as the gifts of Bilbo and Galadriel are for Frodo and Sam.

Merry with Théoden and the Rohirrim
Day 1 of 4 to Dunharrow for Muster

Hornburg

- In early afternoon, Théoden, Merry and the Rohirrim leave.

Travel Light, Travel Fast

Here is another detail Tolkien handled properly. Though Théoden leaves first, he has Aragorn travel faster. Aragorn's small party rides quickly across the open plains, reaching Dunharrow by sunset the next day. Théoden must take his much larger force though the hills to cloak their size and movement and does not arrive until sunset on their fourth day. Once the darkness out of Mordor descends, that will no longer be necessary. Sauron's scheme to blacken the sky will backfire.

The Return of the King, Bk. 5, Ch. 2, "The Passing of the Grey Company." Théoden describes their upcoming journey to Merry during their lunch just before leaving. The journey to Dunharrow is also briefly described in *The Return of the King,* Bk. 5, Ch. 3, "The Muster of Rohan," near the start of the chapter.

Aragorn, Gimli and Legolas with the Rangers
Day 1 of 2 to Dunharrow for the Paths of Dead

Hornburg

- Secretly, Aragorn uses the *palantír* to force Sauron to act hastily.
- In mid-afternoon, Aragorn and the others leave for Edoras.

The Return of the King, Bk. 5, Ch. 2, "The Passing of the Grey Company" and Bk. 5, Ch. 9, "The Last Debate."

Aragorn's Great Gamble

Tolkien knew that one mark of a great leader is a willingness to take calculated risks. Sauron's forces are rapidly growing. The day before this (March 5), Frodo and Sam saw a large army march in the Black Gate. The day after this (March 7), they will watch Faramir battle another army coming up the road that runs along the west side of Mordor. Though Tolkien rarely provides dates for events, those who read the early chapters of Book 4 (which followed Frodo and Sam) did sense this growing military strength. Now in the early chapters of Book 5, we see Aragorn's response. The situation is already desperate, so further delay will only make matters worse. Sauron must be forced to act before he is fully ready.

The origin of World War II offers a contrast. The leaders of Britain and France thought that appeasing Hitler would buy time to build up their armies. But some historians argue that Hitler benefited more than they did by the delay. Germany's economy had been on a wartime footing since 1935, and the resulting increase in weapons was just taking effect when the war began in September of 1939. Starting later, Britain and France had no time to rearm and had been stronger in relative terms in 1935 than in 1939. Others point out that the delay did make one crucial difference. In the last year before the war the arrival of the Chain Home radar defense system and squadrons of Spitfires provided Britain with a desperately needed counter to the air attack known as the Battle of Britain. Whichever is true, the point it that delay is not always best. Sometimes it is better to fight a war now rather than wait for it to start later. A great leader understands that and has the courage to act despite risks.

Frodo and Sam with Gollum

Day 1 of 5 to Minas Morgul, Day 1 of 8 to Cirith Ungol

North of Ithilien

The Two Towers, Bk. 4, Ch. 4, "Of Herbs and Stewed Rabbits." They are so close to the Shadowy Mountains of Mordor that, although the almost full moon rose in late afternoon, it does not clear the mountains to their east until almost midnight.

- After dark, they hike south on the road to save time.
- Gollum forces the Hobbits to hike until dawn.

Fair Ithilien

Unlike the dismal lands to its north, Tolkien made Ithilien habitable and, in the south, well-forested. However, troops from Mordor drove most of the population out of Ithilien in 1301 (a few remained until 1354), so the land they are about to enter has been deserted for 118 years, far less than that around Weathertop. Since Tolkien has Frodo and Sam come across little evidence of human habitation—no more than an occasional stone wall or a growth of once domesticated plants—we can assume that he saw the region as formerly populated with small homesteads made of wood and deliberately burned by the inhabitants as they left. In this fertile land, the forest would quickly reclaim open fields and gardens.

Day 167
March 1

Wednesday, March 7, 1419—Rabbit Stew

Gandalf and Pippin

Day 2 of 4 in Night Ride, Location Calculated

Resting in Firienwood

The Return of the King, Bk. 5, Ch. 1, "Minas Tirith." Karen Fonstad calculated their rest places for *The Atlas of Middle-earth.*

- At dawn, Gandalf and Pippin rest in Firienwood.
- After dark they ride again for Minas Tirith.

Aragorn, Gimli and Legolas with the Rangers

Day 2 of 2 to Dunharrow for the Paths of Dead

Edoras and Dunharrow

The Return of the King, Bk. 5, Ch. 2, "The Passing of the Grey Company." At one point, Tolkien considered creating a romance between Aragorn and Éowyn that ends when she dies saving Théoden. See *The Treason of Isengard,* Ch. 26, "The King of the Golden Hall." For more on Éowyn see *Letters,* No. 244.

- They rest briefly at Edoras and reach Dunharrow at sunset.
- Éowyn wants to travel with Aragorn, but he refuses.

Dunharrow's Geography

Tolkien located Dunharrow in a steep mountain valley that was a natural site for a fortification. The fact that it was difficult to capture but of little strategic importance made it ideal for non-combatants in time of war. Éowyn has good reason to feel useless here. She will get no taste of battle until the war is long lost. (Gondor apparently uses two mountain valleys, Tumladen and Lossarnach, for similar purposes. See *The Return of the King,* Bk. 5. Ch. 1, "Minas Tirith.")

Merry with Théoden and the Rohirrim

Day 2 of 4 to Dunharrow for Muster

White Mountains

- They travel slowly for long hours on mountain trails.

Muster at Dunharrow

This sort of terrain—mountainous, forested and filled with swift streams that must be crossed—is not the sort calvary typically use. At this point, concealment is more important than speed and the delay matters little. Théoden's already marshalled forces must wait for the rest of Rohan's citizen calvary to get their orders and gather.

Frodo and Sam with Gollum

Day 2 of 5 to Minas Morgul, Day 2 of 8 to Cirith Ungol

Ithilien

- At dawn, they camp near a lake and Sam cooks rabbits for Frodo.
- Hearing sounds, Frodo and Sam hide in a thicket.

Almost Shire-like

For a time that proves all too brief, Tolkien lets his two Hobbits relax as if they were on a camping trip in the Shire. Aside from the two Elflands, Ithilien will be the most idyllic spot the Hobbits visit on their journey. How odd that it stands alongside the wastelands of Mordor? Perhaps Tolkien wanted to demonstrated that evil's power is limited.

Frodo and Sam with Faramir

Ithilien

- Frodo and Sam are taken prisoner by Faramir.
- Faramir's men attack Southron troops coming north to join Sauron.

Tactics Repeated

Tolkien likes to repeat plots with small variations. The Orcs will attack Aragorn's army at this same place on March 21, and the Hobbits will use the same sort of trap at the Battle of Bywater on November 3.

Traveling to Henneth Annûn

- In late afternoon, Faramir questions Frodo.
- Frodo and Sam are taken to Henneth Annûn.

Faramir's Background

According to Tolkien, Faramir simply appeared as he was writing this part of the story. Later Faramir became the younger of the two sons of the Steward of Gondor. Tolkien then inserted complicated family dynamics. Faramir respects his older brother, Boromir, but his father treats him as less able. In questioning Frodo, Faramir comes across as shrewder and more intelligent. Only after he has the information he wants, does he tell Frodo his relationship to Boromir and that eleven days earlier (February

Tolkien provided no narrative for this day. This description is based on allusions near the start of *The Return of the King*, Bk. 5, Ch. 3, "The Muster of Rohan." Rohan's citizen army resembles today's Switzerland and Israel. Properly prepared the latter two armies can mobilize in three days. With less rapid communication and transport, Rohan requires six days.

The Two Towers, Bk. 4, Ch. 4, "Of Herbs and Stewed Rabbits."

Tolkien wrote this section in late April of 1944 and mentioned needing to discover when the moon rises when "nearing full" and how to "stew a rabbit." *Letters*, No. 63. See also No. 64 and 66.

The Two Towers, Bk. 4, Ch. 4, "Of Herbs and Stewed Rabbits." For Tolkien's remarks on Faramir's personality, see *Letters*, No. 244.

The Two Towers, Bk. 4, Ch. 5, "The Window on the West." For Faramir's origin, see *Letters*, No. 66. For more on the relationship of the two brothers, see *The Return of the King*, Bk. 6, Ap. A, Sec. 1, iv, under the subheading "The Stewards." Tolkien was writing this in mid-May, 1944. *Letters*, No. 67.

26) he heard Boromir's horn blowing. Three nights after that, he saw Boromir's body drift by in a boat (February 29).

Henneth Annûn, Ithilien

The Two Towers, Bk. 4, Ch. 5, "The Window on the West."

- Blindfolded, the Hobbits are taken to a cave behind a waterfall.
- Faramir questions them again and finds out about the Ring.

Henneth Annûn's History

Henneth Annûn or "Window of the Sunset," is named after the beautiful views of the setting sun visible through the waterfall.

Tolkien has a historical background for almost everything. A little over century earlier, Orc attacks made it difficult for Gondor to retain control of Ithilien. In response, they built secret refugees to enable them to wage guerilla warfare. Henneth Annûn (built in 1301) is the most valuable of those refugees, and that is why Faramir must keep its location secret.

Galadriel and Treebeard with the Ents

Fangorn Forest

The War of the Ring, Pt. 3, Ch. VIII, "The Story Foreseen from Forannest."

- Galadriel sends Treebeard a warning that Sauron will attack Lórien.

Galadriel's Ability to Anticipate

Though little mentioned, Galadriel is one of Tolkien's most powerful characters. On February 15, she told Frodo she could anticipate Sauron's schemes when they concerned Elves. That is what has happened here. Treebeard will battle Sauron's forces on March 11. Like Saruman, it is unlikely that Sauron took into account the military prowess of Ents when he made his plans. Unfortunately, Tolkien says little about this military campaign.

Thursday, March 8, 1419—Paths of the Dead

Day 168
March 2

In 1942 the moon turned full twenty minutes after midnight (Tolkien's UK time) on the March 9. Slight differences may have caused Tolkien's calendar to date it to March 8, as we assume here to avoid confusing readers.

Today Tolkien assumed the moon became full. It rises in the west about 6 p.m. and sets in the east a little before 8 a.m. The muster of Rohan will be completed at Edoras in two days.

Gandalf and Pippin

Day 3 of 4 in Night Ride, Location Calculated

Resting near Erelas Beacon

The Return of the King, Bk. 5, Ch. 1, "Minas Tirith." Karen Fonstad calculated this rest place in *The Atlas of Middle-earth*. On his earlier ride to the Shire, Shadowfax averaged 100 miles a day over a rougher route.

- At dawn, Gandalf and Pippin rest near the Erelas Beacon
- After dark they ride for Minas Tirith and see Gondor's signal fires.

The Ride to Minas Tirith

During these four nights, Gandalf and Pippin average 120 miles per night. It is an impressive feat for Shadowfax and perhaps his finest hour.

Aragorn, Gimli and Legolas with Rangers and the Dead

Day 1 of 8 in Military Campaign

To the Paths of the Dead and the Stone of Erech

- Just before sunrise, Aragorn and the others leave Dunharrow.
- They enter the Paths of the Dead and Aragorn summons the dead.
- Just before midnight they reach the Stone of Erech.

The Pagan Dead

This section is perhaps the furthest that Tolkien moved from his Catholic beliefs to embrace pagan ideas about death. The dead—who really are dead people and not bodies animated by evil spirits or illusions manufactured by Sauron—anticipated Aragorn's arrival and appear to have traveled to the Paths of the Dead for this meeting during the dark of the moon about February 23. Since then they have been waiting for Aragorn to come and free them from their ancient pagan curse.

The Return of the King, Bk. 5, Ch. 2, "The Passing of the Grey Company." For more about this terrifying journey see *The War of the Ring*, Pt. 3, Ch. XII, "The Last Debate." Gimli and Legolas recount their experience in *The Return of the King*, Bk. 5, Ch. 9, "The Last Debate."

Merry with Théoden and the Rohirrim

Day 3 of 4 to Dunharrow for Muster, Location Uncertain

White Mountains

- They travel slowly but long on mountain trails.

Tolkien provided no narrative for this day. For a summary, see the start of "The Muster of Rohan" in *The Return of the King*, Bk. 5, Ch. 3.

Frodo, Sam and Faramir with Gollum

Day 3 of 5 to Minas Morgul, Day 3 of 8 to Cirith Ungol

Henneth Annûn and nearby

- As the moon sets, Faramir awakens Frodo and shows him Gollum.
- Frodo captures Gollum to save his life.
- Faramir and the Hobbits (with Gollum) separate in the woods.

The Two Towers, Bk. 4, Ch. 6, "The Forbidden Pool."

The Two Towers, Bk. 4, Ch. 7, "Journey to the Crossroads." Faramir is bound for Minas Tirith via Cair Andros, where he will get horses.

Faramir's Simple Gifts

Gifts, great and small, play a major role in Tolkien's tale. Some people provide costly or powerful gifts. But Faramir's provision of simple but wholesome traveling food plays a critical role. On February 30, Sam had calculated that their food would run out about March 21. Faramir has enough additional food placed in their packs to get the Hobbits to Mount Doom on March 25.

Tolkien made only one use of the two hiking staffs from Faramir. Sam breaks his fighting Gollum, when he was attacked just after leaving Shelob's tunnel. Thinking Frodo is dead, he leaves his master's staff beside him when he takes on the mission alone. Frodo's hiking staff was probably cast aside by Orcs, when they took his unconscious body away.

Frodo and Sam with Gollum

Traveling to the Morgul-road

- During the day, the three travel south through the forest.
- That night they sleep under a tree.

The Two Towers, Bk. 4, Ch. 7, "Journey to the Crossroads."

Chronological Problems

For a description of the chronological problems Tolkien faced as he wrote and rewrote this part of the story see *The War of the Ring*, Pt. 3, Ch. II, "Book Five Begun and Abandoned" (at the very end of the chapter) and the notes for Pt. 3, Ch. 5, "Many Roads Lead Eastward (2)."

Denethor and Minas Tirith

Minas Tirith

- In the evening, news arrives of an Umbar fleet attacking in the south.
- Denethor sends errand-riders to Rohan bearing the Red Arrow.
- Denethor orders signal fires requesting aid from Rohan.

The Corsairs of Umbar

The Corsairs of Umbar were a pirate-state that battled with Gondor for control of the seas through most of the Third Age. Their last great battle took place 261 years earlier in 1158 at the time of the Long Winter.

Tolkien had Sauron time the arrival of the Umbar fleet, so it reaches Gondor's southern province of Lebennin just before Sauron's army marches from Minas Morgul on March 10. Since soldiers coming from Pelargir have to come only a third as far as those coming from Rohan, Lebennin is a more useful ally at the start of a war. But with Lebennin under attack, no aid could go to Minas Tirith.

Lebennin's inability to aid Minas Tirith makes assistance from Rohan that much more critical and causes the errand-riders to leave for Rohan and the signal fires on mountain tops to be lit. The errand-riders would leave first, probably in early evening just after the news arrives. The signal fires would have to wait for sufficient darkness. On this night the sun sets about 7:30 p.m. so astronomical twilight, when an already set sun is no longer obscuring the stars, comes about 9:30. It is likely that the signal fires were lit shortly after 9:30 and seen then by Gandalf and Pippin.

They cover 21 miles today. Tolkien read this chapter to C. S. Lewis at lunch on Monday, May 15, 1944. *Letters*, No. 69. (He seems to have begun this letter the day before.)

Beregond tells Pippin this in *The Return of the King*, Bk. 5, Ch. 1, "Minas Tirith."

Umbar is located over three hundred miles to the south of Pelagir.

Even Lossernach, between Lebennin and Gondor, feels the threat and sends only ten percent of their men, who arrive on the afternoon of March 9. Aragorn's military campaign from the Paths of the Dead to Pelargir will free Lebennin to aid Gondor. In his conversation with Gimli and Legolas before leaving Hornburg on March 6, Aragorn talked of using his *palantír* to see this threat coming from the south. See *The Return of the King*, Bk. 5, Ch. 2, "The Passing of the Grey Company."

Day 169
March 3

Friday, March 9, 1419—Gandalf at Minas Tirith

Gandalf and Pippin with Denethor II

Day 4 of 4 in Night Ride

Through Anórien to Minas Tirith

- During the night, Gandalf and Pippin ride through Anórien.
- At sunrise they reach Minas Tirith.

Importance of Minas Tirith

Gandalf's concern for the fortifications is justified. Minas Tirith is the free people's strongest city. If it cannot stand against Sauron, no city can. While the War of the Ring can only be won if the Ring is destroyed, the war can be lost at Minas Tirith.

The Return of the King, Bk. 5, Ch. 1, "Minas Tirith." Tolkien placed Minas Tirith at "about the latitude of Florence" in Italy. *Letters*, No. 294.

Minas Tirith

- Pippin tells Denethor of Boromir's death and offers to serve Gondor.
- In late evening, Gandalf warns Pippin the next day will be dark.

The Return of the King, Bk. 5, Ch. 1, "Minas Tirith."

Denethor v. Gandalf

In this first meeting, Tolkien creates tension between Denethor and Gandalf that will nearly lead to disaster during the battle for Minas Tirith. Applying this conflict in the general way that Tolkien approved, we can see Denethor, talented as he is, as the sort of leader whose authority exceeds his judgment. He resents those more capable than he, pursues his own (devious) sources of information, and refuses to accept advice.

For the chronological problems linking Pippin's view of the setting moon shortly before he and Gandalf reach Minas Tirith with a similar sighting by Frodo, see "Shared Sunset, Unshared Moonset" under March 10, 1419.

Merry with Théoden and the Rohirrim

Day 4 of 4 to Dunharrow for Muster

Dunharrow

- Just after sunset, Merry and Théoden reach Dunharrow.
- A grieving Éowyn tells them Aragorn left for the Paths of the Dead.
- In the evening they discuss war plans.
- Hirgon, a Gondor errand-rider arrives, asking for help.

The Return of the King, Bk. 5, Ch. 3, "The Muster of Rohan."

Riders Bearing the Red Arrow

There are hints in the narrative of events that Tolkien seems to have thought about but not worked in detail into the narrative. At one point during the early morning hours of March 9, Shadowfax slows to a walk as three riders rush by at great speed. They were almost certainly Gondor's errand-riders bearing the Red Arrow to Rohan. The number of riders making the entire trip in not given. Only one, Hirgon, is mentioned speaking to Théoden at Dunharrow and two are mentioned traveling with Rohirrim when they leave for Edoras the next morning. Finally, two are found dead near Minas Tirith on March 15. It is possible, given the importance of the message, that Gondor sent out three riders. One rider may have been a spare who dropped out.

One draft of *The Lord of the Rings* referred to these three men as post riders bound for Edoras. See *The War of the Ring,* Pt. 3, Ch. II, "Book Five Begun and Abandoned." The second rider's presence at Dunharrow is mentioned in *The Return of the King,* Bk. 5, Ch. 3, "The Muster of Rohan."

Dunharrow

- Théoden promises to reach Minas Tirith with 6,000 men in a week.
- Hirgon will rest the night and return the next morning.

The Return of the King, Bk. 5, Ch. 3, "The Muster of Rohan."

Rohan's Surprise

With his eye for detail, Tolkien did not expect readers to accept that Rohan could simply ride to Minas Tirith without Sauron receiving a warning. He created a chain of events to make that surprise plausible.

The orders that Gandalf gave on March 6 for the gathering Rohirrim to conceal themselves in the Harrowdale Valley provide the key to the surprise. No Nazgûl has been seen in the valley, and even if one had flown over secretly during the night, it is unlikely, with everything darkened and few fires lit, that it saw anything suspicious. This is one reason Sauron will leave unguarded the northern flank of his forces besieging Minas

"In wartime, truth is so precious that she should always be attended by a bodyguard of lies." Winston Churchill, 1943.

Tirith, and why the Rohirrim will create such a surprise when they arrive in six days. Also, the aid of the Wild Men and the forgotten road allow Rohan bypass Sauron's outlying forces. In all this Tolkien is suggesting that great outcomes often hinge on simple but wise decisions.

Aragorn, Gimli and Legolas with Rangers and the Dead

Day 2 of 8 in Military Campaign

Through Lamedon to Calembel

The Return of the King, Bk. 5, Ch. 2, "The Passing of the Grey Company" and *The Return of the King*, Bk. 5, Ch. 9, "The Last Debate." Karen Fonstad calculated Aragorn's travel distances for *The Atlas of Middle-earth*. I am indebted to her for these figures and for additional details about Aragorn's military campaign. For more information, see her "Pathway Table" and the map on pages 88–89.

- At dawn they leave the Stone of Erech with the Dead following.
- That evening they stop at Calembel.

Calembel

Calembel is a Gondor city at a ford on the River Ciril and the leading town for Lamedon, a Gondor province. On this day they cover about 110 miles. The Dead apparently do not tire. As Legolas notes in "The Last Debate," this is the only day of their campaign that was made in the light. During the preceding day they were in a cave and dark ravine. On the following day the darkness out of Gondor descends. It was apparently on this day, while passing through upper Lamedon, that the Dead tried to race ahead, perhaps in their eagerness to be free of their curse, and were forced back by Aragorn.

Frodo and Sam with Gollum

Day 4 of 5 to Minas Morgul, Day 4 of 8 to Cirith Ungol

To the Morgul-road

The Two Towers, Bk. 4, Ch. 7, "Journey to the Cross-roads."

- They begin early and hike through the woods.
- At dark they reach the valley with the road to Cirith Ungol.
- Staying in the woods, they travel east and sleep in an oak tree.

A Strange Contrast

For more on this topic, see "Tolkien's Natural World" at the end of Chapter 8.

Tolkien has kept a close link between unpleasant environments and danger. Haunted forests, insects, darkness, damp or cold have gone hand-in-hand with threats from Black Riders or Orcs. But for a few days the Hobbits cross a pleasant landscape that still defies Sauron. Unfortunately, even here there are hints of evil. While the trees, bushes and flowers remain oblivious to Sauron, animal life is strangely absent. Tolkien may want us to assume they have fled the growing evil.

Faramir

Day 2 of 3 to Minas Tirith

Cair Andros on the Anduin River

The Return of the King, Bk. 5, Ch. 4, "The Siege on Gondor."

- Faramir sends most of his men to reinforce Osgiliath.
- At dark he and three others leave on horseback for Minas Tirith.

Gondor's Pony Express

In Tolkien's time-scheme, errand-riders carrying the symbolic Red Arrow were apparently dispatched immediately after news arrived of the approach of the Umbar fleet on the evening of March 8. The riders appear to have crossed paths with Gandalf and Pippin that same night. They rode on for Rohan, arriving at Dunharrow late in the evening of March 9.

Is this possible? Could a message be taken from Minas Tirith to Dunharrow in such a short time? Gandalf on Shadowfax takes three full nights of travel to reach Minas Tirith and the Rohirrim will take just over five days. Yet the errand-rider bearing the Red Arrow reaches Théoden in 30 hours at most. The answer lies in the relay stations that Tolkien said were set up to provide fresh horses to messengers from Gondor to Rohan. Fresh horses ridden hard for short distances can travel much faster than horses that must travel hundreds of miles and arrive ready for battle.

America's Pony Express provides a good example of what such a system can do. It operated only briefly, from April 3, 1860 until a telegraph line reached the west coast of the United States in October of 1861, but it covered a far greater distance (2,000 miles from St. Joseph, Missouri to Sacramento, California), and it crossed two major mountain ranges. With some 160 relay stations, a new horse was provided every 10 to 15 miles and a new rider every 75 to 100 miles. In summer, letters typically took 10 days and in winter they took from 12 to 16 days. The most rapid delivery came when President Lincoln's First Inaugural Address reached California in 7 days and 17 hours (185 hours), traveling with an average speed of 10.8 miles per hour.

If we assume some 400 miles from Minas Tirith to Dunharrow and 30 hours continuous riding across grassy plains, then the average speed of Gondor's errand-rider is not much faster, 13.3 miles per hour, and there were no mountain ranges to cross. Even the fact that one rider, Hirgon, seems to have ridden the entire distance is reasonable. One Pony Express rider, Bob Haslam, rode for a grueling 370 miles. So the errand-rider system that Tolkien created is certainly possible.

Faramir describes the alliance between Gondor and Rohan in *The Two Towers,* Bk. 4, Ch. 5, "The Window on the West."

Assuming twelve hours of riding a day, on Shadowfax Gandalf averages a little over 8 miles per hour in his long ride to the Shire over rough roads in September 1418 and about 10 miles per hour to Minas Tirith in early March of 1419. Shadowfax's ability seems to lie in great endurance rather than sheer speed.

More than Chance

From what seems to be a chance meeting between Wizard and Dwarf in 1341 Bree to the arrival at the last possible moment of Gondor's calvary at Minas Tirith in 1419 after the long ride that begins in this chapter, the timing of events in Tolkien's story point to an often recurring theme. In them there is a sense that Someone is working out of sight to achieve much larger ends than any of the participants realize.

Tolkien acknowledged that in a 1956 letter. Behind what we see in the story, he said, is a complex and "monotheistic" way of looking at the

Valar may be from the *vardir* of Norse mythology, where they were gods who protect the world. See Lin Carter. *Tolkien: A Look Behind The Lord of the Rings,* 178.

Letters, No. 181.

world. The One (or God) is indeed remote and reachable only through intermediaries called the Valar. But that does not mean the One has no direct role in this world. Seen through eyes of history, the One has reserved the right to bring the "finger of God into the story."

This means that the future of Middle-earth is not rigidly determined by its past. When the One (God) intrudes—even in ways that at the time seem small—later events are shaped in directions that no one can predict. That is precisely what happens at the beginning of the tale with Bilbo's discovery of the Ring in *The Hobbit*. It continues up to the very end when Frodo's repeated kindness to an undeserving Gollum brings the mission to destroy the Ring to success in a most unexpected way. Small events carefully guided and timed can have large impacts on history.

C. S. Lewis described something similar when he wrote that in the Bible, all of human history "narrows and narrows, until it comes down at last to a little point, small as the point of a spear, a Jewish girl at her prayers." See "The Grand Miracle" in *C. S. Lewis* (Lesley Walmsley, ed.), 7.

Tolkien's Writing Interrupted

Judging by correspondence published in *The Letters of J. R. R. Tolkien*, during 1943 wartime responsibilities kept Tolkien from writing in what he then called his "Hobbit." In a December 7, 1942 letter to his publisher, he mentions the heavy demands on his time, but said that he was nearing the end of Book 3 (Ch. 9, "Flotsam and Jetsam"). He promised to complete in the entire tale in 1943 and said that would require only about six more chapters, although it took another 31. There is, however, no mention of any chapters being completed in his published 1943 correspondence. Instead, over a year later in an April 3, 1944 letter to son Christopher Tolkien in South Africa, he mentions having "begun to nibble at Hobbit again," picking up "the adventures of Frodo and Sam" at the start of Book 4. Most likely, he completed the last two chapters of Book 3 in late 1942 or early 1943 and was too burdened with other demands to begin Book 4 until the spring of 1944. At that time, he began to write rapidly. Between early April and late May, he completed all ten chapters of Book 4 (some 136 pages), noting proudly in a May 31, 1944 letter that he had read the last two chapters to C. S. Lewis on May 29. Lewis, perhaps glad to see his friend writing again, approved of them with "unusual fervour."

Letter to Publisher: *Letters*, No. 47. To Christopher: No. 58. Reading to Lewis: No. 72. Tolkien also mentions his heavy work load or long hours of labor during this period in No. 59, 60, 61, 62, 63, 64, 67, 70, 71 and 73. In No. 69, Tolkien said that he was finding his "moons in the critical days between Frodo's flight and the present situation (arrival at Minas Morgul) were doing impossible things, rising in one part of the country and setting simultaneously in another." Unfortunately, he does not seem to have caught all the problems. That time period, February 26 to March 10, 1419, includes two of the three lunar problems mentioned in Chapter 1, "Dating and Chronology," and in the commentary for March 8, 10 and 24. For his other chronological difficulties during this time, see "Tolkien's Chronology in Shelob's Lair" at the end of Chapter 15.

There are, however, hints in his May 31 letter, that he was pushing himself unusually hard. ("By sitting up all hours, I managed it.") That may explain why a disproportionate share of the chronological difficulties in the entire tale come in Book 4, and particularly in its troublesome last two chapters: "Shelob's Lair" and "The Choices of Master Samwise." We take up their chronological difficulties in the next chapter.

Letters, No. 78 for August 12, 1944 and No. 84 for October 12, 1944. Note, however, that the last two chapters in Book 4 remained, *Letters*, No. 87.

This push to write would not last. In August Tolkien was lamenting to his son Christopher that he was, "absolutely dry of any inspiration for the Ring and am back where I was in the Spring with all the inertia to overcome again." Two months later in October, he began Book 5.

15

Darkness and War

March 10 to 15, 1419

Dawnless Day to victory at Minas Tirith

W. H. Auden captured one of the most important ideas in *The Lord of the Rings* when he wrote, "Evil, that is, has every advantage but one—it is inferior in imagination. Good can imagine the possibility of becoming evil—hence the refusal of Gandalf and Aragorn to use the Ring—but Evil—defiantly chosen, can no longer imagine anything but itself."

At no point in Tolkien's tale is that idea more critical than at this time. Sauron's imagination will fail on two counts. He fails to imagine that Rohan would value loyalty to Gondor above its own safety, and thus does not anticipate the ride of the Rohirrim. He also fails to imagine that anyone possessing the Ring would choose to enter Mordor to destroy it.

W. H. Auden, "At the End of the Quest, Victory" in *The Tolkien Treasury* ed. Alida Becker (Philadelphia: Running Press, 2000), 48. This book has some excellent articles on Tolkien.

Saturday, March 10, 1419—Darkness Begins

Day 170
March 4

By Tolkien's reckoning, the moon is two days past full today.

Day 1 of 6 with Darkness

Gandalf and Pippin with Faramir

Minas Tirith

- Pippin becomes Denethor's squire and learns his duties.
- Gandalf rescues Faramir and his men from five Nazgûl.
- Faramir describes meeting Frodo and Sam.

The Return of the King, Bk. 5, Ch. 4, "The Siege of Gondor."

Line of Stewards

The long line of Stewards reaching to Denethor II replaced Gondor's kings when Eärnur, a king who loved war more than marriage, died childless in 450, after foolishly accepting a challenge to single combat by the Lord of the Nazgûl. Denethor is the twenty-sixth in the line of Stewards, so it is not surprising that he resents Aragorn as a usurper.

The Return of the King, Bk. 6, Ap. A, I, (iv), Gondor and the Heirs of Anárion."

Merry with Théoden and the Rohirrim

Day 1 of 6 in the Calvary Ride to Minas Tirith

Dunharrow, Edoras and beyond

The Return of the King, Bk. 5, Ch. 3, "The Muster of Rohan." On horseback, Minas Tirith, is some 400 miles away.

- Théoden and the Rohirrim leave for Minas Tirith.
- At noon they reach Edoras, eat quickly and depart.
- Merry secretly rides with a knight named Dernhelm.
- That night they camp thirty-six miles from Edoras.

Nazgûl Spies

Tolkien seems to have imagined Sauron's darkness as a sort of twilight. Théoden's horsemen could see well enough that traveling by day was preferable to traveling at night (even with the also darkened moon just past full). But the darkness still provided enough cover that their movements could not be easily spotted by Nazgûl spies.

Here Tolkien illustrates the importance of intelligence gathering in war. When Sauron's Nazgûl saw no evidence the Rohirrim were preparing to ride south, Sauron committed them to the battle for Minas Tirith (note the Nazgûl attack on Faramir on March 13) rather than using them to watch his northern flanks more closely. Sauron also seems to have assumed his allies in the south will be victorious. There too, defeat will come because he lacks intelligence of Aragorn's journey through the Paths of the Dead, something that should have been revealed by the enormous turmoil the Dead created in their wake. In war, Tolkien is saying, knowledge of one's foe often makes the difference between victory and defeat.

Aragorn, Gimli and Legolas with Rangers and the Dead

Day 3 of 8 in Military Campaign

Ringló River

The Return of the King, Bk. 5, Ch. 2, "The Passing of the Grey Company" and Bk. 5, Ch. 9, "The Last Debate." Today they travel 90 miles. Downstream from Calembel, the Ciril joins the Ringló river (a tributary of the Morthond), whose name means "cold flood," probably a reference to icy-cold waters fed by melting snow.

- They rest the night in Calembel on the River Ciril.
- By day, they cross the Ringló River in southern Gondor.

Aragorn's Grand Sweep and Sauron's Darkness

Later, Legolas told Merry and Pippin that he believed the Dead following them gained power because of the darkness that arrives today. Again Tolkien is pointing out that Sauron's darkness failed.

Frodo and Sam with Gollum

Day 5 of 5 to Minas Morgul, Day 5 of 8 to Cirith Ungol

To the Cross-roads

The Two Towers, Bk. 4, Ch. 7, "Journey to the Cross-roads." At this time of year, the sun sets about 6:30.

- Just after midnight, they set out.
- Frodo and Sam rest while Gollum disappears.
- Gollum returns, and they reach the Cross-roads at sunset.

Minas Morgul

The Two Towers, Bk. 4, Ch. 8, "The Stairs of Cirith Ungol."

- Gollum leads them east along the road to Minas Morgul.
- At Minas Morgul they watch an army march out.

Shared Sunset, Unshared Moonset

For Merry, this sunset comes at the very end of "The Muster of Rohan" in *The Return of the King*, Bk. 5, Ch. 3. The moonset is near the start of *The Return of the King*, Bk. 5, Ch. 1, "Minas Tirith."

Perhaps to show that the separated Hobbits still live in the same world, on March 10 Tolkien has Pippin (in Minas Tirith) along with Frodo and Sam (at the Cross-roads) catch the same brief but hopeful glimpse of a sunset. For some reason, Tolkien did not have the last of the Hobbits, Merry, share that experience. Hidden beneath the cloak of Dernhelm, Merry rides only into growing darkness as the sun sets on March 10.

The day before, just before dawn on March 9, they appear to share another common experience. Riding with Gandalf for Minas Tirith, Pippin observed a setting of the moon that Tolkien links to Frodo. Unfortunately, Frodo's narrative for Frodo and Sam on that day contains no mention of the moon and the two Hobbits appear to have been aroused by Gollum at sunrise, after the moon had set. Tolkien may have confused March 9 with March 8, when Frodo is awakened as the moon sets to save Gollum from Faramir's guards. We know nothing of what Merry, riding with the Rohirrim, is doing as the moon sets in the early morning hours of March 8.

For more on Tolkien's difficulties with the moon in this section, see "Tolkien's Writing Interrupted" at the end of Chapter 14.

Frodo's March 8 moonset is at the start of *The Two Towers*, Bk. 4, Ch. 6, "The Forbidden Pool." The March 9 sunrise, with no moon mentioned, is a little over halfway through that same chapter. Pippin's setting moon of March 9 is near the start of *The Return of the King*, Bk. 5, Ch. 1, "Minas Tirith."

Sunday, March 11, 1419—On the Stairs

Day 171
March 5

Day 2 of 6 with Darkness

Faramir and Gandalf

Minas Tirith and Osgiliath

- Denethor forces Faramir to defend the fords at Osgiliath.
- That night a messenger warns that Sauron's forces approach Osgiliath.

A Vindicative Father

Though their personalities differ greatly, almost all the characters Tolkien created who are not allied with Saruman or Sauron have virtues that make them appealing. (Even the gruff and materialistic Dwarves show an impressive loyalty to Bilbo at the Council of Elrond.) Denethor seems to be an exception. Here he almost forces his one remaining son to die in battle, and his 'repentance' from that deed only leads him further into evil, as he tries to kill both his son and himself.

The Return of the King, Bk. 5, Ch. 4, "The Siege of Gondor." With their numbers increased by additional troops coming from the south, this is the same Sauron army that Frodo, Sam and Gollum watched leave Minas Morgul the night before. With its great size, it moves slowly. Sauron believes he has little to fear.

Merry with Théoden and the Rohirrim

Day 2 of 6 in the Calvary Ride to Minas Tirith, Location Calculated

To Firienwood

- The riders may have rested the night in Firienwood.

Calculating the Ride of the Rohirrim

Tolkien left most of the ride of the Rohirrim shrouded in mystery. No text records how far they ride this day or where they rest for the night. Karen Wynn Fonstad estimates that they covered 80 miles and rested in Firienwood, which is near Halifirien, the seventh and last of the beacon hills linking Gondor with Rohan. Firienwood stands on the border between Gondor and Rohan. In draft versions, Tolkien gave other rest stops, but the story changed so greatly that they mean little.

For a summary see *The Return of the King*, Bk. 5, Ch. 3, "The Muster of Rohan."

These calculations of a resting place are from Fonstad's *The Atlas of Middle-earth*, "Pathways." For Tolkien's drafts, see *The War of the Ring*, Pt. 3, Ch. VII, "The Ride of the Rohirrim."

Aragorn, Gimli and Legolas with Rangers and the Dead

Day 4 of 8 in the Military Campaign

The Return of the King, Bk. 5, Ch. 9, "The Last Debate." Despite the battle, they cover 70 miles today.

In *The Return of the King,* Bk. 5, Ch. 9, "The Last Debate" Legolas calls this their third day. It is the third day since they left Erech, but the fourth day of their campaign. For more details, see "Pathways Table" in Karen Fonstad's *The Atlas of Middle-earth.*

The Two Towers, Bk. 4, Ch. 8, "The Stairs of Cirith Ungol." Gollum has slipped away to see Shelob. See *The Return of the King,* Bk. 6, Ap. B, "The Tale of Years" and *The Two Towers,* Bk. 4, Ch. 10, "The Choices of Master Samwise." Tolkien was writing this in October, 1944 and thought he could complete his tale in five books rather than six. *Letters,* No. 87.

The Return of the King, Bk. 6, Ap. B, "The Tale of Years," *The War of the Ring,* Pt. 3, Ch. VIII, "The Story Foreseen from Forannest."

To Linhir and Eastward

- They reach Linhir and battle for the fords over the Gilrain.
- They drive their foes ahead of them and rest briefly in the evening.

Sauron's Two-Front War

Keep in mind a military strategy Tolkien left unstated. Sauron has forced Gondor and its allies into a two-front war. Troops that might have come north to assist Minas Tirith must defend their homes in the south. Aragorn is freeing those allies to come to the aid of Minas Tirith and transforming a two-front war into a single climatic battle.

Frodo and Sam with Gollum—Climbing the Stairs

Day 6 of 8 to Cirith Ungol

Stairs of Cirith Ungol

- They climb the steep Straight Stair.
- They climb the Winding Stair, reaching the top about sunrise.
- The Hobbits sleep into the next day, while Gollum disappears.

Morning or Not?

Here we assume that the red eastern light the Hobbits see is the rising sun of March 11, although Tolkien leaves its meaning ambiguous. It could be the eruption of Mount Doom that is darkening the skies.

Celeborn and Galadriel—Lórien Attacked

Lórien and Rohan

- Lórien is attacked for the first time by the forces of Sauron.

Unnarrated Battles and Ents

Some events in the War of the Ring are only briefly described. Tolkien had Sauron's forces come out of Dol Guldur in Mirkwood (about a hundred miles east of Lórien). Some of those forces go around Lórien to attack Rohan from the north. On this day and the next, they are defeated by the Ents (who left Fangorn on March 7). According to manuscripts quoted in *The War of the Ring,* the Ents (joined by Elves from Lórien) then drove Sauron's forces back across the Anduin, above Emyn Muil and down into Dagorlad. They are approaching Marannon at the same time as Aragorn's troops (March 24–25) and presumably join forces with them, although nothing is said about that in main narrative. The eagles, who clearly were in the battle, could have served as messengers, coordinating the arrival of the two forces from different directions, so they arrive at the same time, increasing the sense of threat that Sauron feels.

The critical role Ents play in this war is little noted. Without them guarding Rohan to the north, Théoden would not have been able to send as many men to the aid of Minas Tirith, and the closely fought battle there might have ended in defeat. Wars are like that. Much praised victories often result from sacrifices by those who get no praise.

Monday, March 12, 1419—Shelob Attacks

Day 3 of 6 with Darkness

Gandalf and Pippin with Faramir

Minas Tirith

- Faramir retreats but plans to hold the Causeway Forts.
- Sauron's forces cross the Anduin.
- Gandalf goes to Faramir's aid.

The Return of the King, Bk. 5, Ch. 4, "The Siege of Gondor."

Tolkien, Darkness, Evil and Pain

Today the darkness is at its greatest, perhaps a hint that it will disappear on the sixth day. Tolkien often links darkness to evil and pain. During World War II, he described to his son Christopher the horror he felt over the suffering of that time. He saw the entire world covered by a "dense dark vapour" that concealed it from the view of heaven.

Letters, No. 64. The letter was dated April 30, 1944, about five weeks before the D-Day landings in France. For Tolkien's use of light and dark, see "Black and White in Tolkien" at the end of Chapter 18.

Merry with Théoden and the Rohirrim

Day 3 of 6 in the Calvary Ride to Minas Tirith, Location Calculated

To Min-Rimmon

- At day's end, they may rest at the foot of Min-Rimmon.

Min-Rimmon

Min-Rimmon is the fifth of the seven beacon hills that are used to communicate between Gondor and Rohan. The name means "towering Rimmon," an indication perhaps of its height or steepness.

Tolkien did not give their location for this day. This rest stop is from Fonstad's *The Atlas of Middle-earth* and assumes they cover about 80 miles today.

Aragorn, Gimli and Legolas with Rangers and the Dead

Day 5 of 8 in the Military Campaign

Across the Plains of Lebennin

- Beginning before dawn, they ride across the Plains of Lebennin.
- Facing fierce opposition, they cover 70 miles, riding through the night.

The Return of the King, Bk. 5, Ch. 9, "The Last Debate."

Fighting Reserve

Talented military leaders are careful not to exhaust their men's 'fighting reserve' of strength unless absolutely necessary. Here Tolkien has Aragorn recklessly expend that reserve, having his men fight all day and ride through the night. The risk he takes is great. With their very last reserves of strength, his men will still be able to fight on the 13th, but they absolutely must win that day or suffer near-certain defeat. Sauron's forces will give them no time to rest and recover. In heroic literature, this situation is called "victory or death." With Minas Tirith about to fall, Aragorn has no other choice.

In a speech at Harrow School on October 29, 1941, Winston Churchill said: "Do not let us speak of darker days; let us speak rather of sterner days."

Frodo and Sam with Gollum

Day 7 of 8 to Cirith Ungol

Top of the Stairs of Cirith Ungol

The Two Towers, Bk. 4, Ch. 8, "The Stairs of Cirith Ungol" and Bk. 4, Ch. 10, "The Choices of Master Samwise. Tolkien refers to Gollum's near repentance at this time being blocked by "rough words" from Sam. *Letters,* No. 96.

- Orcs see Gollum visiting Shelob during the night.
- After sunrise, Gollum returns and finds Frodo and Sam asleep.
- Sam awakes and clashes with Gollum.

Chronological Difficulties

According to "The Tale of Years," Gollum returns to the Hobbits on the 11th. But in "The Choices of Master Samwise, the Orcs say that they spotted Gollum visiting Shelob on the 12th. In "The Stairs of Cirith Ungol" Gollum tells Frodo and Sam that they have slept into the next day (the 12th). This chronology follow the dating of the latter two references.

Torech Ungol, Shelob's Lair

The Two Towers, Bk. 4, Ch. 9, "Shelob's Lair" and *The Return of the King,* Bk. 6, Ap. B, "The Tale of Years."

Gollum knew about Sting but not about the Phial, so he could not anticipate their defeat of Shelob. For more on Shelob, see *Letters,* No. 144.

- Gollum leads the Hobbits into the tunnel and disappears.
- Shelob attacks but is driven off by the Phial and Sting.
- The two Hobbits escape out an exit as night falls.

Late Afternoon of Which Day?

When Frodo and Sam emerge from the tunnel, Tolkien does something he rarely does in this section of his narrative. He states clearly that it is late afternoon when they leave and evening when Shelob is driven off the second time. This fits best with late afternoon on the 12th. If the date were the 11th, the rest at the top of the stairs would have been too brief. If it were the 13th, the Hobbits would have spent so long in the tunnel—perhaps thirty hours—that they would have felt a need to rest, sleep, drink and eat. We hear nothing of that from Tolkien.

Cirith Ungol

The Two Towers, Bk. 4, Ch. 9, "Shelob's Lair."

- Shelob attacks Frodo, while Gollum grabs Sam.
- Sam overpowers Gollum and chases him into the tunnel.

Gollum and Shelob

See *The War of the Ring,* Pt. 2, Ch. VIII, "Kirith Ungol." Several spiders would resemble *The Hobbit,* Ch. 8, "Flies and Spiders."

In early drafts, there were several giant spiders in this tunnel. Reducing their number to one allowed Tolkien to create a strange relationship between Gollum and Shelob, both lonely creatures who have spent most of their lives in underground darkness and loathing the light.

Cirith Ungol

The Two Towers, Bk. 4, Ch. 10, "The Choices of Master Samwise." Tolkien writes of laboring over this chapter, with its revised chronology and motivations, in a May 21, 1944 letter. *Letters,* No. 70. He did not complete it until November, over five months later. *Letters,* No. 89 and 91.

- Sam attacks Shelob and drives her away.
- Exhausted and convinced Frodo is dead, Sam blacks out.

Sam's Long Blackout

We assume Sam remained blacked out from a little after sunset on the 12th to near sunset on the 13th. That time seems overly long, but this is one of the few points where we can insert enough time to reconcile the narrative with a reasonable chronology without distorting the narrative even worse.

Tuesday, March 13, 1419—Minas Tirith Besieged

Day 4 of 6 with Darkness

Gandalf, Faramir and Pippin

Minas Tirith

- In mid-morning Gandalf returns with the wounded.
- Faramir is brought back wounded by a dart.
- Denethor goes to a room high in the Tower and returns to his son's side.
- The city is now under siege.

The Return of the King, Bk. 5, Ch. 4, "The Siege of Gondor." Denethor is consulting his *palantír*.

Changing Views of Leadership

Tolkien has the Houses of Healing make a misdiagnosis. They assume Faramir was wounded by a Nazgûl dart. When Aragorn arrives he corrects that, showing more skill than the professionals. In the age Tolkien was describing, people often assumed a 'true king' would be extraordinarily gifted in many areas. Today our standards are far more modest. We don't expect our political leaders to be able to heal the sick, although we do often expect them to work miracles with the economy, a much harder task. Unfortunately, many today don't expect their leaders to keep their own lives in order. With the disciplined Aragorn in mind, Tolkien might ask, "If they cannot govern themselves, how can they govern a country?"

The Return of the King, Bk. 5, Ch. 8, "The Houses of Healing."

Merry with Théoden and the Rohirrim

Day 4 of 6 in the Calvary Ride to Minas Tirith

To Druadan Forest

- This evening they rest inside Druadan Forest.

Druadan Forest

Druadan Forest lies at the foot of Eilenach and is the second of the seven beacon hills that stretch from Gondor to Rohan. It is about sixty miles from Minas Tirith. In peacetime, they could reach Minas Tirith the next day. But in this situation they must find a way around Sauron's forces, so they do not waste most of their military strength far from where it will do the most good, before the gates of Minas Tirith.

We do not know how far Tolkien had them ride today, but their evening camp is from *The Return of the King*, Bk. 5, Ch. 5, "The Ride of the Rohirrim."

Aragorn, Gimli and Legolas with Rangers and the Dead

Day 6 of 8 in the Military Campaign

Pelargir

- They reach Pelargir and defeat Umbar.
- Aragorn tells the Dead their oath is fulfilled.
- In the night, Corsair ships are readied to sail for Minas Tirith.

A Throw of the Dice

Tolkien understood what every great leader knows in his heart—that situations arise where everything must be risked on a single toss of the

The Return of the King, Bk. 5, Ch. 9, "The Last Debate." The initial Corsair attack is in *The Return of the King*, Bk. 5, Ch. 1, "Minas Tirith."

dice. With Minas Tirith under siege, Aragorn does not have the luxury of a long campaign. He must win quickly or all is lost.

That is why he drove his men so unmercifully. By the time they reach Pelargir, they have been riding and fighting for over 30 hours without rest. It is fortunate that at this point Aragorn could unleash the Dead to fight for them. In is also fortunate that traveling up the Anduin by ship allows his men to get much needed rest. They and their hard-ridden horses are in no condition for another long ride.

Rudyard Kipling described what drove Aragorn and his men to push on against frightful odds when he wrote:

> If you can make one heap of all your winnings
> And risk it all on one turn of pitch-and-toss,
> And lose, and start again at your beginnings
> And never breath a word about your loss;
>
> If you can force your heart and nerve and sinew
> To serve your turn long after they are gone,
> And so hold on when there is nothing in you
> Except the Will which says to them: "Hold on!". . . .
> Yours is the Earth and everything that's in it,
> And—which is more—you'll be a Man, my son!

This last day's ride is about 35 miles. Karen Fonstad describes the various wars between Pelargir and Umbar in The Atlas of Middle-earth.

The quote is from Rudyard Kipling's "If." Kipling is referring to the perseverance to begin again after defeat, but the courage to risk all applies equally well to any situation where we cannot know in advance if we will succeed or fail. For another example, think of Frodo and Sam's grim struggle across the blasted plains of Mordor.

Frodo and Sam

Day 8 of 8 to Cirith Ungol

Cirith Ungol

- Sam takes the Ring and walks toward the Cleft of Cirith Ungol.
- Orcs take Frodo's body to their watch-tower.
- Sam discovers from the Orcs that Frodo is drugged but alive.
- Sam charges against the Undergate only to be knocked unconscious.

A Long Unconsciousness

Again we must use unconsciousness to advance the chronology in large steps. Here we assume Sam remained unconscious from the evening of the 13th to perhaps noon on the 14th. Fortunately, no Orc patrols come along.

The Two Towers, Bk. 4, Ch. 9, "Shelob's Lair." Tolkien read this and the following chapter to C. S. Lewis on Monday, May 29, 1944. Lewis responded with "unusual fevour." Letters, No. 72. This was only a little over a week before the D-Day landing at Normandy.

Gondor's Errand-riders

Day 3 of 3 in Return, Date Estimated

Between the Grey Wood and Minas Tirith

- In the evening, two errand-riders are killed fleeing Sauron's forces.

No Message for Minas Tirith

Since Théoden asked one of the riders, Hirgon, not to return until the next morning (March 10) after he rides with them to Edoras, roughly 60 hours passed between when the errand riders leave Dunharrow and when Elfhlem assumes they were killed not far from Minas Tirith. That is twice

Elfhelm estimated this date, probably from the condition of the bodies, in The Return of the King, Bk. 5, Ch. 5, "The Ride of the Rohirrim."

as long as their ride up. Tolkien probably assumed that the ride down would take longer because the relay system was disrupted by the war. Also, the errand-riders spent time trying to break through Sauron's lines, before being forced to flee. Whatever the timing, their message has not arrived. Minas Tirith does not know Rohan is coming.

We might ask why Tolkien did not use signal fires to carry Rohan's response. The reason probably lay in military secrecy. Gondor's need for aid was so obvious that nothing was revealed when their appeal lit up the sky for hundreds of miles. But Rohan's response was less certain and not something that should be broadcast to the enemy. It was better to entrust that message to errand-riders.

Wednesday, March 14, 1419—Escaping the Tower

Day 174
March 8

Day 5 of 6 with Darkness

Gandalf and Pippin—A City Under Siege

Minas Tirith

- Faramir lies in a fever, his father by his side.
- Gandalf takes charge, but few defend the outer wall.

The Return of the King, Bk. 5, Ch. 4, "The Siege of Gondor."

Middle-earth's Great Debt to Gandalf

This day and the next best illustrate the great debt that the free peoples will owe to a Wizard that many had dismissed as little more than a maker of fireworks or bearer of bad news. At this point, the defense of the city—and thus of all Middle-earth—rests almost solely in his hands.

Merry with Théoden and the Rohirrim

Day 5 of 6 in the Calvary Ride to Minas Tirith

Druadan Forest, East Anórien

- Scouts report the road ahead is blocked by Sauron.
- Wild Men will show them a hidden road through the Stonewain Valley.

The Return of the King, Bk. 5, Ch. 5, "The Ride of the Rohirrim."

Stonewain Valley Road Abandoned

Tolkien had a knack for making plausible the details a plot that other (and lazier) writers would leave vague. Why should a shorter road to Minas Tirith be not only abandoned but completely forgotten? Elsewhere, Tolkien noted that this road had been used long before to transport stone from quarries to Minas Tirith. That demanded a road as short, level and hard-surfaced as possible. After the city was built, its value would decline. As Tolkien notes, it ran through a "long, narrow defile." Such a road put travelers at great risk from robbers eager to steal goods far more valuable than wagons heavily loaded with stones. Useful only for stones, the road would soon be abandoned and forgotten. Its entrance and exit might even be deliberately concealed, so travelers would not mistakenly or foolishly use it. Once concealed, it was soon forgotten.

Tolkien's remarks about the road are in *A Tolkien Compass,* 192.

Forgotten road in the Stonewain Valley

The Return of the King, Bk. 5, Ch. 5, "The Ride of the Rohirrim."

- All that day the Rohirrim are guided along by the Wild Men.
- By late afternoon, they near the plains of Anduin.
- Bodies of two riders (one with the Red Arrow) are found.
- They rest that night.

Darkness and the Wild Men

Rohan's name for Minas Tirith is Mundberg. The Wild Men are called Woses.

At Dunharrow on the evening of March 9, Théoden estimated that he might not reach Minas Tirith until the 17th, eight days away. Riding hard and assisted by the Wild Men, they arrive two days early. Consistent with Tolkien's oft-repeated theme, Sauron's contrived darkness has backfired. It allows the Rohirrim to travel to Minas Tirith quickly and secretly. It also propels the Wild Men into the war at precisely the right moment. Tolkien would no doubt say that this illustrates how evil schemes often go astray.

Aragorn, Gimli and Legolas with Rangers

Day 7 of 8 in the Military Campaign

Up the river from Pelargir

The Return of the King, Bk. 5, Ch. 9, "The Last Debate."

- Aragorn orders four thousand troops to Minas Tirith on foot.
- In the morning, the fleet with soldiers sails for Minas Tirith.

Calculating the Sailing Speed to Minas Tirith

Legolas said that they left in boats on the sixth day *since* they began their fight, making it the seventh day in their campaign

Minas Tirith is over 200 miles away by water, so to reach Minas Tirith by late morning the following day, they must average, over ground, about 8 miles per hour or roughly 11 miles per hour against the river's current. This is an impressive speed, even given how motivated Umbar's ex-slaves would have been, but it is not impossible.

An Internet source gave as a reference two books by Admiral William L. Rogers, *Greek and Roman Naval Warfare* (1937) and *Naval Warfare under Oars* (1939).

According to one source, a Mediterranean *Ousiakos* (in service from A.D. 400 to 1000) had a "battle cruise" speed under oars of 5.2 knots (6.3 m.p.h.) and a maximum (probably 'hull') speed under sail of 12.5 knots (14.4 m.p.h.). The *Ousiakos* was 100 feet long, 13 feet wide and had a draft of 3 feet. (The last allowed it to sail up rivers.) It carried 164 men, including 108 rowers, who could assist in combat.

At this point, Tolkien's Book 6, "The End of the Third Age" begins.

Frodo and Sam—Escaping the Tower

Day 1 of 12 in Mordor

Tower of Cirith Ungol

The Return of the King, Bk. 6, Ch. 1, "The Tower of Cirith Ungol."

- About noon Sam awakes, leaves the tunnel, and enters the tower.
- An Orc escapes the tower with a bundle.
- Sam finds Frodo and they leave the tower.

A Troublesome Bundle

The bundle carried by the fleeing Orc, Shagrat, will be delivered to Barad-dûr in three days and items from it will be shown to Gandalf at the Black Gate 11 days from now on March 25.

Into Mordor

- Frodo and Sam enter Mordor and hide from Orcs.
- During the night, they travel north.

The Return of the King, Bk. 6, Ch. 2, "The Land of Shadow."

The Great Eagles and the Ring

Some Tolkien fans wonder why a great eagle was not used to carry the Ring into Mordor. The main reason is that Frodo had been chosen as the Ring-bearer and that had to be honored. Another reason is suggested by the Nazgûl-bird seen here. Sauron may have had his flying beasts patrolling the sky to prevent spying. Only after the Ring was destroyed, did eagles dare to enter Mordor airspace to rescue Frodo and Sam.

Book 4 focuses on Frodo and Sam, while Books 3 and 5 cover the other characters and Book 6 covers all the characters. Book 6's first three chapters center on events at Mordor. The final six chapters close out the narrative.

Thursday, March 15, 1419—Darkness Ends

Day 175
March 9

A last quarter moon rises in the east-southeast about 1:30 a.m. and sets in the west-southwest at 11 a.m.

Day 6 of 6 with Darkness

Gandalf and Pippin with Denethor and Faramir

Minas Tirith

- About midnight, Sauron attacks.
- Denethor takes his son, so both can meet their death by fire.
- Only Gandalf stands as the Lord of the Nazgûl enters the city.
- Rohan arrives and the Lord of the Nazgûl withdraws.

The Return of the King, Bk. 5, Ch. 4, "The Siege of Gondor."

The Return of the King, Bk. 5, Ch. 6, "The Battle of Pelennor Fields."

A Tolkien Favorite

In a 1967 letter, Tolkien said he found the sounding of the horns of the Rohirrim after the rooster crows to be one of the most moving passages in his entire book. Many readers, including this writer, agree. For sheer drama and importance to the plot, this scene is second only to the destruction of the Ring at Mount Doom.

Letters, No. 294. For the number of soldiers in the battle, see "The Battle of Pelennor Fields" in *The Atlas of Middle-earth.*

Minas Tirith

- Pippin tells Gandalf of Denethor's plans to burn Faramir.
- Gandalf rescues Faramir, but Denethor kills himself.
- Gandalf takes Faramir to the Houses of Healing.

The Return of the King, Bk. 5, Ch. 7, "The Pyre of Denethor."

Denethor's Fears and False Visions

Certain the city will fall, Denethor may fear that his body and that of his son will be dishonored and mutilated by Orcs, hence the importance of burning them and saving what little dignity remaining. Tolkien did not like that sort of defeatism and despair.

Éowyn and Merry with Théoden and the Rohirrim
Day 6 of 6 in the Calvary Ride to Minas Tirith

Riding to Minas Tirith

The Return of the King, Bk. 5, Ch. 5, "The Ride of the Rohirrim" and Bk. 5, Ch. 6, "The Battle of Pelennor Fields."

- In the early morning darkness, the Rohirrim ride for Minas Tirith.
- As day dawns, Rohan attacks.

Rohan's Finest Hour

In the summer of 1940, Britain stood virtually alone against a Nazi Germany that dominated the continent of Europe and threatened to invade Britain itself. On June 4, Winston Churchill would give a speech to the House of Commons in which he said, "Let us . . . brace ourselves that if the British Empire lasts for a thousand years, men will still say: 'This was their finest hour.'"

In much the same way, Rohan's finest hour came when, in fulfillment to its promise to Gondor, it rode out on Pelennor Field, not knowing whether victory or death awaited them.

Pelennor Fields

The Return of the King, Bk. 5, Ch. 6, "The Battle of Pelennor Fields."

- The Lord of the Nazgûl attacks Théoden, knocking him unconscious.
- Éowyn and Merry destroy the Lord of the Nazgûl.
- Théoden dies on the battlefield.

Tolkien and Shakespeare

The prophecy about how the Lord of the Nazgûl was made a little over a thousand years earlier by Glorfindel. See *The Return of the King*, Bk. 6, Ap. A, I, (iv) and the commentary for the years 374–375. Éowyn's stand against the Lord of the Nazgûl may be the bravest single action in the entire tale.

Macbeth, Act 4, Scene 1.

Saruman's attack on Helm's Deep and Sauron's attack on Minas Tirith were both defeated in plots consciously borrowed from Shakespeare. On March 3, we saw how marching trees overcame Saruman's armies. Now we see a *woman* (along with a *Hobbit*) defeat the Lord of the Nazgûl, who has been told that he cannot be stopped by any living *man*. Prophecies have a disturbing tendency to be fulfilled in ways those who trust in them did not expect. Here are the relevant lines from Shakespeare's *Macbeth*.

Following three witches and his ambitious wife, Macbeth murdered to become king. Now he is fearful. The three witches summon an apparition.

APPARITION: Macbeth! Macbeth! Macbeth!

MACBETH: Had I three ears, I'd hear thee.

APPARITION: Be bloody, bold and resolute; laugh to scorn the pow'r of man, for none of woman born shall harm Macbeth.

MACBETH: Then live Macduff; what need of fear of thee? But yet I'll make assurance double sure and take a bond of fate. Thou shalt not live; that I may tell pale-hearted fear it lies, and sleep in spite of thunder. . . .

Later, Macbeth is besieged by an army that walks to his castle disguised as a wood. Still he fights on, certain he cannot be defeated.

Macbeth, Act 5, Scene 7.

MACBETH: They have tied me to a stake; I cannot fly, but bear-like I must fight the course. What's he that was not born of woman? Such a one am I to fear, or none. . . .

The castle is entered and Macduff finds Macbeth.

MACDUFF: Turn, hell-hound, turn.

Macbeth, Act 5, Scene 8.

MACBETH: Of all men else I have avoided thee. But get thee back; my soul is too much charg'd with blood of thine already.

MACDUFF: I have no words—my voice is my sword: thou bloodier villain than terms can give thee out.

Fighting and alarm.

MACBETH: Thou losest labour. And easy mayst thou the intrenchant air with thy keen sword impress as make me bleed. Let fall thy blade on vulnerable crests; I bear a charmed life, which must not yield to one of woman born.

MACDUFF: Despair thy charm; and let the angel whom thou still hast serv'd tell thee that Macduff was from his mother's womb untimely ripp'd.

Macduff was removed from his mother's womb after her death and was thus born of a corpse rather than a living woman. Tolkien's plot hinges on a different technicality in language. In the strictest sense of the word, neither Éowyn nor Merry was a man.

MACBETH: Accursed be that tongue that tells me so, for it hath cow'd my better part of man; and be these juggling fiends no more believ'd that palter with us in a double sense, that keep the word of promise to our ear, and break it to our hope! I'll not fight with thee.

MACDUFF: Then yield thee, coward, and live to be the show and gaze o' th' time. We'll have thee, as our rarer monsters are, painted upon a pole, and underwrit "Here may you see the tyrant."

MACBETH: I will not yield, to kiss the ground before young Malcolm's feet and to be baited with the rabble's curse. Though Birnam wood be come to Dunsinane, and thou oppos'd, being of no woman born, yet I will try the last. Before my body I throw my warlike shield. Lay on, Macduff; and damn'd be him that first cries, "Hold, enough!"

They exit fighting. Later Macduff walks on stage bearing Macbeth's severed head.

Even Macbeth's death by beheading resembles how the Lord of the Nazgûl was killed.

Aragorn, Gimli and Legolas with Rangers

Day 8 of 8 in the Military Campaign

Sailing to Minas Tirith

- Aragorn and the fleet row. At midnight the wind speeds them along.
- They arrive and battle until sunset before Gondor wins.

The Return of the King, Bk. 5, Ch. 9, "The Last Debate" and Ch. 6, "The Battle of Pelennor Fields."

Providential Weather

For six days, a prevailing east window has darkened the skies over Gondor. Now, at precisely the right moment, the wind changes, blowing away the darkness and bringing Aragorn to Minas Tirith. Tolkien is making clear that Sauron's control of the weather, if any, is not absolute. There is a power greater than Sauron.

Aragorn, Gandalf, Merry and Pippin

Houses of Healing, Minas Tirith

The Return of the King, Bk. 5, Ch. 8, "The Houses of Healing." In the exchange between Aragorn and the herb-master, Tolkien may be making fun of those in his profession, philology, who fuss over words without understanding their real meaning or treat ancient tales as simply sources of antiquated words.

- Merry is found by Pippin and taken to the Houses of Healing
- Aragorn treats the sick with *athelas.*

A Parallel to the Battle of Britain

Compare the events of this day with Winston Churchill's words to the House of Commons on August 20, 1940, during the darkest days of World War II, when German bombers were destroying British air defenses and leveling London: "Never in the field of human conflict was so much owed by so many to so few." Gandalf's leadership and the Rohirrim arriving at a critical moment are much like the few hundred RAF fighter pilots who turned the tide of war in the Battle of Britain. Sometimes the bravery and sacrifice of a few can alter the course of history.

Frodo and Sam

Day 2 of 12 in Mordor

Morgai

The Return of the King, Bk. 6, Ch. 2, "The Land of Shadow."

- By daylight Frodo and Sam reach the Morgai Valley.
- They hike north, find water, and sleep under brambles.

Three Battles

Lórien, Mirkwood and Dale

Unfinished Tales, Pt. III, Ch. III, "The Quest of Erebor" and *The Return of the King,* Bk. 6, Ap. B, "The Tale of Years."

- Sauron's forces attack Lórien a second time and are thrown back.
- Sauron's forces attack King Thranduil and the wood Elves.
- Sauron troops from the east attack King Brand in the Battle of the Dale.

Battle Results

Though little noted by Tolkien, in all three cases Sauron's attacks fail. Lórien repulses the attack, and the wood Elves win. The Battle of the Dale will end in defeat for Sauron on March 27. Unlike the Last Alliance at the end of the Second Age, in this war the Elves fight only defensive battles.

Tolkien's Chronology in Shelob's Lair

Frodo and Sam's movements from March 10 to 14 form perhaps the most difficult chronological problem in the entire book. Their weariness and the continual darkness in the sky, on the stairs, and inside Shelob's Lair deprive readers of most clues about the passage of time—an effect Tolkien seems to have deliberately exaggerated by giving readers so few clues as to the time. The chronology given here fits with the available information with one exception. "The Tale of Years" has Gollum slipping away to visit Shelob as the Hobbits talk and sleep, but returning to find Frodo sleeping on the same day (the 11th). That is difficult to reconcile with Gollum's remark when he returned that the Hobbits had slept into the next day. This book goes with Gollum's remark, in part because anything that lengthens the chain of events helps to reconcile these problems.

What happens during this period does not fill the time available. In our attempts to solve that problem, the gaps have been filled with a long sleep by the exhausted Hobbits (11th to daytime on the 12th), Sam's deep shock over Frodo's apparent death (dusk on the 12th to perhaps dusk on the 13th), and Sam's unconsciousness after hurling himself against the under-gate (perhaps the evening of the 13th to noon on the 14th). It is not a perfect solution, but it may be the best that can be done.

Freedom or Slavery

One by-product of Tolkien's popularity is the envy he stirs up among those who will never achieve his success. A generation ago, such people criticized *The Lord of the Rings* as little more than an allegorization of World War II—Sauron was Hitler, the Ring was the atomic bomb, and so forth. In vain, Tolkien said that he was not writing allegory, that parts of the story were written when Hitler was unknown, and that the Ring was the center of the story long before he heard of the atomic bomb.

Today's critics often take the opposite approach. Tolkien, they now claim, is a Hitler-like elitist who believed in the superiority of white, northern Europeans and portrayed dark-skinned people as evil. If you have read other commentary in this book, you know that is nonsense. There we point out the loathing Tolkien had for both Nazism and its close kin, Communism. Hitler, Tolkien bluntly told his son Michael, was a "little ignoramus" under "demonic inspiration."

Tolkien's critics are the ones who cannot think outside a racial box. Describe a member of Group X doing something bad, and they say that you must mean that all members of Group X are bad—displaying themselves a typical racist mindset. Not so. Tolkien's world was far more sophisticated than that. He believed that no enduring line could be drawn between good and evil people. In fact, one central message of his story is

The Atlas of Middle-earth, resolves some of the chronological problems by making Shelob's Lair twelve miles long. For more on how Tolkien wrestled with dating events in this period see: *The End of the Third Age* (Boston: Houghton Mifflin, 2000), Ch. I, "The Story of Frodo and Sam in Mordor." Tolkien also mentioned problems with timing and motivation that arose when his narrative developed differently from what he had planned in "any preliminary sketch." See *Letters,* No. 70 and 71. There are hints in both letters as well as in No. 72, that, due to war responsibilities, Tolkien was tired and getting little sleep as he wrote this section. For more details, see "Tolkien's Writing Interrupted" at the end of Chapter 14.

Tolkien first learned of the atomic bomb on August 9, 1945, when his book was two-thirds completed. *Letters,* No. 102. See also No. 186 and 226. In the last, he claimed the war itself did not influence the story's plot.

Letters, No. 45. See also No. 183, where Tolkien says Frodo's mission was, "the liberation from an evil tyranny of all the 'humane'—including those, such as 'easterlings' and Haradrim, that were still servants of the tyranny." Tolkien then praised the Elves, the most 'superior' of his races, for freeing others at the cost of their own existence in Middle-earth. Nothing could be more removed from Nazi ideas of racial superiority than that.

that no group is immune from the lust for power. No one, Gandalf reminds us, can be trusted with the Ring. Not Elrond, the wisest of Elves. Not Aragorn, the greatest of men. Not even Gandalf himself, chief among Wizards. In the end, even the Hobbit chosen to destroy it, Frodo, proves unequal to his task and is only saved by divine intervention. Read Tolkien's other tales and you will discover that the race most like the Nazism's mythical Aryans—the Númenoreans—turn to evil with such zeal that the Valar are forced to call on the One, who drowns their land in the sea. Not exactly how Hitler would write a history of Middle-earth.

Perhaps the best illustration of Tolkien's attitude comes in *The Two Towers* at the end of "Of Herbs and Stewed Rabbits." Faramir has attacked the dark-skinned Southrons who are allied to Sauron. "Ah," Tolkien's critics might say, "Here is his racism. Dark-skin bad, light skin good. What a bigot!" Hardly. In the battle, one Southron escapes the fighting and dies at Sam's feet. Does Sam gloat over his racial superiority? No. Does he sneer at an inferior race being slain like a wild beast? No. He wonders what the man's name is and where his home might be. Most important of all, he wonders if the man really wanted to go to war, or if he was forced to fight and die in a strange land.

For Tolkien, that is the real distinction between Middle-earth's peoples. Some are fortunate enough to be free, although they must still fight to keep that freedom. That's what Rohan does when it rides to Minas Tirith, and what the Hobbits do after they return to their beloved Shire. Others are not so fortunate. They live as slaves with no choice about the lives they live or the wars in which they fight. Their sacrifices and deaths are in vain.

It is true that in Tolkien's tales, geography plays a major role in determining who is free and who is a slave. Precisely like the world in which he lived, he placed the free peoples in the north and west of Middle-earth and the enslaved to the south and east. But we should never forget that the two points of geography that most threaten the freedom of all are Isengard and Mordor. Placed on a map of Europe, the former might lie in Switzerland at the foot of the Alps, while the latter would be deep inside Germany. Remember too that in *The Lord of the Rings,* evil is very European. Other races enter the picture only as the warrior-slaves of some European power (much like the use of colonial troops in World War I).

For Tolkien, no people, no race, and no place on the map had a monopoly on virtue. Any group could earn its freedom, and any group could fall into slavery and become a tool of evil. If Tolkien had written a tale centered at the end of the Fourth Age, he might have driven that point home by pitting the free peoples of the South and East against the slave armies of the north and west. We can only wonder what his critics would have complained about then. No doubt they would have found something.

Peter Jackson, the New Zealand producer of three major films based on *The Lord of the Rings,* uses this scene to demonstrate that Tolkien was not a racist. For more on Tolkien's political views, see Robert Plank, "'The Scouring of the Shire': Tolkien's View of Fascism" in *A Tolkien Compass.* Plank gave three reasons why Shire Hobbits did not resist Saruman's oppression: 1. cowardice, 2. a "lack of solidarity" and 3. a disturbing willingness to obey orders, however foul. A fourth could be added, one Merry criticized as "getting under cover." Groups that might have resisted more aggressively, such as the close-knit Took family, initially chose isolationism over open warfare. Plank's remark that "courage is more an aristocratic than a democratic virtue" is nonsense. Lacking social connections, wealth and power, ordinary people must depend all the more on courage and determination.

Tolkien "utterly" repudiated the idea that the geography in his tale had a modern application. Mordor was in the east, he said, "due to simple narrative and geographic necessity" and in his tales, "the original stronghold of Evil was (as traditionally) in the North." *Letters,* No. 229. See also No. 294.

16

Marching Against Sauron

March 16 to April 6, 1419

March on Mordor to the defeat of Sauron

Covers 21 Days
Day 176 to 196

There is a danger in trying to see too much, in attempting to anticipate all the risks and foresee all the ends before we act. Sometimes, we must simply do what is right, whatever the potential consequences. Tom Shippey believes Tolkien saw life that way.

They were a major part of his own conviction and a part of his own cure for the defeatism, the appeasement, the lack of will and the weary calculation of odds that he saw dogging the Western democracies as he was writing *The Lord of the Rings* and still after he had finished it. Tolkien's achievement, it may be, was to reintroduce a heroic world view, drawn from the ancient texts he taught as a professor, to a world gone ironic.

And this world view was put across not only by the obviously heroic figures such as Aragorn and Faramir and King Théoden, but by the Hobbits—and, most of all, by the very structure of the story. In this story, all the characters find themselves, literally as well as figuratively, bewildered: their bearings lost, not sure what's for the best, but slogging on regardless. The most important ones, moreover, the Hobbits Frodo and Sam, think they're on their own. All the time, their friends are risking everything to distract the Eye of Sauron from them, but they don't know that. They go on anyway.

In this chapter we will see how a chronology sheds light on what Tolkien was doing. We will follow along as Tolkien has Frodo and Sam "slogging on" against terrible obstacles, not knowing that at the same time their friends are courting death to keep Sauron from turning his attention on them. Everything the free peoples of Middle-earth hold dear will hinge on keeping Sauron diverted—until the last possible moment—from the two small Hobbits who have invaded his fortress on a mission upon which the hopes of all depend.

Tom Shippey, "Tolkien Teaches Us To Take Courage," *National Post*, (January 6, 2003). C. S. Lewis voiced a similar viewpoint when he described how we mistakenly plan our life as if it were a play whose plot and ending we know. But, he went on, "We do not know the play. We do not even know whether we are in Act I or Act V. We do not know who are the major and who are the minor characters. The Author knows. . . . But we, never seeing the play from the outside, never meeting any characters except the tiny minority who are 'on' in the same scenes as ourselves, wholly ignorant of the future and very imperfectly informed about the past, cannot tell at what moment the end ought to come." See "The World's Last Night" in *C. S. Lewis* (Lesley Walmsley, ed), 49.

Friday, March 16, 1419—War Council

The moon is one day past last quarter and rises in the east-southeast about 2:30 a.m. That provides light when a Nazgûl passes over Minas Tirith before sunrise. In the days ahead the moon will be waning, making the nights darker as the army approaches Mordor's northern entrance.

Gimli, Legolas, Merry and Pippin

Houses of Healing, Minas Tirith

The Return of the King, Bk. 5, Ch. 9, "The Last Debate."

- Gimli and Legolas visit Merry and Pippin.

The Stroll of Gimli and Legolas

Note at the Houses of Healing when Gimli says the world would be dull without Elves. That is an amazing statement for a Dwarf to make and an indication of just how much Gimli has been changed by his friendship with Legolas.

For those who have been following how Tolkien has been building the relationship between Gimli and Legolas, their stroll through the streets of Minas Tirith to the Houses of Healing is revealing. Through them we can see that differences between people can be complimentary and beneficial. To provide good human habitats, cities need engineers and artists who work together to create strong and attractive buildings.

Aragorn and Gandalf with Military Leaders

Tents of Aragorn, Minas Tirith

The Return of the King, Bk. 5, Ch. 9, "The Last Debate."

- They agree to march on Mordor in two days with 7,000 men.

Troop Disposition

Total the numbers Tolkien provides, and it becomes clear that the war council divided their offensive and defensive forces equally.

Remaining Behind:

1. Minas Tirith will be protected by 4,000 marching up from Pelargir.
2. Elfhelm will take most of Rohan's remaining calvary, some 3,000 men and horses, north to guard against an attack through Anórien.
Total: 7,000 men

Sent to Attack Mordor:

1. Aragorn will march with the 2,000 men he brought from the south.
2. Imrahil, Steward of Minas Tirith, will supply 3,500 men from Gondor.
3. Éomer will lead 500 calvary-on-foot and 500 horsed calvary from Rohan along with 500 cavalrymen from other sources.
Total: 7,000 men

Later, when they fight at the Black Gate on March 25, their forces will be unequally divided. Aragorn and Gandalf will stand a hilltop on the left flank while Elrond's two sons. Imrahil and Éomer (with Pippin) will fight from a hilltop on their right. The exact size of the two forces is unknown since 1,000 men from all the groups had left to attack Cair Andros.

Frodo and Sam

Day 3 of 12 in Mordor

Morgai

- They climb east, looking for a direct route to Mount Doom.
- They discover camps of soldiers blocking the way.
- Hiding from two Orcs, they hear that Gollum is trailing them.
- They hide until dark and travel north.

The Return of the King, Bk. 6, Ch. 2, "The Land of Shadow."

Following the Ring

There is no indication in Tolkien's writings that Sauron was told that Gollum was following the Hobbits. If he had been told, he might have realized that Gollum was following the Ring and reacted accordingly. A more aggressive search and even a small guard at Mount Doom would have made Frodo and Sam's task impossible.

Saturday, March 17, 1419—Lonely Mountain

Day 177
March 11

Frodo and Sam

Day 4 of 12 in Mordor

Central Morgai

- During the night, the Hobbits travel north.
- During the day, they rest, taking turns watching for Gollum.
- As the sun sets, they travel north again.

The Return of the King, Bk. 6, Ch. 2, "The Land of Shadow." Today, three days after leaving Tower of Cirith Ungol with a bundle containing some of the Hobbits' belongings, Shagrat delivers the items to Barad-dûr. In eight more days, on March 25, the items will be shown to Gandalf. See *The Return of the King,* Ap. B, "The Tale of Years."

The Problem with Few

In the real world, two is not simply twice one nor is three merely fifty percent more than two. Difficult, isolated situations—such as wilderness travel or transoceanic voyages—often create situations that are impossible for one person to handle and difficult for two. It is obvious from the narrative that Tolkien believed if Sam had not been along, Frodo would have never made it to Mount Doom. Even the two Hobbits found tasks that were beyond their ability. Guarding themselves around the clock against Gollum would have meant that both got only half the sleep they needed. Their strength was not sufficient for that.

King Brand and Dáin Ironfoot

Day 3 of 13 in the Battle of Dale

Dale and Lonely Mountain

- King Brand dies fighting at the Gate of Erebor.
- King Dâin Ironfoot stands over his body and dies defending it.
- After dark, men and Dwarves retreat to the Lonely Mountain.

The Return of the King, Bk. 6, Ap. B, "The Tale of Years" and *Unfinished Tales,* Pt. III, Ch. III, "The Quest of Erebor." They will continue to fight from the Lonely Mountain until the Ring is destroyed eight days later.

Light from the Past

Readers who pass over the events of this battle, buried as they are in an obscure and typically unread appendix, miss some of the almost magical light Tolkien often shines on an ancient literary theme and the courageous loyalty it enshrined as men willingly die defending the body of a dead leader or friend. Professor Janet Blumberg, a scholar of Medieval and Renaissance literature, described that theme this way:

> Nothing, however, is more heroic-elegiac than the two famous lines in "The Battle of Malden," an Anglo-Saxon battle poem written in the tenth century right after a terrible English loss to the Vikings, because of which the Vikings overran a large area of East Anglia. The children, the women, the fields, the animals were plundered and taken. Even though such a terrible price was paid because of this disastrous defeat, the poem nonetheless concentrates in the Northern style upon the loyalty of the battle-leader's retainers, as they fight to the death around their slain lord.

From Janet Leslie Blumberg, "The Literary Backgrounds of The Lord of the Rings" in Celebrating Middle-earth, 61–62.

Day 178
March 12

Sunday, March 18, 1419—Marching on Mordor

Aragorn, Gandalf, Gimli, Legolas and Pippin
Day 1 of 8 in the March on Mordor

Osgiliath to Cross-roads

- In the morning, the army leaves without Merry.
- Before noon, they reach the fords at Osgiliath.
- Five miles past the fords, they stop for the night.

Aragorn's Strategy

Tolkien rarely has his leading characters explain the reason behind a particular strategy. But here it is not that hard to discover what it is. Aragorn wants to delay the coming battle as long as possible. That's why, before leaving Minas Tirith, he sends out scouts to make sure Sauron has no troops lurking nearby. Attacking nearby Minas Morgul is also forbidden. That would reveal too soon how weak his forces actually are and draw attention to Frodo and Sam's entry into Mordor. With virtually no chance of defeating Sauron's larger forces, Aragorn must march boldly to Mordor's most distant gate, covering about 25 miles a day. The trumpeters give the impression he is so certain of victory he can give Sauron ample warning. In the Anglo-Saxon and Northern literature that Tolkien studied, horns often symbolize defiance.

The Return of the King, Bk. 5, Ch. 10, "The Black Gate Opens." The attack on Minas Tirith from the north had been turned back, leaving the city safe for now. Aragorn's march speed needed to be fast enough to make his treat credible, but slow enough to maximize the time Sauron would be distracted from Frodo. The timing is perfect. If they had arrived at the Black Gate a day sooner, they would have been defeated and Sauron would have known to look elsewhere for the Ring. If they had arrived a day later, Sauron's preparations might have been completed, and he may have found time to look seriously for the two 'spies.' In either case, Frodo and Sam may have been discovered.

Frodo and Sam
Day 5 of 12 in Mordor

North Morgai and Eastward

- They travel until daylight and hide in a hollow.
- Going for water, Sam gets a glimpse of Gollum.
- After dark, they move out again, hiking east on a road.

The Return of the King, Bk. 6, Ch. 2, "The Land of Shadow."

Timing is Everything

Frodo and Sam separated from their friends 22 days earlier on February 26. They have traveled for five days inside Mordor. About a mile ahead of where they rest today is an heavily traveled road they absolutely must take to reach Mount Doom. Though Aragorn and Gandalf have only the vaguest idea where the Ring-bearer might be, the timing of their march could not be more perfect. Just as Frodo and Sam begin the most dangerous part of their journey, Sauron's attention is suddenly diverted. Forty miles to their north, his forces must rush to prepare for battle. He has no time for reports about a few spies scouting out his land. Timing such as this is where Tolkien most often reveals the presence of the One who otherwise remains hidden.

Monday, March 19, 1419—Marching with Orcs

Day 179
March 13

Aragorn, Gandalf, Gimli, Legolas and Pippin
Day 2 of 8 in the March on Mordor

Cross-roads

- The foot soldiers stop for the night at the Cross-roads.
- Gandalf and Aragorn ride to Morgul Vale.
- The army destroys the bridge to Minas Morgul.

The Return of the King, Bk. 5, Ch. 10, "The Black Gate Opens."

Smashing a Bridge

War, some cynics have observed, is about "killing people and smashing things." In proper military fashion, the bridge to Minas Morgul is smashed to delay any attack coming from that direction.

Frodo and Sam passed through this same Cross-roads nine days earlier on March 10 at sunset. As Tolkien notes, the army begins its march *north* on the same day that Frodo and Sam turn toward the *south*.

Frodo and Sam—Escaping Orcs
Day 6 of 12 in Mordor

Near Isenmouthe

- In the early morning darkness, Frodo and Sam hear Orcs behind them.
- Unable to leave the road, they sit like exhausted Orcs.
- An Orc slave-driver forces them to join the march.

Ugly Orcs, Cute Hobbits

How could Tolkien's cute Hobbits pass themselves off as unspeakably ugly Orcs? The darkness is one reason. Another is the fact that it may have never occurred to the slave-driver that Sauron could have foes so deep within Mordor.

Tolkien's critics often accuse him of being too simplistic. But notice that the distinction Tolkien drew between Hobbits and Orcs is far from

Tolkien's obvious dislike of forced military service, even by Orcs, may be linked to his own unpleasant experiences as a soldier in World War I.

simple. Hobbit goodness is closely linked to the fact that they are *free* to live good lives and serve noble causes—though not all do so. Orc badness comes from being born as *slaves* to evil causes. As a result, they can be driven to serve Sauron with whips, as these Orcs are.

Plains of Gorgoroth

The Return of the King, Bk. 6, Ch. 2, "The Land of Shadow," Bk. 6, Ch. 3, "Mount Doom." Before they begin today's travel, Sam estimates it will take a week to reach Mount Doom. They will reach it in six days, in part because they are able to use the road. Without the use of that road, made possible by Aragorn's march on the Black Gate, they might not have had the strength to reach Mount Doom.

- Frodo and Sam slip away when two columns of Orcs collide.
- The two Hobbits rest until daylight.
- They set out for Mt. Doom across rough ground and on the road.
- That night they sleep by the road.

Moving Troops by Night

Tolkien has thought through Sauron's strategy. Although secure within his own territory, Sauron may be moving his troops at night so his foes, perhaps using eagles flying high outside Mordor (birds as spies is an oft-repeated Tolkien theme), cannot see how numerous they are or where they are being placed. This is yet another case when Sauron's scheming works to his disadvantage. The night movement of troops allows Frodo and Sam to escape in the darkness and use the roads during the day, when they can see large troop columns long before they are seen themselves.

Éowyn, Faramir and Merry

Day 4 of their Recovery

Houses of Healing, Minas Tirith

The Return of the King, Bk. 6, Ch. 5, "The Steward and the King."

- Éowyn goes to the Warden of the Houses of Healing.
- He takes her to Faramir, who encourages her.
- Faramir asks the Warden about Éowyn and is sent to Merry.

Tolkien and Romance

For Sam and Rose, see September 23, 1418 and their meeting just before the Battle of Bywater in *The Return of the King,* Bk. 6, Ch. 8, "The Scouring of the Shire."

If you like romance, enjoy this all-too-brief one. It is a rare instance where Tolkien allowed a romantic interlude to slip into the 'men on a great adventure' narrative of *The Lord of the Rings.* Another, even more lightly covered, is Sam's relationship with Rose Cotton. Both result in long and happy marriages. Just because Tolkien did not dwell on romance, did not mean he had anything against it.

Day 180
March 14

Tuesday, March 20, 1419—To the Black Gate

Aragorn, Gandalf, Gimli, Legolas and Pippin

Day 3 of 8 in the March on Mordor, Day 1 from Cross-roads

Harad Road, north of the Cross-roads

The Return of the King, Bk. 5, Ch. 10, "The Black Gate Opens."

- Scouts go ahead to watch for attacks.
- Soldiers march slowly for Morannon, one hundred miles north.
- Announcements are made that King Elessar has returned.

Taunting Sauron

Marching slowing, blowing horns, and making announcements—Tolkien has Aragorn doing everything he can to taunt Sauron and divert his attention away from Frodo and Sam. You might remember in *The Hobbit* where Bilbo taunts the giant spiders of Mirkwood to distract them and draw them away from the captured Dwarves.

The Hobbit, Ch. 8, "Flies and Spiders."

Frodo and Sam

Day 7 of 12 in Mordor

Plains of Gorgoroth

- They travel south by day on the road and rest at night.

The Return of the King, Bk. 6, Ch. 3, "Mount Doom." Tolkien did not give any specific events for this day.

Éowyn and Faramir

Day 5 of their Recovery

Houses of Healing, Minas Tirith

- Faramir and Éowyn walk together every day, speeding their healing.

An Understated Romance

Here Tolkien introduces his readers to a budding romance, but leaves virtually everything about it unsaid. Tolkien seems to have been more comfortable describing details about wilderness journeys and battles than with relationships between the sexes. Those he kept in soft focus.

The Return of the King, Bk. 6, Ch. 5, "The Steward and the King." Those wanting more vivid romances might read of Gold-mane and Sun-beam in William Morris' *The Roots of the Mountains.*

Wednesday, March 21, 1419—Orc Attack

Day 181
March 15

Aragorn, Gandalf, Gimli, Legolas and Pippin

Day 4 of 8 in the March on Mordor, Day 2 from Cross-roads

Ithilien

- In the afternoon, Orcs and Easterlings attack.
- That night, Nazgûl begin to spy on them from overhead.

The Return of the King, Bk. 5, Ch. 10, "The Black Gate Opens."

Entrapment Again

Again, Tolkien recycles a plot. Sauron's forces use the same trick of entrapment where a road cuts into a hill that Faramir had used at this same location exactly two weeks earlier. But forewarned by scouts, Aragorn's men are ready. Ready learners, the four Hobbits will use a similar trap in the Battle of Bywater on November 3.

Éowyn, Faramir and Merry

Day 6 of their Recovery

Ithilien

- Faramir walks with Éowyn

The Return of the King, Bk. 6, Ch. 5, "The Steward and the King."

Frodo and Sam

Day 8 of 12 in Mordor

Plains of Gorgoroth

The Return of the King, Bk. 6, Ch. 3, "Mount Doom."

Faramir's gift of food is mentioned at the beginning of The Two Towers, Bk. 4, Ch. 7, "Journey to the Cross-roads."

- They get the last cistern water they find in Mordor.

Food and Water

On February 30, Tolkien had Sam calculate that their food supplies would last three weeks, which meant it would run out today. This raises the possibility that at some point in his writing Tolkien may have intended for both food and water to run out at the same time. But before they parted on the morning of March 8, Faramir had additional food placed in the packs of the two Hobbits. That ordinary gift added enough to their food supply to make reaching Mount Doom possible.

Day 182
March 16

Thursday, March 22, 1419—Dreadful Nightfall

A new moon setting about 6:30 p.m. provides Aragorn's army with no light at night. They need campfires to spot attacks.

Aragorn, Gandalf, Gimli, Legolas and Pippin

Day 5 of 8 in the March on Mordor, Day 3 from Cross-roads

North Ithilien

The Return of the King, Bk. 5, Ch. 10, "The Black Gate Opens."

See *The War of the Ring,* Pt. 3, Ch. XII, "The Last Debate." The chapter gives additional reasons why they march on Mordor, including the most telling, a remark that if Sauron had any suspicion about what they intend to do, a few soldiers guarding Mount Doom would make Frodo's mission impossible.

- The troops continue to march north, spied on by Nazgûl.

Power Corrupts

According to Tolkien, Sauron has good reason to fear Aragorn. The Ring's power depends on its bearer. In a draft, Tolkien had Gandalf describe what the Ring would do if someone as powerful as Aragorn, Elrond or himself took it up. Such a person would acquire the ability to dominate others, even Sauron's followers, and rule the world. In this reasoning, Tolkien is echoing the famous statement of his fellow Catholic, Lord Acton (1834–1902), "Power tends to corrupt and absolute power corrupts absolutely." His remark is often shortened to "Power corrupts. Absolute power corrupts absolutely."

Frodo and Sam—Dreadful Nightfall

Day 9 of 12 in Mordor

Plains of Gorgoroth

The Return of the King, Bk. 6, Ch. 3, "Mount Doom."

Tolkien dates this nightfall to March 22 in *The Return of the King,* Ap. B, "The Tale of Years."

- Frodo and Sam are exhausted and their water is almost gone.

Tolkien's Careful Language

Today's sunset began what Tolkien termed a "dreadful nightfall." Casual readers may be confused at this point since Tolkien described it as coming four days after their March 19 escape from the Orcs, which would seem to be March 23. But Tolkien was using his language carefully. He was referring to the four days of daylight travel they have made since March 19. The nightfall comes on the evening of March 22. Since it is also the night of a new moon, it is dark as well as dreadful.

Celeborn and Galadriel

Lórien

- From Dol Guldur, Sauron's forces launch a third attack on Lórien.

The Return of the King, Bk. 6, Ap. B, "The Tale of Years."

Grind before the Storm

For most of his characters, Tolkien made these last days dull. Only faraway Lórien is fighting. Aragorn's army simply marches north, while Frodo and Sam trudge on, thinking of little but water. As in real life, great deeds are often preceded by a period of grind and drudgery.

Friday, March 23, 1419—Desolation of Marannon

Day 183
March 17

Aragorn, Gandalf, Gimli, Legolas and Pippin

Day 6 of 8 in the March on Mordor, Day 4 from Cross-roads

Desolation of the Marannon

- Aragorn's army enters the Desolation of Marannon.
- Some are terrified, so Aragorn sends them to capture Cair Andros.

Aragorn as a Military Leader

Although Tolkien does not explain why Aragorn's decision about the terrified solders is a brilliant one, the reasoning behind this part of his narrative is not hard to discern. Aragorn's army is being constantly watched. Any effort to force these frightened men on would be seen. If they were allowed to flee back to Minas Tirith, the image of invincibility Aragorn was trying to create would be shattered. By sending them to Cair Andros, 40 miles away on the River Anduin, Aragorn enhances his appearance of strength. He creates the impression that the 7,000 men he left with are more than enough to breach the Black Gate. He can do it with fewer than 6,000 men.

The Return of the King, Bk. 5, Ch. 10, "The Black Gate Opens." Sauron took Cair Andros just after the war began. See *The Return of the King,* Ap. B, "The Tale of Years," for March 10, 3019 (1419 in the Shire calendar).

Frodo and Sam

Day 10 of 12 in Mordor

Plains of Gorgoroth

- They leave the road, lighten their load, and travel faster.

The Return of the King, Bk. 6, Ch. 3, "Mount Doom."

Saturday, March 24, 1419—Reaching Mount Doom

Day 184
March 18

By Tolkien's reckoning, today the new moon is four days old rather than two as the lunar calendar indicates. In either case, it provides little light and sets early. Orcs would be at their fighting best on a dark night, but Sauron, filled with doubt, prefers to wait.

Aragorn, Gandalf, Gimli, Legolas and Pippin

Day 7 of 8 in the March on Mordor, Day 5 from Cross-roads

The Return of the King, Bk. 5, Ch. 10, "The Black Gate Opens."

Desolation of the Marannon

- The army marches slowly, prepared for an attack.
- At night they camp surrounded by watch fires.

Frodo and Sam

Day 11 of 12 in Mordor

Approaching Mount Doom

The Return of the King, Bk. 6, Ch. 3, "Mount Doom." Though they apparently have some food left, for the last two days of their journey, they are unable to eat.

- Frodo and Sam struggle on, their mouths too dry to eat.
- Before dark, they collapse at the foot of Mount Doom.

Anglo-Saxon Worldview

As Aragorn's army (as well as Frodo and Sam) move resolutely toward what must seem almost certain death, we do well to remember that this dark vision of life was a theme that Tolkien took from the Anglo-Saxons, for, as Janet Blumberg writes:

> When you think of the legacy of what Tolkien absorbed from Anglo-Saxon literature, then think of a dark and fatalistic worldview that does not fear darkness or run away from the battle. Even in defeat, what matters is *mod*—inward goodness that gleams out more strongly ("*mod* shall be the more") when we are being overwhelmed and defeated.

Janet Leslie Blumberg, "The Literary Backgrounds of *The Lord of the Rings*" in *Celebrating Middle-earth*, 66. Tolkien's tale, set in the world of the Pagan North, does not resolve the issue of life after death. Without dying, Frodo and Sam merely go to a land over the sea where their deeds are honored and their wounds are healed.

Anglo-Saxons often compared this life to the flight of a bird through a Mead Hall in winter. It comes out of the darkness, they believed, and for a few moments enjoys light and warmth. It then returns to the darkness and cold. It was to such a world, much-loved by Tolkien, that Christianity brought news of warmth and light beyond this life and offered victory in death rather than merely an honor that soon faded.

Day 185
March 19

Sunday, March 25, 1419—Ring Destroyed

Aragorn, Gandalf, Gimli, Legolas and Pippin

Day 8 of 8 in the March on Mordor, Day 6 from Cross-roads

Black Gate, Marannon

The Return of the King, Bk. 5, Ch. 10, "The Black Gate Opens." For the possibility that a force of Ents and Elves joins them in this battle, see March 11.

Bilbo's expected role as a burglar and spy is in *The Hobbit*, Ch. 1, "An Unexpected Party."

- The army reaches Marannon and demands that Sauron surrender.
- Sauron's Messenger shows them items from Frodo and Sam.
- Gandalf takes the items and the battle begins.
- Pippin stabs a troll-chief and is buried under the troll's falling body.

Quick Thinking Gandalf

Perceptive readers will spot the mistake Tolkien had the Messenger make—one a quick-thinking Gandalf catches. It comes when the Messenger calls those the items were taken from spies. If the Ring had been discovered, he would have said much more. If Sauron does not have the Ring, all hope is not lost. Tolkien may have intended for Sauron to assume the Hobbits are being used as spies based on what Gollum would have said about them being sneaks and thieves.

The items the Messenger showed Gandalf were in the bundle carried by the Orc Shagrat, who fled the Tower of Cirith Ungol on March 14 and delivered the bundle to Barad-dûr three days later. Although Frodo's escape happened eleven days earlier, first-time readers of *The Lord of the Rings* do not yet know about it. As far as they know, these items mean the Frodo and Sam are prisoners. By confusing his narrative's chronology, Tolkien adds drama and mystery.

The Messenger may not be lying when he claimed they had the Hobbit as a prisoner. Shagrat left before Frodo's escape and may have reported him to be a prisoner to Sauron. The Orcs who know better may be covering up the escape. Tolkien's Orcs are not slaves of Sauron in the same sense as the Black Riders are. It would be more accurate to see them as slaves of evil in general. They grip and grumble at orders and typically serve their own petty interests rather than Sauron.

Finally, notice that Sauron's offer claims that Gondor and Rohan could be disarmed and yet remain free to govern themselves. Tolkien would no doubt regard that as highly unlikely. Even the peaceful Shire needed pitchforks, bows and swords to win and keep its freedom.

The Return of the King, Bk. 6, Ch. 1, "The Tower of Cirith Ungol." For Shagrat, see *The Return of the King,* Ap. B, "The Tale of Years" for March 17. For a map, see *The Atlas of Middle-earth,* "The Battle of the Marannon."

For Orc attitudes toward authority, see the conversation between Gorbag and Shagrat in *The Two Towers,* Bk. 4, Ch. 10, "The Choices of Master Samwise."

Book 6, entitled "The End of the Third Age," now begins.
For the next three chapters the reader's attention will be directed to Frodo and Sam.
Frodo and Sam passed by Marannon on March 5, 20 days earlier.

Frodo and Sam with Gollum

Day 12 of 12 in Mordor

Mount Doom and Crack of Doom

- They climb Mount Doom and reach a path.
- Gollum attacks Frodo and Sam but is overpowered.
- Sam guards Gollum, while Frodo leaves for the Crack of Doom.
- At the Crack of Doom, Frodo puts on the Ring.
- Gollum takes the Ring and falls into the flames, destroying the Ring.
- Frodo and Sam retreat from the spreading lava and wait to die.

The Return of the King, Bk. 6, Ch. 3, "Mount Doom."

Gollum's End Predicted

Almost a year earlier, in the Shire on April 13, Gandalf hinted to Frodo that Gollum might have one more role in the history of the Ring. At the Black Gate on March 5, Frodo warned Gollum that, if he tried to take the Ring, he might be thrown into a fire.

Gandalf's prediction: *The Fellowship of the Ring,* Bk. 1, Ch. 2, "The Shadow of the Past." Frodo's warning: *The Two Towers,* Bk. 4, Ch. 3, "The Black Gate is Closed."

Different Traditions

Reflecting a less accurate tradition, in *The Silmarillion,* "Of the Ring of Power and the Third Age" Frodo is credited with casting the Ring into the fire. But Tolkien believed that without Gollum, Frodo would never have destroyed the Ring. The mercy both Frodo and (at the very end) Sam showed Gollum saved them from failure. Those who forgive are forgiven. Jesus said something much like that in his Sermon on the Mount.

For Tolkien's remarks about the Frodo's failure, see *Letters,* No. 191, 192 and 246. For Jesus' remarks, see Matthew 6:14–15.

Gandalf, Frodo and Sam with Gwaihir

Morannon

The Return of the King, Bk. 6, Ch. 4, "The Field of Cormallen." Mount Doom is some 90 miles away, so even with a wind from behind, the journey took about two hours.

- Gwaihir and other eagles help in the battle.
- With Sauron defeated, Gandalf races for Mount Doom with eagles.

Mount Doom

J. R. R. Tolkien, "Guide to the Names in the Lord of the Rings," *Tolkien Compass*, 201.

- Gandalf and the eagles rescue Frodo and Sam from the rising lava.

Exactly Three Months

Tolkien said that he planned for the mission of the Fellowship of the Ring to take exactly three months (December 25 to March 25). He gave no reason, but perhaps setting that as a goal gave him in a structure in which to place events.

The date for Easter is linked to the Jewish Passover, which is based on the moon. The closest year in which Easter came on March 25 was 1951. If Sunday, March 25 corresponded to Easter, however, then the dreadful nightfall on the evening of Thursday, March 22 corresponds exactly in time to Jesus' ordeal in Gethsemane. See Luke 22:39f.

Another possibility, given Tolkien's Catholic faith, is that the starting and ending dates for the mission were intended to span the period from Christmas to Easter. But that match is precise only at the beginning. Easter is the first Sunday after a Pascal Full Moon, which is the full moon coming between March 21 and April 18. In 1942, the year whose calendar Tolkien used to calculate the moon's phases in his tale, Easter comes on April 5. In fact, the date the Ring was destroyed is the first Sunday after a *new moon* and thus could never be Easter.

Éowyn and Faramir

Day 10 of their Recovery

Houses of Healing, Minas Tirith

The Return of the King, Bk. 6, Ch. 5, "The Steward and the King."

- An eagle brings Faramir and Éowyn news of Sauron's fall.

Éomer as King

For how Éomer succeeded Théoden as king see: *The Return of the King*, Bk. 6, Ap. A, "Annals of the Kings and Rulers" in "The Kings of the Mark: Line 3."

Day 187
March 21
Spring Equinox

Tuesday, March 27, 1419—Victory at Dale

Today is the Spring Equinox. Both day and night are of equal length.

Bard II and Thorin II

Day 13 of 13 in the Battle of Dale

Dale and the Lonely Mountain

The Return of the King, Bk. 6, Ap. B, "The Tale of Years." For the family tree of Dwarf kings see "Durin's Folk" in Bk. 6, Ap. A of *The Return of the King*.

- Bard II becomes King in Dale.
- Thorin II becomes King of the Lonely Mountain.
- Sauron's demoralized forces are forced away from the Dale.

Wars Have Messy Endings

As someone who served in World War I, Tolkien knew that there are always some who "don't get the message" and, as a result, fighting can continue after a truce is declared or defeat is obvious. Here some of

Sauron's forces fight on. It is unfortunate that in the two decades after *The Lord of the Rings* was released, Tolkien's publishers did not give him encouragement and a financial incentive to write more about these events. The stories might have proved interesting.

Wednesday, March 28, 1419—Dol Guldur

Day 188
March 22

Celeborn

Dol Guldur

- Celeborn destroys Dol Guldur to rid Mirkwood of evil.

Completing the Circle

The darkest events of *The Hobbit* came in Mirkwood. Tolkien completes the transformation from evil to good by cleansing the forest. Although buried in an appendix, this event adds to the sense that an important, world-changing task has just been completed.

Of course, Saruman remains and can do much harm. Orcs still lurk underground awaiting a new leader. More important, the possibility of evil entering into any heart remains a part of the logic of genuine freedom and real choices. Evil has been purged from Mirkwood, but the potential for some new evil arising always remains.

The Return of the King, Bk. 6, Ap. B, "The Tale of Years." Sauron ruled Dol Guldur for 1969 years. Tolkien placed the very last blow to evil on a fitting day. He was married on this date in the modern calendar, March 22, 1916. In May he was shipped off to face World War I and "the carnage on the Somme." *Letters,* No. 43.

Thursday, April 6, 1419—Mirkwood Renamed

Day 196
March 30

Celeborn and Thranduil

Wood of Greenleaves

- Celeborn and Thranduil divide Mirkwood.

The Return of the King, Bk. 6, Ap. B, "The Tale of Years."

Mirkwood Divided

With the fall of Sauron, Mirkwood is renamed the Wood of Greenleaves and divided into three parts. Thranduil gets the northern portion. The Beornings and the Woodmen get the middle, while Celeborn gets the southern portion.

The Ring and Totalitarianism

The quotes that follow are from *The Origins of Totalitarianism* (New York: Harcourt Brace Jovanovich, 1973), Ch. 13, "Ideology and Terror." Elsewhere, Arendt clarified the distinction by noting: "The decisive difference between totalitarian domination, based on terror, and tyrannies, and dictatorships, established by violence, is that the former turns not only against its enemies but against its friends and supporters as well, being afraid of all power, even the power of its friends. The climax of terror is reached when the police state begins to devour its own children, when yesterday's executioner becomes today's victim." Hannah Arendt, *On Violence* (New York: Harcourt Brace Jovanovich, 1969), 55. Historical examples include the Great Terror of the French Revolution, the Nazi 'Night of Long Knives,' and the Soviet show trials of the 1930s (dramatized in Arthur Koestler's *Darkness at Noon*). In Tolkien the Ring personifies this totalitarian obsession with absolute power, binding all to its will so completely that, as Gandalf warns just before the march on Mordor, "none can foresee the end of it while the world lasts."

For free speech, see the conversation at *The Ivy Bush* near the start of "A Long-expected Party" in *The Fellowship of the Ring*, Bk. 1. Ch. 1. For a contrast, see the start of *The Return of the King*, Bk. 6, Ch. 8, "The Scouring of the Shire."

Those who want a chilling glimpse into what life under Sauron would have been like may want to read a book that was being written at the same time Tolkien was working on *The Lord of the Rings*. Authored by Hannah Arendt, a Jewish intellectual who fled Hitler's Germany, and entitled *The Origins of Totalitarianism*, it takes a grim and unblinking look at the twentieth century's two great horrors, Communism and Nazism.

In her book, Arendt made a bold claim. When the ancient Greeks listed all possible forms of government, she said, they failed to include one that has appeared only in modern times. The totalitarianism of Stalin and Hitler, she told readers, is more than an exaggerated form of "despotism, tyranny and dictatorship." At the heart of totalitarianism is a reliance on "suprahuman forces" such as the "law of History" (Communism) or the "law of Nature" (Nazism). With such an ideology anything can be justified—even the extermination of millions of innocent people. That ideology then becomes the rationale for ruling over every thought and action. The parallel with what Tolkien wrote is obvious, particularly when what Arendt said is paraphrased to read:

One Ideology to rule them all, One Ideology to find them,
One Ideology to bring them all and in the darkness bind them.

Much like Tolkien, Arendt believed that the foundation for totalitarian rule rested on terror—the possibility that anyone could be branded an enemy of the State and crushed—noting: "If lawfulness is the essence of non-tyrannical government and lawlessness is the essence of tyranny, then terror is the essence of totalitarian domination." Terror exists, she explained, to allow "the force of nature or of history to race freely through mankind, unhindered by any spontaneous human action." Terror, she goes on, exists to bind all of humanity into "One Man of gigantic dimensions." Think of people so paralyzed by some great danger that they are unable to think or act independently and you get her point. She further explains:

Totalitarian government does not just curtail liberties or abolish essential freedoms; nor does it, at least to our limited knowledge, succeed in eradicating the love for freedom from the hearts of man. It destroys the one essential prerequisite of all freedom, which is simply the capacity of motion which cannot exist without space."

To get a taste of that difference, think of the Shire as it is at the start of the story, a place where people have the room to act and think much as they please. Contrast that to the Shire after only a short time under Saruman—a place dominated by rules and those who enforce them with the threat of confinement in lockholes—a place without space.

What does Arendt tell us is the greatest enemy of a totalitarian state? Oddly enough, it centers on the most ordinary of events, the birth of a child. "From the totalitarian point of view, the fact that men are born and die can be only regarded as an annoying interference with higher forces." No matter how complete the rule, no matter how cowed into silence a people has become, each child offers the potential that, with that new birth will come someone who refuses to bow before the terror.

Her belief that humanity's hope lies in each "new birth" enabled Arndt to close perhaps the most depressing book ever written on a note of hope, as she quoted from the Christian thinker, St. Augustine, who wrote during the last years of a collapsing Roman empire.

But there remains also the truth that every end in history necessarily contains a new beginning: this beginning is the promise, the only "message" which the end can ever produce. Beginning before it becomes a historical event, is the supreme capacity of man; politically, it is identical with man's freedom. *Initium ut esset homo creatus est*—"that a beginning be made man was created" said Augustine. This beginning is guaranteed by each new birth; it is indeed every man.

It is important to realize that the person whose birth she is describing is not simply someone who does not believe in the One Ideology. Mere unbelievers, she said, pose no threat. The totalitarian state needs only a few who actually believe (or pretend to believe) its ideology. For the rest, "The aim of totalitarian education has never been to instill convictions but to destroy the capacity to form any." It is enough that the great majority merely endure evil. They need not embrace it.

Gandalf, Aragorn, Elrond and Galadriel are Sauron's greatest foes precisely because they hold strong convictions about good and evil. The essential difference between the four fear-filled Hobbits who fled the Shire at the beginning of the story and the same four who boldly return at the end is the growth in their convictions. That is why they do not hesitate to challenge the legitimacy of Saruman's rules and those hired to enforce them. That is why they fight and are willing to die if necessary. Someone who is not willing to die for freedom is already a slave.

For Arendt, the critical factor that prepares modern societies for totalitarian rule is loneliness or, as she puts it elsewhere, the "atomization" of society. Loneliness, she stresses, is different from solitude. In solitude we talk with ourselves, in loneliness we lose the ability to talk with anyone about what really matters. But our ability to talk with ourselves and remain sensible, she emphasizes, is dependent on our relationship to others. It is in talking to others, that we learn to talk wisely with ourselves. When a totalitarian state destroys genuine communication between people, individuals are left with no "self" with whom they can talk.

To see that in concrete terms, think of the dark nights Sam experiences on the plains of Mordor and how, in solitude, he faced the fact that his journey across that blasted landscape would be one way, ending with his death. That alone would be enough to drive some to madness and still more to despair. Only a sense of himself and his place in the world,

Recall Chapter 5, "A Time of Preparation," and the importance Tolkien attached to births and family ties.

The Origins of Totalitarianism, 479. The quote is from Augustine's *The City of God*, Bk. 12, Ch. 20. Recall the importance one boy, grown to manhood, has against the machines in the movie series, *The Terminator*.

A similar lack of conviction can result from value-free education. Tolkien's friend, C. S. Lewis, blasted that in his *The Abolition of Man*. The first chapter closes with an apt summary: "We make men without chests and expect of them virtue and enterprise. We laugh at honour and are shocked to find traitors in our midst. We castrate and bid the geldings be fruitful." Lewis described how England might lose its freedom to technocrats in the third volume of his science fiction trilogy, *That Hideous Strength*.

In a May 1944 letter, Tolkien compared Britain's wartime regimentation to "attempting to conquer Sauron with the Ring." That, he said, would "slowly turn men and Elves into Orcs." *Letters*, No. 66. Tolkien's Orcs, you might remember, gripe and complain about orders, but in the end do as they are told.

nurtured over many years by his fellow Hobbits, enabled him to go on, giving his life on a mission that, as far as he knew, would provide him with no benefit.

That, you may also remember, was precisely why Gandalf was impressed with the kindness that Hobbits displayed for one another as so many lay dying during the Long Winter of 1158 to 1159. It was why he came to believe that, given the proper inspiration, these small, fun-loving Hobbits could achieve a greatness equal to that of Elves and men.

In "Wartime Wisdom" Peter Kreeft notes that, "The single force most responsible for winning the War of the Ring is Sam's friendship and love of Frodo." See *Celebrating Middle-earth,* 48.

Different Reactions to Sauron

In the past that Tolkien created for Middle-earth, Elves, Dwarves, and men were not as united in their opposition to Sauron as they are in this tale. Of the three, Tolkien felt that Sauron found men the easiest to seduce into evil—as shown by the alliances he is still able to make with nations to the south and east of Mordor. Elves were more difficult to tempt, but some could be flattered and deceived. That is why Sauron was able to use them to make the other Great Rings. Only after Sauron put on the One Ring—which he forged in secret—did they see through his schemes and become his undying foes. (Given their long lives, the Elves are less troubled by a problem that haunts others races. One generation of humans may learn a lesson well, but with each new generation, that lessons fades until the mistake is repeated yet again.) Tolkien's Dwarves are perhaps the most surprising. They are corruptible, but only by greed. Proud, strong-willed and unwilling to serve others, they are as ill suited to be Sauron's servants, as they were to share their wealth at the end of *The Hobbit.* But what was in most circumstances a serious character flaw, became a virtue in the special circumstances of *The Lord of the Rings.*

For more about each of Middle-earth's peoples, see the last chapter in *The Silmarillion,* "Of the Rings of Power and the Third Age." See also *Letters,* No. 181. For a discussion of how various individuals and races followed evil, see *Letters,* No. 153.

The Hobbits, newcomers to Middle-earth history, are the great unknown in Tolkien's tale. He will use the War of the Ring to test their character, and in the end they do surprisingly well, much as Gandalf had hoped. But notice that Tolkien did not believe any of his races, including the lovable Hobbits, were without fault. Near the end of Tolkien's tale, we discover that Saruman corrupted a few of them and demonstrated that, in the absence of strong leadership, most of the rest could be intimidated. But, as Tolkien has Gandalf observe, there is a strength about them that surprises those who see only their love of comfort and dislike of adventure. Among the many creatures that Tolkien created, the Hobbits may be the most interesting.

For a discussion of Tolkien's different peoples, see Deborah C. Rogers, "Everyclod and Everyhero: The Image of Man in Tolkien" in *A Tolkien Compass,* 69f.

17

Peace Returns

April 7 to August 22, 1419

War's aftermath to dividing the Fellowship

Covers 139 Days
Day 197 to 335

"Anguish," C. S. Lewis tells us, is "almost the prevailing note of *The Lord of the Rings*." But it is not the anguish "typical of our age, the anguish of abnormal or contorted souls." No, it is that of healthy-minded Hobbits who love nothing better than "a snug fireside and many an hour of good cheer." It is that of "those who were happy before a certain darkness came up and will be happy if they live to see it gone."

All of the darkness and much of the anguish is now gone and much that has been delayed so long—marriage, coronation and homecoming—blossoms forth as life in Middle-earth returns to normal.

From his August 14, 1954 review in *Time and Time*, republished in Lesley Walmsley's *C. S. Lewis*, 521.

Friday, April 7, 1419—Pippin Recovers

Day 197
March 31

Pippin

Ithilien

• Pippin is able to walk about.

The Return of the King, Bk. 6, Ch. 4, "The Field of Cormallen."

Comparing Illnesses

Tolkien gave three Hobbits illnesses of equal severity to be cured with a similar treatment—a deep sleep induced by Aragorn. Pippin, crushed beneath an Orc during the battle at the Black Gate twelve days ago, is able to walk today. Sam will come out of a coma the following day, oblivious to how long has passed. Tolkien left unclear when Frodo recovered. But Frodo seems to know as little about what has happened as Sam, suggesting that he too recently awoke.

Saturday, April 8, 1419—Renewing Friendships

Day 198
April 1

A full moon rises in the east about 8:30 p.m. and sets in the west just before eight the next morning.

Aragorn, Gandalf, Gimli Frodo, Legolas, Merry, Pippin and Sam

Field of Cormallen, Ithilien

The Return of the King, Bk. 6, Ch. 4, "The Field of Cormallen."

- About noon, Sam awakes.
- That evening they feast and meet friends.

The Return of the King, Bk. 6, Ch. 5, "The Steward and the King."

Of Boats and Horses

There is a hint in Tolkien's writings that he considered boat travel less demanding for the injured than carts or horseback, probably because the jostling is more gentle. On an unknown day sometime before this date, Merry, still recovering from his clash with the Lord of the Nazgûl, was brought by boat up the Anduin to rejoin his friends. In 20 days, the still-recovering Hobbits will make a similar journey down the Anduin. Perhaps when Tolkien was recovering from wartime injury and illness, he found boat travel easier than train.

Early to Mid-April, 1419—Engagement

Éowyn and Faramir

Date Approximate

Minas Tirith

The Return of the King, Bk. 6, Ch. 6, "Many Partings." For Tolkien's description of the romance between Faramir and Éowyn, see Letters, No. 244.

- Faramir and Éowyn become engaged.

Dating Faramir and Éowyn's Engagement

The date of Faramir and Éowyn's engagement was not given by Tolkien, but it came some time after Faramir became busy preparing for Aragorn's return and before Aragorn arrived—perhaps early to mid-April.

Friday, April 28 to Sunday, April 30, 1419

Day 218–220
April 21–23
3 Days

The first quarter moon rises on April 30 in the east-northeast just after noon and will set the next day in west-northwest shortly after 2 a.m.

Aragorn, Frodo, Gandalf, Gimli, Legolas, Merry, Pippin and Sam with the Captains of the West

Cair Andros to Minas Tirith

The Return of the King, Bk. 6, Ch. 4, "The Field of Cormallen" and Bk. 6, Ch. 5, "The Steward and the King."

- On April 28, they voyage to Osgiliath, staying overnight and a day.
- On April 30, they travel to Minas Tirith, arriving in the evening.

To Minas Tirith for Coronation

A look back illustrates just how much change Tolkien has compressed in so little time. A little over ten weeks have passed since the travelers left Lórien on February 16 to travel down the Anduin at a point about 500 miles upstream from where they start this day. Fifty-nine days have passed since Faramir saw his brother's body drifting in a canoe down this stretch of the river on February 29. Finally, a little over a month has passed since the Ring was destroyed.

The ruins of Osgiliath are about 50 miles away, so Tolkien needs them to leave early on April 28 and paddle rapidly to fit this journey into one day. Karen Fonstad estimates that upstream in their earlier journey they covered 40 miles a day drifting for long hours and 55 miles by paddling.

Tolkien gives no reason for their one day stay in Osgiliath. If pressed, he might suggest that Frodo, Pippin and Sam were still recovering and needed a rest before taking a land journey to Minas Tirith. Though the city was in ruins, it could have had housing for soldiers stationed there.

For some reason, Tolkien chose to have Aragorn arrive only the day before his crowning. The timing may be a matter of official protocol. It limits the time in which a king is present but uncrowned to an absolute minimum. It also spares Aragorn, a man more accustomed to wilderness than royal courts, the unfamiliar burden of planning the celebration. Similarly, Arwen arrives the day before her wedding. Unlike most brides, she did not have to concern herself with wedding preparations.

See her Pathways Table in "Pathways," The Atlas of Middle-earth and the entries in this book for February 17 and 29, 1419.

Monday, May 1, 1419—Aragorn's Coronation

Day 221
April 24

Aragorn, Faramir, Frodo, Gandalf, Gimli, Legolas, Merry, Pippin and Sam

Minas Tirith

• Aragorn becomes King Elessar and allows Faramir to remain Steward.

A Symbolic Transfer of Power

Born during the reign of Queen Victoria, Tolkien was accustomed to long-established traditions, such as the ceremonies that accompany the coronation of a king or queen. Here he makes the transfer of power complex and many faceted. Faramir, Steward of the city, willingly gives up his office while the people, in a form of verbal democracy, agree to recognize their new king. In such ceremonies, significance is often attached to who places the crown on the king's head. Aragorn refuses to do that for himself (he will not be a 'self-made' king). Instead, he has Frodo bring the crown and Gandalf place it on his head. It is symbolic of the great debt he owes to both.

The Return of the King, Bk. 6, Ch. 5, "The Steward and the King."

G. K. Chesterton wrote that: "Tradition means giving votes to the most obscure of all classes, our ancestors. It is the democracy of the dead. Tradition refuses to submit to the small and arrogant oligarchy of those who merely happen to be walking about. All democrats object to men being disqualified by the accident of birth; tradition objects to their being disqualified by the accident of death." *Orthodoxy,* Ch. 4, "The Ethics of Elfland."

Arwen and Elrond

Day 1 of 61 in Journey, Day 1 of 20 to Lórien

Rivendell for Lórien

• Accompanied by her father Elrond, Arwen leaves Rivendell.

The Return of the King, Bk. 6, Ap. A, "The Tale of Years."

Aragorn and Arwen's Romance

See *The Return of the King,* Bk. 6, Ap. A, "Annuals of the Kings and Rulers, Sec. I, v, "Here Follows a Part of the Tale of Aragorn and Arwen."

In storybooks, a man of wealth and power often marries a beautiful woman. Tolkien saw no reason to violate that well-established custom. Now that the care-worn Aragorn has become a powerful king, the pretty (although far from young) Arwen is free to marry him.

Arwen begins her journey to Minas Tirith to marry Aragorn on the very day he is crowned king. Elrond, it seems, is being quite literal in his insistence that his daughter may only marry a king.

Day 228f
May 1f

Monday, May 8, 1419 and After

Éomer, Éowyn and the Riders of Rohan

Minas Tirith to Rohan

The Return of the King, Bk. 6, Ch. 5, "The Steward and the King."

• On May 8, Éomer and Éowyn leave to prepare Théoden's funeral.

An End and a Beginning

At this point Tolkien weaves into his story two of life's major passages, the funeral for Théoden and the marriage of Aragorn and Arwen. Notice that he often selected memorable days for historic events. Aragorn is crowned on May Day and marries on Midyear's Day.

Aragorn, Frodo, Gandalf, Gimli, Legolas, Merry, Pippin and Sam

Minas Tirith

The Return of the King, Bk. 6, Ch. 5, "The Steward and the King." For more about what Gandalf told the others during those days together, see: *Unfinished Tales,* Pt. III, Ch. III, "The Quest of Erebor."

• During this time, they live together and Gandalf tells of the past.
• Gandalf tells Frodo that Aragorn is preparing a surprise.

Unfinished Tales

Unfortunately, in the 1950s Tolkien's publishers did not get Tolkien to complete Gandalf's fascinating tales. Of course, it is also true that any time a publisher suggested another book, Tolkien would offer drafts of *The Silmarillion.* Publishers who saw it did not think it would sell well.

Day 240–266
May 13–June 8
27 Days

Saturday, May 20 to Thursday, June 16, 1419

Arwen and Elrond

Day 20–46 of 61 in Journey

From Lórien to Departing Edoras for Minas Tirith

The Return of the King, Bk. 6, Ap. B, "The Tale of Years."

• Arwen travels from Rivendell to Edoras, passing through Lórien.

Comparing Travel Times

The journey to Lórien from Rivendell took 20 days (May 1 to 20). Since Tolkien has the nine travelers (reduced to eight in Moria) make the

Arwen has probably traveled between her relatives in Rivendell and Lórien many times in her long life.

same journey in 22 days of mostly night travel done as rapidly as possible, Tolkien seems to have intended for Arwen's party to move quickly.

After resting for six days in Lórien, Tolkien has Arwen venture into unfamiliar landscapes, leaving for Edoras on May 27. Éomer's remarks when he first meets Aragorn on the plains of Rohan suggest that few Elves went into his unwooded land. Even the much closer Galadriel (the 'Lady of the Wood') was regarded as little more than a legend, so the well-protected and reclusive Arwen's trip through Rohan is extremely unusual.

After 18 days on the road, Arwen reaches Edoras on June 14. With Sauron now defeated and his Orc allies scattered, Tolkien can regard the mountain passages as safe even for a sheltered queen-to-be. Since Arwen arrived in Edoras on the 44th day of her journey and left on the 46th (June 16), she spends but a single day in the city, far less than in Lórien, where she felt more at home. Given that she will reach Minas Tirith the day before her wedding (1 Lithe), she did not have time to stay longer.

> For Rohan's view of Elves, see *The Two Towers,* Bk. 3, Ch. 2, "The Riders of Rohan." In drafts, Arwen was named Ellonel and Finduilas. See *The End of the Third Age,* Ch. 7, "Many Partings," 66.

Thursday, June 23 to Friday, June 24, 1419

> Day 273–274
> June 15–16
> 2 Days

Aragorn and Gandalf

Mount Mindolluin above Minas Tirith

- On June 23, Gandalf takes Aragorn to Mount Mindolluin.
- On June 24, Gandalf shows Aragorn a young White Tree.
- Aragorn plants the tree in the city, where it blossoms.

> *The Return of the King,* Bk. 6, Ch. 5, "The Steward and the King."

The White Tree

Gondor has been without a king for 969 years (since 450), so Aragorn needs a special sign to confirm he is the lawful king. Aragorn's discovery of this young tree supports his claim to the throne. The city's last White Tree (a descendant of Teleprion, the Eldest of Trees) died 167 years before in 1252 without leaving a seed. How and when this young tree came to be plated is a mystery Tolkien never answered.

> For the date of the tree's sprouting, see the discussion in this book for 1412.

Friday, 1 Lithe, 1419—Arwen at Minas Tirith

> Day 281
> June 23

Arwen, Elrond, Celeborn and Galadriel

Day 61 of 61 in Journey, Day 16 of 16 to Minas Tirith

Minas Tirith

- Arwen arrives at Minas Tirith after 15 days of travel.

Cutting It Close

Tolkien cut Arwen's arrival rather close. She reaches Minas Tirith the day before her wedding. As with Aragorn's coronation, the chief participant has no time to play a role in the preparation for the ceremony.

> *The Return of the King,* Bk. 6, Ch. 5, "The Steward and the King" and *The Return of the King,* Bk. 6, Ap. B, "The Tale of Years."

Midyear's Day, 1419—Aragorn's Wedding

Day 282
June 24

Aragorn and Arwen

Minas Tirith

- King Elessar (Aragorn) and Arwen marry.

The Return of the King, Bk. 6, Ch. 5, "The Steward and the King" and *The Return of the King,* Bk. 6, Ap. B, "The Tale of Years." Midsummer's Day and Midyear's Day refer to the same day.

A Long Engagement and Marriage

Arwen has waited a long time to marry. Born in the 241st year of the Third Age and remarkably pretty, she is 2778 years old. In contrast, Aragorn, born in 2931 of the Third Age, is a mere youngster of 88 years. They have known each other for 68 years and have been engaged for 39 of those years. To say the least, it has been a most unusual romance.

Their relationship divides easily into four distinct periods.

1. 1351–1380 During the first 29 years they knew each other, Aragorn wanted to marry Arwen, while she remained uncommitted.

2. 1380–1409 During the second 29 years, the two are engaged, but Elrond has not given permission for their marriage.

3. 1409–1419 During the following 10 years, they wait until Aragorn meets the conditions Elrond set for their marriage.

4. 1419–1541 The final period is their 122 years of marriage. At the time of Aragorn's death they will have known each other for 190 years.

Day 298
July 10

Sunday, July 15, 1419

Aragorn, Arwen and Frodo

Minas Tirith

The Return of the King, Bk. 6, Ch. 6, "Many Partings."

- Frodo tells Aragorn he wants to return to the Shire.
- Aragorn suggests he accompany Théoden's funeral party.

Frodo's Rapid Decline

Tolkien wants us to sense that Bilbo's decline into old age has been very rapid. Arwen noticed it even though she was only in Rivendell for five weeks after the destruction of the Ring.

Day 301
July 13

Wednesday, July 18, 1419

On this night, the moon is new, so the nights will be dark.

Éomer and Gimli

Minas Tirith

The Return of the King, Bk. 6, Ch. 6, "Many Partings."

- Éomer of Rohan arrives with a picked set of knights.

Chivalry and Symbolism

Tolkien knew the emphasis Medieval knighthood placed on honoring women, and you see that attitude here. That evening Éomer calls Gimli to tell him Lady Galadriel is not the fairest in the world, instead Queen Arwen is the more beautiful. Gimli replies that, although they do not agree, they can remain friends—Éomer has chosen the evening, while he has chosen the morning. It is a clever way to settle their disagreement and contains a symbolic meaning. As Gimli suggests, the morning or Age of Elves (Galadriel) is passing, while the evening or Age of Man (now that Arwen is married to a man) has arrived.

Although Sauron has been destroyed, the possibility of renegade Orc bands requires an armed guard for the slow-moving funeral procession.

Thursday, July 19, 1419

Day 302
July 14

Funeral Escort

Minas Tirith to Edoras

- An escort leaves to prepare the way for the main funeral party.

The Return of the King, Bk. 6, Ap. B, "The Tale of Years."

The Role of the Escort

Like Secret Service advance teams who prepare for a Presidential trip, this escort will look for bands of Orcs and make sure any bridges or sections of road destroyed in the war are repaired.

Sunday, July 22 to August 7, 1419

Day 305–320
July 17–August 1
16 Days

The moon is full on August 2, so they will be traveling north during a time when the nights are brightly lit. That provides them with additional protection from Orcs.

Aragorn, Frodo, Gandalf, Gimli, Legolas, Merry, Pippin and Sam with Arwen and numerous others

Day 1–16 of 16 in the Funeral Journey

Minas Tirith to Edoras

- On July 22, the funeral party leaves for Rohan with the king's body.

Edoras

The Return of the King, Bk. 6, Ch. 6, "Many Partings."

- On August 7, King Théoden's funeral procession reaches Edoras.

The Return of the King, Bk. 6, Ch. 6, "Many Partings" and *The Return of the King,* Bk. 6, Ap. B, "The Tale of Years." Their journey to Edoras takes three times longer than Théoden's frantic ride down

Chronology of the Funeral Escort

According to "The Tale of Years," the funeral escort for King Théoden left the day after Éomer arrived in Minas Tirith on July 18. But Aragorn's words to Frodo in "Many Partings" indicate that most of the funeral party left with Théoden's body four days after Éomer's arrival. A July 22 departure is also easier to fit with their August 7 arrival and the specified 15-day travel time. (It is either 15 or 16 days of travel to August 7, depending on whether partial days of travel are counted. Here we count portions of days for a total of 16.) Leaving on July 19, however, gives either 18 or 19 days. This chronology assumes a scouting party left on the 19th and the main party left on the 22nd.

Day 321–322
August 2
2 Days

Tuesday, August 8 to Wednesday, August 9, 1419

Aragorn, Frodo, Gandalf, Gimli, Legolas, Merry, Pippin and Sam with Arwen

Edoras

The Return of the King, Bk. 6, Ch. 6, "Many Partings."

For Théoden's linage see *The Return of the King,* Bk. 6, Ap. A, "Annals of the Kings and Rulers," under the subsection, "The Kings of the Mark."

• Preparations are made for Théoden's funeral.

Théoden's Linage

The meticulous Tolkien created a long family linage for Théoden. The last king, Théoden's father Thengle, died in 1380. This is the first funeral for a king that Rohan has had in almost 40 years. Only older members of the population remember the last one.

Day 323
August 4

Thursday, August 10, 1419—Théoden's Funeral

Aragorn, Frodo, Gandalf, Gimli, Legolas, Merry, Pippin and Sam with Arwen

Edoras

The Return of the King, Bk. 6, Ch. 6, "Many Partings," Bk. 6, Ap. A, "Annals of the Kings and Rulers," Sec. v and Bk. 6, Ap. B, "The Tale of Years." For Tolkien's remarks about the romance between Faramir and Éowyn, see *Letters,* No. 244.

• Théoden is buried.
• Éomer announces his sister's engagement to Faramir.
• Arwen has her last conversation with her father Elrond.

The Bitter and the Sweet

Tolkien mixes both bitter and sweet in this day. The bitter is the funeral for Théoden and Arwen's parting from her father, their relationship not to be renewed in this life. There is also the sweet—the feast after the funeral and Éowyn's engagement. Even in the midst of grief, Tolkien is saying, life must go on.

Day 327
August 8

Monday, August 14, 1419

Aragorn, Frodo, Gandalf, Gimli, Legolas, Merry, Pippin and Sam with Arwen

Day 1 of 37 to Rivendell

Edoras to Helm's Deep

The Return of the King, Bk. 6, Ch. 6, "Many Partings."

• Éomer and Éowyn give Merry an ancient horn.
• The Companions of the Ring leave Edoras for Helm's Deep.

Merry's Horn

The horn illustrates how magic plays a distinctly secondary role in Tolkien's tale. Boromir's horn brought no aid. Merry's horn will play only a minor role in freeing the Shire, with most of the credit going to careful planning and Hobbit bravery. In many folk tales, magic is more powerful than any character. In Tolkien, except for the Ring, the reverse is true.

Tuesday, August 15, 1419

Day 328
August 9

Treebeard with Saruman and Gríma

Orthanc, Isengard

- Treebeard allows Saruman and Gríma to leave Orthanc.

The Return of the King, Bk. 6, Ch. 6, "Many Partings."

Sympathetic Ents

Each of Tolkien's races has certain traits. Elves are artistic and elusive, Dwarves are blunt and good at making money, and so forth. As a race whose mission is shepherding slow-growing trees, the Ents are patient, kind and sympathetic. Here Treebeard shows sympathy. Saruman imprisoned himself inside Orthanc over five months earlier on March 3. Even the damage he inflicted on Fangorn does not prevent Treebeard from feeling that the evil Wizard has suffered enough and is now harmless. Events soon demonstrate he was naive.

The separation between Ents and Entwives can be blamed on the great sympathy each feels for a different sort of tree. See Treebeard's remarks in *The Two Towers,* Bk. 3, Ch. 4, "Treebeard."

Friday, August 18 to Sunday, August 20, 1419

Day 331-333
August 12-14
3 Days

Aragorn, Frodo, Gandalf, Gimli, Legolas, Merry, Pippin and Sam with Elrond, Celeborn and Galadriel

Day 4 to 6 of 37 to Rivendell

Helm's Deep and Glittering Caverns

- The travelers reach Helm's Deep on the 18th and rest the 19th and 20th
- On the 19th or 20th, Legolas goes into the Glittering Caves with Gimli.

The Return of the King, Bk. 6, Ch. 6, "Many Partings," *The Two Towers,* Bk. 3, Ch. 8, "The Road to Isengard."

Glittering Caves

Tolkien wanted to show that even Elves and Dwarves can be friends. On March 4, after the Battle of Hornburg, Gimli and Legolas agree to show each what the other deemed beautiful. Gimli would show the Elf the Glittering Caves, while Legolas would take the Dwarf deep within Fangorn Forest. This is the first of those visits.

The Two Towers, Bk. 3, Ch. 8, "The Road to Isengard." The caves are also known as *Aglarond,* Sindarin for "Halls of Glory."

Tolkien's relationship with C. S. Lewis shows that Dwarf/Elf sorts of differences have little to do with friendship. Lewis put it this way: "At my first coming into the world, I had been (implicitly) warned never to trust a Papist, and at my first coming into the English Faculty (explicitly) never to trust a philologist. Tolkien was both." Yet in the end, neither mattered because, as Lewis put it, "You become a man's friend without knowing or caring . . . how he earns his living. What have all these . . . to do with the real question, *Do you see the same truth?* In the circle of true Friends, each man is simply what he is: [he] stands for nothing but himself."

Trust: C. S. Lewis, *Surprised by Joy* (London: Fontana, 1955), 173. This is near the start of Ch. 14, "Checkmate." Friend: C. S. Lewis, *The Four Loves* (London: Fontana, 1960), 66. This is one third of the way through Ch. 4, "Friendship."

Monday, August 21, 1419—For Isengard

Day 334
August 15

Aragorn, Frodo, Gandalf, Gimli, Legolas, Merry, Pippin and Sam with Elrond, Celeborn and Galadriel

Day 7 of 37 to Rivendell, Date Estimated

Helm's Deep to Isengard

The Return of the King, Bk. 6, Ch. 6, "Many Partings."

- They leave for Isengard.

The Stay at Helm's Deep

Tolkien's remark that they rested for two days at Helm's Deep is ambiguous. Here we assume they arrived on the 18th, rested on the 19th and 20th, and leave for Isengard on August 21. That gives them all that day and part of the next to reach Isengard, roughly 50 miles away.

Day 335
August 16

Tuesday, August 22, 1419—Fellowship Divides

Aragorn, Frodo, Gandalf, Gimli, Legolas, Merry, Pippin and Sam with Elrond, Celeborn and Galadriel

Day 8 of 37 to Rivendell

Isengard

The Return of the King, Bk. 6, Ch. 6, "Many Partings." Saruman was freed on August 15. On August 28, they catch up with him.

Their promises were made in *The Two Towers,* Bk. 3, Ch. 8, "The Road to Isengard." Legolas also mentioned visiting Fangorn to Treebeard in *The Two Towers,* Bk. 3, Ch. 10, "The Voice of Saruman." Treebeard was understandably suspicious about an axe-bearing Dwarf entering his forest.

- At Isengard, Treebeard says he let Saruman go.
- Gimli and Legolas go to visit Fangorn Forest.
- The others leave Isengard southward and Aragorn leaves them.

Promises Made and Kept

In Tolkien's tale much of the enmity between Dwarf and Elf was the result of perceptions by each that the other had violated a trust. After the Battle of Hornburg, Gimli and Legolas had discussed visiting the Caves of Helm's Deep and the forest of Fangorn together. Here Tolkien has his representative Dwarf and Elf keep their promises. Gimli and Legolas had visited the Glittering Caves a few days earlier. Legolas now takes Gimli to visit Fangorn Forest. There we can assume that Gimli acquired an understanding of the Elves and their great love for woods.

CHAPTER

18

Returning Home

August 23, 1419 to Late 1419

Departing for Bree to freeing the Shire

G. K. Chesterton once began a book by describing how a journey can change how we view our home. He used as an example a tale he never wrote.

> I conceived it as a romance of those vast valleys with sloping sides, like those along which the ancient White Horses of Wessex are scrawled along the flanks of the hills. It concerned some boy whose farm or cottage stood on such a slope, and who went on his travels to find something, such as the effigy and grave of some giant; and when he was far enough from home he looked back and saw that his own farm and kitchen-garden, shining flat on the hill-side like the colours and quarterings of a shield, were but parts of some such gigantic figure, on which he had always lived, but which was too large and too close to be seen. That, I think, is a true picture of the progress of any really independent intelligence today; and that is the point of this book.

G. K. Chesterton, *The Everlasting Man,* at the beginning of "Introduction: The Plan of the Book."

That never-written tale illustrates how the four Hobbits will find their view of the Shire forever altered by the new vistas and distant perspectives they acquired during their travels. It is also resembles the impact Tolkien has on many of his readers.

Wednesday, August 23 to Sunday, August 27, 1419

Day 336–340
August 17–21
5 Days

Frodo, Gandalf, Merry, Pippin and Sam with Elrond, Celeborn and Galadriel

Day 9 to 13 of 37 to Rivendell

Gap of Rohan to Dunland

- The travelers ride through the Gap of Rohan and into the wastelands.
- They turn north into Dunland.

The Return of the King, Bk. 6, Ch. 6, "Many Partings."

Dunland's Alliances

For more about Dunland, see *Unfinished Tales*, Pt. 3, Ch. IV, "The Hunt for the Ring," Note 18. For Dunland fighting with Rohan, see *The War of the Ring*, Pt. 3, Ch. II, "Book Five Begun and Abandoned."

The people of Dunland have good reason to fear the victors in the War of the Ring. When Saruman had goods from the Shire shipped south, it appears they were transported openly to Dunland and then taken secretly to Isengard. This suggests Dunland was covertly allied with Saruman. On the other hand, in draft versions, Tolkien had some men from Dunland fighting with Rohan. Perhaps, like many small countries caught up in great wars, they tried to play on both sides.

Day 341
August 22

Monday, August 28, 1419—Meeting Saruman

Frodo, Gandalf, Merry, Pippin and Sam with Elrond, Celeborn and Galadriel
Day 14 of 37 to Rivendell

Central Dunland

The Return of the King, Bk. 6, Ch. 6, "Many Partings." For how Tolkien developed his account of their trip home, see: *The End of the Third Age*, Ch. 8, "Homeward Bound." Saruman locked himself inside Orthanc on March 3, 1419 and was allowed to leave by Treebeard over five months later on August 15, 1419.

- Near sunset the travelers meet Saruman and Wormtongue.
- To avoid them, Saruman turns west.

Two Journeys, One Destination

As readers, we can lament that the travelers were not perceptive enough to wonder where Saruman was going or take seriously his hints that all was not well in the Shire. If they had, they might have shortened their journey and reached the Shire sooner.

A little geography will help us understand how Tolkien calculated Saruman's journey and their own. Saruman will reach the Shire, roughly 350 miles away, on September 22, after 24 days on foot, traveling just under 15 miles a day. Going through Rivendell and traveling about twice as far in twice as long (47 days on the road), as well as staying 12 days in Rivendell, the Hobbits will take two months to reach the Shire on ponies, not arriving until October 30.

Day 342–348
August 23–29
7 Days

Tuesday, August 29 to Monday, September 5, 1419

Frodo, Gandalf, Merry, Pippin and Sam with Elrond, Celeborn and Galadriel
Day 15 to 21 of 37 to Rivendell

The moon is full on September 1, so these nights are well-lit. That is why Tolkien described the month beginning with nights of silver.

North Dunland to Eregion

The Return of the King, Bk. 6, Ch. 6, "Many Partings."

- On August 29, the travelers enter uninhabited northern Dunland.
- They cross the Swanfleet River into Eregion.

A Pleasant Wilderness

Tolkien's unpopulated wildernesses are typically unpleasant places. Like Ithilien, northern Dunland is an exception, and even here he hints that this is the sort of place where people *ought* to be living. Tolkien believed people could live in harmony with nature.

See "Tolkien's Natural World" at the end of Chapter 8.

Tuesday, September 6 to Tuesday, September 20, 1419

Day 349–363
August 30–September 13
15 Days

The moon is at its last quarter on September 9, so the nights are growing darker. It will be new on September 17.

Frodo, Gandalf, Merry, Pippin and Sam with Elrond, Celeborn and Galadriel

Day 22 to 36 of 37 to Rivendell

Near the Gates of Moria

- On September 6, the travelers halt near the Gates of Moria.
- Gandalf has long mental conversations with Celeborn and Galadriel.

The Return of the King, Bk. 6, Ch. 6, "Many Partings."

Much Melancholy

Tolkien passes quickly over the six days spent here, but there is a deep sadness accompanying the thoughts that were exchanged. One disadvantage to living for many centuries, as have Gandalf and the Elves, is that the pain becomes all the greater when relationships built up over vast expanses of time must be broken. Parting may be 'sweet sorrow,' but it is sorrow nonetheless.

To Rivendell

- On September 13, the Elves from Lórien head for the Redhorn Gate.
- The others leave for Rivendell.

The Return of the King, Bk. 6, Ch. 6, "Many Partings."

Redhorn Gate

Much has happened in Middle-earth during the eight months since January 11, when the travelers made their ill-fated attempt to cross Redhorn Gate. Since it is late summer, the Elves should have no problem with blizzards.

Wednesday, September 21, 1419—Rivendell

Day 364
September 14

Bilbo, Frodo, Gandalf, Merry, Pippin and Sam with Elrond

Day 37 of 37 to Rivendell

Rivendell

- In the evening the travelers reach Rivendell and find Bilbo.

The Return of the King, Bk. 6, Ch. 6, "Many Partings."

Timing their Arrival

It is unlikely that their arrival on the very eve of Bilbo and Frodo's birthday was an accident. No doubt Tolkien intended for them to arrive in time for Bilbo and Frodo's birthday. Given the role that birthday parties play in his stories, Tolkien seems to have had a great fondness for them.

Much has happened since a near-dead Frodo first reached Rivendell on October 20, 1418, almost exactly 11 months (336 days) earlier.

Thursday, September 22, 1419—Two Birthdays

Day 365
September 15

Bilbo, Frodo, Gandalf, Merry, Pippin and Sam

Day 1 of 12 in Rivendell

Rivendell

The Return of the King, Bk. 6, Ch. 6, "Many Partings."

• Bilbo celebrates his 129th birthday and Frodo celebrates his 51st.

Saruman and Wormtongue

Shire

The Return of the King, Bk. 6, Ch. 8, "The Scouring of the Shire" and *The Return of the King*, Bk. 6, Ap. B, "The Tale of Years."

• Saruman (known as "Sharkey") and Gríma reach the Shire.

Saruman and the Shire

It seems likely that Tolkien, who spent quite a bit of time fussing over the chronology that lies behind this tale, deliberately had Saruman reach the Shire on Bilbo and Frodo's birthday. That backs up remarks Saruman makes which suggest he is getting revenge for the destruction of Isengard. In addition to the harm his thugs have already done, Saruman will have over a month to wreck the Shire before the Hobbits return.

See *Unfinished Tales*, Pt. 3, Ch. 4, "The Hunt for the Ring," Sec. iii.

Tolkien placed the historical roots for this tragedy almost seventy years earlier. Probably just after the Fourth White Council in 1353, Saruman visited the Shire in disguise. He was curious about Gandalf's interest in the place and suspicious enough to study the Hobbits and put agents there. Fortunately, he did not link Hobbits with the Ring. He saw only a people and land he could exploit.

Day 366–375
September 16–26
10 Days

Friday, September 23 to Sunday, October 2, 1419

The moon is first quarter on September 24 and full on October 1.

Bilbo, Frodo, Merry, Pippin and Sam

Day 2 to 10 of 12 in Rivendell

Rivendell

The Return of the King, Bk. 6, Ch. 6, "Many Partings."

• The four Hobbits spend much time with Bilbo.

Tolkien's Elderly Scholars

The gap between Bilbo's desire to write and his constant naps or distractions, perhaps hints at how Tolkien regarded the lives of elderly scholars such as himself. Having escaped the grind of grading papers, they find they no longer have the energy for literary pursuits.

Monday, October 3 to Tuesday, October 4, 1419

Day 376–377
September 26–27
2 Days

Bilbo, Frodo, Gandalf, Merry, Pippin and Sam
Day 11 to 12 of 12 in Rivendell

Rivendell

• On October 3, Sam tells Frodo he wants to be back in the Shire.

Hurting Heroes

Tolkien hints that Frodo's homecoming will be different from Sam's. Like Bilbo, as a Ring-bearer Frodo is a marked man and must eventually leave Middle-earth to seek his healing over the sea. In that respect, Tolkien's ending differs from the typical heroic tale. Elsewhere, the hero typically lives happily and long, benefiting from the fame he has achieved. But Frodo achieves no great fame at home and must soon travel far away. Perhaps Tolkien's views were influenced by seeing World War I heroes who never recovered from their experiences.

Rivendell

• On October 4, Elrond tells Frodo and Sam to leave the next day.

The Return of the King, Bk. 6, Ch. 6, "Many Partings."

Bilbo's Gifts

Tolkien was as fascinated by gifts as he was by birthday parties. Bilbo gives Frodo three books of translations from the Elvish, no doubt the product of long labors. Sam gets a practical gift—a small bag of gold for his marriage. (For Bilbo to know of the marriage, Sam must have talked of his anticipated reunion with Rose Cotton, which comes on November 2.) Along with pipes for smoking, Merry and Pippin get friendly advice, perhaps having something to do with how the dull Shire will regard two returning adventurers. (Bilbo knew that well.) Finally, before they leave Bilbo gives Frodo his notes and papers to be sorted and arranged. It is those notes, added to by Frodo and Sam, that Tolkien wants us to assume eventually became *The Hobbit* and *The Lord of the Rings*.

Wednesday, October 5, 1419—Leaving Rivendell

Day 378
September 28

Frodo, Gandalf, Merry, Pippin and Sam
Day 1 of 23 to Bree

Leaving Rivendell

• The travelers leave for Bree and the Shire.

The Return of the King, Bk. 6, Ch. 6, "Many Partings." Bilbo and Elrond will pass through the Shire almost exactly two years later.

Prophetic Wisdom

Today we see prophecy as a supernatural vision of the future with no connection to how well the prophet understands the world around him. That sort of vision could come to the smallest child as easily as to the most mature of adults. But for Tolkien, the ability to predict the future was often part of an ability to link what we see in the present with what we have observed in a long life of thought and reflection. From this perspective, life has patterns that constantly recur and can be understood by the wise. When Elrond says that Bilbo will return to the Shire about this time of year, he is simply being observant. In the past, Bilbo and Frodo took to the road in the fall when their shared birthday arrived. They will do so again.

Day 379–380
September 29–30
2 Days

Thursday, October 6 to 7, 1419

Frodo, Gandalf, Merry, Pippin and Sam
Day 2 to 3 of 23 to Bree

Near the Ford of Bruinen

The Return of the King, Bk. 6, Ch. 7, "Homeward Bound."

- On October 6 at the Ford of Bruinen, Frodo is in pain.
- By the end of October 7, Frodo's pain has eased.

One Year to the Day
This is an anniversary flashback. Exactly one year earlier, on October 6, 1418, Frodo was wounded by a Nazgûl knife on Weathertop.

Day 381–400
October 1–20
20 Days

Saturday, October 8 to Thursday, October 27, 1419

The moon is new on October 10, first quarter on the 17, and full on the 24th.

Frodo, Gandalf, Merry, Pippin and Sam
Day 4 to 22 of 23 to Bree

Westbound on the Great East Road

The Return of the King, Bk. 6, Ch. 7, "Homeward Bound."

- The party travels slowly along the Great East Road.
- Frodo hurries past Weathertop (perhaps on October 23).

Calculating the Date for Weathertop
Given the care that Tolkien exercised in getting his travel times right, it is possible to calculate when the travelers passed Weathertop. In the other direction the previous fall, they reached Weathertop on their seventh day out of Bree. But that journey began late (mid-morning on September 30) and ended early (mid-day on October 6), so it involved six days of travel on trails. On good roads, hurried along by bad weather, and pushing hard on the last day to arrive late in Bree, it seem reasonable to assume that the returning travelers took five days to travel the roughly 100 miles between Weathertop and Bree. That would have them passing Weathertop in late afternoon on Sunday, October 23 or 382 days after Frodo was wounded. The next day, when the weather turns bad, would then be October 24.

Riding fast on Shadowfax and staying on the Great East Road, Gandalf took three days to go from Bree to Weathertop, arriving on October 3, 1418.

UNTANGLING TOLKIEN

Friday, October 28, 1419—Reaching Bree

Frodo, Gandalf, Merry, Pippin and Sam

Day 23 of 23 to Bree

The Prancing Pony, Bree

- About sunset, the travelers reach Bree.
- Butterbur tells them of trouble with thieves and troublemakers.
- Sam discovers Bill the pony returned safely.

Comparing Travel Times

Tolkien took care to make sure that his chronology reflected their leisurely rate of travel. The year before, traveling through the wilderness with a wounded Frodo and only one pony, he had them take 21 days to travel from Bree to the Ford of Bruinen. Their return on horses and ponies along a well-established road takes 23 days.

The Return of the King, Bk. 6, Ch. 7, "Homeward Bound." The pony was released at the entrance to Moria on January 13, 1419.

The Hobbits' first visit to Bree was on the night of September 29, 1418, almost exactly 11 months earlier.

Saturday, October 29, 1419

Frodo, Gandalf, Merry, Pippin and Sam

Day 1 of 1 in Bree

The Prancing Pony, Bree

- In the evening a crowd comes to the inn to ask questions.
- Frodo promises a book about his adventures.

Tolkien's Own Feelings

If we pretend along with Tolkien, the book promised by Frodo, with contributions from Bilbo and others, became known as "The Red Book of Westmarch" and was the imagined literary foundation for *The Hobbit* and *The Lord of the Rings.* In a 1971 interview on BBC radio, Tolkien explained how he felt in 1949 as he completed the first draft of the latter: "I actually wept at the denouement."

The Return of the King, Bk. 6, Ch. 7, "Homeward Bound."

A denouement is the final dramatic outcome of a complex literary work.

Sunday, October 30, 1419—Trouble in the Shire

Frodo, Gandalf, Merry, Pippin and Sam

Riding to the Shire

- In early morning the five travelers depart Bree.
- Gandalf leaves them to visit Tom Bombadil.

Missing Gandalf

In Tolkien's early drafts, Gandalf remained with the Hobbits, and Frodo played a much more aggressive role in the Shire. Tolkien probably removed Gandalf to demonstrate how much the four Hobbits have matured. He may have also made Frodo less involved to emphasize how deeply hurt the Hobbit was.

The Return of the King, Bk. 6, Ch. 7, "Homeward Bound."

See *The End of the Third Age,* Ch. 9, "The Scouring of the Shire."

Frodo, Merry, Pippin and Sam

Day 1 of 5 to Rescue the Shire

Brandywine Bridge

The Return of the King, Bk. 6, Ch. 7, "The Scouring of the Shire."

- After dark they reach the Brandywine Bridge and are bared by a gate.
- Merry forces Bill Ferny to open the gate and leave the Shire.
- The four Hobbits take charge, ignoring posted rules.

A Hurried Day

The Hobbits have good reason to feel tired and irritable. Tolkien had them cover the 50 miles between Bree and the Shire in a single day, quite a distance on ponies. (They cover only 22 miles the following day.) After many weeks of procrastination, the four Hobbits are finally becoming serious about what is happening in their little Shire.

Day 404
October 24

Monday, November 1, 1419—Frogmorton

The Hobbits will have well-lit nights for their return to the Shire. This evening the moon is full, rising in the east-northeast a little after 7 p.m. and setting in the west-northwest about 9:30 a.m. the following day.

Frodo, Merry, Pippin and Sam

Day 2 of 5 to Rescue the Shire

Bridge of Stonebows to Frogmorton

The Return of the King, Bk. 6, Ch. 7, "The Scouring of the Shire." They cover 22 miles today.

- By evening, they reach Frogmorton.
- Sam questions Robin Smallburrow.

A Literary Tragedy

It is unfortunate that Tolkien's friends persuaded him that the public would not be interested in stories about day-to-day Hobbit life. Sam's conversation with Robin Smallburrow gives a hint what those tales might be like. They would describe a people so easy going and law-abiding that someone becomes a shirriff not to fight crime and arrest evildoers, but simply to walk about the countryside and check out the beer at various inns. Perhaps because their lives were as quaint and sheltered as those of Hobbits, Tolkien's academic friends found such tales boring. Modern readers with more hectic lives might have found them interesting.

Day 405
October 25

Tuesday, November 2, 1419—Bywater

Frodo, Merry, Pippin and Sam

Day 3 of 5 to Rescue the Shire

Frogmorton to Bywater

- At ten in the morning the travelers leave for Bywater.
- Near sundown they reach Bywater and force six ruffians to flee.
- A large fire is lit and the road is blocked at each end of the village.
- Ruffians discover they are outnumbered, and all but one surrenders.

The Return of the King, Bk. 6, Ch. 7, "The Scouring of the Shire." Bywater is about 25 miles from Frogmorton. This evening Pippin, a Took himself, goes to get help from the Tooks. For the leadership role of the Tooks, see *The Fellowship of the Ring,* "Prologue," Sec. 3, "The Ordering of the Shire."

Blinding the Foe

Rohan horsemen used a similar technique to blind their opponents on February 29 when they attacked Orcs out of a rising sun. Tolkien may have learned it in the trenches of World War I, facing German foes who would attack out of a rising sun. Fighter aircraft in 'dog fights' use a similar technique, attacking their opponents by diving out of the sun.

Wednesday, November 3, 1419—Battle of Bywater

Day 406
October 26

Frodo, Merry, Pippin and Sam with Saruman

Day 4 of 5 to Rescue the Shire

Bywater

- Tooks arrive to help local Hobbits.
- A hundred ruffians are surrounded and defeated.

The Return of the King, Bk. 6, Ch. 7, "The Scouring of the Shire."

Battle of Bywater

This battle is the first fought in the Shire in almost 300 years. The lower death toll among the smaller Hobbits shows that their tactics were superior to those of the human thugs who were working for Saruman. Most of the praise for that belongs to the four newly returned Hobbits. Their adventures in the larger world have taught them something about war and the advantage of choosing where you fight. Trapping the ruffians on a road where it cuts through a hillside is identical to the tactic Faramir used against the Southrons in Ithilien on March 7 and that the Orcs unsuccessfully tried against Aragorn's army on March 21.

The earlier battle was the Battle of Greenfields in 1147. The Tooks also played a major role in it.

Bag End

- The Hobbits travel to Bag End.
- Saruman tries to stab Frodo with a knife.
- Gríma kills Saruman and is killed by Hobbit arrows.

The Return of the King, Bk. 6, Ch. 7, "The Scouring of the Shire."

War's Grim Side

Tolkien may have believed that war was necessary, but he had no illusions about what it meant. Fighting in World War I, he lost all but two of his close friends. In this story, he does not shield Hobbits from the pain of war. The death toll for the Battle of Bywater was grim. Seventy ruffians are killed and a dozen become prisoners. Nineteen Hobbits are dead and thirty wounded. Saruman has hurt many people.

Day 407f.
October 27f.

Thursday, November 4, 1419 and After

Frodo, Merry, Pippin and Sam

Day 5 of 5 to Rescue the Shire and After

Michel Delving and the Shire

The Return of the King, Bk. 6, Ch. 7, "The Grey Havens."

- Frodo releases prisoners from the Lockholes.
- Led by Merry and Pippin, the ruffians are thrown out of the Shire.

Hobbits of the Shire

Shire

The Return of the King, Bk. 6, Ch. 9, "The Grey Havens." For another portrayal of the ugliness of industrialization, see *Hard Times* by Charles Dickens.

- Saruman's ugly buildings are torn down by Sam and others.

Reversing the Industrial Revolution

Tolkien hated what the Industrial Revolution had done to England, particularly the growth of ugly factory cities and meddlesome rules dictated from above. Here he reverses that process, leveling the factories and running the rule-makers out of the Shire.

Sam

Shire

The Return of the King, Bk. 6, Ch. 9, "The Grey Havens." Sam seems to have led much of the restoration. That may explain why Tolkien thought he would become a popular mayor.

- Sam plants seedlings, each with one grain of Galadriel's soil.
- He plants a *mallorn* seed to replace the party tree.

Bringing Good Out of Bad

The Shire's restoration brings something even better than before out of the evil Saruman had done. The party tree was an ordinary tree with sentimental attachments. This *mallorn* will be a special tree, the only one of its kind for hundreds of miles around, and one with sentimental attachments to Frodo and Sam's journey.

Tolkien and "Lunatic" Aryan Myths

From an early age, Tolkien was fascinated by northern European mythology. As a result of that interest, he became an Oxford professor and literary scholar. With that background, it is hardly surprising that there are numerous parallels between his stories and those myths (particularly the Finnish epic *Kalevala*). That has led some to link Tolkien with those who used those same mythologies for evil purposes, particularly in Germany during the 1930s. The link is an unfair one.

What the evidence does demonstrate is the importance of a person's basic beliefs in determining how they handle the other influences in their life. Because of his mother, Tolkien was a devout Catholic, and that guided how he interpreted northern sagas. You see it in the importance *The Lord of the Rings* attaches to the pity and kindness Frodo displays for Gollum. The vengeful and harsh attitudes of some pagan tales simply could not find a foothold in Tolkien's post-pagan, Christianized mind.

In 1930s Germany, the situation was different. During the late nineteenth century one of Germany's best known exports was an approach to the Bible called Higher Criticism. According to it, one bold and creative hand (Moses) could not have written the first five books of the Bible. It had to have be written by squabbling priests, each obsessed with seeing his particular word for God given preeminence. It was a grossly inaccurate description of Judaism in the second millennium B.C., but it did accurately reflect the pedantic, status-obsessed world of the scholars who created it. Even more disturbing was the anti-Semitism inherent to the idea. If the Jews forged their holy book, what other evils might they do? The Jewish writer, Herman Wouk, summarized the now-discredited theory as once advanced by its premier scholar, Julius Wellhausen (1844–1918).

> Wellhausen starts by announcing his grand theme: the forging priests, the non-existent tabernacle, and the phony doctrine of central worship. Then he plunges into his main task: getting the Bible to retell its story according to Wellhausen, in its own words.
>
> His method is simple, but the working out in detail is grandiose. Whatever passages of Scripture support his thesis, or at least do not contradict it, are authentic. Whenever the text contradicts him, the verses are spurious. His attack on each verse that does not support him is violent. He shows bad grammar, or internal inconsistencies, or corrupt vocabulary, or jerkiness of continuity, every time. There is no passage he cannot explain away or annihilate. If he has to change the plain meaning of Hebrew words he does that too. He calls this "conjectural emendation."
>
> Early in the game he seems to realize that he will not quite be able to shout down one haunting question: how is it after all that hundreds and hundreds of Bible verses refute his theory in plain words? Wellhausen

In a 1914 letter to his fiancee, Edith Bratt, Tolkien wrote of the "great delight" that lay in the *Kalevala*. *Letters,* No. 1. He also wrote of wanting to write short stories that resembled the historical romances of William Morris.

As a specialist in ancient languages, Tolkien saw the English version of this speculative scholarship, and both he and C. S. Lewis loathed it. Lewis criticized it in an article entitled "Fern-seed and Elephants" (in a book with the same name). These scholars, Lewis wrote, claim to see a tiny fern-seed hidden deep within a text, and yet they cannot see the literary equivalent of an elephant "ten yards away in broad daylight." In that same article, Lewis blasts those who think Tolkien's Ring "was suggested by the atom bomb. . . . Yet in fact, the chronology of the book's composition makes the theory impossible."

Herman Wouk, *This is My God* (Garden City, NY: Doubleday, 1959), 315. Wouk also wrote *The Winds of War* and *The Cain Mutiny*.

answers this challenge by unveiling an extraordinary hypothetical figure, the Interpolator, a sort of master forger. Seeing across the span of twenty-three centuries, this man (or men) obviously anticipated the Wellhausen theory, and went through all of Holy Scripture carefully inserting passages that refute it!

With the discovery of the Interpolator, Wellhausen's difficulties were at an end. As a tool of controversial logic this figure is wonderful. Sections of the Bible that appear to contradict Wellhausen are not only shorn of their genuineness, they turn around to become arguments in his favor. . . . When all else fails Wellhausen—grammar, continuity, divine names, or outright falsifying of the plain sense of the Hebrew—he works an interpolator.

Higher Criticism provided career paths for scholars, but it also led many Germans into skepticism, particularly in liberal Protestant churches where its influence was greatest. The resulting spiritual vacuum led many to seek a fashionable new religion. The more educated found it in the worship of culture, particularly Germanic culture. Others found it in an intense nationalism that would lead the nation into two disastrous wars.

But whether that devotion centered on German culture or the nation, the result was not a religion. It lacked proper ceremonies and a sense of being part of something rooted in the distant past. For that, some began to turn to pre-Christian Paganism (or what they imagined it to be). Hitler disdained that and preferred his own blend of nineteenth-century free thought and vague nature mysticism. But Nazism used this interest in old Germanic Paganism to counter the influence of the churches, particularly with the young.

To give but one example, in February of 1937, *Schwarze Korps,* a magazine published by the Nazi SS, had an article on the "Veneration of Ancestors in Former Times and Today." It attacked Christianity for putting an "end to the customs of our forefathers" and called for a return to the worship of the "eternality of our people." The agenda was obvious. The God of all people was to be replaced by the worship of the blood of One People (*eine Volk*).

Nazism met with disturbingly little opposition from most German institutions. But in this area, resistance from churches was open and fierce. In his 1937 New Year's Eve sermon, the Catholic Bishop of Trier blasted the Nazi agenda when he said: "You have heard of the so-called Winter-Solstice celebrations. A few years ago I said: "I am not sure whether there lies therein a hidden danger for our youth. Today I am sure. This artificially stirred-up old Germanic pagan Consecration of Fire is meant as a direct challenge to the highest mystery of our religion, the Incarnation of Jesus Christ on the Holy Night of Bethlehem."

Some of Hitler's rambling, disjointed thinking about philosophy, religion and science is in *Hitler's Secret Conversations: 1941–1944.* Hitler's love for Wagner does demonstrate an interest in 'high culture' Germanic mythology.

The quote is from *The Persecution of the Catholic Church in the Third Reich* (London: Burns Oates, 1940), 498. The author or authors was living in Germany at that time and remained anonymous.

The bishop's remarks are from *The Persecution of the Catholic Church,* 487–88.

Those who ask why a people as educated and cultured as the Germans could believe Hitler's mad theories about a shadowy Jewish conspiracy, should ask the same questions about Wellhausen's similar arguments. Those who did not accept Wellhausen's theories also seem to have also been more resistant to political anti-Semitism and more willing to cooperate with Jews. One Jewish historian, Uriel Tal, notes that in the late nineteenth-century, Protestant "Conservatives began to cooperate more and more with the 'ultramontane' Catholics, and to some extent with Jewish Orthodoxy and political Zionism, recognizing their common interests based on a common religious and even national-religious heritage." All four groups shared a common interest, ensuring that parents retained control of their children's education rather than the state. When Hitler took power, he would use already established, state-run schools to indoctrinate German youth.

Tolkien knew what was happening in Germany. In 1938 he was contacted by his publisher, Allen & Unwin. A Potsdam publisher wanted to bring out a German translation of the The Hobbit, but needed to know if the author was of proper *'arish'* (aryan) origin. Though desperately in need of money for his family, Tolkien's reply was blunt. Their laws were "lunatic" and as far as he was concerned a German translation could "go hang." He saw no honor in not having "Jewish blood."

But Tolkien recognized that his publisher had a financial stake in his book. For their sake, he enclosed two letters they could send to Germany. Only one is in Unwin's files, so it is likely the other was sent. The one that remains is riddled with sarcasm. He feigns confusion about what they mean by "arish" since in academic circles that meant his ancestors spoke languages like Hindustani, Persian, or Gypsy. To the other meaning, that he is of Jewish origin, he replies that he regrets he does not know of any ancestors from "that gifted people." He goes on to assert that, although in the past he has regarded his German name with pride, if this continues, a German name "will no longer be a source of pride." The result speaks for itself. *The Hobbit* was not published in Nazi Germany.

In 1941 he wrote his son Michael that the "little ignoramus Adolf Hitler" was "ruining, perverting, misapplying, and making for ever accursed, that noble northern spirit, a supreme contribution to Europe, which I have ever loved, and tried to present in its true light. Nowhere, incidentally, was it nobler than in England, nor more early sanctified and Christianized."

For a detailed exploration of this complex issue, see Uriel Tal's *Christians and Jews in Germany* (Ithaca: Cornell University Press, 1975), particularly Chapter 4, "Protestantism and Judaism in Liberal Perspective." For the quote, see pages 220–221. "Ultramontane" Catholics were those who looked 'over the mountains' to Rome for spiritual guidance.

Tolkien's remarks about Germany are from his *Letters,* No. 29 and 30, both dated July 25, 1938.

For more on Tolkien's contempt for racist "Nordic" ideas, see "Blending the Northern with the Mediterranean" at the end of Chapter 3.

Tolkien's criticism of Hitler is from *Letters,* No. 45, June 9, 1941.

Black and White in Tolkien

You see similar reasoning in explanations for the colors in various national flags.

In literature, it is common for colors to be symbolic. Red may stand for violence, green for life, and black for evil. Red, after all, is the color of blood, the typical product of violence. Green is the color of growing plants and of a fertile, well-watered land. In our well-lit age, however, it is often hard for us to see the close link between darkness, whose color is black, and evil. When we hear a noise outside our homes, we flip a light switch and call the police. We forget that for most of human history, the setting sun shifted the balance of power from good to evil. Tolkien was born in an age less well-lit than our own, perhaps the last humanity will ever know. He understood that imagery and used it in his writing. Recall the terrifying night on Weathertop and the journey through Moria. Recall too the close connection he makes between light and safety. In the tunnel with Shelob, a single lamp makes the difference between life and death.

Unfortunately, those who are perhaps a bit too obsessed with race themselves have equated Tolkien's link between evil and darkness with racism. "Was Tolkien a racist?" they ask, although it is all too obvious they have prejudged him and think they know the answer.

Letters, No. 61.

They could not be more wrong, and a letter Tolkien wrote his son Christopher in South Africa proves it conclusively. In it Tolkien notes that the treatment of colored people there always "horrifies" those who go to South Africa from Britain. Unfortunately, he goes on, that "glorious sentiment" typically doesn't last long. Long before it was politically fashionable to deplore South African racism, Tolkien was doing so. As he notes in that 1944 letter, he had a "special interest" in South Africa since he was born there and his mother often talked of it.

For the Black Rider's white faces, see *The Fellowship of the Ring,* Bk 1, Ch. 11, "A Knife in the Dark," at the end of the chapter.

Finally, the Black Riders are used by some to demonstrate Tolkien's alleged racism. They are, these people tell us, both black and unspeakably evil. But at the risk of stating the obvious, those particular servants of Sauron are called black because of the *clothes* they wear and the *horses* they ride rather than the color of their *skin.* When Frodo uses his Ring on Weathertop, he sees them as they really are—with "white faces."

One revealing historical parallel to Tolkien's Black Riders is Nazism's terrifying "Black Corps" (*Schwarze Korps*) or Nazi SS, whose uniforms were also black. Their racial ideal was a tall, blue-eyed blond, and they were expected to obey Hitler without question—just as the Black Riders obey Sauron. When Tolkien began writing *The Lord of the Rings* in late 1937, the black uniforms of the S.S. were well known. During World War II, they would terrify occupied Europe much as the Black Riders terrorized Middle-earth. Tolkien may not have deliberately intended to draw a parallel between the two, but it is there none the less.

CHAPTER

19

Aftermath

1420 to 1541

Wounds of war to the last departure over the Sea.

In a book review, C. S. Lewis wrote that, "Almost the central theme of the book is the contrast between the Hobbits (or 'the Shire') and the appalling destiny to which some of them are called, the terrifying discovery that the humdrum happiness ...which they have taken for granted as something normal, is in reality a sort of local and temporary accident." Unfortunately for Bilbo and Frodo, that "appalling destiny" included an inability to adapt afterward to the "humdrum happiness" of a normal life. Lewis noted that when he wrote Tolkien in 1949: "And the long *coda* after the eucatastrophe, whether you intended it or no, has the effect of reminding us that victory is as transitory as conflict ... and so leaving a final impression of profound melancholy."

C. S. Lewis, 521. Based on a book review in the August 14, 1954 *Tide and Time.* Lewis's 1949 remarks came in a letter to Tolkien just after he had read the completed manuscript, (Joseph Pearce, *Tolkien, Man and Myth,* 78–79.) In the terminology of Tolkien and Lewis, a *eucatastrophe* resembled a catastrophe except that the sudden and surprising event was good rather than bad.

Tuesday, March 13, 1420—Shelob's Sting

March 7

Frodo with Farmer Cotton

First Anniversary of the Shelob's Sting

Bag End, Hobbiton

• Farmer Cotton finds Frodo in bed, lost in a nightmare.

Recurring Nightmares

Recurring nightmares are a classic symptom of Post Traumatic Stress Disorder. Perhaps because Tolkien saw it among those he fought with in World War I, he anticipated what psychology would later discover.

The Return of the King, Bk. 6, Ch. 7, "The Grey Havens" and *The Return of the King,* Bk. 6, Ap. A, "The Tale of Years." For more on Post Traumatic Stress Disorder, see October 6, 1420.

Sunday, March 25, 1420—Living with Sam

March 19

Frodo, Sam and Rose

Bag End, Hobbiton

• Frodo asks Sam and Rose Cotton to move in with him after they marry.

The Return of the King, Bk. 6, Ch. 7, "The Grey Havens."

March 30

Thursday, April 6, 1420—Mallorn Blooms

Frodo, Merry, Pippin and Sam

Bag End, Hobbiton

- In the spring, the newly planted *mallorn* flowers.

The Shire's Solitary Mallorn

The Return of the King, Bk. 6, Ch. 7, "The Grey Havens" and *The Return of the King,* Bk. 6, Ap. A, "The Tale of Years." *Mallorn* means "tree of gold," a reference to its golden leaves. In his *The Napoleon of Notting Hill,* G. K. Chesterton advocated small communities with their distinctive customs and way of life unhindered. Of course, Tolkien could make exceptions. He did not mind that the tobacco grown in the Shire originally came from elsewhere.

This is the only *mallorn* to grow outside Lórien. Given their great beauty, we might ask why Tolkien did not have Elves, Hobbits and men scatter their seeds all across Middle-earth. That may have been because Tolkien, who was in some ways ahead of his time, believed in keeping native species where they had always grown, avoiding many of today's problems with invasive plants and animals that take over an new environment. In much the same way, under Aragorn's rule the lovely little Shire will be reserved exclusively for Hobbits. We can imagine how, many generations hence, that law prevents it from being dominated both culturally and economically by the vacation homes of wealthy residents from distant Minas Tirith. Tolkien wanted a world in which the little places retain their own unique way of life.

April 24

Monday, May 1, 1420—Sam Married

Frodo, Sam and Rose

Bag End, Hobbiton

- Sam marries Rose Cotton and they join Frodo at Bag End.

Rose, the Archetypical Hobbit

The Return of the King, Bk. 6, Ch. 7, "The Grey Havens" and Bk. 6, Ap. A, "The Tale of Years." Sam marries exactly one year to the day after Aragorn became king. For various epilogues to this tale that Tolkien ascribed to Sam, see: *The End of the Third Age,* Ch. 11, "The Epilogue."

Sam's great love, Rose, is a typical Hobbit, focused on down-to-earth, here-and-now matters and unconcerned about the great issues that weighed so heavily on Gandalf and Lady Galadriel. If some evening Sam were to begin to talk of his adventures with his children, it is easy to imagine Rose interrupting him with an insistence that there were more important things to be done, perhaps firewood to be chopped.

June 24

Midyear's Day, 1420 and after

Frodo, Merry, Pippin and Sam

Bag End, Hobbiton and Crickhollow

- Merry and Pippin ride about as soldiers.
- Frodo and Sam return to their old way of life.

The Most Changed are the Least Marked

The Return of the King, Bk. 6, Ch. 7, "The Grey Havens" and Bk. 6, Ap. A, "The Tale of Years." At this time, Frodo resigns as mayor.

The two Hobbits that most in the Shire would regard as most changed by their adventures, Merry and Pippin, seem to have been the least deeply affected. It is they who slip back into their old, fun-loving ways. Those who were most affected, Bilbo, Frodo and to a lesser extent Sam, never quite fit in and must eventually seek relief over the Sea.

Thursday, September 22, 1420—Two Birthdays

September 15

Frodo, Merry, Pippin and Sam

Bag End, Hobbiton

- On this birthday, Bilbo is 130 years old and Frodo is 52.

Birthdays, Birthdays, Birthdays

Tolkien seems almost obsessed with this birthday. Aragorn may let his March 1 birthday pass without a celebration, but the Hobbits never let this one pass without at least a small party. Oddly, Tolkien tells us nothing about the birthdays of Merry, Pippin and Sam, even though the nearly day-to-day portion of the narrative covers an entire year—late September, 1418 to early November 1419. Their birthdays slip by unannounced.

The Return of the King, Bk. 6, Ch. 7, "The Grey Havens" and Bk. 6, Ap. A, "The Tale of Years."

Thursday, October 6, 1420—Frodo's Wound

September 29

Frodo, Merry, Pippin and Sam

Second Anniversary of the Weathertop Wounding

Bag End, Hobbiton

- Frodo is again sick from his knife wound, but recovers the next day.

Post Traumatic Stress Disorder

Tolkien was describing what is now known as the "Post Traumatic Stress Disorder." Accidents, war, natural disasters and criminal attacks often interfere with a victim's ability to function normally for many years afterward. Among the symptoms is a vivid recall of the event, often on an anniversary date. The disorder can result in a generalized numbness about life, a withdrawal from others, and increased anxiety. It can affect anyone, but is more common among women and less common among the elderly.

The Return of the King, Bk. 6, Ch. 7, "The Grey Havens" and Bk. 6, Ap. A, "The Tale of Years."

Tuesday, March 13, 1421—Shelob's Sting Again

March 7

Frodo, Merry, Pippin and Sam

Bag End, Hobbiton

- Frodo is sick on the second anniversary of Shelob's sting.

A Cumulative Effect

In Post Traumatic Stress Disorder, a series of terrible events can have a cumulative effect. The dangers Frodo faced fleeing the Shire and elsewhere magnified the impact of his knife wound on Weathertop and Shelob's sting.

The Return of the King, Bk. 6, Ch. 7, "The Grey Havens" and Bk. 6, Ap. A, "The Tale of Years." Frodo conceals his pain from Sam and Rose.

Sunday, March 25, 1421—Elanor Born

Frodo, Merry, Pippin and Sam

Second Anniversary of the Ring's Destruction

Bag End, Hobbiton

The Return of the King, Bk. 6, Ch. 7, "The Grey Havens" and Bk. 6, Ap. A, "The Tale of Years." Tolkien compared *elanor* flower to a pimpernel. *Letters,* No. 312.

- Elanor the fair, daughter of Sam and Rose, is born.

Elanor

Tolkien often repeated important dates. He had Elanor born on the second anniversary of the destruction of the Ring, perhaps to symbolize the world being reborn. The daughter's name comes from *elanor* or "Sunstar," a small golden flower that booms in Lórien.

The Return of the King, Bk. 6, Ap. A, I, iii, Eriador, Arnor, and the Heirs of Isildur."

Later, leaving Bag End, Elanor becomes one of the maids of Queen Arwen, quite a rise in social status for the granddaughter of a common laborer. Perhaps because of his impoverished childhood, Tolkien seems to have had little of the class-consciousness common among the English of his generation.

Wednesday, September 21, 1421

Frodo and Sam

Day 1 of 15 to Grey Havens and Return

Bag End, Hobbiton to Green Hills

The Return of the King, Bk. 6, Ch. 7, "The Grey Havens" and Bk. 6, Ap. A, "The Tale of Years."

For more on the history of the Red Book and the copies that were made of it, see the Prologue to *The Lord of the Rings.* For how Tolkien developed his account of the trip to Grey Havens see: *The End of the Third Age,* Ch. 10, "Grey Havens."

- In the morning, they leave Bag End on ponies.
- That evening, they camp in the Green Hills.

Red Book of Westmarch

At this time, there is a passing of literary responsibilities from Frodo to Sam. According to Frodo, this book, which would become the Red Book of Westmarch, contained 80 chapters. The early ones were by Bilbo and, we are to assume, became *The Hobbit.* The later ones were by Frodo and became *The Lord of the Rings,* with part of the last chapter completed by Sam after Frodo's departure from Grey Havens. Frodo's title for his part was "The Downfall of the Lord of the Rings and the Return of the King." Today's editions of *The Hobbit* (19 chapters) and *The Lord of the Rings* (62 chapters) total 81 chapters, so we can pretend, for the sake of the story, that one of the longer chapters was split in two.

Thursday, September 22, 1421—Two Birthdays

Bilbo, Frodo and Sam with the Elves

Day 2 of 15 to Grey Havens and Return

Through the Shire

- They retrace the steps they took fleeing from Black Riders.
- In the evening they meet Gildor, Elrond and Galadriel.
- All night they ride through the Shire.

Still More Partings

In the aftermath of the War of the Rings, so many friendships were broken up that Tolkien entitled one chapter "Many Partings." The last chapter in the narrative will have still more separations. The Elves are leaving Middle-earth and Frodo and Gandalf must say goodbye to Sam, Merry and Pippin. Victory over Sauron has brought sadness as well as joy. Despite what some Tolkien critics say, the book is not escapist and does not end on a light and happy note. There is a deep sadness in the last chapter that the victories over Sauron and Saruman cannot conceal.

The Return of the King, Bk. 6, Ch. 7, "The Grey Havens" and Bk. 6, Ap. A, "The Tale of Years." In the latter, this journey is called the "Last Riding of the Keepers of the Rings." For a history of the Grey Havens, see the last chapter in *The Silmarillion,* "Of the Rings of Power and the Third Age." For Tolkien's description of the voyage, see *Letters,* No. 325.

Thursday, September 29, 1421—Grey Havens

September 22

Bilbo, Frodo, Gandalf, Merry, Pippin, and Sam with the Elves and Círdan the Shipwright

Day 8 of 15 to Grey Havens and Return

Grey Havens

- Bilbo's party reaches Grey Havens and meets Gandalf.
- Just before they leave, Merry and Pippin ride up.
- After last farewells, the ship leaves.

Shadowfax

In a 1965 letter, Tolkien said that he believed Shadowfax traveled over the sea with Gandalf. It was logical, he argued for the two who had shared so much to remain together.

The Return of the King, Bk. 6, Ch. 7, "The Grey Havens," Bk. 6, Ap. A, "The Tale of Years" and *The Silmarillion,* "Of the Rings of Power and the Third Age,"

Letters, No. 268. For legal complications of Bilbo and Frodo's departure without dying, see *Letters,* No. 214.

With this departure, some say the Third Age came to an end.

Thursday, October 6, 1421—Return to the Shire

Merry, Pippin and Sam

Day 15 of 15 to Grey Havens and Return

Returning to the Shire

- The three remaining Hobbits reach the Shire.

The Return of the King, Bk. 6, Ch. 7, "The Grey Havens" and Bk. 6, Ap. A, "The Tale of Years."

The Hobbits took eight days to reach Grey Havens and seven to return. For Tolkien's original plan for the book's ending, see *Letters*, No. 91 and 93. For the epilogue, see *The End of the Third Age*, Ch. 11, "The Epilogue."

Tolkien mentioned this sequel in *Letters*, No. 256, written in May of 1964 and No. 338, written in June of 1972.

Letters, No. 117 dated October 31, 1948. The dates the three volumes were released are given where their portion of the story begins and in "Tolkien's Outline of the Book" at the end of Chapter 20.

Epilogues and Sequels

At least as early as when he was beginning to write the fifth book, Tolkien anticipated that Frodo would leave Middle-earth and Sam would settle down to a normal family life. At one time Tolkien planned to have the book end with Sam reading to his children and telling them what happened to the other characters in the tale. That became an epilogue set fifteen years later in March of 1436. It placed Sam with his children talking of his adventures and telling them of an upcoming visit by their king. Unfortunately, on the advice of others, he abandoned it.

On the other hand, it is probably fortunate that Tolkien dropped a sequel set about 100 years after the death of Aragorn. In it, Gondor had grown decadent. Tiring of the good, it was dabbling in "dark cults" with young boys pretending to be Orcs. Tolkien found what he was writing "sinister and depressing," and concluded it was, "Not worth doing."

Thanks to a summer retreat that gave time for writing, Tolkien was able to announce in the fall of 1948 that the draft of his tale was finished. Almost six years of editing and negotiating with publishers would follow before the first volume was published in July of 1954

1422 to 1541—The Rest of the Story

Sam and Rose Gamgee

Bag End, Hobbiton

The Return of the King, Bk. 6, Ap. A, "The Tale of Years." Sam leaves Bag End for the Havens only one calendar day later than Bilbo and Frodo.

For Sam's ancestry and details about their children, see: "The Longfather Tree of Master Samwise," in *The Return of the King*, Ap. C, "Family Trees."

- In 1442, Sam, Rose and Elanor spend a year at Gondor.
- On Midyear's day of 1482, Rose dies.
- On September 22, 1482, Sam goes to Grey Havens and over the sea.

Prolific Sam and Rose

Tolkien gave Sam, the most down-to-earth of the Hobbits, the largest family. They fill Frodo's large Bag End home with 13 children, among them a Bilbo, Frodo, Merry and Pippin. His long and happy life included a political career in which he is elected mayor of the Shire seven times. He was, nevertheless, one of the Ringbearers and joins Bilbo and Sam over the sea when he is 99 years old.

Merry and Estella Brandybuck

Buckland and Rohan

The Fellowship of the Ring, "Prologue," *The Return of the King* and Bk. 6, Ap. B, "The Tale of Years." For Merry's family tree, see: "Brandybuck of Buckland" in *The Return of the King*, Ap. C, "Family Trees."

- Merry marries Estella Bolger (born in 1385).
- In 1432 he becomes master of Buckland.
- In 1484 (at 102), he and Pippin visit King Éomer in Edoras.
- Merry is buried alongside King Elessar (Aragorn), perhaps in 1541.

Meriadoc the Magnificent

Merry's career parallels that of Tolkien. He becomes a well-recognized historian, a scholar on the relationship between the languages of Hobbits and those of Northern Men and a respected botanist. Given his interests, it may be he who carries the "Red Book of the Periannath" (on which *The Lord of the Rings* is said to be based) from the Shire to Rohan.

The year of Merry's death is unknown, but probably came before 1490. That year Merry would have been 108 years old, an impressive age for a Hobbit. Saradoc, Merry's father, lived to be 92.

Pippin and Diamond Took

Shire and Gondor

- In 1427 Pippin marries Diamond and in 1834 becomes Shire Thain
- Their son, Faramir I (born in 1430) marries Goldilocks in 1463.
- In 1484 (at 94) he and Merry visit King Éomer in Edoras.
- Pippin is buried alongside King Elessar (Aragorn), perhaps in 1541.

Éomer, Merry and Pippin

Both Merry and Pippin kept up their friendship with Éomer throughout their lives. Like Sam, Merry and Pippin, Éomer's life as a public official would be long and successful, and he reigned as king for 65 years. Given the timing of his invitation to Merry and Pippin, it is likely that he knew he was dying in 1848. The year of Pippin's death is unknown, but may have been before 1490, when he would have been 100 years old.

The Fellowship of the Ring, "Prologue" and *The Return of the King,* Bk. 6, Ap. B, "The Tale of Years." For Pippin's family tree see Peregrin I under "Took of the Great Smials" in *The Return of the King,* Ap. C, "Family Trees." For Éomer's reign, see "The Kings of the Mark: Third Line" in *The Return of the King,* Bk. 6, Ap. A, "Annals of the Kings and Rulers." Paladin II, Pippin's father, lived to be 101.

Aragorn and Arwen

Gondor

- Aragorn rules Gondor and Anor for 122 years.
- In 1436, seventeen years after the War of the Ring, he visits the Shire.
- He gives the Westmarch to the Shire in 1452.
- In 1541, he allows himself to die on his 210th birthday, March 1.

Love and Grief

Aragorn retained a special affection for Merry and Pippin. There are hints that a provision in his will had Merry and Pippin reburied alongside him roughly half a century after their deaths.

In a good marriage, the death of one partner is often very difficult for the other. After Aragorn's death, Arwen's life looses all meaning. She goes to the woods of Lórien, where no one now lives. On Cerin Amroth, where she and Aragorn became engaged, she lays down and dies. Her death illustrates Tolkien's belief that in this life we can never have complete happiness. Tolkien's friend C. S. Lewis put it this way:

> There is no safe investment. To love at all is to be vulnerable. Love anything, and your heart will certainly be wrung and possibly be broken. If you want to make sure of keeping it intact, you must give your heart to no one, not even to an animal. Wrap it carefully round with hobbies and little luxuries; avoid all entanglements; lock it safe in the casket or coffin of your selfishness. But in that casket—safe, dark,

The Return of the King, Bk. 6, Ap. A, "Annals of the Kings and Rulers," Sec. I, v, "Here Follows a Part of the Tale of Aragorn and Arwen," and Bk. 6, Ap. B, "The Tale of Years." Aragorn was king for almost 122 years.

Lewis' own grief at the death of his wife is chronicled in his 1961 *A Grief Observed* and dramatized as both play and film in *The Shadowlands.*

C. S. Lewis, *The Four Loves,* (London: Collins, 1960), 111–12. For those with other editions, this is about one quarter the way through the last chapter.

motionless, airless—it will change. It will not be broken; it will become unbreakable, impenetrable, irredeemable. The alternative to tragedy, or at least to the risk of tragedy is damnation. The only place outside Heaven where you can be perfectly safe from all the dangers and perturbations of love is Hell.

Legolas and Gimli

Glittering Caves and Ithilien

- Gimli founds a Dwarf colony in the Glittering Caves
- Legolas starts an Elf colony in Ithilien.
- In 1541 Gimli and Legolas may have sailed to the Undying Lands.

The Greatest Friendship

Of all the friendships in *The Lord of the Rings,* that between Gimli and Legolas is perhaps the greatest, because it joined two people as different as Dwarf and Elf. With the deaths of Aragorn and Arwen in 1541 and the passage of Gimli and Legolas over the sea that same year, the tale of the Fellowship of the Ring finally comes to an end.

The Return of the King, Bk. 6, Ap. A, "Annals of the Kings and Rulers," Sec. II, "Durin's Folk" at the very end of the appendix and Bk. 6, Ap. B, "The Tale of Years." Gimli lived to be 262 years old. In a 1971 letter, Tolkien said that the Glittering Caves were based on caves at Cheddar Gorge, that he visited on his honeymoon. *Letters,* No. 321.

That ends the story of the Fellowship of the Ring.

Never Absent and Never Named

Erik Davis, "The Fellowship of the Ring" *Wired* (October 2001), 124.

In the closing years of the Soviet dictatorship, a young Russian woman came across a translation of the first volume in *The Lord of the Rings* and it brought her to tears. Two years later, she borrowed, all too briefly, the remaining two volumes. Blessed with a photographic memory, she memorized what she had read to recite to friends. Later she taught herself English, so she could read the book exactly as Tolkien had written it.

Why did the book have such an impact on her? "Soviet people have been raised as atheists," she explains today. "Tolkien's books offered me hope for our world, the hope that Tolkien's Elves call *estel*. Tolkien does not mention God in *The Lord of the Rings* at all, but you feel something really wonderful when you read it. Later I recognized it as faith."

Letters, No. 192. See also: No. 131, 142, 156, 181, 183, 250, 269, 310 and 328. The letter written to his son Michael three weeks before the death of C. S. Lewis (No. 250) is especially revealing.

Judging by remarks made in his letters, Tolkien would heartily approve of what she said. In a 1956 letter, he remarked about Frodo's inability, in the end, to carry out his mission to destroy the Ring. At that point, he said, Frodo had done all that he could do, "The Other Power then took over: the Writer of the Story (by which I do not mean myself), 'the one ever-present Person who is never absent and never named' (as one critic has said)."

20

Tolkien's Great Puzzle

Understanding Tolkien's writing style

Whether you realized it or not, when you last read *The Lord of Rings*—whether for the second or twentieth time—you were inside one of the most complex puzzles in modern literature. That puzzle centers on the dating of events in the book and the cause/effect relationships that are so closely linked to chronology. With amazingly few exceptions, the dates simply aren't there. For hundreds of pages, all Tolkien gives his readers are off-hand remarks such as "the next day" or "the third day." The next day after what? The third day from when? Although you undoubtedly found the experience pleasant, the truth is that Tolkien has sailed us out onto a vast sea, virtually devoid of chronological landmarks, and abandoned us. Even more surprising, we can be quite certain he did that on purpose.

This chronological puzzle is easily demonstrated. If you have a one-volume edition of *The Lord of the Rings,* take it out. If you have a three-volume edition, pick up *The Two Towers.* For the one-volume edition, flip to a random page in the middle of the book. For *The Two Towers,* open it to any page from front to back. In either case, your chance of finding the current date on the page you've chosen is virtually zero. In the middle 60 percent of *The Lord of the Rings*—that's 38 chapters and 595 pages—Tolkien gives the current date precisely once. By one count, in the entire narrative of *The Lord of the Rings* (the book less prologue and appendices), the current date is given 23 times. But that doesn't tell the whole story. Here is some chronological data based on a one-volume 'movie cover' edition.

That rare and illusive date is in Book 3, Chapter 9, "Flotsam and Jetsam." Pippin wants to know what day it is and Aragorn tells him it is March 5. In a one-volume edition you will read 267 dateless pages before you come to that date and another 328 pages before Tolkien gives you the date again.

Chronological Data

In the first chapter of *The Lord of the Rings,* the narrative moves so slowly that many first-time readers give up, shaking their hands and wondering why Tolkien fans think a book about the birthday party of an elderly bunny-like Hobbit is worth reading. In that chapter, Tolkien gives the date once and in the two chapters that follow, he gives it three more times or once every 21 pages. That's followed by a terrifying time when the Hobbits flee for their lives into the wilderness, pursued by deadly

In his book review in the August 14, 1954 issue of *Time and Tide,* C. S. Lewis wrote that in the first chapter Tolkien, "writes almost in the manner of the earliest and far lighter book," referring to *The Hobbit.*

riders clad in black. For the next nine chapters, the current date is only mentioned once, on October 5 in Chapter 11 when they are six days out of Bree bound for Rivendell. The next time it is given is on October 24, when they are safely in Rivendell. Over two months later, the travelers depart Rivendell on a day that's vaguely described as in late December. The first date in their journey that's clearly given does not come until over two weeks later on January 12. That's followed by no less than 15 chapters and 53 days of often great hardship and danger during which the date is not given once. Only on March 5, when several of the travelers who had been separated, reunite and have a brief moment of rest, is the date given. Tolkien's writing technique is obvious. In rare moments of safety, the date may be given. In oft-present times of danger, it almost never is.

At this point the narrative becomes so intense it takes 328 pages and 22 chapters to cover the next nine days (36 pages per day). Despite that great wealth of detail, during this period the date is not given at all, and readers are left wandering in a chronological fog. On March 14 and 15, perhaps to offer a glimpse into what Frodo and Sam's friends were doing as the two Hobbits enter hostile Mordor, Tolkien relents for a brief moment and gives readers the date on two adjacent days. That's followed by 63 pages (including the climax of the book) with no date and still more chronological uncertainty. With the main drama complete, Tolkien returns to providing dates, the first coming on April 8. Over the next 73 pages he gives the date 12 times, or once every six pages. Only one of the twelve comes during an even mildly dramatic moment.

The numbers drive that point home. In the book as a whole, the current date is given 23 times in 987 pages of narrative or an average of once every 43 pages. The specific date for other events is given seven times or once every 141 pages and vague references to the date (such as "the last days of October") are given four times or once every 247 pages. The 53 chapters and 865 pages that comprise the most dramatic part of the book have only five current dates, or one for every 173 pages. Even more telling, within the most intense 38 chapters and 595 pages with 60 percent of the narrative, readers are given the date only once.

Letters, No. 199.

Did Tolkien do this out of spite? Certainly not. Did he do it because he wasn't clear himself when things were happening? Again no. Although I have not seen them, he apparently had elaborate charts and calendars tracking characters and events. In a June 1957 letter, he referred to a "many columned calendar" (presumably using Shire dating) describing where each character was on each day and what he was doing. He went on to say that he reconciled problems as they developed by "constantly re-writing backwards." My many months of research certainly indicates that, to be as accurate and consistent as he was, he must have had some way of keeping track of everyone's movements.

Interlacing Literature

If Tolkien was so careful to get the dates right, why did he go to so much trouble to conceal them? The answer lies in literature. Those who call *The Lord of the Rings* the greatest literary work of the Middle Ages are not far from the mark. The key lies in a single word, "interlace." Understand what that means, and you have taken a giant step toward understanding what makes *The Lord of the Rings* so special, as well as why the story seems so real to many of its readers.

For a moment we must dip into literary theory. Dr. Richard West summarized the literary background to interlace by contrasting it with the "organic unity" style of writing that makes up virtually all the fiction you find on bookstore shelves.

Organic unity seeks to reduce the chaotic flux of reality to manageable terms by imposing a clear and fairly simple pattern upon it. It calls for a progressive and uncluttered narrative line [chronology] in which there is a single major theme to which a limited number of other themes may be related as long as they are kept subordinate. . . . It is considered preferable to have a limited number of characters and to have no more than one or two dominate the action. . . .

Interlace, by contrast, seeks to mirror the perception of the flux of events in the world around us, where everything is happening at once. Its narrative line is digressive and cluttered, dividing our attention among an indefinite number of events, characters, and themes, any one of which may dominate at any given time, and it is often indifferent to cause and effect relationships. The paths of characters cross, diverge, and recross, and the story passes from one to another and then another but does not follow a single line. . . .

Interlace reached the peak of its development in the French cyclic romances of the thirteenth century, but variations of the form can be found at best as early as the Roman poet Ovid's *Metamorphoses* and at least as late as Spenser's *Faerie Queene*. It is easy to see how the form could become bewilderingly complex, and the preference in the later Middle Ages for shorter narrative units indicates that authors and audiences came to desire briefer and clearer stories. Out of this movement toward singleness came the modern novel, which remained for the most part associated with the structural techniques of organic unity until recently, when writers like James Joyce, Marcel Proust, Gunter Grass and William Faulkner once again began experimenting with varieties of the interlace.

Because it mirrors how we experience life—as a bewildering array of often unrelated people and events—the sheer complexity of an interlaced novel leaves readers with a strong sense that they are encountering something very real. On the other hand, the rapid shifts in time and locale between many major characters makes the narrative confusing for those

Tolkien described his formal education and early career in a 1925 letter. See *Letters,* No. 7. The letter shows his life-long interest in ancient Northern European languages.

Dr. Richard C. West, "The Interlace Structure of *The Lord of the Rings,*" in *A Tolkien Compass*, 78–80. Italics added.

Interlacing can also be used in films. For an example, see a Vietnamese film, Tran Anh Hung's *The Vertical Ray of the Sun.*

Dr. West suggest that Tolkien's exposure to interlacing may be through *Beowulf,* an ancient tale for which he was one of the world's leading experts.

who want to examine the inner workings of story, whether as scholars or as engaged readers who have read the narrative through many times. Most novels focus on, at most, two or three people. Tolkien typically follows nine characters, picking up Gollum, for instance, just after Boromir is killed. This means that, for serious readers of Tolkien, a well-done chronology is as necessary as a saw is for a carpenter. In fact, if you look at what has been written about the other modern interlacing authors Dr. West mentioned, you will find that an independent chronology of the author's fiction is a critical to understanding what the author is saying.

Take James Joyce as an example. The theme for Joyce's much praised *Ulysses,* could hardly be more different from *The Lord of the Rings. Ulysses* is intensely personal and concerned with petty affairs of one man in Dublin in the late nineteenth and early twentieth century. In contrast, Tolkien's epic is set in the far-distant past and its theme is no less than the salvation of the world from the most terrible of tyrannies. Nevertheless, the parallels are significant enough that Tom Shippey, Tolkien's successor as Professor of Anglo-Saxon at Oxford University, devoted several sections of his *J. R. R. Tolkien: Author of the Century* to comparing the two authors.

That similarity suggests that the importance of a chronology for one would equal that of the other. John H. Raleigh explained why he developed a book-length chronology of *Ulysses* this way.

Just prior to assuming this office, I had become interested in the chronologies of the lives of the Blooms which Joyce has scattered—and thus in a sense buried—throughout *Ulysses.* I was quite sure that these chronologies had been carefully put together before they were shredded and the pieces distributed randomly throughout the book to the respective memories of the Blooms. It was not until I had been able to reconstruct and set in chronological order, the greater part of Bloom's past by working only with the text of *Ulysses* that I turned to investigate the known chronologies for the book that Joyce himself had left behind in manuscript form.

Raleigh developed his chronology for much the same reasons and in much the same way as the chronology in this book was built—by looking first to the narrative and only secondarily to the author's own chronology. As Raleigh goes on to relate (and as I discovered about Tolkien), the chronology buried within the narrative is far more detailed and complex than anything in the author's papers or published works.

Tolkien himself understood the need for a chronology. He included (some would say hid) one in Appendix B, "The Tale of Years" of *The Return of the King.* But that chronology is far from complete. This chronology is over fifty times larger for the period covered by *The Lord of the Rings.* The chronology that was published after his death in *The Peoples of Middle-earth* is even less helpful. For the War of the Ring, it is

So pornographic it was initially banned in the United States, *Ulysses* is more popular with the *literati* than with the general public, and its status as a masterpiece rests with them. In general, the opposite is true of *The Lord of the Rings.*

John Henry Raleigh, *The Chronicle of Leopold and Molly Brown:* Ulysses *as Narrative* (Berkeley: University of California Press, 1971), 1. At this time Raleigh was Vice Chancellor of Academic Affairs at the University of California's Berkeley campus.

less than one percent as long as this book, and events are only broken down to the year, making it virtually useless as a chronology.

How was this chronology created? Although I'm simply a writer with an interest in Tolkien, I approached the almost dateless narrative as seriously as any university-endowed scholar, looking for every clue to the date of an event from whatever source. I tried to look beneath the surface of the narrative to establish Tolkien's intentions. As a writer, he wanted to place what happens in this book on the proper days based on scheme that was hidden from readers. Engaging in "reverse engineering," I established what those days were and whether he was successful at getting it right. In the process, I do not hesitate to point to examples (thankfully few) where Tolkien's chronology as written doesn't seem quite right. But given the thousand of details he had to juggle, the result is nothing short of amazing.

Now is as good a place as any to note that in the sidebar on each page, you'll find references to other books that offer far more detail than I can provide here. Those books fall naturally into four categories. The first are books that Tolkien completed himself and that were published in his lifetime (a copyright date of 1973 or earlier), including *The Hobbit* and *The Lord of the Rings*. If you are serious about Tolkien, you should own those books (perhaps along with *The Letters of J. R. R. Tolkien*) as a matter of course. The second category includes books such as *The Silmarillion* and *Unfinished Tales*. These are books whose text was drafted by Tolkien and completed by his son Christopher. They are not as polished in a literary sense as the first category, but well worth owning if you want to understand more about Middle-earth. This book will point you to some of the information you can find in them. The third category are the books in Christopher Tolkien's "The History of Middle-earth" series. Unless you're a great fan of trivia, they are of limited value. Your understanding is not improved by discovering that Bilbo was originally named Bingo. The fourth category are books about Tolkien's tale written by others. Along with this chronology, it is a good idea to own at least one encyclopedia and an atlas. You may also want to pick up a book such as Michael Stanton's *Hobbits, Elves and Wizards*. You can enjoy the marvelous insights Professor Stanton developed teaching a class on *The Lord of the Rings* for over a quarter of a century at a fraction of the price of college tuition. Remember, it is important to support independent writings like these. No author, much less one as brilliant as Tolkien, should be trapped in a Mordor-like world where what is said and written has to be authorized or approved by others. Tolkien's own professional career was as an *independent* literary commentator and critic.

Now we look briefly at the structure of the book and how it came to be written.

Because many Tolkien books have or may in the future be issued in editions with differing pagination, most of the references in this book are to the letter number (*Letters*) or to a chapter number and title. That should make this book useful to more readers. Also, sometimes overly complex section numbering schemes are simplified slightly.

Tolkien gave a description of the deficiencies of *The Silmarillion* manuscript in *Letters,* No. 294, February 8. 1967. In 1954 C. S. Lewis described other difficulties in Tolkien's writing when he wrote that "though *The Fellowship* in one way continues its author's fairy tale, *The Hobbit,* it is in no sense an overgrown 'juvenile.' The truth is the other way round. *The Hobbit* was merely a fragment torn from the author's huge myth and adapted for children; inevitably losing something by the adaptation. . . . Misunderstanding on this point might easily be encouraged by the first chapter [of *The Fellowship*], in which the author (taking a risk) writes almost in the manner of the earlier and far lighter book. With some who will find the main body of the book deeply moving, this chapter may not be a favourite." From "Tolkien's *The Lord of the Rings*" in *C. S. Lewis* (Lesley Walmsley, ed.), 520.

Tolkien's Outline of the Book

Tolkien wrote *The Lord of the Rings* as six short books. Publishing constraints united pairs of book into three volumes, and his names for the books were left out of published editions. For those who are interested, Tolkien intended to divide *The Lord of the Rings* as follows:

Volume I: The Fellowship of the Ring

UK Release: July 29, 1954, U.S. Release: October 24, 1954

Book 1: The First Journey—189 pages or 19.4%

- Twelve chapters that include the discovery of the Ring's origin and the Hobbits' flight from Shire to Rivendell.
- Covers from early September of 1401 to October 20, 1418 (18 years).

Book 2: The Journey of the Nine Companions—186 pages or 19.2%

- Ten chapters on what happens to all the travelers from Rivendell until the fellowship breaks up at Parth Galen.
- Covers from October 20, 1418 to February 25, 1419 (4 months).

Volume II: The Two Towers

UK Release: November 11, 1954, U.S. Release: April 21, 1955

Book 3: The Treason of Isengard—184 pages or 18.9%

- Eleven chapters describing the capture and pursuit of Merry and Pippin as well as the war with Saruman. No account is given of what is happening to Frodo and Sam.
- Covers from February 26 to March 5, 1419 (10 days).

Book 4: The Journey of the Ring-bearers—137 pages or 14.1%

- Ten chapters describing Frodo and Sam's journey from when they separate from the other travelers until they enter Mordor. No account is given of the other travelers.
- Covers from February 26 to March 13, 1419 (18 days).

Volume III: The Return of the King

UK Release: October 20, 1955, U.S. Release: January 5, 1956

Book 5: The War of the Ring—144 pages or 14.8%

- Ten chapters describing the war with Sauron until the battle begins at the Black Gate. All the major characters are covered.
- Covers from March 6 to 25, 1419 (20 days).

Book 6: The End of the Third Age—132 pages or 13.6%

- Nine chapters giving the defeat of Sauron, the aftermath of the war, the Shire's liberation, and the departure of Bilbo, Frodo and Gandalf over the sea. All the major characters are covered. Includes six appendices (104 pages) covering many topics.
- Covers from March 14, 1419 to October 6, 1421 (31 months).

The page count and percentage for each book is for the narrative and come from the 1987/1994 Houghton Mifflin single-volume edition. Note that the first three books are close to 19% and the last three are close to 14%. The date range with each second bullet is for the narrative itself or soon-stated remarks that look back a few days. All the books describe events in other time periods.

In a March 1953 letter, Tolkien suggested a different set of names: 1. *The Ring Sets Out*, 2. *The Ring Goes South*, 3. *The Treason of Isengard*, 4. *The Ring Goes East*, 5. *The War of the Ring*, and 6. *The End of the Third Age*. For the volumes he suggested: I. *The Shadow Grows*, II. *The Ring in the Shadows*, and III. *The War of the Ring* or *The Return of the King*. See *Letters*, No. 136.

On August 8, 1953, Tolkien suggested the three volumes be named: 1. *The Return of the Shadow*, II. *The Shadow Lengthens*, III. *The Return of the King*. See *Letters*, No. 139. The version that was finally adopted is in *Letters*, No. 140, dated August 17, 1953.

A Quick Reference to Important Dates

Aragorn
  Born—Mar. 1, 1331
  Crowned—May 1, 1419
  Dies—Mar. 1, 1541
  Engaged to Arwen—1380
  Gandalf first met—1356
  March on Mordor—Mar. 18, 1419
  Married—Midyear's Day, 1419
  Meets Arwen—1351
  Paths of Dead—Mar. 8, 1419
  Pursues Orcs—Feb. 26, 1419
Battle of Bywater—Nov. 3, 1419
Battle of Osgiliath—June 20, 1418
Battle of Pelennor Fields—Mar. 15, 1419
Battle of the Hornburg—Mar. 4, 1419
Bilbo
  Birthday party—Sept. 22, 1401
  Born—Sept. 22, 1290
  Grey Havens—Sept. 29, 1421
  Hobbit adventures—1341–42
Council of Elrond—Oct. 25, 1418
Darkness
  Begins—Mar. 10, 1419
  Ends—Mar. 15, 1419
Frodo
  Adopted—1389
  Black Gate—Mar. 5, 1419
  Born—Sept. 22, 1368
  Bree—Sept. 29, 1418
  Bree again—Oct. 28, 1419
  Faramir—Mar. 7, 1419
  Gandalf warns—Apr. 12, 1418
  Gollum joins—Feb. 29, 1419
  Grey Havens—Sept. 29, 1421
  Escapes Cirith Ungol—Mar. 14, 1419
  Leaves Bag End—Sept. 23, 1418
  Leaves Bree—Sept. 30, 1418
  Leaves Lórien—Feb. 16, 1419
  Leaves Rivendell—Dec. 25, 1418
  Leaves Rivendell again—Oct. 5, 1419
  Leaves with Sam—Feb. 26, 1419
  Lórien—Jan. 16, 1419
  March with Orcs—Mar. 19, 1419
  Meets Gollum—Feb. 29, 1419

  Moria—Jan. 13, 1419
  Rabbit stew—Mar. 7, 1419
  Ring destroyed—Mar. 25, 1419
  Rivendell—Oct. 20, 1418
  Rivendell again—Sept. 22, 1418
  Shelob attacks—Mar. 12, 1419
  Shire—Oct. 30, 1419
  Stairs—Mar. 11, 1419
  Weathertop—Oct. 6, 1418
Gandalf
  Alive—Feb. 14, 1419
  Balrog attack—Jan. 15, 1419
  Bree—Midyear's Day
  Dies—Jan. 25, 1419
  Dol Guldur—1250
  Escapes Isengard—Sept. 18, 1418
  Isengard—July 10, 1418
  Meets Aragorn—May 1, 1418
  Minas Tirith—Mar. 9, 1419
  Tom Bombadil—Oct. 30, 1419
  Weathertop—Oct. 3, 1418
Gimli
  Born—1279
  Grey Havens—1541
Glorfindel
  Finds travelers—Oct. 18, 1418
  Leaves Rivendell—Oct. 9, 1418
Gollum
  Aragorn captures—Mar. 1, 1418
  Dies—Mar. 25, 1419
  Escapes Sauron—1417
  Goes Underground—870
  Mirkwood—1344
  Mordor—1351
  With Frodo—Feb. 29, 1419
Great Plague—35-40
Legolas
  Grey Havens—1541
Long Winter—1158–59
Merry
  Born—1382
  Captured by Orcs—Feb. 26, 1419
  Escapes Orcs—Feb. 29, 1419
  Leaves for Minas Tirith—Mar. 10, 1419
  Minas Tirith—Mar. 15, 1419
  Treebeard—Feb. 29, 1419
  Visits Éomer—1484

Nazgûl
  Attack Minas Ithil—400
  Invade Shire—Sept. 23, 1418
  Isengard—Mid-Sept., 1418
  Occupy Mordor—380
Pippin
  Born—1390
  Denethor's squire—Mar. 10, 1419
  Marries Diamond—1427
  Minas Tirith—Mar. 9, 1419
  Visits Éomer—1484
Sam
  Born—1383
  Elanor born—Mar. 25, 1421
  Grey Havens—Sept. 22, 1482
  Marries Rose—May 1, 1420
  Rescues Frodo—Mar. 14, 1419
  Takes Ring—Mar. 13, 1419
Saruman
  Dies—Nov. 3, 1419
  Ent attack—Mar. 3, 1419
  Freed—Aug. 15, 1419
  Meets travelers—Aug. 28, 1419
  Shire—Sept. 22, 1419
  Spies on Shire—1353
  Takes over Isengard—1159
Sauron
  Dark Tower rebuilt—1351
  Defeated—Mar. 25, 1419
  Dol Guldur again—860
  Launches war—Mar. 10, 1419
  Moves east—463
  Moves east again—1341
  Occupies Mordor—1342
Treebeard
  Attacks Isengard—Mar. 3, 1419
  Frees Saruman—Aug. 15, 1419
  Meets Hobbits—Feb. 29, 1419
War Council—Mar. 16, 1419
White Council
  First—863
  Second—1251
  Third—1341
  Fourth—1353
White Tree
  Dies—1252
  Replanted—1419
  Sprouts—1412

Printed in the United States
1532100002B/1-58